WHOSE LAND?
WHOSE PROMISE?

WHOSE LAND?
WHOSE PROMISE?

What Christians Are Not Being Told
about Israel and the Palestinians

Gary M. Burge

THE
PILGRIM
PRESS
Cleveland

To Mitri, Bishara, Naim, Salim, Nora, and Abuna.

Courageous ministers of the gospel in their homeland.

The Pilgrim Press
700 Prospect Avenue
Cleveland, Ohio 44115-1100
thepilgrimpress.com

© 2003 by Gary M. Burge

Scripture quotations unless otherwise noted are from the New Revised Standard Version Bible, copyright © 1989 by the Division of Christian Education of the National Council of the Churches of Christ in the U.S.A.

All rights reserved. Published 2003

Printed in the United States of America on acid-free paper

08   07   06   5   4

Library of Congress Cataloging-in-Publication Data
Burge, Gary M., 1952-
    Whose land? whose promise?: what Christians are not being told about Israel and the Palestinians / Gary M. Burge.
        p.   cm.
    Includes bibliographical references and index.
    ISBN 0-8298-1545-7 (cloth : alk. paper)
    ISBN 0-8298-1660-7 (pbk. : alk. paper)
    1. Palestine in Christianity. 2. Arab-Israeli conflict – Religious aspects – Christianity.   I. Title.
BT93.8.B87 2003
263'.0425694 – dc21
                                                     2003043360

Isaiah's Song of the Vineyard

Let me sing for my beloved
my love-song concerning his vineyard:
My beloved had a vineyard
on a very fertile hill.
He dug it and cleared it of stones,
and planted it with choice vines;
he built a watchtower in the midst of it,
and hewed out a wine vat in it;
he expected it to yield grapes,
but it yielded wild grapes.

And now, inhabitants of Jerusalem
and people of Judah,
judge between me
and my vineyard.
What more was there to do for my vineyard
that I have not done in it?
When I expected it to yield grapes,
why did it yield wild grapes?

—Isaiah 5:1–4

The Lord's Prayer in Arabic

CONTENTS

Preface ix

1. The Dilemma of Israel/Palestine for Christians 1

Part One
THE BACKGROUND TO THE PROBLEM

2. Knowing the Land 17

3. Knowing the History of the Land 33

Part Two
THE OLD TESTAMENT AND THE LAND

4. The Land Promises of Abraham 67

5. The Nation of Israel and the Land 80

6. The Prophets and the Land 94

7. Jerusalem 112

8. Modern Israel in the Land 130

Part Three
THE NEW TESTAMENT AND THE LAND

9. Jesus and the Early Christians 167

10. The Palestinian Church 190

11. Living Stones in the Land 205

12. Evangelicals and the Land 233

13. Where Do We Go from Here? 260

Index of Subjects and Names 273

Index of Scripture 280

Index of Websites 285

PREFACE

Whoever walks four cubits in the Land of Israel is assured of a place in the world to come.
                                        —Babylonian Talmud, Kethuboth 110b–111a

On March 20, 2000, Pope John Paul II fulfilled one of his life dreams at the age of seventy-nine. He visited the Holy Land. He began in Jordan and first traveled to Mt. Nebo in order to glimpse the Land as Moses saw it for the first time thousands of years ago. But in addition to visiting various holy sites in Jerusalem, John Paul said that a visit to Bethlehem lay "at the heart" of his trip. On March 22 in Bethlehem's Manger Square, he met thousands of Christians and Muslims who had just festooned the square with Palestinian and Vatican flags. They shouted "Viva Al-Baba" ("Al-Baba" is the Arabic word for the pope) as John Paul was presented with a golden bowl of Palestinian soil, which he kissed — something generally reserved for nations he visits. Following a worship service, the pontiff remarked, "This is a place that has known the yoke and the rod of oppression. How often has the cry of innocents been heard in these streets? Your torment is before the eyes of the world," he declared. "And it has gone on too long."

And then he did something unexpected — and virtually ignored in the Western press. At 4 p.m., John Paul visited Dheisheh refugee camp outside Bethlehem. Home to over ten thousand people who lost their homes in 1948 when Israel was born, the camp is a tragic example of squalor and poverty. About 650 buildings are squeezed onto Dheisheh's one square kilometer. That's over fifteen people per small home. Unemployment is 60 percent. On the Hebron Road that leads to the camp, John Paul was greeted by "The March of the Keys" — hundreds of Dheisheh schoolchildren who were carrying keys to the homes their grandparents lost so many years ago. These keys are handed down now to a third generation as a reminder of the families' loss and displacement. Most children carried signs bearing the names of their ancestral villages, now bulldozed into the hillsides of Israel.

At a public gathering inside the camp, John Paul spoke again:

> I greet each one of you and I hope and pray that my visit will bring some comfort in your difficult situation. You have been deprived of many things which represent basic needs of the human person: proper housing, health care,

education and work. Above all you bear the sad memory of what you were forced to leave behind, not just material possessions, but your freedom, the closeness of relatives, and the familial surroundings and cultural traditions which nourished your personal and family life.

Dear refugees, do not think that your present condition makes you any less important in God's eyes! Never forget your dignity as his children! Here at Bethlehem the Divine Child was laid in a manger in a stable; shepherds from the nearby fields were the first to receive the heavenly message of peace and hope for the world. God's design was fulfilled in the midst of humility and poverty.

The tableau was astonishing: John Paul standing in a Bethlehem scene as poor as that which greeted Jesus on Christmas morning. John Paul embracing children who carried their grandparents' iron keys.

The pope's decision to visit Dheisheh Camp reminded me of the tough dilemma I face as a Christian who thinks about Israel today. Since the birth of this nation — a moment in history celebrated by millions of Christians around the world — countless people have suffered. Since 1948, 531 Arab villages have been either destroyed by bulldozers or occupied by Israeli residents despite U.N. resolutions calling for the rightful return of these homes and lands to their Arab owners. According to U.N. records in June 1999, about 3.6 million Palestinian refugees are the victims of Israel's nationhood.[1]

As an evangelical I have a theological interest in Israel's history and future. As a Christian I recognize the ancestral connection between Jews today and Abraham, Moses, and David. And yet I am confused and troubled when I try to interpret the meaning of this small country and I learn about one more village story, one more set of keys to a lost home, one more house being bulldozed, and more refugees being pushed away from their homeland.

The Arab village of Halhoul just outside Hebron illustrates our dilemma nicely. Anyone driving from Jerusalem to Hebron on the main road drives right through it. This ancient village has a history that goes all the way back to the Bible. Halhoul is mentioned in the NIV as "Halhul" and is listed in Joshua 15:58 as among those towns awarded to the tribe of Judah following Joshua's conquest. Now here is the question: *Who owns Halhoul?* Should the Arab residents who have lived there for countless centuries be displaced based on a promise given to Joshua? If a Jewish settlement is built tomorrow called, perhaps, Kiryat Halhul, and its settlers claim that they have arrived to fulfill the pledge given by God to Jews — is this claim justified? What

---

1. For a catalogue of villages, see J. Fayez, *Lest the Civilized World Forget: The Colonization of Palestine* (New York: Americans for Middle East Understanding, 1992). Such lists are also available throughout the Internet. See also below, p. 44 n. 13.

happens to the thousands of people who live in Halhoul today? *Does such a claim from the Bible trump a claim to historic residence?*

I also found myself in a similar dilemma almost ten years ago during the height of the Gulf War when Iraq invaded Kuwait. In January 1991, Dr. John Walvoord, formerly president of Dallas Seminary, was being interviewed on Moody Radio in Chicago. While American warplanes were attacking Saddam Hussein's forces in Iraq and Kuwait, Dr. Walvoord spoke eloquently about Bible prophecy and its fulfillment in the modern Middle East.

The presentation was exciting and compelling. Could this configuration of Arab and Western armies spell the beginning of the countdown that would end history? In 1948, Israel had returned to its ancient homeland and reestablished its nationhood — an astonishing twentieth-century miracle. Some orthodox Jewish groups in Jerusalem were even talking about rebuilding the Temple. The puzzle pieces were coming together. As short-range Scud missiles landed in Tel Aviv, many Bible-believing Christians echoed Dr. Walvoord's sentiments as they studied Ezekiel, Daniel, and the book of Revelation, searching for clues to help decipher each day's newspaper headlines. Perhaps Armageddon was around the corner. Some were even calling Hussein the Antichrist.

Becoming caught up in that enthusiasm was easy. In fact, just before the outbreak of hostilities, many of us cheered the prospect of war. *If war means that the second coming of Jesus is approaching, then let the fighting begin! If war means that the eschatological clock will tick a little faster, so be it.* Not only were we on the winning side militarily, but we knew that the host of heaven would be drawn into the action soon.

But then we saw something disturbing. A laser-guided bomb plowed directly into a bomb shelter and incinerated hundreds of Iraqi children and women hiding there. Reports after the war described that our carpet bombing of the front with B-52s may have ended over 100,000 Iraqi lives. That's 100,000 people! Many were men and boys who had no desire whatsoever to be there. Saddam's elite troops had fled. As the allies moved forward, Iraqi soldiers surrendered eagerly. They were conscripts, many of whom were kept in their bunkers on threat of death. Minefields were laid *behind* them (to keep them from fleeing) as well as in front of them. By the war's end, about 115,000 Iraqi soldiers died, 3,000 Arab civilians died in the air war, and almost 120,000 civilians died after the cease fire from civil unrest or war-related ailments.[2] In a word, the war completely destroyed the Iraqi

---

2. *Newsweek*, January 20, 1992, 18. *Newsweek*'s sources came from the Department of Defense, the U.S. Central Command, the U.S. intelligence agencies, and Greenpeace, USA.

infrastructure (water, electricity, agriculture). For example, of six hundred poultry farms in the country, only three were left. Factories that once processed food or medicines were in rubble, which has led many to question whether or not the war fulfilled what once was called a "just war." In the years immediately following the war, masses of Iraqi children (five hundred per day under the age of five by some estimates) were still dying from the war's delayed effects.[3]

In light of the outcome of the war, I have had to ask myself some hard questions. Did I have room in my heart for the suffering that this war created? Was my commitment to eschatology greater than my commitment to these people, whom God surely loved? I could not justify or excuse the ruthless and unpardonable Iraqi conquest of Kuwait, but something had happened to me. My eschatological zeal, my fervor to see prophecy fulfilled, had made me stereotype the Arabs, making them pawns in some game I was playing with my faith and my Bible. I was in a dilemma.

Following the Gulf War, the allied forces led by the United States imposed a strict embargo on Iraq with devastating results. From 1991 till 1998, over 500,000 children in Iraq under the age of five died needlessly according to UNICEF (a welfare unit of the United Nations focused on children).[4] According to the United Nations, as many as 1 million children are in need of food. Over 1.2 million people have died because of medical shortages or the effects of malnutrition. Denis Halliday served as the first Humanitarian Coordinator for the United Nations in Iraq, and when he resigned in October 1998 he remarked, "We are in the process of destroying an entire society. It is as simple and as terrifying as that. It is illegal and immoral."[5] In February 2000, Hans von Sponeck, the second U.N. Humanitarian Coordinator, likewise resigned. He commented: "How long should the civilian population, which is totally innocent of all this, be exposed to such punishment for something that they have never done?"[6]

These figures compare with 305 American troops killed (146 killed in action, 159 killed outside combat) and 244 fatalities among the other allied armies.

3. C. Scriven, "Second Thoughts about the War," *Christianity Today,* January 13, 1992, 11. For a complete report, see A. Arnove, ed., *Taken from Iraq under Siege: The Deadly Impact of Sanctions and War* (Cambridge, Mass.: South End Press, 2000).

4. Children under the age of five were dying at the rate of 6,000 per month (up from 506 per month prior to the war).

5. *The Independent,* October 15, 1998.

6. BBC Online, February 8, 2000. For complete information on Iraq, see the website sponsored by students at Cambridge University, CASI [Campaign Against Sanctions Against Iraq], at *www.cam.ac.uk/societies/casi/.* For thorough Christian research on Iraq and an active humanitarian mission, see the work of Dr. Jim Jennings at Conscience International, 4685 Chamblee-Dunwoody Rd., Suite A7, Atlanta, GA 30338. For a website devoted to the Iraqi sanctions and its consequences, see *www.megastories.com/iraq/index.htm.*

And then there are the Christians who suffered in this war. Most estimates indicate that 4 percent of Iraq's 25 million population is Christian — 1 million people with whom I am linked by faith.[7] Today, if 25 percent of an Iraqi village is Christian, the Christian faith must be taught in the schools. Churches can be built freely and open worship is protected. Iraqi Christians who are my friends remind me that they are not being persecuted at all in their country.

Of these Christians, who worship in over 250 Iraqi churches, many of them are Presbyterian, exactly like my own denomination. More than 10 churches identify themselves as evangelical! On a recent visit to Iraq, I preached in a congregation in Kirkuk, Iraq (within the northern no-fly zone). During the potluck dinner after the service, you would think you were in any evangelical church anywhere in the United States. Without the approval of the American government, many American Christians have crossed into Iraq bringing aid to the suffering. Some churches are trying to build "partnership relations" with Iraqi churches, supporting them in their need.

But wait. What happened to my zeal during the Gulf War? What happened to the simple and clear categories of "right and wrong" so smoothly outlined on CNN? What happened to those evangelical sermons announcing that we were doing God's work with our military?

Many of us in the evangelical community live with a troubled conscience.[8] We are learning that our vision is not what it should be. Our excitement at living in "the last days" has led us to overlook some devastating facts about our faith, the Middle East, and what God would have us do. In some cases, we have not been told things, important things, about life as it really is in the Middle East. This situation is even more true today, as our government contemplates further military action against Iraq. In a day of increasing militarism, many of us are deeply disturbed.

As an evangelical Christian, as a professor of New Testament at a large evangelical college, and as a pastor, Israel and the Middle East confront me with an impossible problem. How do I embrace my commitment to Judaism, a commitment to which I am bound by the Bible, when I sense in my deepest being that a profound injustice is afoot in Israel? How do I celebrate the birth of this nation Israel when I also mourn the suffering

---

7. Current estimates: Chaldeans (800,000), Assyrians (90,000), Catholic and Orthodox Syrian (90,000), others [Armenians, Melkites, Copts, Protestants, others] (20,000).

8. D. Neff, "Love Thy (Arab) Neighbor," *Christianity Today,* October 22, 1990, 22. Neff writes, "When international disputes escalate to this extent, the church has a special responsibility to douse the flames of hatred."

of Arab Christians who are equally my brothers and sisters in Christ? And how do I love those Palestinian Muslims who are deeply misunderstood by all parties in this conflict? As I write (August 2002), the region has just witnessed almost twenty-four months of breathtaking conflict. Palestinians have traded stones for automatic weapons and bombs — while Israelis have employed attack helicopters, fighter jets, and tanks in a conflict that has now witnessed thousands of causalities throughout the country. Palestinians have died at four times the rate of the Israelis, and so I am forced to ask: How should I feel about this? Where should my sympathies be lodged?

This book is not written for the academic historian or the technically trained theologian, although its conclusions and observations are based on many academic works. This book is practical, written for the average Christian who, like me, struggles on a basic personal level with the dilemma of Israel and the Palestinians within conservative theological framework.

Discerning readers will at once see that this book has been a personal exploration of my own. In it I have tried to explore and distill the essential ideas that we must acknowledge if we are to understand Israel fully. Some will quickly look to see "where I come out": Is he pro-Israeli or pro-Palestinian? I have tried to enter both communities — Israeli and Arab — in order to listen with compassion. I have likely spent more nights sleeping in Israeli *kibbutzim* than in Arab homes. I am as comfortable riding an Israeli Egged bus out of Tel Aviv's Central Bus Station as I am taking an Arab taxi into central Hebron. I have stayed in Gaza City as well as Israeli West Bank settlements. Hopefully, such readers will patiently and thoughtfully weigh the evidence as I have done and discover that grave problems lie within Israel/Palestine.

Throughout the book I have been careful in my use of words that are loaded with special meanings. Virtually everything — from the color of one's license plate to one's address — has some political meaning in Israel/Palestine. The same is true of vocabulary. For example, I use "Israel/Palestine" when referring to the larger country which includes the lands occupied in the 1967 war (particularly the West Bank and Gaza). This term respects both peoples' desire for national identity. Palestine is an ancient word that has been used since Roman times to describe this land.[9] And today, "Palestinian" has become the preferred title of the people who live

---

9. In fact, Palestine goes back further. It originates with the word "Philistine," which occurs throughout the Old Testament.

there. When I refer to Israel or Israeli, I generally mean the Jewish nation formed in 1948.

Many people contributed to the writing of this book, and I want to render thanks where it is due. An original version was published in 1993 as *Who Are God's People in the Middle East? What Christians Are Not Being Told about Israel and the Palestinians.* The bulk of its research was done while I was on sabbatical at North Park University. Since 1993 my interest in Israel/Palestine has continued leading me to travel to the country annually. After I joined the faculty of Wheaton College, I continued my interest by leading numerous trips and most recently conducting a thorough research trip on the future of the Palestinian church. Thanks are due to Wheaton's generous Aldeen Fund for faculty research which financed this work.

One of the chief changes to research today is the use of the Internet. Today Palestinians are talking with each other and with people around the world thanks to e-mail, websites, and instant messaging. They are cataloguing their grievances (visit: *www.electronicintifada.net*) and cataloguing the data of their struggle.[10] Jewish sites are doing the same. When I cite figures for home demolitions, for instance, I generally use the Israeli site B'Tselem (*www.btselem.org*), since it cannot be accused of bearing pro-Palestinian bias. Within hours of a death on either side of the war, digital images are circulating to any who are connected. In most cases, when an especially helpful website has served to give insight to a problem or a movement, I have supplied the web address in the footnotes.

Many friends in Israel/Palestine invited me to enter their world in a way that few visitors have an opportunity to experience. They trusted me, and for this trust I cannot express enough appreciation. Many of their names and their stories are found in the pages of this book, and I deem it a high privilege to be representing them and their concerns. The first person to invite me to have a glimpse of this story was the late Audeh Rantisi, once an Anglican pastor in Ramallah. Audeh and his wife Pat brought me to their home during the hard days of the first Uprising (the *Intifada*), and from that vantage I saw firsthand what violent occupation looks like. Personal experiences like these are not forgotten.

Over the last ten years a number of people have become friends in a network of people who are committed to the Palestinian church and are able to bridge these interests to Christians in the West. A few deserve mention: Na'im Ateek, Nora Kort, Bishara Awad, Salim Munayer. Many Westerners have likewise devoted their energies to this enterprise, and their wisdom has

---

10. See the list of links at *www.sabeel.org/links.html.*

been essential: Don Wagner, Tom Getman, Ken Bailey, David Neff, and the many friends in the advocacy group *Evangelicals for Middle East Understanding.* Students have also served as research assistants. Kathy Marsh, now working in Bosnia, served as my assistant in 1993. Recently Rachel Weissburg worked tirelessly updating the book's historical sections and has provided helpful editorial suggestions throughout. Editorial readers have also included Issam Smeir and Ashleigh Burge. The maps were drawn with the expert hand of one of my students, Laura Brosius. Thanks are also due to Bob Land and John Eagleson, whose editorial work improved the text enormously. Finally, the index was compiled by Robert Rectenwald, a Wheaton College graduate student.

A special thank-you goes to my wife, Carol, who has generously encouraged me to make so many trips to Israel/Palestine (as well as most of the other Arab countries). Her support has helped me pursue this issue for many years. Likewise our daughters, Ashleigh and Grace, have been patient during my many absences, and they have inherited something of these issues. I will never forget watching Ashleigh in 1995 (when she was twelve) impatiently listening to a predictable lecture on land rights by an Israeli professor while he stood in front of fifty college students at Jerusalem University College. Much to everyone's amazement, single-handedly Ashleigh challenged him from the audience, asking him all of the hard questions that I hope the church will ask today.

SINCE THE PUBLICATION of the original hardcover edition of this book (Spring 2003), the tensions in Israel/Palestine have shown no sign of abating. The so-called "Second Intifada" (or Al Aqsa Intifada) that began in September 2000 has continued to expand, and the Israeli occupation has tightened its grip on the West Bank and Gaza. Yasser Arafat's administrative compound in Ramallah has been virtually destroyed, thus crippling its ability to govern. And this has empowered increasingly violent resistance groups such as Hamas.

Casualty numbers are a telling indicator of the suffering on both sides of this conflict: From September 2000, 2,780 Palestinians have died and 25,201 have been injured (*Palestine Red Crescent,* to March 19, 2004). On the Israeli side, there have been 834 deaths and 5,394 injuries (*Israeli Ministry of Foreign Affairs,* to March 1, 2004). When these casualty statistics are compared with the respective size of the Palestinian and Israeli populations, their impact on this small nation is undeniable.

Overtures for peace have completely stalled. President Bush's "Roadmap for Peace," announced in March 2003, rightly identified the critical issues for peace, but these calls have fallen silent as talks have ended and conflict escalated. Palestinian suicide bombings have brought the pain of this war to most major Israeli cities, and Israeli military violence — seen clearly in the assassination of Palestinian leaders by helicopter gunships — is Israel's attempt to quell the violence.

This violence reached its symbolic peak on Monday, March 22, 2004. At 5:30 a.m. in Gaza City, Israeli gunships fired three rockets, killing the wheelchair bound Sheikh Ahmed Yassin, the notorious sixty-six-year-old founder and leader of Hamas. Hamas has no doubt become the critical opponent of Israel. Yassin directed numerous violent operations against Israel and opposed any peace overture that acknowledged Israel's existence, even opposing the "two state" solution. Such "targeted killings" (which killed 337 people since 2000) have raised troubling moral questions for many even when they strike overtly dangerous people. And so they have been widely condemned around the world. But they have also been defended, particularly by the United States, as Israel's necessary strategy for self-defense. This killing, however, is symbolic, striking at the heart of Palestinian resistance. And it will only accelerate the cycle of violence.

Readers of the first printing of this book have expressed enthusiastic appreciation and strong criticism for the theological and political views expressed in these pages. And as I have represented these views in lectures around the country and listened to critics and supporters alike, I have heard three points that continue to surface. These points are not new, and careful readers will see them expressed in full in the following pages. They are also represented in the unofficial "Geneva Accord" launched on December 1, 2003, by two courageous diplomats from opposing sides, former Israeli Justice Minister Yossi Beilin and former Palestinian Information Minister Yasser Abed Rabbo. The fact that Israel's Ariel Sharon and Palestine's Yasser Arafat dislike the accord is a signal that it is getting to the heart of matters.

According to many — myself included — three principles must be held together in order to build a lasting peace in the region.

1. *Israeli Security.* We need to make an unequivocal statement affirming Israel's right to exist as a nation in the region. Israeli anxiety about the rejection, about the denial of its own legitimacy, is profound and grounded in the reality of decades of both Christian and Arab rejection of the right to Jewish self-expression in a sovereign Israel. This must be followed by an equally strong rejection of Palestinian violence that targets civilians.

2. *Palestinian Displacement.* We must likewise acknowledge the violence absorbed by the Palestinian people through the Israeli occupation, their loss of land, and their denial of nationhood. They too experience the rejection of

legitimacy by Israelis and need to be reassured that, indeed, a self-sustaining homeland will be theirs. This also must be followed by an equally strong rejection of government-sanctioned Israeli violence, which is not always self-defense but rather an ongoing effort to control and confiscate more land. Israeli settlements must be withdrawn and Palestinian worries about permanent exile addressed.

3. *Anti-Judaism.* It is simply incorrect to say that critics of modern Israel are anti-Semitic. However, Christians must be warned that there are those who will read this book and conclude that the opponent here is Judaism, not the domestic policies of the State of Israel. Further, some who are genuinely anti-Semitic may exploit this theological and political presentation for their own purposes. *I loathe such efforts.* My primary audience is Christians who believe that the Bible bears a direct relevance to the future of the Middle East, who see in Israel a rich fulfillment of biblical prophecies — and yet have never heard another side to this story. In particular I wish to engage Christian Zionists, whose blend of politics and religious fervor has been particularly ill-informed in recent years.

But I want to be certain that I am not misread. Indeed some of the Scriptures used in this book contributed over time to the *adversus Judaeos* tradition, a tradition that persecuted Jews and fostered a theological justification for it in the Christian church and the world of western European society. It culminated in the hellish culture that ultimately resulted in the destruction of European Jewry. This tradition will make many of the words in this book particularly difficult for my friends in the Jewish community. I would ask them to bear with me. And I would ask them to remember that my ethical and political critique is merely an echo of what countless courageous Jewish voices are already saying. I will argue that even if Christian theologians reject the position that modern Israel inherits the land promised to Abraham (thanks to a new covenant that abrogates the old), this should not diminish the church's respect for Judaism nor the rights of the Jewish people to live in the land of Israel.

The political and theological issues that intersect in Israel/Palestine are complex if not daunting. It will take men and women of genuine courage who can trust the "other," set their fears aside, and let go of strategies that are in the end self-defeating.

Chapter One

THE DILEMMA
OF ISRAEL/PALESTINE
FOR CHRISTIANS

Blessed are the meek, for they will inherit the land;...Blessed are the peacemakers, for they will be called children of God.   — Matthew 5:5, 9

Certain memories remain fixed in the imagination. They are personal and they become indelible symbols as they help us to understand what transpired in our past. Each of us lives with an archive of such memories, and occasionally we redraw those landscapes, we reconstruct those conversations and crises, making them seem as though they happened yesterday. In some fashion, their power is still with us.

LEBANON, 1973

I was an exchange student in Beirut, Lebanon, in the early 1970s during the outbreak of the Lebanese civil war. Palestinian refugees who had lost their homes in Israel lived in squalid camps around Beirut, and they had upset the uneasy balance of Lebanon's politics. The year I was at the American University of Beirut, the Lebanese army had begun its fight with these Palestinian camps, and from the balcony of my dormitory I could watch French Mirage jets strafing the refugee camps less than three miles away. One lead fighter would shriek downward with its partner close behind. If the first plane drew the aim of the antiaircraft gunner, the first pilot would pull out of his approach while the second jet attacked with awesome ferocity. The roar was deafening. And when the bombs made impact, the rumble vibrated through our building. We would sit, eating pita bread, tuna fish, and Arabic hummus (a chick-pea and garlic purée) on the sixth-floor balconies of the dorm on Bliss Street as if we were watching an arcade game.

The Palestinian students on my floor were crazed with anger. How could an army destroy civilians like this? When the angry students started throwing furniture out of the dorm windows into the busy street below, the Lebanese

1

army rolled a tank up Bliss Street and parked it one-half block away, aiming its barrel at the top floors of the dorm. It was tough even to get a peek at the thing. A squad of soldiers fired hardened rubber bullets at anyone who showed his or her profile in a window. We slept at night with wet towels crammed under the door of our room to keep the tear gas out. My Palestinian roommate, Samir El Far, made it his mission to keep this naive American out of harm's way. We spent the days and nights talking about what these things meant.

Since college classes usually do not prosper under such circumstances — the furniture from one of my classrooms had been taken to form a barricade — most of us thought it would be good to get away. I joined a teacher and a busload of students and headed south into the beautiful, rolling hills of southern Lebanon. Our destination was the village of Hesbiya. Palestinians fleeing the war in Beirut and Palestinians wishing to return to their homeland in Israel were settling in southern Lebanon not far from the Israeli border. Many had become guerrilla fighters in their own right, some were simply gangsters, but most were families living in abject confusion, wandering from place to place.

The Israelis had plans for southern Lebanon as well. They wanted to depopulate it, to drive the Palestinians away from Israel's northern border, so they sent fighter jets into these hills to attack the Palestinians. In the process, they attacked any Lebanese village that gave refuge to the Palestinian refugees.[1]

When we entered Hesbiya, I saw firsthand the results of an attack from fighter jets: the crumbled buildings, the panic, and the dismay. I remember seeing brightly colored children's toys locked under the weight of massive broken concrete blocks. The misshapen steel reinforcement rods stuck into the air like arms reaching nowhere. The toys were red and plastic, and I wondered where the children were who played with them. Kids were everywhere telling us in indecipherable Arabic and hand gestures how the jets swooped down on them firing. These kids saw themselves as heroes. Bravado was on their little faces. They had survived.

We had come to build a bomb shelter for Hesbiya. Before we finished the foundation, a village elder slaughtered a chicken to bless the structure.

---

1. In the late 1970s Israel finally occupied southern Lebanon, made an alliance with the Christian militias there, and created a buffer zone. In order to stop Palestinian reprisals, Israel went as far as laying siege to Beirut in 1982. After twenty-two years of occupation, Israel unilaterally withdrew from southern Lebanon on the night of May 23, 2000. Abandoned Christian communities, fearing for their lives, fled to the new Israeli border. Thousands were then let in. These "Christian" communities use this designation as a cultural-political identifier. In many cases, however, it represents a deep and profound faith.

Then stone upon stone, we constructed the walls of the underground shelter. The people mainly wanted a place for the children to hide when the jets returned. And they did return many times later after we left. I often wonder what became of that shelter and how it fared in those days of attack.

In the span of just a few weeks I witnessed the crisis of the Palestinian world. Attacked by the Lebanese, attacked by the Israelis, these people had nowhere to go. They were becoming the refuse of Middle Eastern history. They were of no use to anyone. I remember walking in the hills outside the village at night. It was very dark and very quiet. The stars seemed crowded in this sky that didn't suffer from the light pollution of my native southern California. God seemed very near to this place, and yet it was a place of tragedy beyond description.

ISRAEL/PALESTINE, 1990

In the following eighteen years I returned to the Middle East many times: sometimes as a pilgrim, frequently as a professor with students, and often as a researcher hoping to understand more of this turbulent world. I found a profound dilemma.

The Middle East was a land of miracles. This was the Holy Land — the land of Abraham, Moses, and Jesus. This place had witnessed the miraculous rebirth of the nation of Israel, surely a triumph that has no parallel elsewhere in history. Once after reading Hal Lindsey's book *The Late Great Planet Earth*,[2] I stood in the Valley of Armageddon and reflected on Israel's fulfillment of prophecy and the coming wars that would torment these lands and bring about the end of human history as we know it. Surely God was at work in this place.

But I also witnessed suffering and sinfulness in an unprecedented way. Both Arab evil and Israeli evil abounded. Whenever I left the usual tourist trail and looked behind the scenes, I caught glimpses of an Israel I barely recognized.

I was in Israel/Palestine in 1990 visiting an Arabic Christian pastor and his family in the city of Ramallah. This pastor's home had become a refuge for many who sought support and protection. At 7:00 in the morning an elderly Palestinian woman burst into the kitchen where we were eating breakfast. Her story riveted us. The Israeli army had come that night to homes on her street looking for stone-throwing boys. It was about midnight, and the

---

2. H. Lindsey (with C. C. Carlson), *The Late Great Planet Earth* (Grand Rapids, Mich.: Zondervan, 1970).

children were in bed. In panic they fled as soldiers with weapons tore through the bedrooms. Ziena, a twelve-year-old girl, fled out the front door and there on the porch was shot point-blank by a soldier with an automatic weapon. She was barely alive.

The woman fell to the floor, and her weeping — her incessant weeping — paralyzed us all. I knew what she was talking about. Just the day before I had been walking up Al Tireh Street, Ramallah's main boulevard, and watched a platoon of soldiers shake down a row of homes. An officer told me that a child had thrown a rock out of the yard and it had hit the new car of an Israeli settler. Now the soldiers were looking for him. They could find only women and young children since school was in session and the men were away at work. The residents were told to line up in the field in front of the houses while the soldiers searched more carefully. I squatted down next to a jeep, watching in amazement. A girl of about five ran into the street, her mother screamed as she pursued her, and the soldiers yelled for them to get back in line. Then the rocks started falling. Soldiers on the top of the buildings nearby started targeting the young woman and her child with apple-sized stones. It was their laughter that disturbed me; it was their grisly sport here in Ramallah that I found stunning. The young mother swept up her child with tears streaming down her face and fled for the cover of trees. And there she wept. To this day I can still see and hear her weeping in the trees of Ramallah and laughing, young Israeli soldiers targeting her with rocks.

I deduced what happened next. The frustrated platoon decided to come back that night and in a surprise raid catch whomever they could. The young critically wounded girl was just one more accidental victim.

We returned to breakfast, and the Palestinian Christian pastor said grace in a way I will never forget: "Lord, thank you for this food you give us this day. And please Lord remember those of us who suffer in this land and remember to bring justice to us."

It was time to leave Ramallah. I joined a communal taxi already filled with Arab riders and headed south toward Jerusalem. I climbed out of the taxi on the Nablus Road just north of the Old City's Damascus Gate. I bought a popsicle from a vendor, and as I watched, an army patrol stopped its truck on the road in front of me and began to abuse the passengers in the waiting cars. They were the dreaded Border Regiments that work primarily in the Occupied Territories and are known for their forest-green berets and their bravado. I watched as soldiers reached into the windows of the filled taxis and slapped people across the face. My anger was brimming — I had been with these people; my car had Arab medical students in it. But I had an overwhelming sense of powerlessness. I did not know how to control my rage at the injustice, the provocation.

Cameras are always a threatening weapon before soldiers, so I opened mine, slipped off the lens cap, and rested it on my chest. At once the patrol spotted me, the only blonde in a sea of Arab faces. With clubs poised inches from me they screamed in Hebrew something about photos. It was surreal. There I was standing face-to-face with a squad of heavily armed, arrogant young men. Each had a white-knuckled grip on his club and had weapons loaded with live clips. Clearly this roll of film was going to be a very expensive one.

Compassion is a Latin word that means "to suffer with." I had crossed an invisible yet tangible line somewhere. Deep within me fear and courage were at work. For a moment I was sure I wanted to be arrested — to confront the system, to dare them to do to an American citizen what they were doing to these people.

Suddenly a Russian Israeli officer approached, intervened by yelling at the men, and escorted the squad back to the truck. Palestinian faces everywhere were looking at me — from the taxis to the sidewalk crowds. I turned to look at a shopkeeper behind me, and he smiled a smile like no other — a smile of grace, of sorrow, and of thanks — as the Israelis drove off. All I could say, as if he represented his entire people, was, "I'm sorry." And I walked on into the old city of Jerusalem.

Inside the Damascus Gate I could tell that a demonstration was about to erupt. Shops were slamming closed and people were running. Israeli patrols had mounted the high walls surrounding the gate, and they were distributing tear-gas canisters and locking them on to the underside of their rifle barrels. About seventy-five teenage girls packed a narrow street in that quarter of Jerusalem chanting and clapping. An Arab shopkeeper grabbed me, saying that it was not good for me to stay there, but I felt compelled, intoxicated by the surge of voices and curious to witness the fate that awaited them. A patrol of soldiers — I could see them — was about four hundred yards ahead. The girls sang as men in sunglasses loaded and aimed tear-gas guns, M-16s, and Uzi machine guns. There was a scream, gas, panic, a stampede, and retching. The girls retreated from their demonstration as I sprinted up an alley to move away from the gas.

My head was still swimming from the adrenaline. I needed a place to sort out my feelings, to clear out my thinking. I followed a small road called the El Wad going south and then headed east on the Via Dolorosa, the Way of Suffering that Jesus walked on as he headed toward the cross of Golgotha. It was also the street where the women of Jerusalem wept for him.

I knew of a private place — a quiet place, a place to settle down — and was anxious to weave through the crowds to get there. For a shekel the Sisters of Zion (a Catholic order) will let you into the remains of the ancient Roman Antonia Fortress. There underground, beneath the streets of Jerusalem, in perfect solitude, are pavements and cisterns built by the Romans to equip the Roman occupation army of the first century. The deepest ladder took me far from the awful world above. And there my surroundings hit me like nothing before: I was sitting amid the ruins of the Roman army that terrorized and battered this land in Jesus' day — an army that Jesus knew all too well; an army that slapped him, mocked him, and crucified him.

So it had been Jesus' experience too. Did he feel what I felt? Did his followers not want him to do more? Were the Israelis now behaving like the Romans once had? And I wept for the first time since I had visited this land.

ISRAEL/PALESTINE, 2002

For the next twelve years, I worked to sort out my assumptions about this land. In 1993, I published a book, *Who Are God's People in the Middle East?*[3] as much as an act of personal disclosure as anything. So many stories of suffering had come to me, that when I wrote these up I felt a sense of release. When a refugee gives you the sacred trust of his or her story, you carry it like a burden, wondering how to use it. When NATO troops and aid workers entered Kosovo in June 1999 following the Serbian invasion, they were overwhelmed with story after story of astonishing despair. The troops didn't know what to do with all of the pain. I felt the same.

The most remarkable thing that happened following the publication of the book was the response I received from the evangelical community. Many letters came in, some thanking me profusely, others reserving a place for me in the lower levels of Dante's inferno. At conservative Wheaton College (where I work), some alumni even wrote our president urging I be dismissed for not affirming a proper biblical perspective on Israel! I was invited to speak on a dozen radio programs and one television show where callers could engage in conversation. The passion and the anger my stories evoked simply astounded me.

I learned quickly that many did not want to hear about this difficult side of Israel's life. One well-known Christian leader I know has led over eight church-based pilgrimage trips to Israel using an Israeli guide and has *never*

---

3. G. M. Burge, *Who Are God's People in the Middle East?* (Grand Rapids, Mich.: Zondervan, 1993).

met an Arab Christian. Each summer Wheaton College takes fifty students to the Middle East for an extensive exposure to the historical geography of the Bible. I quickly learned that our Christian leaders could choose to walk through biblical sites without meeting a single Palestinian Christian. Imagine spending a month in Israel and never having a personal conversation with an Arab who is not a shopkeeper. Imagine being in a despair-filled country surrounded by Christians and not making an effort to learn about them, to meet them, even to embrace their struggles. In 1995, I led one of these trips and brought in Nora Kort from the Arab Orthodox Society to speak to the group one evening about her work as a Christian in the Old City of Jerusalem.[4] The next day after Nora spoke, the president of the evangelical college where we stayed rebuked me angrily for letting her come to campus.

I also became active in a Christian advocacy organization called *Evangelicals for Middle East Understanding.*[5] And through our annual conferences around the country I began to see that when evangelicals take the time to hear "the other side," to meet their first Palestinian pastor, to share a meal with an Arab family, suddenly their hearts are changed. For a long time, many assumed that things were going quite well as the Middle East worked toward peace. Israel made peace with Egypt (1979), Jordan (1994), and has pulled out of Lebanon (May 23, 2000). Israel is now in negotiation with Syria, its most contentious opponent, normalizing relations. In two years we have witnessed the deaths of the leaders of Jordan (King Hussein, February 7, 1999) and Syria (President Assad, June 10, 2000), making way for new configurations for leadership in the region.

Yet, behind the scenes, behind all of the talk about "the peace process," a dangerous and treacherous struggle is being waged for the land of Palestine. A Palestinian national homeland — which was merely a dream in 1990 — now seems inevitable. And yet, in these years of "peace," Israel has accelerated its acquisition of Palestinian land, its building of settlements, its destruction of Arab neighborhoods, and its bulldozing of Arab homes. By changing the "facts on the ground," Israel hopes that final negotiations for this Palestinian homeland will take into account what Israel already possesses. And when Palestinian resistance occurs, violence often erupts. Since 1987, at least 16,700 Palestinians (including 7,300 children) have been made homeless in the West Bank and East Jerusalem through the demolition of over 2,650 homes. Today in East Jerusalem alone, 10,000 Palestinian homes — one-third of the Arab population of the city — are threatened by

---

4. Today Nora works for the evangelical Venture International Organization bringing aid to the women of Jerusalem's Old City.

5. See the website *www.emeu.net.*

demolition orders.[6] People who watch the region closely were not surprised when the entire country erupted in September 2000, and the world witnessed some of the worst bloodshed and fighting it had ever seen. By mid-2002, no one knew how the fight would ever stop.

Rather than simple statistics, these numbers represent families no different than our families in our own homes. On January 26, 1999, more than a hundred Israeli soldiers accompanied by bulldozers arrived at the village of Isawiyeh on the outskirts of East Jerusalem. In this village the fourteen-member Awais family had outgrown their home and had built a four-room house *on their own property.* They were refused a building permit by Israel — as so often happens in these villages — so that the family would leave. But on this Tuesday, bulldozers arrived and began demolishing their new home. About a hundred local people gathered and started to throw stones. Soon the army used batons to suppress them. Next the troops shot rubber-coated metal bullets at close range and killed Zaki 'Ubayd, the twenty-eight-year-old father. The troops then left quickly, leaving the children in shock and tears, standing in the midst of rubble and death.

Such stories pour out in an endless stream if one listens carefully in this land. The Halaseh family (with its eleven children) had their family home demolished twice and were living in a tin shack on land that belonged to their family near the Jewish settlement of Kedar. Without warning on July 25, 1999, Israeli troops bulldozed their little home. The father (who was paralyzed) and his sixteen-year-old daughter were then arrested for "attacking soldiers" during the raid.

I wish you could stand with me in the rubble of a destroyed Palestinian home. To lose your home in the course of war is one thing. To have it destroyed before your eyes by government authorities when you are holding your property deed, when you know that your children will be homeless that very night, is quite another.

FOUR COMPLICATIONS

Why do we sense we cannot get anywhere when it comes to Israel and the Palestinians? Why have Christians been peculiarly — and sometimes rightly — paralyzed on the matter of this subject? Passions always flare when someone brings up aid for Israel or the settlement of the West Bank or the Palestinian resistance. We are torn. We are drawn to this subject

---

6. Amnesty International Executive Summary, December 1999. See *www.amnesty.org/ailib/aipub/1999/MDE.*

instinctively. If rioting takes place in Bethlehem, the story may well make the national news, but if hundreds die in Sudan or Pakistan, we may never hear. As Christians our interest is heightened because we attribute a spiritual importance to this part of the world.

One of the most popular books circulating among evangelicals today is Bodie Thoene's multivolume sets *The Zion Covenant* and *The Zion Chronicles,* which trace the story of Jewish families surviving Holocaust Europe and establishing the State of Israel. This romantic story of suffering, endurance, and hope does not want to be complicated by another story of suffering and endurance among people whom Thoene's fictional characters displace. Today the nationally best-selling series *Left Behind* paints a similar portrait of political crisis centered around Israel's fate in world history.

Four factors seem to continue to influence and complicate our thinking when we reflect on modern Israel today.

1. We bear a subliminal sense of guilt for the horrors of the twentieth century that have been perpetrated on Judaism. We share the guilt of men and women who, in the name of Christ, pursued, persecuted, and massacred Jews. From Moscow to Chicago, anti-Semitism is a part of the heritage of Western Christendom. Jews were killed by the Byzantine armies, the Holy Roman Empire, and even the Crusaders. When the Crusaders entered Jerusalem in 1099 C.E. in the name of Christ, they massacred everyone who looked Middle Eastern, Muslims and Jews alike. Few in the Middle East have forgotten this.

Twentieth-century Jews have had to face similar horrors. That Jewish synagogues on the north side of Chicago have metal fireproof doors on their buildings is no accident. Congregation members can often be seen scrubbing off swastikas from the alleyway entrances. Kristallnacht, the night of November 9, 1938, commemorates the day when the Nazi SS began destroying Jewish businesses and synagogues in Munich. Its anniversary is still remembered each year, especially in Skokie, north of Chicago, among the neo-Nazis. Jews in the synagogues there pray that the night will pass without incident.

Our relationship with Israel is thus complicated by a collective feeling of guilt. These people have suffered severely in history, and our debt to their future is great. Judaism deserves a place of security — a place to protect itself from outsiders. I cannot imagine the restraint it took for the Israelis not to respond with force when Saddam Hussein was lobbing Scud missiles at Tel Aviv in early 1990. "To defend yourself and not rely on someone else's guns" is a vow that was born somewhere in the Warsaw ghetto in the 1930s. I recall standing on the top of the mountain of Masada, the "last stand" of the Jews against the Romans, and watching the bar mitzvah of a young man in the ruins of the two-thousand-year-old synagogue. As he vowed in the silence of the desert to embrace his faith and his land with his entire life, an F-16 fighter barreling down the Jordan Valley screamed defiantly over the mountain and its synagogue with a deafening roar. Judaism will never be desecrated in a ghetto again. Ever. And this is good.

Israel has not hesitated to remind the West of this obligation. Comments about the "debt" of the West are heard frequently. Well-known theologian Dr. Rosemary Ruether was recently traveling in Gaza and there watched a Palestinian demonstration. A car full of Israeli settlers drove past, threatening the marchers. "Why are you doing this?" she asked them. "Because of the war!" one Israeli yelled back. My friend continued, "But these people didn't do anything to you." The settler responded, "But they must pay. The whole world must pay."

2. Evangelical Christians have rightly concluded that we of all people have a shared sense of spiritual destiny with Judaism. Our branches spring from the same Middle Eastern olive tree. We share a parallel faith. The Lord is the same God both of synagogue and church. Every autumn, thousands of evangelical Christians flood into Jerusalem from the United States and Europe to celebrate the Festival of Tabernacles. They march around the walled city of Jerusalem arm-in-arm with Jewish worshipers, waving palms and praising God for the harvest of vine and tree. Jerusalem's mayor usually gives a speech praising the evangelicals' presence, and every Israeli prime minister (except Ehud Barak) has celebrated with them.

We know that Jesus was Jewish. He was of the tribe of Judah, a descendant of David. Paul was from the tribe of Benjamin, a rabbi. Eighty percent of our Bible belongs to the Hebrew canon. The Lord's Supper is actually a Jewish Passover Seder. Above all, we are commanded in Scripture to bless the children in Abraham. Paul's life witnessed intense hostility from the Jewish synagogues: he was jailed, cursed, arrested, flogged with forty lashes five times, beaten with rods three times, and nearly stoned to death once. Still he could say (in Romans 11) that for the sake of the promises God made to their ancestors, the Jewish people — especially those who refuse to believe in Christ — are still beloved (Rom. 11:28). Judaism holds an incomparable place in divine history.

So our relationship with Israel is further complicated by the kinship we feel with this Israeli state that overtly professes faith in the God of Jesus. Even the Israeli Parliament building, the Knesset, is architecturally designed to recall the Ten Commandments — ostensibly the basis of secular Jewish law. Christians can only wish that our American Supreme Court could do as well.

3. Deep within our instincts we have concluded that we are witnesses to a miracle in the twentieth century. The nation of Israel is God's doing. The return of the Jews to Israel after two thousand years, Israel's survival against inestimable odds — are these not signs of something larger than history? How many cultures alive today are thirty-five hundred years old, have suffered multiple exiles, and then after two thousand years of assimilation into the European world have resurrected their dead language and political life in a self-sustaining state?

After the miraculous Israeli victory in 1967's Six-Day War, evangelical Christians throughout America and Europe were freely and confidently exclaiming that God had stepped in and won the victory on behalf of the Israeli defense forces. Legends circulated widely from one Christian pulpit to the next of besieged Israeli soldiers whose Arab enemies were quickly closing in on them with overwhelming firepower. Then suddenly a reversal of fortune occurred — the intervention of an angelic army? — and the Arab soldiers retreated in droves. Clearly, many of us have claimed, this victory and the others — 1948, 1956, 1973 — were miracles. God was defending Israel.

As we look at Israel through this lens, we are cautious. If this little nation in the eastern Mediterranean is God's handiwork, if Israel's history is being orchestrated from on high, then we should be slow to criticize, careful about our chastisements, and supportive at all costs. Evangelicals are prone to cite Genesis 12:2–3 as a reasonable approach to Middle Eastern foreign policy. In this passage God says to Abraham, "I will make of you a great nation, and I will bless you, and make your name great, so that you will be a blessing. I will bless those who bless you, and the one who curses you I will curse; and in you all the families of the earth shall be blessed."

4. In 1991 we rediscovered the fourth factor that influences our judgments about Israel. At the height of the Gulf War, many people realized that this event might be the configuration of nations that will bring about the end of history. Hal Lindsay's *The Late Great Planet Earth* topped the 25 million mark in sales. John F. Walvoord's *Armageddon, Oil and the Middle East Crisis* sold 2 million copies thanks to the Gulf War. Both authors said the same thing: Israel will play a role in the end times. In fact, the hostility of the Arabs figures into a prophesied scenario in which Israel is backed up against the sea, total war breaks out in the Middle East, and Armageddon erupts, bringing about the end of human history as we know it today.

I heard a news commentator reflect on this idea one night in early January 1991 as American bombers were racing to Saudi Arabia. This announcer made the one deduction that evangelicals everywhere were pondering: If

Armageddon is upon us, we had better be on the right side. No matter what happens militarily in the Middle East, evangelical eschatology demands that we keep a firm commitment to Israel. John Walvoord wrote during the Kuwait war, "The rise of military action in the Middle East [such as that taken by Iraq against Kuwait] is an important prophetic development. While wars in Korea, Vietnam, and Europe were not necessarily prophetically significant, all end-time prophecy pictures the Middle East as the center of political, financial, and military power at the end time."[7]

I once received a publication called "The Jerusalem Prayer Letter," distributed by a conservative Christian organization called *Bridges for Peace*. These Christians earnestly support Israel and endeavor to foster Christian/Jewish understanding. Reflecting on the Gulf War, Jim Gerrish, the editor of the prayer letter, compared hostility against Israel during the war with the rise of Nebuchadnezzar in the Old Testament. Nebuchadnezzar, like Hussein, plotted the destruction of Jerusalem. Gerrish remarks:

> Today we now see presidents and nations taking their stand against the covenant people [Israel]. It would seem that all the odds are against Israel. Israel, however, has one thing in her favor. The King of the Universe is on her side and will remain so forever. It is Israel who will be the ultimate winner in any contest. Nations who come against her will vanish away (Psalm 129:6). Those who stand with her will be blessed both now and hereafter.[8]

When we look at Israel through this lens of eschatology, or prophecies of the end times, we are sobered, lest we find ourselves playing on the wrong side of the table if the Lord should return during the next major conflict.

Together these four factors have made it difficult, if not impossible, to see Israel as just another nation. We have become paralyzed and perplexed, unable to launch appropriate criticisms of the Middle East. Just possibly, we have been unable to see other features of the land and its difficulties.

WHERE DO WE GO FROM HERE?

Many complicated technical works have given exhaustive attention to the problems of Israel/Palestine. Our goal is to distill these works, decipher their leading arguments, and digest them as Christians might who have a heartfelt commitment to this Holy Land. As a Christian writing to other Christians, I am hoping to make two simple points:

---

7. J. F. Walvoord, *Armageddon, Oil and the Middle East Crisis* (Grand Rapids, Mich.: Zondervan, 1991), 48.

8. J. Gerrish, "Jerusalem Prayer Letter," November 18, 1991. Published by Bridges for Peace, International Headquarters: 7 Shaul Adler, Jerusalem, Israel. See *www.bridgesforpeace.com*.

1. *If Israel makes a biblical claim to the Holy Land, then Israel must adhere to biblical standards of national righteousness.* Land promises are a by-product of a covenant with God. Therefore, all aspects of biblical nationhood must be at work. In chapters 4–8 we examine what the Old Testament says about the land promises and how God's people should live on the land. We also study Jerusalem — a flashpoint in conflict today — and examine modern Israeli ambitions for their country.

2. *Christians must look more closely at their commitments.* The New Testament must be read alongside the Old Testament when we interpret the land promises of the Bible. Further, Israel/Palestine has a body of Christian believers who today look to us for support. As fellow Christians we must ask if we have a spiritual obligation here as well. Chapters 9–13 give insights from the Christian community that lives in Israel/Palestine today. Arab and Jewish Christians together struggle to live in this land.

An outline of each chapter and how it addresses these questions is given below:

Part 1: The Background to the Problem

Chapter 2. Knowing the Land. As we begin we need to understand the land itself. What is its geography? Where is the West Bank? On what issues do the border disagreements focus? Why do the Palestinians fight against the "Israeli settlers"?

Chapter 3. Knowing the History. We also need some savvy for the history of this land. When did Abraham come here? What sort of kingdom did David build? How long did the Arabs possess Jerusalem? What about the wars fought by the Israelis since 1948? These historical facts provide the context of the present struggle.

Part 2: The Old Testament and the Land

Chapter 4. The Land Promises of Abraham. What are the promises God has given concerning this land? Are the promises conditional? How does God's covenant connect with the land? Does the land ever belong to anyone, or is it always God's land?

Chapter 5. The Nation of Israel and the Land. What obligation does the land bring to its occupier? Is the conquest of Joshua an apt parallel to the modern growth of the state of Israel? How did the Israelites treat non-Israelites (called "aliens" or "sojourners")? Was the Old Testament kingdom of Israel an ethnically exclusive Jewish state?

Chapter 6. The Prophets and the Land. How do the prophets of the Old Testament relate the land of Israel to the people of Israel? What unique message did they bring? When they considered this inheritance, how did they explain Israel's loss of land during the exiles of the eighth and sixth centuries B.C.E.?

Chapter 7. Jerusalem. What about the city of Jerusalem? How was this city established? To whom was it given? What were its purposes? The ownership of this city lies at the heart of present-day struggles between Palestinians and Israelis.

Chapter 8. Modern Israel in the Land. Is the modern state of Israel claiming a historical connection between biblical Israel and its own nationhood? If so, how do we apply the Old Testament to this modern nation? How does the modern state compare to Old Testament Israel?

Part 3: The New Testament and the Land

Chapter 9. Jesus and the Early Christians. Does the New Testament say anything about the land? What do Jesus and Paul say? If Christians are the descendants of Abraham by faith, what does this mean for the promises to Abraham's descendants? What did the earliest Christians think about the land of Israel?

Chapter 10. The Palestinian Church. Who are the Palestinian Christians? What are their concerns? What have Western Christians not been told? What struggles do Palestinian Christians face?

Chapter 11. Living Stones in the Land. Who are the Palestinian Christian leaders whose voices need to be heard today? Who are some of the "silent saints" within the Palestinian church? What are they saying? What must Western Christians hear from them?

Chapter 12. Evangelicals and the Land. How have Western evangelicals approached the question of Israel and the Palestinians? How should evangelicals relate to the Palestinian church? Should Israel be treated like "just any other nation"?

Chapter 13. Where Do We Go from Here?. The epilogue brings many of the most recent developments into focus. This chapter also asks, "Is it right to be critical of Israel? Is such criticism anti-Semitic?"

Part One

THE BACKGROUND
TO THE PROBLEM

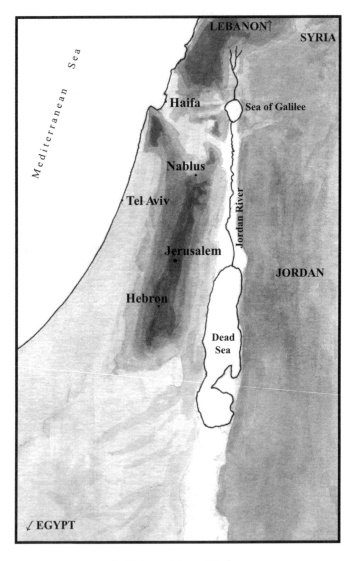

Relief Map of Israel/Palestine

Chapter Two

KNOWING THE LAND

The land that you are crossing over to occupy is a land of hills and valleys, watered by rain from the sky, a land that the LORD your God looks after. The eyes of the LORD your God are always on it, from the beginning of the year to the end of the year.   —Deuteronomy 11:11–12

The countryside of Israel is dotted with a series of peculiar-looking forts that date back to the British occupation of the country during the first part of the twentieth century. Tour guides generally pass these by since today most are simply outposts for the Israeli army (known as the Israeli Defense Forces, or the IDF). They all have a distinctive architecture and are easy to identify. Sir Charles Teggart built them around 1937, and the British used them to maintain control during the turbulent years before the founding of the modern state of Israel (1948). Teggart had come from India, where he had a reputation for effective police enforcement. In Palestine he introduced a system of sixty-five military-police forts situated strategically throughout the land.[1]

When I have a group of students with me, I like to stop the bus and ask them to examine their maps in order to tell me why Teggart chose to build a fort in this particular place rather than elsewhere along the highway. A good place is Latrun on the main highway between Tel Aviv and Jerusalem (Hwy. 1). Teggart's advisors were keen strategists who studied geography and history. They knew the mountains and valleys, and they understood which routes had to be controlled, which highways needed protection if the British were to be successful administrators of this region in the 1930s and 1940s. This particular highway is the primary artery that gains access to the central mountains and Jerusalem from the coast. Today its edges are dotted with wrecked military vehicles from the 1940s, preserved by the government to show the courage and perseverance of fighters who kept West Jerusalem linked to Tel Aviv.

---

1. R. John and S. Hadawi, *The Palestine Diary,* 2 vols. (New York: New World Press, 1970), 1:280; M. Begin, *The Revolt* (Los Angeles: Nash, 1948), 91.

Once we see the strategic importance of the landscape, I then ask students if this route was important in antiquity. Did the ancient Israelites and Philistines fortify this area as well? Nine times out of ten, nearby we discover a crusader fort and an archaeological tell, a mound that looks like a man-made hill which hides the remains of some ancient fortress or city. The conclusion is clear: ancient conquerors, just like Teggart, knew which valleys and passes had to be fortified. Strategic considerations have never changed in Israel. King David, King Herod, Titus, the Crusaders, Saladin, the Ottoman Turks, General Teggart, King Abdullah I of Jordan, and Moshe Dayan of Israel all were concerned about the same valleys. While long-range artillery and air power may have changed the strategic military equation, the struggle for control of the central hills of Israel will never change.

MAJOR FEATURES OF THE LAND

Most political conflicts have a great deal to do with geography. The location of mountains, valleys, highways, bodies of water, and rainfall for agriculture all define the problem. For example, the Black Sea just north of Istanbul, Turkey, held vital warm-water ports for the Soviet Union's naval fleet. Now with the breakup of the U.S.S.R., Ukraine has inherited these advantages. These geographical questions have a direct bearing on a country's sense of well-being.

Understanding the complex problems of Israel/Palestine is impossible without at least a cursory knowledge of the land itself. Look carefully at the map on the following page. Israel is a small country approximately the size of the state of Vermont. For the sake of convenience, we discuss the major regions of Israel by dividing the country north-to-south into four zones.

ZONE 1: GALILEE

The northern area is called Galilee and is dominated by a large, pear-shaped lake that is about thirteen miles long, eight miles wide. Mountains having an east-west pattern rise to the west of the lake and continue all the way to the Mediterranean Sea. To the north, these mountains ascend to Mount Hermon, which stands in all of its ninety-three hundred feet of majesty. In the Bible the dew of Mt. Hermon, falling on the country, is a sign of rich blessing (Ps. 133:3). Water drains down from these mountains into a wide basin called the Huleh Valley that eventually makes its way to the Sea of Galilee. Therefore the "headwaters" of the Jordan River, which runs like a

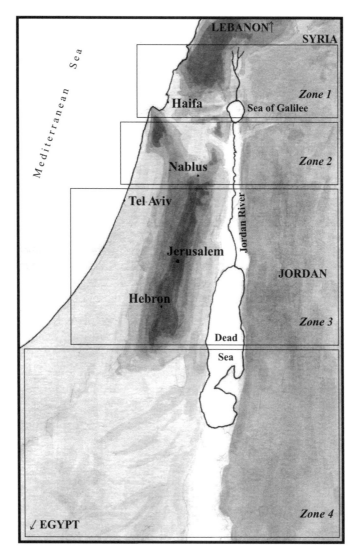

Israel/Palestine: Geographic Zones

north/south ribbon through the land, begin in the far north, on the shoulders of Hermon.

East of Mount Hermon is an elevated plateau called the Golan Heights. This plateau continues south around the east side of the Sea of Galilee and towers over it from 2,500 to 3,000 feet. Considering that the Sea of Galilee is about 650 feet below sea level, the Golan offers a huge strategic advantage over the region.

The value of this area for any nation's economy — from the Old Testament to today — cannot be missed. It receives generous rainfall and has good soil. Virtually any crop can be grown in abundance in Galilee. Even the Golan Heights receives enough rainfall to support cereal crops. Overland caravan traffic in the ancient world traveled south down the Golan Heights into the Huleh Valley above the Sea of Galilee. In Old Testament times, this valley possessed one of the largest fortress cities in the ancient Near East, Hazor. It stood as an imposing obstacle to any who would travel this route and perhaps try to lay siege to it. Today Hazor displays a massive archaeological tell that covers twenty-five acres. In New Testament times, Capernaum, located on the north coast of the sea, was a station for taxation along this route. This fact explains why Matthew, a tax collector, was found at Capernaum (Mark 2:1, 13–14) and why there was a contingent of Roman soldiers with its centurion there (Matt. 8:5).

Galilee is a vital source of fresh water for modern Israel. In fact, Israel's national water carrier (which supplies Tel Aviv) begins here and runs the length of the country. In some respects, Israel views the sea as its one great natural reservoir and so will protect and control at all costs the sources that feed this sea. Its outflow is the Jordan River, which continues south all the way to the Dead Sea. As it travels the Jordan is joined by other rivers coming from the great eastern plateaus. In particular, the Yarmouk Gorge has a river that supplies a flow almost equal to that of the Jordan. The Yarmouk is also an essential supplier of water for the region.

ZONE 2: JEZREEL

Galilee is bordered on the south by the prominent Jezreel Valley. It is a break in the mountains that connects the Mediterranean Sea on the west with the Jordan River valley on the east. This valley has been the site of many wars, especially during the Judges and early kingdom periods. Any foreign army that could control this valley with chariots could essentially cut Israel in half, which is why the great judge Deborah decided to confront the nine hundred iron chariots of Jabin, the king of Hazor, in Galilee (Judges 4). King Saul also fought to control this place and, with his son Jonathan, lost his life in its eastern borders. To control access to the valley from the east, a tremendous fortress, Beit Shean, was built. Even in New Testament times when the movements of commerce replaced that of armies, Beit Shean was a large commercial city, Scythopolis, which today holds one of the largest theaters in Israel. Israeli archaeologists are working at high speed to uncover and reconstruct this beautiful city for modern tourism.

Considering the number of biblical wars in the Jezreel Valley, it comes as no surprise that this valley is called the "Valley of Armageddon." Megiddo is a fortress in the mountains of the southwest portion of the valley. "Har" means "mountains of." This *valley* beneath the "*mountains* of Megiddo" is the one that will witness, according to Revelation 16:16, the final conflict of human history.

The valley has also proven to be an agricultural asset. Generous rainfall can enter the region from the Mediterranean Sea and give it a fertility that is unsurpassed elsewhere in the country. Today the Jezreel is cultivated intensely by the Israelis.

ZONE 3: THE CENTRAL MOUNTAINS AND JORDAN VALLEY

From the Jezreel Valley to the southern end of the Dead Sea, the land follows a consistent pattern. A central mountain range follows the Jezreel Valley diagonally (northwest to southeast beginning south of Haifa), turns south when it nears the Jordan River, and then continues south for many miles. It rises to about twenty-six hundred feet around Jerusalem and three thousand feet around Shechem and Hebron. These central mountain regions today are called "Samaria" and "Judea" by Israel and are the ancient homeland of the Israelite tribes. Palestinians, on the other hand, refer to it as the "West Bank," meaning the west bank of the Jordan River. Israelite life — with Jerusalem at its center — found in these relatively remote cities safety from Egyptian and Mesopotamian armies moving along the coast.

The western flank of the mountain range is made up of low rolling hills (called the Shephelah) that decrease until they become a plain near the Mediterranean Sea. This side of the mountains (the west side) is extremely fertile since it catches the moist western rainfall from the Mediterranean Sea. Thus the west is a good agricultural region. The climate has also made it a much-sought-after region: witness the conflicts in the central mountains between the Philistines (who controlled much of the Shephelah and the coast) and the Israelites. The historic ambition of ancient Israel was to move west, to enter these hills and turn them into agricultural regions. The historical ambition of the Philistines was to keep them out. Today that rivalry continues. Numerous Arab villages were destroyed in this area from 1948 till 1967, and today many new Israeli towns have appeared.

The eastern flank of the central mountains drops quickly into the Jordan Valley. These descending hills are desert because they are in a rain shadow from the central mountains. Average rainfall here is five to ten inches per year, while in the western Shephelah rainfall is twenty to twenty-five inches per year. This area is often called "the Judean desert," which begins just over the hill from Bethel, Jerusalem, Bethlehem, and Hebron. The site of Jesus' wilderness temptation, these parched hills provide a formidable obstacle for anyone entering the land from the east. When Joshua entered the land this way, he had to climb more than thirty-seven hundred feet in as few as fifteen miles since he began at Jericho (well below sea level). When the Roman conqueror Pompey attacked Israel in 63 B.C.E., he came through this "back door" since it was the least expected approach.

The Jordan Valley, one of nature's miracles, is the lowest place on earth. The Jordan River flows south out of Galilee and culminates in the Dead Sea (about 1,275 feet below sea level). While the Jordan River is picturesque up near Galilee, in the south it winds through dreadful, deserted badlands where summer temperatures regularly exceed one hundred degrees. Winter is almost the only time to appreciate this region. Herod the Great built a "winter palace" for himself near Jericho to escape the winter winds in Jerusalem. Although few tourists visit it, today his pools and villas can still be seen. Along the western edge of the Dead Sea, numerous important archaeological sites have been found: Qumran, the home of the Dead Sea Scrolls, and Masada, the mountaintop fortress built by Roman engineers and finally defended by Jews in their last great struggle against Rome in the first century.

East of the Jordan Valley are the mountains of Moab and Edom. The valley climbs dramatically up almost four thousand feet until it levels off on a high desert plateau. Today these mountains are in the country of Jordan. This plateau was the location of biblical Edom, Moab, and Gilead (south to north) and contained a desert highway used by Moses and the Israelites as they finished their forty-year wanderings and moved toward the Promised Land. The plateau is broken by a number of gorges that bring water down from the mountains to the Jordan Valley below.

ZONE 4: THE NEGEV DESERTS

The central mountains descend and fan out into the deserts in the southernmost reaches of the country. The high Jordanian Plateau still follows the eastern border; the Jordan Valley (now waterless) is still a rift that continues beyond the Dead Sea; and in the west, deserts (called "the Negev") have populations that must live near natural springs. Isaac, for instance, decided to live in Be'er Sheva (Beersheba), which in Hebrew means "seven springs." Modern Israeli settlements here prosper only with great effort, but native Bedouin tribes still wander the region. Lucky visitors can still see camels roaming the hillsides or south of Be'er Sheva visit the splendid Museum of Bedouin History.

SUMMARY

This brief tour of the land clearly shows that the land of Israel/Palestine has dramatic differences in quality. Life in Galilee cannot be compared with life in the Negev. Farming in Israel's western hills near, say, Beit Shemesh, is good. An identical farm in the Jordan Valley near Jericho must use completely different agricultural techniques. Travel three miles north of Jericho and agriculture is virtually impossible. The distribution of land here must always consider the location of water. Israel/Palestine is not like Illinois or Michigan where land quality and rainfall are somewhat even. The country's primary river system remains in the center of a deep valley, and water cannot be carried or piped up to Jerusalem's mountains. Therefore every region is valued by how much agriculture it can sustain. Most ancient towns in biblical times survived in the central mountains by catching rainfall and holding the water in underground cisterns.

An interesting approach is to study the settlement patterns of the twelve Israelite tribes with geography in mind. Benjamin (the last son of Rachel) fortunately gained the central hill country and the hills and valleys west. This fact is really a theological comment, showing that this treasured son of Judah obtained the very best land in the country. Judah, Ephraim, and Manasseh (all privileged tribes) gained the rest of the central mountains, including the city of Jerusalem. Dan, on the other hand, lived so far down in the western hills that conflict with the Philistines made the Danites migrate north to Galilee (Judg. 18). Reuben, the firstborn son of Jacob, who should have inherited the best land, settled in the high deserts on the other side of the Dead Sea. Jacob's last words to his sons in Genesis 48 and 49 describe their fate and give insight into the future life of their people.

The modern significance of this distribution is that good land is so precious in Israel/Palestine that it is passed down from generation to generation. Even the ancient Israelite Jubilee year returned lost land to families again. Today Arabs name their land — as well as every significant feature it holds (such as caves and trees and springs). Land is a treasure. When someone is forcibly moved from the land, or when someone says "you get 50 percent" of the land, of utmost importance is the answer to the question, "Which 50 percent?" It is important to note which 50 percent we are talking about. Is this land desert (east of Jerusalem)? Is this land fertile (west of Jerusalem)? Can this land be cultivated? Hebron, for instance, grows some of the best grape harvests in the entire region! The Dotan Valley just south of Jenin and north of Nablus has rich fertile valleys that welcome intense agriculture. But villages east of Bethlehem such as Beit Sahour have such little rainfall that they must rely entirely on light industry for economic development.

ISRAEL'S NEIGHBORS

Of equal importance is understanding what countries surround Israel/ Palestine, because they have frequently played a role in Israel's internal politics. All of these countries are Arab, and each has fought Israel at some point since 1948. Today, however, many have signed peace treaties.

These countries are also relative newcomers to the world scene. For four hundred years (from 1517), the Ottoman Empire based in Istanbul, Turkey, dominated this entire land. While regional differences persisted, Ottoman control was complete, and any local expressions of autonomy were brutally suppressed. Jerusalem and its holy sites were sorely neglected for centuries. An excellent record of this neglect is clearly apparent in photographs made by the Bonfils family from Beirut, who visited the Holy Land in the 1870s.[2]

North

Israel shares a forty-nine-mile border in the north with *Lebanon.* Lebanon is a breathtakingly beautiful country with Mediterranean beaches backed by mountains rising to ten thousand feet; even in biblical times the "Cedars of Lebanon" were famous as symbols of majesty and strength (Judg. 9:15; Ps. 92:12; 104:16). The most famous delivery of its precious wood came to King Solomon and was used in building the Jerusalem Temple (1 Kings 5:1–14; 2 Chron. 2:1–16).

Following the defeat of the Ottomans in World War I, Lebanon came under French control (which explains why French can be heard along with Arabic in the capital of Beirut) and gained its independence in 1943. Its population of 3.5 million is well educated (87 percent literacy), and its European links made it a commerce and culture capital of the region. This reputation for being the "Paris" of the Middle East came to an abrupt halt in 1975 when Lebanon was plunged into a sixteen-year civil war that devastated

---

2. The Bonfils collection can be seen in many museums today and is frequently published. On the web, see *http://almashriq.hiof.no/general/700/770/779/historical/pcd0109/ pcd0109.html.*

the country. Today, Lebanon's militias have been weakened or disbanded with the help of twenty-five thousand Syrian troops that are found behind the scenes in Beirut, the central valley, and the north. Beirut is now being rebuilt with the ingenuity, creativity, and hard work so characteristic of the Lebanese. Since 1991, Lebanon has invested over $31 billion in the complete rebuilding of Beirut. Its downtown banking district hosts perhaps the most beautiful French colonial architecture in the Middle East, with cafés and restaurants crowded every night.

But Lebanon also lives with an uneasy religious balance that has often led to strife: 70 percent Muslim and 30 percent Christian. The government recognizes thirteen Christian groups (four Orthodox, six Catholic, and three Protestant).

When Israel gained nationhood in 1948, over a hundred thousand Palestinian refugees (14 percent of the total) fled to Lebanon and were blocked by Israel from returning home. This situation led to the development of refugee camps throughout the southern half of the country and made Lebanon a natural base for Palestinian resistance groups. By 1990, there were thirteen huge camps and the refugee population had climbed to over 300,000. Lebanon's Palestinian refugee population today is about 383,000, of whom 215,000 still live in camps.

From 1971 until 1982, the Palestine Liberation Organization (the PLO) was based in Lebanon and waged numerous conflicts with Israel in an attempt to redress the refugee problem.[3] The PLO was driven out in 1982 when the Israelis invaded Lebanon, moving right to the outskirts of Beirut. Israel made a buffer zone by controlling the south with its own armies and alliances with Christian militias. However, this severe Israeli occupation gave birth to an equally severe resistance movement — Hizbullah (or the Party of God) — which fought the Israelis and led to their unilateral withdrawal from the area on May 23, 2000, ending over twenty years of occupation. Today, Hizbullah still controls the south, and their distinctive yellow and green banners can be seen in almost every village.

Israel also shares a similar border with *Syria* (forty-seven miles). This large desert country sited on a semi-arid plateau is almost twenty times the size of Lebanon. Only 28 percent of Syria is arable, which means it values those regions that can be cultivated (particularly in the south). About 74 percent of Syria is Muslim, 16 percent belongs to Muslim sects (Druze, Alawite),

---

3. The PLO is a confederation of multiple Palestinian political, resistance, and humanitarian organizations headed by Yasir Arafat. It even formed a "government in exile" and today has provided the nucleus of the "Palestinian National Authority" that may eventually shape a Palestinian state.

and 10 percent is Christian; between 1 million and 1.5 million Christians live in Syria today. In fact, Syria hosts some of the most ancient Christian villages in the world. For instance, the well-known "Christian Valley" (in the southwest, near Krac de Chevaliers) hosts forty Christian villages and a living monastery with twenty monks in residence. In the northwest at Qal'at Sam'aan, one can see the ruins of a huge monastery complex that once flourished for five hundred years (before the advent of Islam). The village of Maaloula (in the hills north of Damascus) still speaks Aramaic (the language of Jesus) and has chapels dating from the early 300s. Damascus itself, a city of 5 million, has hundreds of thousands of Christians and numerous churches.

Syria lived under Ottoman rule until the end of World War I, when it declared itself an independent state ruled from Damascus in 1919. But the European powers had other plans. Backed by the League of Nations, France defeated its weak Arab army and ruled the country from 1920 until 1946 when Syria gained independence. A military regime has ruled since 1963, and following a coup, Hafez al-Assad ruled from 1971. Assad died June 10, 2000, and his thirty-four-year-old son, Bashar Al-Assad, succeeded him. Syrian Christians today speak positively of the Syrian government, claiming that they have more freedom and protection today than at any other time. Churches can be built anywhere. When they are completed, they pay no taxes and all their utilities are paid by the government. Christians even sit on Assad's ruling cabinet.

In 1948, Syria also received numerous Palestinian refugees (about 75,000) and today this number has grown to 392,000 (of which 110,000 live in camps). Syria supported the Palestinian cause and has always held a militant posture with Israel. In the failed war of 1967, Syria lost to Israel its southern link to the Galilee region and the elevated Golan Heights — both deeply valued to the country. Today the Golan has over 42 Israeli settlements (about 19,000 settlers) and is a point of sharp contention with Israel as both countries seek a way to normalize relations. Israel takes a Syrian threat quite seriously; Damascus boasts a considerable military budget of about $1 billion per year.

East

Immediately to the east, Israel shares a 148-mile border with *Jordan,* whose capital is Amman. This small desert kingdom has always seen its history as closely tied with Palestine. Following Ottoman rule, British control continued until 1946 when Jordan became independent. However — and this fact is important — Jordan possessed valuable lands west of the Jordan

River in present-day Israel. East Jerusalem and the central hills north and south were Jordanian from 1948 (Israel's independence) until 1967, when Israel conquered Jerusalem, the West Bank, and all lands up to the Jordan River. Many older Palestinians still remember "Jordanian" Jerusalem, which continues to be a point of contention. One friend who was an official in the Jordanian government in Jerusalem now runs a well-known gift shop at the Seven Arches Hotel on the Mount of Olives. Such stories are common.

Jordan emerged into nationhood as a resource-poor country populated by Bedouins and Palestinians living on a desert plateau with virtually none of the tools for building a strong economy. Water is scarce (only 4 percent arable land), and even pasture land is hard to find (9 percent). Its few resources are in mining (phosphates, potash), and most Jordanians work in industry or services. The forty-six-year rule of Jordan's King Hussein which began in 1953 made Jordan into a modern state. Despite a number of wars with Israel and Israeli possession of vast lands once claimed by Jordan, Hussein signed a peace treaty in 1994. Since then, borders have opened and trade moves between the countries. Jordan's capital, Amman, is today a modern city where English is spoken freely and Western institutions live alongside Arab culture. Its downtown sparkles with European stores, expensive cars, and billboards promoting the Internet.

Hussein was dearly loved, as was his American wife, Queen Noor, who promoted many humanitarian and environmental causes. When Hussein died on February 7, 1999, the country was grief-stricken. Within hours, Hussein's eldest son, Abdullah, was crowned as king. Respect for the nation can be seen in the tremendous number of dignitaries who deeply admired Hussein and attended the state funeral.

About 1.6 million Palestinian refugees now live in Jordan (from both the 1948 and the 1967 wars), which gives the country an inherent sympathy for Palestinian causes. Even though militant Palestinian groups were expelled in 1971, Jordan still holds a keen interest in the fate of Palestinians living under Israeli occupation. Many still have family connections, and Palestinians frequently travel to Amman for medical care and business. Today about 288,000 of the Palestinians live in refugee camps.

Christianity spread to these deserts early. When Jerusalem was destroyed by the Roman army in 70 c.e., the first Christian historian (Eusebius) tells us that the apostles and their followers moved to Pella (today a Jordanian city) to avoid the war. A strong Christian community about 200,000 strong (4 percent of the population) lives here today, and Amman hosts one of the best evangelical seminaries in the region. A number of Catholic priests currently in leadership in Palestine have come from the Jordanian city of Madaba, home to a particularly strong Roman Catholic community.

While not sharing a border with Israel, *Iraq* has always been deeply involved in the wider Arab opposition to Israel. Iraq is a large country with rich natural resources and an important history. This land is the home of the great empires of antiquity (Assyria, Babylonia), thanks to its strategic geographical location on a plain watered by the great Tigris-Euphrates river system. When Jerusalem was taken into exile in the Old Testament, its captives were brought to Babylon — a city about fifty miles south of Baghdad, the capital of Iraq. During the New Testament era, Babylon had a huge Jewish population stemming from the exile and soon found many Christian communities growing as well. In fact, its present Assyrian population (not to be confused with "Syrian") in the north is proud of the antiquity of its faith, dating from the earliest Christian centuries. This enthusiasm can lead to exaggeration, however, as one Assyrian told me, "We've been Christians since the days when Jonah preached in Nineveh!"

Following Ottoman rule, Iraq came under British control until gaining full independence in 1932, which explains the frequent use of English throughout the country. Its monarchy was pro-Western until 1958, when a period of turmoil overthrew the government. The military dictatorship of Saddam Hussein began in 1979 and continues to this day for Iraq's 25 million people. About 20 percent of Iraq is not Arab, and this population is divided between Kurds and Assyrians. About 4 percent of the population is Christian; thus, 1 million Christians live in Iraq.

For the last twenty-five years Iraq has been known for its wars. From 1980 until 1988, its struggle with Iran cost millions of lives and lost the country over $100 billion. But the invasion of Kuwait in August 1990 suddenly brought Iraq to America's attention. Iraq annexed Kuwait and filled it with three hundred thousand troops. During the Gulf War, a huge coalition of allied troops led by the United States brought seven hundred thousand personnel to the region. Following a devastating air bombardment in January 1991, a land assault in February freed Kuwait City in three days. Hoping to divide Arab support of the allied offensive, Iraq launched many long-range missiles against Israeli cities. At the end of the war, Baghdad, a city of 5 million, was crippled. Not only did it lose every bridge across the Tigris River, but its infrastructure (water, electricity, etc.) was completely ruined.

The Palestinians — always eager to champion anyone who attacks its longtime enemy in Tel Aviv — gave moral support to Iraq. This move, which also made sense because thousands of Palestinians were living and working in Baghdad, backfired entirely. Not only was Western sympathy for Palestinians hurt, but over five hundred thousand Palestinians working in Kuwait were immediately expelled.

Iraq lives today with a harsh trade embargo because it refuses to cooperate with U.N. inspection teams examining the country's nuclear, chemical, biological, and long-range missile programs. However, an oil-for-food program begun in 1996 has permitted Iraq to trade some of its vast oil reserves for food and medicine, which has alleviated some suffering but has not gone far enough to halt the catastrophic loss of life — particularly among children.[4]

But make no mistake about Iraq's attitude toward Israel. Saddam Hussein sees Israel as the singular opponent who has fractured Arab solidarity and disrupted the balance of power, bringing American interests to the region. On July 17, 2000, former U.N. inspector Richard Butler gave a lecture in Jerusalem in which he summarized comments made by the Iraqi Deputy Prime Minister Tariq Aziz. Aziz told him that his country has biological weapons now "to deal with the 'Zionist entity.'"[5] Washington sees itself as having "unfinished business" in Iraq, which was pursued in 2003 with the return of vast military resources to the region.

South

Underestimating the significance of *Egypt* in the larger scheme of Middle East life is simply impossible. This is one of the great empires of antiquity. In the Bible Joseph prospered here and Moses led Israel out of this land after a four-hundred-year sojourn. Even Jesus spent some of his childhood in Egypt. That religious heritage has not been forgotten today. The Christian church in Egypt — called the Coptic Orthodox Church — has about 10 million members in Egypt and another 1.2 million living overseas. It traces its history to the ministry of St. Mark, who was martyred in the city of Alexandria (on Easter Monday), and today the leader of the Copts, Pope Shenouda III, claims to be Mark's 117th successor.[6] Many Christians who have interviewed Pope Shenouda are at once impressed with his pastoral wisdom and wit, and his near-perfect ability to recite any passage of Scripture.

---

4. For a brief outline of the embargo and its effects see *www.megastories.com/iraq/index.htm*.

5. *Jerusalem Post*, July 18, 2000.

6. For a fascinating survey of this church, visit the official website of the Christian Coptic Orthodox Church at *www.coptic.net*.

Egyptian Christianity also has a rich tradition of Christian theology. Its great libraries and schools in Alexandria produced some of the church's most profound thinkers (Clement, Origen) as well as thousands of copies of the Bible and libraries of Christian works. The New Testament may even have been translated into Coptic first (in the third century). Christian monasticism began here with the first monk, St. Anthony, who was a Copt from southern Egypt.

But this church bears its own cross. The Muslim conquest of Egypt in 641 brought the end of Christian leadership, and since then so many Christians have died that today Copts commonly use "The Calendar of the Martyrs" to remember them. Fortunately, one of Muhammad's wives was Egyptian, and so he gave generous concessions to the Copts, permitting them to freely exercise their faith. Egypt's large majority of Muslims nevertheless makes clear that this large church will always find its power checked. Islamic fundamentalist groups like the Muslim Brotherhood today would like to change entirely the tolerant complexion of Egypt's religiously pluralistic world.

Egypt's vast arid desert (three times the size of New Mexico) is blessed with one gift that made its great civilizations possible: the Nile River. Today while only 2 percent of Egypt has arable land, twenty-two thousand square miles are irrigated from the Nile, which provides food for the country's 75 million people. European interest in Egypt also comes from the Suez Canal connecting the Mediterranean Sea to the Red Sea, making a passage to the East that avoided transit around Africa. British interests in Iraq and India until the late nineteenth and early twentieth centuries made this canal a vital strategic asset.

Since the fall of Ottoman rule, British control of Egypt continued until 1922 when independence was gained. Egyptian nationalism and defiance against Israel was shaped under Gamal Abdel Nasser (1956–70), but Anwar Sadat, Nasser's vice president and successor, helped bring Egypt into the community of world states. Despite two defeats to Israel (1967, 1973) and the loss of the Sinai Peninsula, Sadat still sought peace. In November 1977, Sadat shocked the world by asking to come to Israel to speak at its parliament. While this led to the Camp David Accords (with Jimmy Carter in 1978), a peace settlement with Israel (1979), and the return of the Sinai, Sadat alienated himself from many former Arab allies. In October 1981, Sadat was assassinated during a military parade for this overture to Israel. On October 11, 1981, England's *Sunday Times* wrote, "By that one act, committed in the third most holy city of Islam [Jerusalem], he branded himself a traitor to his own religion and invited the 'execution' that finally came from the guns of his own soldiers."

Egypt has always held firm sympathies with the losses of the Palestinians and so joined in most wars against Israel. Few refugees came to Egypt in 1948 (seven thousand people) because of its distance, but over two hundred thousand Palestinians fleeing south packed into Gaza, a coastal region under Egyptian control. Gaza came under the control of Israel in 1967 and the refugee population grew considerably. By the 1990s, the Gaza refugee population exceeded 1.1 million, creating a truly explosive environment where extremist movements have been born. But Egypt will not be pushed by Palestinian calls for justice and statehood. Egypt's current president, Mohammed Hosni Mubarak, believes firmly that his country's national interests will continue to dominate its relation with Israel, with whom peace and increasing trade are priorities. But his people are also mindful of Palestinian suffering. Four hundred thousand Palestinian refugees within Egypt's borders won't let them forget.

SUMMARY

The Arab states surrounding Israel have been consistent in their resistance to Israel's statehood. They are sympathetic to the Palestinian loss of land and see Israel as one more extension of Western imperialism in the Middle East. This time, however, French and English interests are not the problem, but rather Jewish interests backed by American dollars. Therefore while Israel is not a threat, say, to Jordan or Egypt, Israel is viewed as an offense to Arab sensibility and pride. As Israel has conquered and acquired more and more land — creating more and more refugees — Arab states have unified in their opposition.

However, to stereotype these countries as trying to "push Israel into the sea" would be incorrect. Arab belligerence was a luxury of the cold war era when Russian dollars financed Arab armies. Those days are over, and a new generation of Arab leaders sees Israel as a permanent resident in the neighborhood. Jordan and Egypt now hold peace accords with Israel. Israel has withdrawn its troops from southern Lebanon. Beirut is being rebuilt, and Cairo is more keen to promote economic modernization than military threats. Moreover today a new leadership is just over the horizon. Two young men in their thirties now rule in Damascus and Amman. In Iraq, Saddam Hussein's eldest son, Odai Hussein, won a seat in the Iraqi Parliament (March 28, 2000), will likely become the speaker of the house, and is the heir apparent. Abdullah, Jordan's new king, already shuttles between Washington and the Middle East brokering peace.

This situation bodes well for regional peace, but it comes at the price of taking Arab support away from the Palestinians. Without the help of military intervention from across the border, Palestinian national movements — in all of their chaos and powerlessness — stand alone facing Israel, which continues to build itself internally. Today, however, these hopeful signs of peace have been utterly shattered by levels of conflict never predicted even three years ago, making some wonder if the current Israeli/Palestinian struggle begun in September 2000 might unravel the optimism of even the most hopeful leaders. We tell that story in our next chapter.

Chapter Three

KNOWING
THE HISTORY

My final purpose is to take possession in due course of Palestine and to restore to the Jews the political independence of which they have now been deprived for two thousand years. Don't laugh. It is not a mirage. There will come that splendid day prophesied by Isaiah. Then the Jews, if necessary with arms in their hands, will publicly proclaim themselves master of their own ancient fatherland.   — Ze'ev Dubov, one of the first Zionists to reach Palestine, 1882

One of the most difficult things to understand about Israel/Palestine is its history of conquest and occupation. Most books give more detail than we need. Modern descriptions assume we know, for instance, why the Palestinians are angry about land "taken" by Israel in 1967. Where do the British fit in? And what about these "wars" whose dates writers often parade out (1948, 1967, etc.)? At the risk of oversimplifying, I shall attempt a concise summary of the last four thousand years, beginning with the tribes of Abraham and concluding with the modern era. Keep in mind that the earlier dates are debated. This outline is designed for reference and comparison.

THE BIBLICAL PERIOD

Tribal Period (2000–1000 B.C.E.)

In the earliest period, Abraham's tribe migrated from Mesopotamia (Iraq) into the land. Israel/Palestine was an Egyptian province called Canaan. The descendants of Abraham through his grandson Jacob (Israel's twelve tribes) migrated to Egypt and remained there for more than four hundred years. Moses led them back to Canaan, and Joshua led their conquest of the land. They were loosely organized around God's tabernacle in the central mountains. However, Israel yearned to have a king and a kingdom like other nations. Saul was the first king, which was Israel's first overture to self-conscious nationhood.

The Kingdom of Israel (1000–538? B.C.E.)

Saul, David, and Solomon gave Israel international status in the region, but this era of successful nationhood lasted only about seventy-five years. A civil war following the death of Solomon divided the land north and south. The north (Samaria; capital: Samaria) was conquered by the Assyrians in 721 B.C.E. The south (Judah; capital: Jerusalem) was conquered by Babylon in 586 B.C.E. Survivors from the south remained in Babylon in exile until they were freed by the Persians about fifty years later.

The Persian Period (538?-332 B.C.E.)

The Persian defeat of Babylon sent the Israelites back to Jerusalem, but they were not permitted to rebuild a completely autonomous nation. Israel/Palestine was a Persian province ruled from Samaria. Jerusalem was rebuilt (Ezra, Nehemiah), and the Jews lived under Persian domination for two hundred years.

The Greek Period (332–164 B.C.E.)

Alexander the Great conquered the Middle East after he defeated the Persians in 333 B.C.E., went on to subdue Israel in 332 B.C.E., and made the entire region a part of the Greek Empire. For 150 years Judaism lived as a vassal under Greek rulers and adopted much of Greek culture.

The Jewish Hasmonean Kingdom (164–63 B.C.E.)

Jewish armies defeated their Greek overlords and established the first Jewish "kingdom" since the monarchy of the Old Testament. However, following its victory the leadership quickly fell to corruption and internal conflict, with warring factions (Pharisees and Sadducees) paralyzing the government. Many Jews dissented and departed, forming enclaves of communal life in the desert (such as the Dead Sea community at Qumran).

The Roman Empire (63 B.C.E.–324 C.E.)

The Romans conquered the entire Middle East in the century before the birth of Christ (63 B.C.E.) and made it one of its provinces for more than four hundred years. The Jews were given some autonomy, but persecution was common and revolts against Rome frequent. In 66–70 C.E., Rome suppressed a major revolt and utterly destroyed Jerusalem. In 132–35 C.E., a second revolt was likewise defeated, and the Jews were expelled from Jerusalem permanently. Jewish leadership migrated to Galilee. Countless other Jews found themselves forming communities throughout Europe, North Africa, and the Middle East.

THE MEDIEVAL PERIOD

The Christian Roman Empire (324–638 C.E.)

From 324 to 638 C.E., Israel/Palestine was controlled by rulers in Constantinople (today called Istanbul, Turkey). This civilization (called Byzantine) was the grandchild of the Roman Empire and embraced Christianity as a national religion. Jerusalem witnessed the construction of many of its most famous churches in these centuries, because many Christians began to travel on pilgrimage to the "Holy Land." Likewise the Christian communities of Lebanon, Syria, Egypt, and Jordan grew rapidly. Pilgrimage to Syria, for instance, was common among Byzantine Christians, and vast ruins of Christian monastic complexes are still visible in the country today.

The Emperor Constantine's mother, Helena, claimed to find the original cross in Jerusalem, and with her inspiration, Constantine consecrated three important churches centered on three caves, recalling Christ's birth, death/resurrection, and ascension. Soon pilgrims were traveling in vast numbers. Monasteries were turning desert valleys into cities. At one point, twenty-four churches surrounded by their monasteries populated the Mount of Olives. Despite devastating attacks by Persians (614) and later Muslim clerics (e.g., the Caliph Hakim, 1009), the Church of the Holy Sepulchre still stands today as a great and historic monument to Byzantine devotion.

Islamic Period (638–1099 C.E.)

Arabs from present-day Saudi Arabia swept north bearing the religion of Muhammad (Islam) with evangelistic zeal. All "Byzantine" provinces in the Middle East were put under siege, and an exhausted Byzantine military could not resist. In 636, a major army lost in battle to Arab invaders at the Yarmouk River gorge (in western Jordan), and two years later (638) Jerusalem surrendered to the second successor of Muhammad, the Caliph Omar. Omar respected both Jews and Christians and did not slaughter the residents of the city. In fact, he refused to pray in the Church of the Holy Sepulchre despite the invitation of the patriarch because, he argued, "If I had prayed in the church it would have been lost to you, for the Believers [Muslims] would have taken it saying: Omar prayed here." Islamic control continued until 1099. Impressive architectural remains (such as the famous "Dome of the Rock") originated in this era.

The Crusaders (1099–1187 C.E.)

Christian knights from Europe traveled to Israel/Palestine and recaptured the city of Jerusalem in 1099, slaughtering most of the city's residents, Jew and Muslim alike. Even today, Muslims have not forgotten the fanaticism and brutality of that act, and "crusader" is a name that can evoke passionate anger.[1] Their control was brief, however. The Arab leader Saladin (or Salah Aldin) defeated the Crusaders in Galilee in 1187. The Europeans barely held a few remaining fortresses (such as Acco in the western Jezreel Valley and Krac de Chevaliers in Syria) with the help of reinforcements from France and Britain. Nevertheless, internecine conflict reigned for many years. Finally in 1291, the crusaders were utterly driven out (their remaining armies fleeing to Cyprus).

The Egyptian Mamlukes (1250–1517 c.e.)

In 1250, armies from Egypt defeated the regime of Saladin, and for more than three hundred years, Israel/Palestine was a defensive province for an Egyptian Islamic empire that needed to guard its northern frontier. The land and its people were neglected terribly even though Christian pilgrims, particularly from the Latin west, continued to travel to Jerusalem.

The Ottoman Turks (1517–1918 c.e.)

In 1517, a rival Islamic power in Istanbul, Turkey, defeated the Mamlukes and took Israel/Palestine into its realm. Ottoman control lasted four hundred years, giving the old city of Jerusalem its distinctive character we see today. For instance, the ancient walls of the city were built by Ottoman ruler Sulayman the Magnificent from 1537 to 1540. Despite Turkish dominance, an Arab society lived in Palestine (along with a very small Jewish minority) and flourished. While some claim that Palestinian life barely existed through this period, excellent written and photographic histories depict a thriving culture.[2]

In the nineteenth century, European Jews began to migrate because of persecution, and Palestine was one of their destinations. They had been expelled from England in 1290, from France in 1394, and from Spain in 1492. Most had gone to Eastern Europe and the Ottoman Empire. But in the nineteenth century, European persecutions — particularly in Russia — became acute, and the dream of a homeland was born. By the late nineteenth century, only about twenty-five thousand Jews were in Palestine, and most of these lived in Jerusalem surrounded by a vast Arab majority.

---

1. In October 2000, Wheaton College abandoned its historic mascot, the Crusader, following two years of debate and study. Our campus wisely decided not to associate with this era of Christian brutality.

2. See W. Khalidi, *Before Their Diaspora: A Photographic History of the Palestinians, 1876–1948* (Washington, D.C.: Institute for Palestine Studies, 1992).

This dream — called Zionism — was rooted in a Jewish theological vision that sustained a hope for return to the land of Israel. "Next year in Jerusalem" was a centuries-old Passover refrain everyone knew, but this vision found expression between 1880 and 1900 when Russian persecution had reached its peak. In 1897, Theodor Herzl organized the first "Zionist Congress" in Basel, Switzerland, and gathered Jewish intellectuals from twenty-four countries. Following this meeting, Herzl wrote in his diary, "At Basel I founded the Jewish state."[3] Within a couple of years, over ten thousand Zionist settlers had moved to Palestine. Many purchased land from absentee Arab landlords who had no investment in the local people, but other Zionist leaders understood that one feature of their strategy had to be removing the Arab population. Herzl wrote in his diary on June 12, 1895, that the removal of the Arabs bodily from Palestine is part of the Zionist plan "to spirit a penniless population across the frontier by denying it employment. Both the process of expropriation and the removal of the poor must be carried out discreetly and circumspectly."

The only obstacle to Herzl's plan for a Jewish homeland in Israel was Ottoman rule, which was about to be overturned by World War I.

THE MODERN PERIOD

The British Mandate (1918–48 c.e.)

Because the Turks had sided with Germany in the war, the victors dismembered the Ottoman Empire and took the spoils. France and Britain divided up the Middle East and created most of the borders we know today. Britain initiated its control over "Palestine" (they termed it) and Jordan (as well as other areas such as Iraq and Egypt). The Zionists saw clearly that if they were to establish their homeland, they had to win British support. In 1916, the key was found when Arthur Balfour, a friend of the Zionist cause, became Britain's foreign minister. Balfour successfully convinced the government to support Zionism because it would wear well in America, which they wanted to bring into the war. The "Balfour Declaration" (1917) did not support the formation of a Jewish state, but it affirmed British support for a "national home" for Jews in Palestine with the condition that the civil and religious rights of non-Jews in Palestine would not be lost. Five weeks after the declaration, British troops entered Jerusalem.

---

3. Cited in T. M. McAleavy, *The Arab-Israeli Conflict* (Cambridge: Cambridge University Press, 1998), 11.

British control over Palestine continued until the outbreak of World War II. Many Jewish families emigrated to Palestine, joining courageous communities of Zionist pioneers who at first truly worked to coexist with the Arabs. Their numbers were small (fewer than one hundred thousand living with five hundred thousand Arabs) but they were well-organized, bringing with them skills honed in European universities. They also built organizations that would eventually become the seeds of the Israeli state. Arab anxiety was strong, however, as they watched the balance of power and influence shift under British rule. Fighting in numerous cities tore the fragile peace between Jew and Arab. In 1929, for instance, sixty Jews were killed in rioting in the Arab town of Hebron, and conflicts like this evoked memories of European persecutions — which only galvanized Zionist determination. Israeli settlers in downtown Hebron today have a museum for this massacre, and it contributes to their "siege" mentality, framing their relation to the Arabs as if they were once again living in Germany.

The shock of the Nazi Holocaust created a fervor among Zionists to move out of Europe that much sooner. As British troops tried to govern a now-divided country, Jewish pressure for immigration increased. The British had changed their minds, though, knowing that the creation of a Jewish state would explode the fragile peace in the region. Nevertheless, ships continued to force their way to the coastline, and British troops found themselves in the unenviable position of stopping refugee-survivors from the European Holocaust. Zionist soldiers began attacking British positions and using terrorism, such as blowing up part of Jerusalem's King David Hotel (July 1946) where British officials kept their offices. American public opinion and the sympathies of Washington soon became critical of Britain's posture and openly supported the formation of a Jewish state.

Exhausted and further depleted by World War II, Britain could not retain control of the lands mandated to it following World War I. In 1947, Britain announced that it would leave the region, handing "Palestine" over to the United Nations. That year, the United Nations proposed a partition of Palestine in order to make an Arab and a Jewish state.[4] But the divisions of land barely reflected the size of each population. Despite extreme Arab resentment, Israel raised its new flag with the star of David on May 14,

---

4. A detailed map showing the borders of the partition is difficult to find. An excellent scholarly edition can be found in H. Cattan, *Palestine, the Arabs and Israel: The Search for Justice* (London: Longman, 1969), 207. Generally, the land was to be partitioned in three sections: forty-five hundred square miles for the Jewish state, and Jerusalem to be set off as an international island for both parties and all religions.

1948. Within eleven minutes, President Truman of the United States gave Israel formal recognition. At once the Arabs declared war.

The First War: 1948, "The War of Independence"

Known as Israel's War of Independence, Israeli and Arab armies (from Egypt, Syria, Jordan, Lebanon, Saudi Arabia, and Iraq) fought viciously to change the boundaries. King Abdullah I of Jordan no doubt had dreams of taking everything, including land promised to Israel. Other Arabs were offended even by the notion of an Israeli state or the presumption that a European-American assembly (the United Nations) could determine the destiny of the region.

Israel won decisively and redrew the map, acquiring more land than was even offered in the U.N. partition. At the close of the war, Israel occupied 77 percent of the land (33 percent more than the U.N. proposal). Nevertheless, Jordan occupied the West Bank of the Jordan River (all the way into the central mountains, including the cities of Nablus, Ramallah, and Hebron). Jordan also possessed the eastern half of the city of Jerusalem. Even though the Partition Plan of 1947 anticipated a Palestinian state, Jordan later annexed the West Bank (issuing Jordanian citizenship papers and passports there). In the end, hopes for a Palestinian state free of Israeli and Jordanian rule evaporated.

In response to the fighting thousands of refugees fled from the war zone into the West Bank and neighboring countries (see notes below). According to U.N. estimates, about 750,000 people were displaced. Seeing this activity as an opportunity to move a population, Israel then closed its borders, refusing reentry to most of the refugees following the war. Soon hundreds of Arab villages were destroyed (over 350 of them), making any return an impossibility. As Joseph Weitz, director of the Jewish National Land Fund, remarked in 1940, "It must be clear that there is no room for both peoples in this country. If the Arabs leave the country, it will be broad and wide open for us. If the Arabs stay, the country will remain narrow and miserable. The only solution is Israel without Arabs. There is no room for compromise on this point." David Ben-Gurion, Israel's first prime minister, was specific about his strategy. In a letter to his son in 1937 he wrote, "We will expel the Arabs and take their place."[5]

In order to accomplish the "ethnic cleansing" of important regions, Jewish military regiments, the Irgun (led by Menachem Begin), the Stern Gang (led by Yizhak Shamir), and the Haganah launched terrorist offensives to

---

5. Cited in McAleavy, *The Arab-Israeli Conflict*, 22.

remove villagers. The most famous took place on April 9, 1948, when the village of Deir Yassin near Jerusalem was attacked. Over 250 people were slaughtered, and the news spread quickly. Israeli propaganda distributed in Arab villages referred frequently to "Deir Yassin" as the fate of villages that resist. Some of Deir Yassin's villagers were even driven through Jerusalem in a "victory parade" before being taken back to the village and shot.[6] (The survivors of Deir Yassin have kept these memories alive and even have their own website publishing their personal accounts and photographs.[7])

Within days, 50,000 Arabs fled from both Haifa and Jaffa. By May, 250,000 Arabs were running. More than any other event, the massacre at Deir Yassin was responsible for breaking the spirit of the civilian population. In June 1948, Israeli leader Ben-Gurion made his policy clear: "I do not accept that we should encourage their return. I believe we should prevent their return. We must settle Jaffa. Jaffa will become a Jewish city. We must prevent at all costs their return."[8] Ben-Gurion wrote in his diary on December 19, 1947, how a village must be approached: "In each attack, a decisive blow should be struck, resulting in the destruction of homes and the expulsion of the population." In order to guarantee that the Arabs would not return, the villages were generally destroyed and their village wells poisoned, generally with typhus and dysentery bacteria. The Arab village at Acre, for instance, could not be conquered, so in 1948 soldiers placed dysentery bacteria in the spring feeding the town (called the Capri); once the entire town became sick, Jewish forces occupied the town.[9] Today the Israeli water authority, Mekorot, regularly checks wells in rural areas since, according to many technicians, soldiers poisoned virtually every Arab well they captured.

Israelis frequently dispute this tragic story, but today it cannot be denied. A new generation of historians — such as Benny Morris — have opened this painful chapter for all Israelis to see. Morris's most recent book, *Correcting a Mistake — Jews and Arabs in Palestine/Israel 1936–1956,* is a shocking exposé of government half-truths that covered up plans to "cleanse" a land and exterminate an entire people.[10]

---

6. A. Shlaim, *The Politics of Partition* (New York: Columbia University Press, 1988), 136.

7. *www.deiryassin.org.*

8. Cited in McAleavy, *The Arab-Israeli Conflict,* 24. Today the Internet has become a mine of information about specific village histories. For a sample, see *http://alcor.concordia.ca/~pal/History/Villages/village@.html.*

9. *The Link* 34, no. 1 (January–March 2001): 4–6, citing S. Laybobis-Dar in the Hebrew newspaper *Hadashot* (August 13, 1993).

10. B. Morris, *Correcting a Mistake — Jews and Arabs in Palestine/Israel 1936–1956* (Tel Aviv: Am Oved Publishers, 2000). Also see B. Morris, *Israel's Border Wars, 1949–1956: Arab Infiltration, Israeli Retaliation and the Countdown to the Suez War* (Oxford: Clarendon Press,

It has always struck me as ironic that if you stand in the right place at the Jewish Holocaust Memorial in Jerusalem (Yad Vashem), you can almost see the village of Deir Yassin. Even the family home of Menachem Begin (the leader of the massacre) is just across the valley. But Deir Yassin was not an exception to the Israeli's ethnic cleansing. Countless villages received severe treatment. In the end, over 350 villages were turned to rubble. From the Palestinian view, these events were the first use of "terrorism" in the country.

The Second War: 1956, "The Sinai War"

Hostilities continued for eight years, generally in the form of guerrilla attacks. Egypt's fury was expressed by nationalizing the Suez Canal in 1954 and by closing the canal to Israeli shipping the next year. Egypt also blockaded the Israeli port of Eilat, disrupting all Asia-bound shipping. Seeing this move as an act of war, Israel attacked Egypt on October 29, 1956, with a land assault across the Sinai. British and French forces then bombed Port Said and Port Fu'ad at the north end of the canal and landed troops. In response to exhaustive U.N. condemnations (and American pressure), Britain and France left Egypt; Israel withdrew in 1957. U.N. troops entered the region to secure a fragile peace on the promise that Egypt would not stop Israeli shipping from Eilat through the Gulf of Aqaba.

The Third War: 1967, "The Six-Day War"

The struggle was obviously not going to end that easily. Border skirmishes continued between Israel and the Arab countries of Syria, Jordan, and Egypt for eleven years. By 1966, all of the countries clearly were bracing for war. Egypt termed it "a holy war" to defeat the Jews. By spring 1967, Egypt called for the withdrawal of all U.N. troops in Sinai. Egypt then blocked the Gulf of Aqaba again and began moving heavily armored divisions to the border. Syria did the same. The Arabs were poised to field about 540,000 troops, 2,500 tanks, and 950 aircraft. The Israelis had 265,000 troops, 800 tanks, and 300 aircraft. The odds could not have been stacked more firmly against Israel.

Anticipating an attack, on June 5, 1967, Israel struck first by launching an air strike in the early morning and virtually wiped out the Egyptian air force on the ground. By nightfall, Israel had destroyed 416 Arab planes. Within two days (June 7), Israel occupied all of east Jerusalem — meaning that for the first time since the days of the Roman Empire, Jews now

---

1993), and *The Birth of the Palestinian Refugee Problem, 1947–1949* (Cambridge: Cambridge University Press, 1987). See the review of G. Levy, *Am Ha'aretz*, November 3, 2000.

occupied Jerusalem in its entirety. Within a week (June 10), the war was over. With lightning speed and superior organization, Israel had defeated an overwhelming Arab army and succeeded in taking the Sinai, Gaza, the West Bank (to the Jordan River), and the Golan Heights.

Following the war, another million Arabs were now under Israeli military control, and over 350,000 Arabs fled as refugees to neighboring countries. By December, 245,000 fled the West Bank, 11,000 fled Gaza, and 116,000 Syrians fled the Golan Heights. *And again Israel closed its borders to them.* The United Nations concluded that Israel had no intention of returning to its "pre-1967" borders and in November 1967 demanded that it do so. This U.N. decision — Resolution 242 — is famous and is still cited today as a call for Israel to return conquered lands and set captive people free.[11]

The Fourth War: 1973, "The Yom Kippur War"

Calculating the wound to Arab pride that came in 1967 is impossible. Syria and Egypt — with massive aid from the Soviet Union — began rebuilding their armies almost immediately. This time, however, both were equipped with sophisticated surface-to-air missiles that would halt another Israeli air attack. Incredibly Israel was complacent, basking now in its victory of 1967 and enjoying the "buffer" zones created on most frontiers.

On October 6, 1973 — the Jewish holy day of Yom Kippur — Jewish farmers relaxing near Gaza suddenly heard the scream of Egyptian fighters overhead. They couldn't believe what they were seeing. At the Suez Canal, 400 Israeli soldiers were quickly overrun, and in minutes 8,000 Egyptian troops were across the border, followed by wave after wave of tanks. Israelis scrambled to counter the attack by air, but Soviet missiles shot them down. On the Golan Heights, 1,100 Syrian tanks overran 157 Israeli tanks, and in a handful of days, Syrian forces had penetrated Israel. The seriousness of the attack was sobering and frightening. In one month, Israel lost 2,378 soldiers.

Resupplied by American arms stores in Europe ($2.2 billion), the Israeli army counterattacked within the week, pushing the Syrians back. American satellite reconnaissance fed Israel the exact positions of all Egyptian troop movements in Sinai, and by mid-October the Egyptian army had lost over 250 tanks (compared to 10 Israeli tanks destroyed). Israeli speed, resolve, and discipline joined with superior American equipment and intelligence made victory inevitable. The Arab armies were fighting not simply Israel,

---

11. Today the boundary that marks the division between lands captured in 1948 and lands captured in 1967 is called "the green line." One often hears, "that village is on the other side of the green line."

but America — a note not later forgotten. In late October, the Egyptian Third Army was surrounded in Sinai, and though Israel wanted to completely destroy it, American pressure made Israel withdraw, ending the war on October 26.

With the help of the United States (and Henry Kissinger's "shuttle diplomacy"), Egypt was willing to make concessions to Israel if Egypt would regain the oil fields of Sinai. Kissinger won this point in 1975, and with generous American aid now flowing to Egypt, Cairo's hostilities eased. In this less tense atmosphere, Egyptian President Anwar Sadat made a surprise visit to Jerusalem in 1977, paving the way for the famous meeting at Camp David in 1979 with Jimmy Carter. The accords reached at the meeting included a formal peace treaty, establishment of diplomatic relations, and Israel's complete withdrawal from the Sinai. They also stipulated that this peace "be linked" to full autonomy for the Palestinians. Sadat's courageous overture cost him his life, however, as he was killed in October 1981 by Egyptian radicals opposed to the peace process.

The Fifth War: 1982, "The Invasion of Lebanon"

With its southern border secured, Israel turned its attention to Palestinian military attacks on the Lebanese border in the north. Palestinians exiled since 1948 were waging a guerrilla war on northern Galilee, angry that they could not return home. In 1978, Israel launched its first land assault into Lebanon in order to create a buffer zone that it could control with the aid of Christian militias in the region. Still, the Palestinian forces were numerous and aggressive. Therefore, in June 1982, Israel launched a full-scale invasion of Lebanon (called "Operation Peace for Galilee") in order to drive out the confederation of resistance groups called the Palestine Liberation Organization (known simply as the PLO). Refugee camps in southern Lebanon were destroyed, and Israeli armor rolled to the edge of Beirut. For three months, Israeli artillery shelled the city, indiscriminately killing many thousands of Lebanese civilians until the Lebanese themselves agreed to usher the Palestinian leadership out of the country. Terror became another tactic as Lebanese militias under Israeli protection committed atrocities in refugee camps (e.g., the Sabra and Shatila camps). Finally, in August 1982, the PLO leadership was given safe passage out of Beirut and departed for Tunisia. In their wake, sixteen thousand Arabs and seven hundred Israeli soldiers had died.[12]

12. For an outstanding study of the invasion of Lebanon written by a Christian pastor, see P. Crooks, *Lebanon: The Pain and the Glory* (Eastborne, Sussex: Monarch, 1990). Formerly an Anglican chaplain in Beirut and Damascus, Crooks now lives in England. The

Many Arabs in Lebanon viewed America as responsible for financing Israel's siege of their country. American hardware attacking them by air and land was easy to see. One popular Arab song in the period called Israel "the snake" to be watched — and America as "the head of the snake." In July 1983, an Arab suicide bomber vented this hostility by destroying the U.S. Marine headquarters in Beirut, killing hundreds of American soldiers. For any astute observer of the region, the attack was an utterly predictable episode focused on a poorly defended target.

Refugees

Most of the major military conflicts just discussed produced refugees who fled their homes because of the war and then were refused permission to return. The numbers are simply staggering. Entire families have grown up in the squalor of these camps, and young adults have known no other life.

According to the United Nations, today more than 3.6 million Palestinian refugees are scattered throughout the West Bank, Gaza, and the countries surrounding Israel. Palestinians have also migrated to Western countries such as Australia and the United States. Today in Chicago and Detroit, for example, entire Palestinian communities have their own stores and neighborhoods — and long memories of the land left behind. What is surprising is how these refugees still remember their villages and their histories. In the large camp of Jalazone outside Ramallah, a family once explained their history to me in detail. Their home once had been located where today we find Tel Aviv's Ben-Gurion International Airport. In 1948, the family was driven out by the army. Some extent of the disaster to Palestinian villages can be seen in the following statistics: of about 807 registered Palestinian villages in 1945, only 433 were still standing by 1967. Put bluntly, 45 percent of the Palestinian villages were emptied and demolished as a result of the creation of the state of Israel.[13] As Israel acquired land, one of its specific goals was to depopulate the areas acquired. Today we refer to such activity as "ethnic cleansing." The Palestinians fell victim to propaganda campaigns

---

book is enthusiastically endorsed by the Anglican bishop of Jerusalem. More recently, see the article by B. Belsham, "Why Four Corners Was Perfectly Entitled to Accuse Sharon," at *www.theage.com.au/articles/2002/05/01/1019441390497.html.*

13. S. Jiryis, *The Arabs in Israel*, trans. from Arabic by Inea Bushnaq (New York: Monthly Review Press, 1976), 70. Lists of Palestinian villages can be found in official Israeli publications. For 1967, see Census of Populations 1967 (Central Bureau of Statistics), West Bank of the Jordan, Gaza Strip and northern Sinai, Golan Heights, Publication 1 (Jerusalem, 1967), 45–49, 163–65. For a catalogue of villages, see J. Fayez, *Lest the Civilized World Forget: The Colonization of Palestine* (New York: Americans for Middle East Understanding, 1992). Increasingly the Internet is a repository for catalogues of these villages and their stories.

telling them to flee. Many Arab countries affirmed the wisdom of flight on the assumption that everyone could return home once the fighting was over.

One of my former Jewish neighbors spent most of his life in a kibbutz near Gaza during those turbulent years. He tells how in 1948 Israeli planes dropped leaflets in the Palestinian villages warning the people to get out or else they would all be killed. After they left, Israeli settlers simply moved into the Palestinian homes. Some of the villages were destroyed by dynamite, and some were plowed under for agricultural areas. Others are now buried in reforestation projects.

Consider, for instance, the Galilee village of Lubya (or Louba). Not far north of Nazareth and Kana is a small hill just off the Tiberius-Nazareth highway where Lubya was once located (about five miles west of Tiberius). Its history goes back before the Crusaders, who called the town Lubia. Nearby are the ruins of a medieval caravansary known as "Khan Lubya," which refreshed travelers a thousand years ago. Even nineteenth-century pilgrims leaving Nazareth made note of it in their diaries. During the early twentieth century, about seven hundred people lived here.

The village was attacked at night on January 20, 1948, by Zionist forces who were repelled. More attacks continued through March, but in April when Tiberius fell, Lubya looked to Nazareth for aid. In July, Nazareth surrendered to Israeli soldiers and the residents of Lubya were terrified. On July 16, most of the village fled northwest toward Lebanon, leaving behind some armed men and the elderly. When the Israelis arrived, they shelled the village and then began destroying homes. The elderly hid in caves and some escaped, but little is known of their fate. The villagers became refugees in Lebanon and have never been permitted by the Israelis to return.

Today the Lavi Pine Forest planted by the Jewish National Fund stands on the site. The debris of Lubya's houses is buried in these forests, and one can still find the cacti, the fig, and the pomegranate trees marking another generation's work. Random stone walls and the village's cisterns are still visible. Ironically, an Israeli military museum has been built adjacent to the site in honor of an Israeli brigade's heroism.[14]

The Sixth War: 1987–93, "The First Intifada"

During each of the previous wars, the Palestinians residing in and around Israel were becoming the pawns in a larger Middle Eastern chess game.

---

14. The secondary road which once led from the village to the Tiberias-Nazareth highway can still be located on the roadside. See also B. Morris, *The Birth of the Palestinian Refugee Problem* (Cambridge: Cambridge University Press, 1987).

As one Arab leader after the next came to terms with Israel's existence, Palestinian frustration became acute. *Who would champion their cause?* In fact, an entire generation had now grown up under Israeli occupation, and 70 percent of the Palestinians were under twenty-five years of age. An estimated 120,000 of them traveled daily into Israel as manual laborers, and they could see the enormous inequities of their lives. Israeli appropriation of Arab land had grown at an alarming rate. Almost 50 percent of the West Bank and 30 percent of Gaza had been taken by the Israeli government. Water rights likewise provoked anger. In Gaza, 750,000 Palestinians consumed about 30 percent of the water available while 45,000 Jewish settlers were allotted the remaining 70 percent. Furthermore, in 1985, Israel's Defense Minister Yitzhak Rabin introduced his "Iron Fist II" policy to crush any Palestinian resistance. Within a month, twelve Palestinian political leaders were deported out of the country with no formal trial, sixty-two activists were placed under administrative detention, and five people were killed by the military. Israeli prisons were being filled with Palestinians, most under twenty-one. That same year, Israel bombed the new headquarters of the PLO in Tunis, killing more than seventy Palestinian leaders.

These compressed feelings erupted with a fury on December 8, 1987. A small group of tired Palestinian men were waiting in their cars on a narrow Gaza road at a military checkpoint. They were returning from a day's work in Israel, crossing back into the territory where they lived. Suddenly, an Israeli tank appeared and swerved into the line of cars, crushing everything in its path. Four men died instantly, seven were critically injured. Official military reports stated that the tank's brakes had failed. Rumor among those living in Gaza told a different story — that the crash was deliberate, in retaliation for the death of an Israeli soldier's relative. The Palestinians found the rumor more believable, and the following day six thousand people attended the four men's funeral. Soon there were demonstrations and protests, which were quickly confronted by Israeli soldiers in the streets of Gaza. Arab injuries were everywhere as tear gas, beatings, and arrests spread and Israeli troops poured in. This funeral was to be the most significant in Palestinian history. *The Intifada had begun.*

Palestinians took to the streets throughout the country, disengaging from the Israeli economy and fighting their occupation with civil disobedience (throwing stones, etc.) to thwart Israel's control and inspire international sympathy. Soon the world's televisions were showing heavily armed Israeli soldiers with Uzi submachine guns squaring off against teenagers with slings and rocks. It was made for TV: David and Goliath revisited, except that now the Jews were playing the role of the giant. In many cases, women took to the street and dared the soldiers to harm them. When harm came in the form of rubber bullets, toxic tear gas, or glass pellets shot from guns, the rage in the villages was uncontrollable. During the first year of fighting, 300 Palestinians were killed and 11,500 were wounded. To enter the street, to resist the soldier, even to be wounded — these became marks of heroism in villages and refugee camps. At last, Palestinians said, "we're doing something." Soon the uprising was guided by a central authority — The Unified National Command of the Uprising — which worked closely with the PLO. Momentum was growing.

Intifada does not mean "uprising." Palestinians say it means to shake off aggressively as if a scorpion had suddenly appeared on your arm. The Intifada was the first unifying expression of Palestinian solidarity that could not be stopped. The Israelis did everything to halt it: beatings, arrests, deportations, shootings. Nothing worked. The Palestinian school system was closed for two years, the university system was closed for four. In five years, over 1,000 Palestinians were killed by soldiers and 230 of these were under sixteen years old. Over 16,000 people were imprisoned, and over 1,882 homes were demolished as punishment. On any given day, 25,000 Arabs could be found under curfew. Some villages witnessed mass arrests where all males between the ages of fourteen and sixty were taken away to detention camps where torture became a frequent policy of the Israeli Secret Police (Shin Bet). Only in the last three years has Israel admitted these policies and made them public in its national press.

A June 1994 report of the Palestine Human Rights Information Center offers some idea of the impact of the Intifada. By their estimate, the total deaths resulting from shootings, beatings, or tear gas was 1,392. Of this number, 362 were children under the age of sixteen. Injuries stemming from actions of the Israeli army were about 130,787. The number of property demolitions numbered at almost 2,000, and about 382 houses had been sealed shut. Given statistics such as these, it is little wonder that the world raised an outcry at the images the media captured from the streets. In fact, one of the main reasons that the Intifada had some definite, positive consequences was because of the media's role in the conflict. Thousands of protests erupted throughout the world in countries such as West Germany, Italy, Canada, the United States, the Netherlands, and Japan. Gallup polls in the United States revealed that 41 percent of Americans thought U.S. aid to Israel should be decreased, and 20 percent wanted it stopped altogether. Twenty-two percent of these people gave Israel's handling of the Intifada as the reason for their opinion.

The effect on Israel was paralyzing. Israelis suddenly were engaged in an *internal war* that could not be won. Young Israeli men and women, trained in field combat, were now in the streets brutalizing average people, and it wounded the Jewish conscience. Numerous Israeli peace groups spoke out, condemning Israeli behavior. Many Jewish families, shaped by the heroism of other wars, viewed these deeds as demolishing Israeli virtue. The government had worked hard in many cases to improve life in the West Bank. The number of clinics and hospitals, for instance, had grown from 113 to 378 since 1967. The roster of schoolteachers had grown from 5,316 to 17,373. Nevertheless, three times more Arabs had died under Israeli occupation than the number of blacks killed under South African apartheid. No Israeli could be proud of this record.

In 1988, King Hussein of Jordan made a bold move. He gave up all claim to the West Bank, thus making way for a Palestinian claim to statehood. As a result, peace in Bethlehem and East Jerusalem had to be negotiated directly with the Palestinians and no one else. In December 1989, a yet more remarkable event occurred. The leader of the PLO, Yasir Arafat, spoke to the general assembly of the United Nations and not only recognized the State of Israel (by embracing U.N. Resolution 242 [see p. 42 above]), but he denounced terrorism. While Israel refused to talk to the PLO, the United States announced that it would accept direct diplomatic discussions with Arafat, thus acknowledging the PLO as the legitimate representative of the Palestinian people.

The Gulf War, 1990–91

If the Six-Day War of 1967 inspired many Christian writers to wonder about the biblical fulfillment of prophesy, the Gulf War in 1990 helped these writers identify the enemy clearly: Saddam Hussein. While eschatological zeal among Christians was evaporating in the 1980s, Hussein's invasion of Kuwait in August 1990 resurrected prophetic speculation again. Did Iraq's mighty army represent that configuration of armies that would meet in Armageddon?

As hundreds of thousands of allied troops raced to the gulf along with the largest arms airlift in military history, Iraq knew that it had to fracture the Arab coalition arrayed against it. Israel stayed out of the conflict (because of American pressure) given that no Egyptian or Saudi soldier would ever fight *alongside* an Israeli against another Arab. On December 27, 1990, Saddam Hussein unofficially began Israel's involvement in the Gulf War by broadcasting his intentions publicly: "If aggression were to take place, we should assume that Israel has taken part in it. Therefore, without asking any questions we will strike at Israel." Less than a month later, on January 18 the first of 42 Scud missiles hit Israeli cities. Thanks to President Bush's immediate order to deploy U.S. Patriot antimissile batteries to protect Israel, the damage was fairly minimal. A total of 2 deaths, 230 injuries, and 4,100 damaged buildings resulted from the attacks. Israeli military restraint not to retaliate was phenomenal. Israel had thorough surveillance of Iraqi war capabilities. In 1981, for instance, Israel had attacked Iraq's Osirak nuclear plant, fearing the development of nuclear warheads. One week prior to Iraq's invasion of Kuwait, Israel's Defense Minister Moshe Arens perfectly predicted the Iraqi offensive by warning the American State Department.

Hussein's strategy to play the Israeli card failed. In fact, his actions probably strengthened the allied coalition. The common threat that he posed to such countries as Egypt, Saudi Arabia, Kuwait, Oman, Syria, and Turkey provided the glue that held these unlikely friends together. Ironically one by-product of the war may have been the many peace talks between Israel and its neighbors throughout the 1990s.

The situation that the Palestinians found themselves in at the time of the Gulf War can be illustrated simply by reading the headlines of newspapers around the world at the time: "In Time of Trouble," "Caught in a Crossfire," "The Other Occupation," "The Biggest Losers of the Gulf War," "The Palestinians Back Another Loser." The Gulf War put in bold relief the Palestinian dilemma in the early 1990s. The Intifada was losing steam and the world's television cameras had gone elsewhere. Saddam Hussein had welcomed the Palestinians for years and was a champion of their cause. A Palestinian doctor in Gaza said it poignantly in 1991, "Everyone has closed the door to us. . . . There's just one light coming through, and it's coming from Saddam Hussein. Can you blame us for wanting to follow that light to the end?"

No matter how ludicrous it seems now, Hussein had dedicated his cause to the liberation of these Palestinians living in Occupied Territories like the West Bank and Gaza. Arafat and the Palestinians thus threw in with Hussein, and many hoped and prayed that the war would bring them freedom. This alliance did not make their lives any easier. For the Palestinians living under Israeli occupation, the war meant strict curfews that were enforced at gunpoint. The Palestinian economy was paralyzed, and many feared hunger. Gas masks were distributed to all Israeli citizens but not to Arabs in the West Bank. When the shooting started, one nineteen-year-old Arab boy remarked, "We don't have shelters or gas masks. If there's an attack, we'll die in flocks. If we make any problems, Israeli soldiers will flatten the whole area."

During the war, perhaps 10 percent of Kuwait was made up of Palestinian workers. Open Palestinian support for Iraq after the invasion put them under immediate suspicion by the Kuwaitis. Some of them helped administer the occupation; many simply stayed out of sight. Following the war, Kuwaiti courts sentenced 29 Palestinians to death. Most of the rest fled or were expelled, but few Arab countries opened their doors. Jordan accepted over 300,000 people with no place to put them. Refugee camps spilled over. Amman was filled with men and women who had no place to go. Abdul Fatah, a former researcher for the Kuwait government, took a job at a small plastics factory in Jordan but could not make ends meet on his monthly salary of $102. "We had a comfortable life in Kuwait and were content," said his wife, Ne'meh, sitting in the family's shack on the outskirts of Amman. "Now that's all gone." Muhammad Ayyash Milhem, head of a Jordanian committee for the new arrivals, estimated in March 1992 that about 188,000 of the Palestinian refugees were in complete poverty.

Another consequence of the war was the disengagement of many Arab countries with the PLO. Saudi Arabia, for instance, provided $250 million per year to the PLO budget but cut off all funds. Arafat was being discredited by many. His people were angry and despairing. In Jerusalem's Old City, Mohammed Kamel said it well: "We are depressed and desperate because we have no friends and no allies. This is the story of our lives."

The Peace Process in the 1990s

By the close of the Gulf War, the eyes of the world were no longer on the Palestinians, and the sympathy the Intifada had created had all but dissipated. Street conflicts continued, but they were sporadic. Many of the world's leaders knew that something had to be done to address this unresolved problem. The United States, recently buoyed by the victory over Iraq, now viewed itself as a genuine leader in the region. In October 1991, the United States and the Soviet Union sponsored a Middle East peace conference in Madrid between Arab and Israeli delegates, and they invited leaders from the PLO. Israelis and the Palestinians were negotiating for the first time, but the meetings were a disappointment. Palestinian national aspirations were dashed as Israel and the United States only offered autonomy over civilian affairs, which the Palestinians rejected.

More meetings — this time secret — came in Oslo, Norway, in January 1993. After lengthy negotiations, both Israel and the PLO signed the "Declaration of Principles" in Washington, D.C., on September 13, 1993. This declaration (also called the "Oslo Accords") brought formal mutual recognition to both parties and affirmed that both the West Bank and Gaza would be progressively handed over to the Palestinians over five years. By May 1994, Israel fulfilled the beginning of its promises by removing its troops from Gaza. In July, Arafat entered Gaza with great fanfare and soon swore in the members of the new "Palestinian Authority." By the end of the year, the "PA" had assumed control of education, social welfare, health, tourism, and taxation.

But the peace process did not please many extremists, particularly among the Israeli settlers. On November 4, 1995, Yigal Amir took out his rage by assassinating Israel's Prime Minister Yitzhak Rabin in Tel Aviv.[15] Rabin was a hero of the peace process and the winner (along with Peres and Arafat) of the 1994 Nobel Peace Prize. His death profoundly shocked the Israeli public.

For the next seven years, Palestinians and Israelis continued to negotiate about how the West Bank — or which parts of it — would come under Arab control. Large Arab cities like Bethlehem, Hebron, Ramallah, Nablus, and Jennin would have Palestinian police and no more Israeli military patrols (except in limited areas where settlers lived). The entire countryside would be divided into zones, some planned for Palestinian control, others reserved for Israeli development, making the West Bank a patchwork or regions without contiguous borders. According to many Arab leaders, these disconnected areas eliminated the possibility of a Palestinian state altogether.

Many questions remain. How could Gaza and the West Bank be united when they share no contiguous border? Would Israeli settlers be placed under Palestinian authority? Would the PA be able to control borders with the outside world? And what about East Jerusalem, now annexed by Israel along with its large Palestinian population? Many Palestinian leaders view Jerusalem as the heart of their country. As progress on these matters continues, Palestinian optimism will grow. But when negotiations continue year after year and more and more Israeli settlements are built on Arab land, the prospect for continued violence remains and Palestinian optimism dissipates quickly. Afaf Mikki, a Palestinian woman who owned an embroidery shop in Gaza, commented in 1995, "I only feel that we are in a big prison, and the Israelis have the keys, and they will open the door only when they want."

After seven years of living under the Oslo Accords (by mid-2000), Palestinian frustration reached a peak. Rather than using this time to advance peace, the Israeli government accelerated its acquisition of Palestinian land. The West Bank is today a bewildering array of disconnected "cantons" that

---

15. Today Amir is serving a life sentence in a Beer Sheba prison. In an interview with Mark Lavie from the Associated Press five years later, Amir boasted about his deed and only expressed regret that he did not do it sooner.

have no territorial contiguity. Early Palestinian worries have been confirmed. This fragmentation makes the building of any Palestinian state impossible. Most observers today see it as a new form of apartheid. One Palestinian described it thus: This is like two teenagers arguing over the last slice of pizza, except that one of them is eating it.

But in addition, settlements expanded at a rate not seen before. Prime Minister Benjamin Netanyahu accelerated settlement growth to four times what it was previously, despite promises made at Oslo. Palestinians were commonly denied building permits for homes. Hundreds of their houses — built on their own land — have been destroyed since 1993. The key fact, though, is that Israel built a matrix of bypass roads in the West Bank that avoid the villages and link the settlements, making a web of well-connected settlement life. In 1999, the U.S. government even gave Israel $1.2 billion for building these roads.[16] The roads cut through Arab land, further fragmenting Arab society and restricting the growth of Arab villages.

Rather than offering peace, the ongoing consequences of Oslo for Arabs became tragic. In 1993, for example, Israel "closed" Jerusalem to Palestinians who do not have a travel permit; as a result, access to hospitals, religious centers, and educational institutions is off-limits. A close look at Bethlehem shows the effects of this policy. The main checkpoint between Jerusalem and Bethlehem is one of the busiest in the country. But today the Israelis have built an alternate checkpoint[17] reserved for Palestinians. Diplomats, tourists, and Israeli settlers use the old checkpoint known for years, but Palestinians will be routed out of sight 650 meters away to a parking lot for 700 cars. Here the Israelis will limit Arab entry without the scrutiny of foreign visitors. As one writer describes it, this practice of separating travelers based on race is "tantamount to apartheid."[18] But more, Bethlehem is utterly dependent on greater Jerusalem for its economic growth. This "closure" starves Bethlehem while non-Arabs are free to move smoothly in and out of Jerusalem, bypassing the town itself.

Camp David II, July 12–25, 2000

Such conditions inevitably lead to conflict since people without hope soon become desperate. In May 2000, when Israel celebrated its 52nd "Independence Day," the Palestinians commemorated what they term "the Nakbah" which in Arabic refers to "the catastrophe." For them, the founding of the

---

16. The Wye River aid package passed by the U.S. House of Representatives, November 5, 1999. Four million dollars was given to the Palestinian Authority.
17. Palestinians call it "Erez 2" after the Erez checkpoint in Gaza.
18. S. Jones, "Report: Erez 2, Bethlehem Checkpoint," *Cornerstone* 17 (Winter 1999): 7.

Israeli state has been just that, a catastrophe. Street fighting erupted on a scale not seen in years with many deaths. But for the first time in memory, Palestinian police did not stand passively when they watched Israeli soldiers firing on civilians. The newly armed police fired back — which brought a sobering realization to Israel how an armed struggle would look if the Palestinians traded in stones for weapons. The old images of the Intifada from ten years earlier seemed like paradise compared with live fire from Palestinian rifles. Since 1993, the Palestinians had been permitted to equip and train a professional police force of forty thousand. Suddenly the threat no longer looked like rioting. This new dimension could lead to civil war.

On July 12, 2000, President Bill Clinton invited Israeli Prime Minister Ehud Barak and Palestinian President Yasir Arafat to Camp David in order to discuss the future of the peace talks. This meeting was to be an important one, evoking memories of the famous talks hosted by President Jimmy Carter at Camp David in 1979 when Anwar Sadat of Egypt and Israel's Menachem Begin negotiated genuine peace for the first time. Expectations ran high, and all onlookers realized that a meeting producing a halfway settlement would be a disaster.[19] The incendiary issues of Jerusalem and land confiscation and refugees could no longer be ignored.

After nine days of intense negotiations (to July 20), both sides declared that a resolution was impossible. President Clinton intervened, urging the parties to remain and work further. Secretary of State Madeline Albright worked with negotiators day and night. But at last on July 25, after fifteen days of exhausting work, both Israeli and Palestinian leaders announced that the meeting was a failure. While the media represented Arafat as walking away from Barak's generous offers — offers that were never placed in writing — the PLO negotiators found the Israeli proposals impossible to accept. For example, they planned to divide up the Palestinians into four cantons, each separated by Israeli land (the northern West Bank, the central West Bank, the southern West Bank, and Gaza). The Arabs would not have control over their own water, borders, or air space. Months later the details of the map used by the Israelis came to light, clearly showing their intentions.[20] Another sticking point turned on the ownership of Jerusalem. One of Arafat's aids commented about him, "He is very angry and he doesn't believe the Israelis are willing to make peace. It's a waste of time to stay here any longer." Barak was also in a dilemma. Conservatives at home threatened to destroy

---

19. C. Krauthammer, "The Last Deal, or No Deal," *Time*, July 17, 2000, 88.

20. A. Eldar, "What Went Wrong at Camp David. The Official PLO Version," *Ha'aretz*, July 24, 2001. For a map of the divisions of Palestine, see *www.fmep.org/maps/v11n4_Barak_Sharon_map.jpg*.

his fragile political coalition if he should make any concessions on Jerusalem — while progressives were urging him to provide the Palestinians with
genuine access to the city. On July 26, three hundred American rabbis calling
themselves "The American Committee on Jerusalem" met at the University
of Maryland and called for a halt to Israeli demands on Jerusalem. For them,
Jerusalem should be a shared city that recognizes a "divine ownership" over
its precincts. But their three hundred voices were not heard.[21]

The Violent Aftermath: The Second Intifada

Before long, Palestinian frustration with this process exploded. On September 28, 2000, the spark that lit the fuse arrived at Jerusalem's Old City in the
form of retired general Ariel Sharon, the leader of the conservative Likud
party with a grim history as leader of Israel's invasion of Lebanon. Together
with hundreds of armed Israelis and with the full permission of Ehud Barak,
he entered the Muslim sanctuaries of the Haram al-Sharif (to Muslims "the
noble sanctuary," or to Jews, the Temple Mount), stood near the Al-Aqsa
Mosque, and announced Jewish sovereignty over even this region. Rioting
broke out immediately. Within two weeks, over 90 Arabs were dead and
2,000 in the hospital. Worried Israeli and Palestinian leadership wondered
how they might stop an anger that showed no signs of abating. Two months
later, the fighting continued to escalate. Soon no one knew how to stop it.
By late summer 2001, over 800 Arabs were dead (150 of them children)
and over 12,000 wounded. Over 7,000 Arab homes and 50 public buildings were destroyed. The Israelis even pulled up over 23,000 Arab fruit and
olive trees as punishment.[22]

These conflicts forced an early election in Israel and challenged Barak's
ability to broker a peace deal with the Palestinians. In a remarkably ironic
twist, in late January 2001, Barak found himself running against the notori-
ously hawkish Ariel Sharon who started the entire incident. On February 6,
the Israeli public, exhausted by months of violence and failed negotiations,
elected Sharon as prime minister in the largest landslide in Israel's history (Sharon won 62.6 percent of the vote). Within days he announced
that all peace concessions engineered by Barak were "off the table" and
soon declared the Oslo Peace Accords "dead." Saeb Erekat, the chief Palestinian negotiator, told CNN, "I'm afraid that we will not have a peace
process anymore. I would say 'God help Palestinians and Israelis', because
to have a meaningful peace process means that we would continue where

---

21. For a thorough study of the Peace Talks, see D. Sontag, "Quest for Middle East Peace:
How and Why It Failed," *New York Times,* July 26, 2001.
22. *Chicago Tribune,* July 20, 2001.

we left off." In spring 2002, Sharon launched a full-scale military assault on the Palestinian territories, arresting Arabs by the thousands, destroying the infrastructure of Arab towns (phone lines, water, sewers), ruining administrative buildings and offices (such as the education ministry and the office of land deeds), and confiscating all documents of the Palestinian government.

The Palestinians announced a "Day of Rage" and street conflicts escalated. Neighboring Arab governments saw these conflicts as ominous and asked publicly if they indicated a future of renewed tensions in the region. At a funeral for a fallen Israeli soldier and friend, Chaim Azran, nineteen, commented to the *New York Times*, "I voted for Ariel Sharon so there will be war, because only through war can we put an end to this."[23]

No one imagined where this so-called "second intifada" would go. Conflict raged for months. Palestinian gunmen were no match for Israel's army, one of the best in the world. Soon tanks, armored personnel carriers, attack helicopters, and jet fighters were laying siege to Palestinian cities that had not seen occupation for years. Yasir Arafat's personal compound in Ramallah was surrounded, bombed, and occupied, leaving the leader and his small circle of aides in just a handful of rooms. The death toll climbed. Palestinian deaths outpaced Israeli causalities four to one until suicide bombs brought unspeakable terror to Israeli streets. Many observers viewed the two peoples in a death grip, pulling each other toward national suicide. By the end of July 2002, Palestinian deaths beginning in September 2000 totaled 1,674. In addition, 19,938 people had been wounded.[24] During the same period, 577 Israelis were dead with 4,122 wounded.[25] And the killing showed no sign of ending. On July 23, 2002, an Israeli F-16 jet fighter destroyed a residential building in Gaza City. The missile successfully killed the military leader of the militant group Hamas. However, the missile also killed 15 civilians who were sleeping in the same building and wounded scores of others. But the loss of life among the children grieves us most. In eighteen months, 286 Palestinian children under the age of eighteen have died. During the same time, Israel lost 54 children.[26]

---

23. "Israeli Town's Adieu to 4 'Finest Sons and Daughters,' " *New York Times,* February 16, 2001.

24. These numbers are updated weekly by the Palestinian Red Crescent Society and are available at their website: *www.palestinercs.org/Latest_CrisisUpdates_Figures&Graphs.htm.*

25. These numbers are updated weekly by the Israel Ministry of Foreign Affairs and are available at their website: *www.israel.org/mfa/go.asp?MFAH0ia50.*

26. See the recently published free book "Who Will Save the Children?" published by Americans for Middle East Understanding, New York, 212-870-2053, or go the website: *www.whowillsavethechildren.org.*

In order to comprehend the shock of these figures, American congress persons supportive of Israel have translated these casualty figures into American demographics. If America had lost the same proportion of lives as Israel, our losses would have equaled 24,000 people. They rightly argue that this would be intolerable to us. But we need to do the same math and ask what the Palestinian losses look like if projected into the American population. These losses would be the equivalent of America losing 125,550 people.[27] To sharpen this further, Palestinian deaths are the same as if the United States underwent the tragedy of the New York World Trade Center crisis (of September 11, 2001) twenty-five times in twenty months.

THE MODERN STRATEGIC EQUATION

The challenge for us today is to weave these many threads of history and geography into a coherent pattern, making some sense of this modern conflict. We continue to live in a remarkably tense situation in which Israel struggles for moral credibility in the world (few nations have been condemned as many times by the United Nations), where Israel's neighbors have grievances based on war and loss of land, and over 3 million Palestinian refugees seek their home in the midst of the conflict. Some Palestinians would like to see Israel pull back to its borders in 1967, which will likely not happen. But what we can hope for is a resolution that meets most of the needs of both parties.

More is at stake. Arabs grieve the loss of control in this land where Islamic empires have had the upper hand for twelve hundred of the last two thousand years. The success of Israel — militarily as well as economically — has shamed Arab pride significantly, which is one reason the Arab world is pleased to see Western dependence on its oil. Since the 1970s, oil has reaped considerable political leverage for the Arab world.

Israel is a remarkably small country: about 40 miles from the western Mediterranean coast to the Jordan River in the east, and about 140 miles from the far north (Mount Hermon) to the southern desert city of Be'er Sheva. From the mountains in the center of the country, a good artillery unit could easily reach Tel Aviv. From the Golan Heights, a mortar round could land almost anywhere in northern Galilee. An F-16 fighter flying out of Amman, the capital of Jordan, could reach Jerusalem in seventy-five seconds

---

27. In these figures, I am assuming an Israeli population of 5.5 million and a Palestinian population of 3 million.

and Tel Aviv in three minutes.[28] Syrians and Iraqis alike can easily target Israel with modern missiles. Today if Egypt were to place Scud missiles with a 160-mile range on the Suez Canal, they could target both Jerusalem and Tel Aviv. If these missiles were advanced 50 miles east into the Sinai, they could hit any city in Galilee. This close proximity explains the paranoia that so often accompanies negotiations and the preoccupation with security. Every piece of real estate has some strategic value. So when people begin to talk about slicing up the country to build, say, a parallel Palestinian state, almost every Israeli shudders to think how this might alter the military equation.

Lebanon borders Israel in the north above Galilee and is well known among Israelis as the source of "terrorist" infiltration. The country is perceived today as unstable, and yet occupying a buffer zone in southern Lebanon for twenty years has come at a high price in Jewish lives. When Israel pulled out of Lebanon in May 2000, it abandoned its Christian allies there — many of whom have now been allowed to "come through" the fence and enter Israel. Israel watches southern Lebanon closely today using world-class reconnaissance. Palestinian refugees still populate the region and have harbored anger toward Israel for generations.

Syria once owned the Golan Heights but lost them in the war of 1967. The Golan's elevation (to almost three thousand feet) offers a serious advantage over the lowlands of Galilee. So many mortars have been fired on the kibbutzes of northern Galilee that most have underground shelters today. Above ground the Israelis devised an ingenious means of protection: loose stone boulders are held in place with heavy fencing, forming small twenty-by-twenty-foot shelters that can absorb the impact of a direct hit. After many years of these attacks, Israel could not tolerate the security risk any longer and so conquered the plateau in 1967. In 1973, Syria tried to regain the region but failed in the midst of one of the largest tank battles of modern history. Israel later annexed this region in 1981. Traditional underground shelters today are popular places for kibbutzes to sponsor dances. The bomb-proof walls are likewise rock music–proof.

The Golan Heights are an eerie no-man's land. An abandoned Syrian city called Quneitra sits on the plateau like a ghost town. The flank of Mount Hermon nearby bristles with high-tech surveillance devices that keep an eye on everything that moves. The United Nations maintains a buffer zone between the two armies. If Israel eventually makes peace with Syria, this region will have to be negotiated.

---

28. M. Widlanski, *Can Israel Survive a Palestinian State?* (Jerusalem: Institute for Advanced Strategic and Political Studies, 1990), 32–33.

Jordan shares a long border with Israel from south of the Sea of Galilee (along the Yarmouk River gorge), along the Jordan River itself, to the Gulf of Aqaba in the south. Hot springs on the Yarmouk River date back to Roman times (Hammet Gader). Visitors who like adventure can sit in the hot springs and then climb the hill to watch Israeli guards and Jordanian soldiers staring at each other with high-powered binoculars.

From 1948 until the war of 1967, the Jordanian border used to cross over the Jordan River and extend into the central mountains, encompassing the Arab cities of Nablus (biblical Shechem), Ramallah, Bethlehem, and Hebron. In fact, just north of Jerusalem (in the village of Shuafat) are a curious little airport and palace that were being built by King Hussein of Jordan before he lost the mountains to Israel. The Israelis redrew the border of Jerusalem and annexed this region so that the airport could be theirs.

In the war of 1967, Jordan lost the central mountains to Israel. From a strategic standpoint, this victory was a significant achievement for Israel. Today Israel occupies all of the highlands inside the country and uses the deep gorge of the Jordan River as a natural barrier against attacks from the east. High-tech sensors and electric fences stretch along this eastern frontier. Near the Israeli highway that skirts the border, a double fence is separated by soft sand that is combed daily by an army patrol looking for the footprints of intruders. But since Israel has negotiated a peace accord with Jordan, traffic now moves across multiple crossings every day.

In the far south are the great deserts that extend from the region south of the Dead Sea all the way west to the Mediterranean. As we noted above, these deserts are a buffer between Israel and Egypt. Israel conquered them in 1956, returned them, reconquered them in 1967, nearly lost them in 1973, and then as a result of a 1979 treaty returned them again in 1982.

THE CENTRAL ISSUE: TAKING LAND

The form of the equation is evident: Israel has a genuine security problem. It is surrounded by Arab nations who are suspicious of its intentions because Israel occupies land that is hotly disputed. In each of the major wars, Israel strategically increased the size of its holdings at the expense of Lebanon, Egypt, Syria, and Jordan. Consider the following statistics gleaned from the records of the United Nations: When the U.N. Nations General Assembly approved a plan to divide the country into an Israeli state and a Palestinian state on November 29, 1947, the breakdown of land and population looked like this:

	Arabs (Muslims and Christians)	Jews
% of population	69	31
% of land owned or settled	94	6
% of land offered in U.N. plan	48	52

At once the relative inequity is clear: 31 percent of the population living on 6 percent of the land was being given half the country! Let us look at one district (as the British organized the area) and see how this worked out. In Nazareth District in 1945, the Arab population was 84 percent and the Jewish population was 16 percent. Land ownership broke down thus: Arab, 52 percent; Jewish, 28 percent; public lands, 20 percent. Therefore it made sense to give this region to the Palestinians. But consider the neighboring Galilee District: Arab population, 67 percent; Jewish population, 33 percent. Land holdings: Arab, 51 percent; Jewish, 38 percent; public lands, 11 percent. Yet this area near the Sea of Galilee was given to Israel.[29]

When Israel declared itself a state on May 14, 1948, the Arabs took offense that Westerners would divide their land and then offer them such a slice. King Abdullah of Jordan no doubt saw this as an attempt to limit his growing control. At the close of the war, Israel even exceeded its allotted holdings significantly; instead of possessing 52 percent of the land as the United Nations urged, Israel held 77 percent of it — one-third more than the original U.N. plan.

The next major territorial increase came in the spring of 1967. Within a week, Israel captured the entire Sinai desert, the "West Bank" including east Jerusalem, Gaza, and the Golan Heights. This was a watershed event, for in one campaign, Israel virtually doubled its size by taking huge chunks of Syria, Jordan, and Egypt.

These lands are called today "the Occupied Territories" in the political jargon of the Middle East, and they are sorely disputed. On November 22, 1967, the United Nations passed Resolution 242 (perhaps the most famous resolution for Israel and the Palestinians), declaring that Israel must withdraw from these territories. The United States agreed to the resolution, and ever since then Resolution 242 has played a pivotal role in all discussions. Even though Israel returned the Sinai to Egypt in 1982, Israel still holds the Golan

---

29. See the government statistics given in H. Cattan, *Palestine, the Arabs and Israel. The Search for Justice* (London: Longman, 1969), 18–30, 207–10. This data is based on U.N. Statistics, British Administration reports, and village land records.

Heights (annexed in December 1981) and most of the West Bank. Israel even increased the size of Jerusalem significantly and annexed it for its own.

Look once more at the map on p. 16. Consider the military advantages that come to anyone holding the mountains (the West Bank) and the Golan Heights above Galilee. Consider the religious and psychological importance of capturing Jerusalem in its entirety and making it a new capital. Israeli strategists, like Joshua long ago, know precisely what they are doing.

But today another problem is surfacing in the Israeli consciousness: the rapid growth of the Arab population within its borders. The survival of Israel is not simply tied to its ability to hold on to disputed land, but its ability to be viable amid a growing population of Arabs. U.N. demographers predict huge population growth in the next fifty years in the Middle East. The population of the Palestinian "Occupied Territories" (the West Bank and Gaza) is growing twice as fast as Israel. Those 3 million Palestinians living under occupation will become 12 million by 2050 since Palestinian women have five or six babies each (Israelis have about two). Israel will have only 8 million people. But alongside Israel, Syria's population will swell from 17 million to 36 million — Iraq from 21 million to 53 million. Imagine the stress on land and natural resources such as water.[30] One day the Arabs within Israel's own borders — Israeli citizens — will be able to outvote their Jewish neighbors by sheer numbers.

ANCIENT AND MODERN TIMES COMPARED

The story I have just summarized is nothing new to the Middle East. Since the earliest days when Joshua surveyed this land with his lieutenants, every leader has been forced to consider how to control this narrow strip of real estate. Four facts must be kept in mind:

1. *Israel/Palestine is an ancient highway.* Thousands of years ago, the superpowers of the ancient world were Egypt in the south and the kingdoms of Mesopotamia in the north (particularly Assyria and Babylon, today in modern Iraq). Because the deserts of Arabia and Syria do not permit easy passage, caravans (in peacetime) and armies (in war) traveled along a coastal route between the desert and the sea, directly through Israel/Palestine. They would hug the coast, traveling between the hills and the coastal swamps, finding easy passage to their destinations. Keep in mind that Abraham and Sarah were from Iraq. When God called them to travel south, they followed this ancient highway.

---

30. See the U.N. report *www.unfpa.org/swp/swpmain.htm.*

As a result, even today, Israel/Palestine plays a pivotal geographical role. Travel from Turkey, Syria, or Lebanon to Egypt must pass through Israel/Palestine to avoid a major detour. Some strategists in Washington see the American alliance with Israel as serving a similar modern purpose. Israel is an outpost, a Western friend, a point of access to the larger Middle East.

2. *Life in Israel/Palestine is dangerous.* In peacetime long ago, the coastal regions offered access to the great trade route, but in war, armies moving north and south laid waste to every city and fortress in the region. Abraham must have known this when he climbed into these mountains and settled there, leaving the ancient highway behind. In later years, Israel became a mountain kingdom, extending west through the hills and into the coast only when it was safe (see the stories of Samson and the Philistines and of Eli and his sons as examples). This is why Jerusalem (the capital of King David) is tucked away high in the mountains — as is Samaria, the capital of the breakaway northern kingdom in the Old Testament. These were good places to build defenses against marauding foreigners.

Is it any surprise that Israel refuses to give up the West Bank? This area is much more than just the west bank of the Jordan River! The West Bank is really the highlands, the mountains from Nablus to Hebron called "Samaria and Judea" by Israeli leaders. These mountains provide refuge and safety. In war they offer the possessor an astonishing advantage. Foreign armies from distant places — such as Greece and Rome in the ancient world, the Crusaders in medieval times, and the British in the twentieth century — have learned the hard way the awesome advantage of these mountains.

3. *Life in Israel/Palestine is precarious.* Perhaps the most precious commodity in Israel is water. When Moses described the land to the Israelites, this item was one of the first he wanted to clarify: "For the land that you are about to enter to occupy is not like the land of Egypt, from which you have come, where you sow your seed and irrigate by foot like a vegetable garden" (Deut. 11:10). In the next verses, Moses goes on to tell the people that rainfall is one tool that God uses in this land to bless or to discipline the people. Why is this a problem? The Jordan River is in a deep gorge almost four thousand feet below the central mountains. The Sea of Galilee has abundant water, but only this century has the Israeli government effectively pumped its water throughout the country by pipe. In the winter of 1991–92, record snow and rain fell, bringing up the water levels, and the entire nation celebrated!

Israel struggles for some of its natural resources. The land is a hard land that requires the people who would subdue it to have faith in God. Every century the use of these limited resources must be negotiated carefully with

Israel's neighbors. Today, considering the value of Galilee's water, what does it mean if Jordan has lost access to it? What does it mean when Palestinian villagers are not permitted to dig new wells while neighboring Jewish settlements have sprinkler systems for their lawns with piped-in Galilee water? Within Israel, hundreds and hundreds of Palestinian villages have been destroyed by bulldozers because they sat on excellent land. Today careful observers can identify these silent villages because the cactuses (the Sabra) used by the Arabs for fencing continue to grow back.

4. *"When the cat's away, the mice will play."* In the absence of dominating superpowers (ancient Egypt, Assyria, Babylon, Greece, Rome — or today, Turkey and Britain), the regional nations struggle for dominance. In the Old Testament the Israelites fought against the Philistines (on the coast), the Edomites and the Moabites (in modern-day Jordan), the Ammonites (in modern Syria), and the Phoenicians (in modern Lebanon). Each country leveraged its power against others. Unusual treaties were formed — such as Ahab's alliance with Phoenicia.

This pattern of regional struggle is no different today. The desert kingdom of Jordan has precious few resources and historically has always laid claim to lands west of the Jordan River. For example, Amman, the capital of Jordan, gets less than half the rainfall that Jerusalem does. Syria likewise values the good agricultural potential of the Golan Heights and Lebanon. In New Testament times, the Golan (called Gaulinitis and Batanea) was used for grain production by the Romans because it receives sufficient rain each year for a cereal crop.

SUMMARY

In order to win at Monopoly, we have to know the playing board. In order to understand the life-and-death game being played in Israel/Palestine, we have to understand the major political and geographical issues that have been weighed for thousands of years. Who will occupy the best land in this country? Where will they live? Can they defend themselves?

The struggle for this land is not new. Its contours have been known from earliest times. When Alexander the Great conquered the land in 332 B.C.E., he wisely built his regional administrative center in Samaria. He knew the advantages. The remains of his buildings can be seen today just west of modern Nablus. When General Teggart surveyed the land for the British in 1937, legend has it that he studied the Bible, especially the book of Joshua. From these notes and the input of his Middle Eastern advisors, he planned the British occupation of Israel/Palestine. Ancient principles are still at work.

ISRAEL/PALESTINE IN THE TWENTIETH CENTURY

Boxed dates (e.g., 1967) indicate a major strategic war.

1918–48	British mandate Period
	• 1922 League of Nations grants Mandate
1948	War of Independence (May 1948–July 1949)
	• Israel's strategic goal: the coastal corridor, Galilee and Eilat
	• Independence: May 14, 1948
1956	The Sinai Campaign
	• Israel's strategic goal: South (Sinai) and a buffer zone with Egypt
1967	The Six-Day War
	• Israel's strategic goal: East (West Bank, Golan Heights, Sinai, Jerusalem)
1973	The Yom Kippur War
	• Arab retaliation led by Syria (Golan Heights) and Egypt (Sinai)
1978	Camp David Accords (September 17)
	• Washington peace conference led by J. Carter, M. Begin, A. Sadat
1979	Treaty with Egypt (March 26)
1982	Invasion of Lebanon
	• Israel's strategic goal: North (southern Lebanon) and the defeat of the PLO
1987–93	The Uprising/Intifada
	• Popular Palestinian resistance against Israeli occupation
1990–91	The Gulf War
	• Iraq invades Kuwait
1993	Treaty with PLO
	• Oslo Accords, "Declaration of Principles," September 13
1995	Treaty with Jordan (July 28)
	• Y. Rabin assassinated, November 4
	• S. Peres forms government, November 22
1996	B. Netanyahu Elected (May 29)
1999	E. Barak Elected (May 17)
2000	Israel Withdraws from Lebanon (May 23)
	Camp David II
	• A failed attempt at peace between E. Barak and Y. Arafat, July 12–25
	The Al-Aqsa Uprising/Intifada (September 28–)
2001	A. Sharon Elected (February 6)

Part Two

THE OLD TESTAMENT
AND THE LAND

Chapter Four

THE LAND PROMISES
OF ABRAHAM

On that day the LORD made a covenant with Abram, saying, "To your descendants I give this land, from the river of Egypt to the great river, the river Euphrates, the land of the Kenites, the Kenizzites, the Kadmonites, the Hittites, the Perizzites, the Rephaim, the Amorites, the Canaanites, the Girgashites, and the Jebusites."   —Genesis 15:18–21

The land shall not be sold in perpetuity, for the land is mine; with me you are but aliens and tenants. Throughout the land that you hold, you shall provide for the redemption of the land.   —Leviticus 25:23–24

The ancient walled city of Jerusalem is divided into four quarters. For centuries this tradition has been respected, giving the city its distinctive character. The Jewish Quarter (southeast), the Armenian Quarter (southwest), the Christian Quarter (northwest), and the Muslim Quarter (northeast) all preserve ancient communities that venerate unique holy sites.[1] The Christian Quarter, for example, consists of about forty-five acres and is centered on the magnificent Church of the Holy Sepulchre, the traditional place of Jesus' crucifixion and burial. Christians from all over the world pilgrimage to this place and there can witness worship in progress as Latin and Eastern traditions celebrate mass and Protestant Christians sing and pray in chapels carved into the stone walls.

In early 1990, a group of Israeli settlers broke with tradition. Carefully disguising their plan, they purchased St. John's Hospice in the Christian Quarter under false pretenses and began to move in—a move that offended even Jerusalem's mayor, Teddy Kollek, who respected the privileges of each faith community in the city. The hospice, which stands between the Greek Convent of St. John and the sacred Church of the Holy Sepulchre, has

---

1. Both the Armenian and the "Christian" quarters are Christian. The former is dominated by the Armenian Orthodox Church and the latter mainly by the Greek Orthodox Church. Armenia was the first nation to embrace Christianity (fourth century C.E.). Even without land of their own, Armenians have remained an important Christian presence in the Middle East. In the early twentieth century, they suffered under a systematic massacre when the Turks killed more than 2 million of them.

been owned for centuries by the Greek Orthodox Church, and in the Old City of Jerusalem, *no one sells property like this*. In April that year, David Levy, Israel's minister of Housing, admitted that he had secretly provided $1.8 million for the Jewish settlers to move into the Christian Quarter.

During Holy Week, on Maundy Thursday, 150 Jewish settlers moved in, protected by the Israeli army. When the traditional Orthodox Holy Week procession came through the city, they stopped at St. John's and tried to remove Israel's flags, which covered sacred Christian symbols. The entire crowd was teargassed.

Protests erupted everywhere. The Church of the Holy Sepulchre was closed down on Easter for the first time in history. Christians throughout the Middle East — Protestant, Catholic, and Orthodox — saw this as an unprecedented offense.[2] In fact, when the Greek patriarch Diodoros and many of his bishops came to the building in protest, these elderly dignified men were roughed up by soldiers and teargassed in front of television cameras. Bishop Timothy, the general secretary to the patriarch, commented that "it was a violation of the status quo of church property" in Jerusalem.

I happened to be in Jerusalem that spring and thought it would be interesting to see what all the fuss was about. The government had demanded that most of the settlers leave, and only a "symbolic group" remained to occupy the property. As I rounded the corner, soldiers were everywhere, and I could see Hebrew graffiti that aggressively laid claim to the property. What looked like sheets covered up the Christian symbols on the building, and the star of David was spray-painted generously on the walls.

As I looked on at the tense scene, two teenage boys from the settlement stopped me. They were eager to explain to a tourist what this meant, and so I listened.

"We have bought what is ours anyway, and how we did it doesn't matter," they said.

I asked if it were not true that the Greeks had owned this property for hundreds of years — maybe even a thousand years.

"It doesn't matter," they answered. "God gave us this country and this city, and Jews can live anywhere."

I reflected on the fact that Greek Christians could not buy land in the Jewish Quarter.

"We are only taking what is ours by right. These people have no right even to be in this city," they replied.

---

2. "Christians in Israel Express Their Unease," *Christian Century* 107 (April 25, 1990): 419–20. Cf. "Palestinian Christians Fear for the Future," *Christianity Today*, August 20, 1990, 43.

This last thought enticed me. I pursued this idea of "rights" with these seventeen-year-old zealots.

"God gave this land to Abraham, and we are his descendants. It belongs to us. Everything that happened in between simply doesn't matter. The Palestinian Christians should just get out."

The conversation struck me as odd because these boys were American. They were from New York and had been in the country only a few years. Yet they were ejecting an ancient Christian community that could trace its history to this bit of real estate for more than a thousand years. And, ironically, this community likewise claimed descent from Abraham. Did God promise the land to Judaism? What do the Scriptures say? Was the promise confirmed later? Did it come with conditions?

THE ORIGINAL PROMISES

The source of this argument used by the Israeli teenagers in Jerusalem can be found in Genesis 12. When God called Abraham, he made two promises. One promise concerned Abraham's children — whose number would exceed the stars in the sky. The other concerned land, since Abraham was nomadic and had no land of his own. These two items — children and land — reside at the center of Middle Eastern life even today. One promises the continuing survival of name and heritage; the other promises a place, a refuge, a locale called "home." Today an Arab man is commonly known as "the father" of his firstborn son.[3] Arab village farmers likewise esteem their land by giving personal names to its trees, its springs, and its caves.

The introductory verses of the Abraham story begin with an outline of God's promise.

> Now the LORD said to Abram, "Go from your country and your kindred and your father's house to the land that I will show you. I will make of you a great nation, and I will bless you, and make your name great, so that you will be a blessing. I will bless those who bless you, and the one who curses you I will curse; and in you all the families of the earth shall be blessed." (Gen. 12:1–3)

Strikingly, this promise fails to mention the land. Virtually every scholar who studies the passage notes that this omission is peculiar.[4] In some sense, the primary thrust of the story is that Abraham is going to be the father of a nation, and their identity as God's people is most important, not necessarily

---

3. I know a Palestinian student named Nakhleh Hussary. His father is called Abu Nakhleh. *Abu* in Arabic means "father of."

4. Typically, see G. von Rad, *The Problem of the Hexateuch and Other Essays* (New York: McGraw-Hill, 1966), 83–84.

where they live. This point makes sense when we consider that Abraham was nomadic, traveling between Mesopotamia (his home, Iraq) and the Egyptian province of Canaan (what we commonly call Israel/Palestine today). This original promise addressed the migratory life of the patriarch. The promise is for new pasture for the nomad, his clan, and his animals to escape the threat of starvation.[5] As Abraham's story continues, it is interesting that Abraham interestingly does not settle down. He moves his tents among the cities of Shechem, Bethel, Hebron, and Be'er Sheva. He does not buy any land or possess any land until Sarah dies and he needs a burial site.

A brief form of this promise is mentioned in Genesis 13:14–17. After Abraham scans the countryside in all directions, God says, "The land that you see I will give to you and to your offspring forever.... Rise up, walk through the length and the breadth of the land, for I will give it to you."

This promise is formally reaffirmed in Genesis 15 when God makes a covenant with Abraham. In 15:1–6 the land is omitted once again, but in 15:18–21, God speaks clearly about the land inheritance that Abraham will receive.

> On that day the LORD made a covenant with Abram, saying, "To your descendants I give this land, from the river of Egypt to the great river, the river Euphrates, the land of the Kenites, the Kenizzites, the Kadmonites, the Hittites, the Perizzites, the Rephaim, the Amorites, the Canaanites, the Girgashites, and the Jebusites." (Gen. 15:18–21)

Again in Genesis 17, when Abraham's name is changed (formerly it had been Abram), God repeats the twofold promise for progeny and land:

> I will establish my covenant between me and you, and your offspring after you throughout their generations, for an everlasting covenant, to be God to you and to your offspring after you. And I will give to you, and to your offspring after you, the land where you are now an alien, all the land of Canaan, for a perpetual holding; and I will be their God.
>
> God said to Abraham, "As for you, you shall keep my covenant, you and your offspring after you throughout their generations." (Gen. 17:7–9)

One thing is exceedingly clear. This gift of land is intimately connected to the covenant, or contract, that God is making with Abraham. This "package deal" includes the following elements:

- Abraham will receive the land as an everlasting possession;
- Abraham's posterity will become a great nation;

---

5. C. Westermann, "Promise to the Patriarchs," in *The Interpreter's Dictionary of the Bible,* supplemental volume, ed. K. Crim (Nashville: Abingdon, 1962), 690–93; also R. Ruether and H. Ruether, *The Wrath of Jonah: The Crisis of Religious Nationalism in the Israeli-Palestinian Conflict* (New York: Harper & Row, 1989), 7.

- An everlasting covenant will bind Abraham and his descendants to God.

- All of the people of the earth will be blessed through Abraham and his people.[6]

In order to make clear that this promise extends to Abraham's children, Genesis repeats these promises for Isaac (Abraham's son) in 26:2–4 and for Jacob (Abraham's grandson through Isaac) in 28:13–15. But in all cases — even when repeated elsewhere in the Old Testament — the promise to Abraham is the anchor passage. In fact, when Israel later disobeys the Lord and the prophets announce punishment, God's promise to Abraham brings hope of restoration and forgiveness (Jer. 7:7; 16:15; cf. Deut. 8:18). Micah 7:20 says it succinctly: "You will show faithfulness to Jacob and unswerving loyalty to Abraham, as you have sworn to our ancestors from the days of old."[7]

As we read the story of Abraham carefully, three things stand out. First, the native residents of this province called Canaan are not displaced. They are not ejected from their homes. Instead, Abraham becomes a neighbor (not a conqueror) who enters into trade relations with the indigenous people of the land. This point cannot be stressed enough. When Sarah dies (Gen. 23), Abraham does not presume that he can simply take any burial ground he desires. He must buy it. In fact, Genesis 23 records a lengthy negotiation in which Ephron the Hittite who owns the field Abraham desires to buy tries to give the property to Abraham as a gift. Abraham refuses to accept it. He insists on buying it. Before an array of legal witnesses at Hebron's city gate, Abraham finally purchases the cave of Machpelah near the Oaks of Mamre.[8] Keep in mind that Ephron was a *Hittite* — one of the very people listed in Genesis 15:20 whose land Abraham was going to inherit. Yet here Abraham treats the Hittites with considerable respect.

Second, the story emphasizes that land is linked with covenant. Genesis 17:9 affirms Abraham's responsibility, and this verse follows right on the heels of 17:8, which contains the land promise. It is not as if a "title deed" had been handed to Abraham and God was no longer part of the picture. Rather, the land is an outgrowth of the relationship between Abraham, Abraham's descendants, and God. In this relationship, the land is certain to be an everlasting possession, but responsibility for it assumes faithfulness to a relationship with God. The law books Leviticus and Deuteronomy

---

6. C. Chapman, *Whose Promised Land?* (Herts, Eng.: Lion, 1983), 100–101.

7. In the New Testament, even the apostle Paul makes this appeal. In Romans 11:28, he admits that the Jews have been "enemies" of the gospel, but for the sake of their ancestors, "they are beloved."

8. The details of the passage underscore how carefully land transactions are understood in the Middle East: trees, caves, springs, irregularities, and all assets are commonly itemized.

make this assumption clear. The prophets likewise remind Israel that this dimension cannot be ignored.

Finally, God emphasizes that Abraham's children will become "a great nation" and through them "all of the peoples of the earth will be blessed." Frequently Christians have taken Genesis 12:2–3 out of context:

> I will make of you a great nation, and I will bless you, and make your name great, so that you will be a blessing. I will bless those who bless you, and the one who curses you I will curse; and in you all the families of the earth shall be blessed.

The idea here is not that the Gentiles must somehow support Israelite efforts at greatness and nationhood and in so doing discover the blessing of God. Nor (in its original setting) does the passage mean that the blessing of the families of the earth will come about because Israel will bring the world its messiah, Jesus Christ.[9] Rather, these verses suggest that through Israel's greatness, through Israel's goodness, because Israel is blessed, God's people will in turn be able to bless and enrich the lives of others living nearby. In other words, an *ethical* dimension exists to Israel's relation with God. The covenant is not designed simply to satisfy Israel's nationhood and give it land. Nor is the covenant designed to satisfy Israel's self-interest. The covenant with Israel is God's strategy to bring his goodness and righteousness to the rest of humanity. Israel is to be a nation of priests (Exod. 19:6; Deut. 7:6), mediating God's presence and goodness to the earth.

PROMISES WITH CONDITIONS

The connection between covenant fidelity and the promise of land is evident throughout the Torah (the five traditional books of Moses). Possessing the land was contingent on Israel's consistently living by God's righteous standards.[10] One of the most surprising discoveries for me was how rarely this theme is sounded by evangelical writers. For example, John Walvoord's *Armageddon, Oil, and the Middle East Crisis* contains a discussion of the promises of land to Israel but neglects this material completely.[11]

---

9. In Galatians, 3:8 Paul interprets the blessing of Abraham as referring to Christ. From this vantage, since Christ has come, Genesis 12:2–3 has been fulfilled and Israel's task of "blessing" is complete.

10. W. Eichrodt, *Theology of the Old Testament*, 2 vols. (Philadelphia: Westminster, 1961, 1967), 1:457–67; W. Kaiser, *Toward an Old Testament Theology* (Grand Rapids, Mich.: Zondervan, 1978), 182–219.

11. J. F. Walvoord, *Armageddon, Oil, and the Middle East Crisis* (Grand Rapids, Mich.: Zondervan, 1990). Walvoord does refer to the condition of obedience (71) but believes it

Both Leviticus and Deuteronomy warn Israel about righteousness and the land in dramatic terms. In fact, the images are shocking. If Israel does not obey God's laws, then the land itself will vomit the nation out. Leviticus 18 and 20 were given at Mount Sinai, where God was exceedingly explicit about his covenant and its obligations. Chapter 18 warns Israel against taking on the lifestyle of the Canaanites:

> Do not defile yourselves in any of these ways, for by all these practices the nations I am casting out before you have defiled themselves. Thus the land became defiled; and I punished it for its iniquity, and the land vomited out its inhabitants. But you shall keep my statutes and my ordinances and commit none of these abominations, either the citizen or the alien who resides among you (for the inhabitants of the land, who were before you, committed all of these abominations, and the land became defiled); *otherwise the land will vomit you out for defiling it, as it vomited out the nation that was before you.* For whoever commits any of these abominations shall be cut off from their people. So keep my charge not to commit any of these abominations that were done before you, and not to defile yourselves by them: I am the LORD your God. (Lev. 18:24–30, emphasis added.)

Chapter 20 turns its attention to the expectations of ritual holiness within the covenant:

> You shall keep all my statutes and all my ordinances, and observe them, *so that the land to which I bring you to settle in may not vomit you out.* You shall not follow the practices of the nation that I am driving out before you. Because they did all these things, I abhorred them. But I have said to you: You shall inherit their land, and I will give it to you to possess, a land flowing with milk and honey. I am the LORD your God; I have separated you from the peoples. You shall therefore make a distinction between the clean animal and the unclean, and between the unclean bird and the clean; you shall not bring abomination on yourselves by animal or by bird or by anything with which the ground teems, which I have set apart for you to hold unclean. You shall be holy to me; for I the LORD am holy, and I have separated you from the other peoples to be mine. (Lev. 20:22–26, emphasis added)

Note how Moses emphasizes holiness, and note how in each case the land itself will eject its inhabitants. The land has a life of its own and can suffer abuse and be defiled. Unrighteousness defiles the land of Israel/Palestine. Just as grievous sinners were ejected from the camp of Israel lest further wrongdoing increase, so, too, Israel could be ejected from the camp or land of God.

---

applies only to the occupation under Joshua and is not a feature of the covenant itself. He completely overlooks the balance of the Torah and all of the prophets.

After the wilderness wanderings, Moses led the people across the south end of the Dead Sea, up onto the plateau that is today Jordan, and then north until he was adjacent to Jericho, across the Jordan River. Here on "the plains of Moab" he delivered his final words of counsel concerning entry into Canaan. Again, the same theme is sounded. Possession of the land is linked to covenant fidelity. To break the law is to lose the land. Note his words in Deuteronomy 4:

> When you have had children and children's children, and become complacent in the land, if you act corruptly by making an idol in the form of anything, thus doing what is evil in the sight of the LORD your God, and provoking him to anger, I call heaven and earth to witness against you today that you will soon utterly perish from the land that you are crossing the Jordan to occupy; you will not live long on it, but will be utterly destroyed. The LORD will scatter you among the peoples; only a few of you will be left among the nations where the LORD will lead you. (vv. 25–27)
>
> Keep his statutes and his commandments, which I am commanding you today for your own well-being and that of your descendants after you, so that you may long remain in the land that the LORD your God is giving you for all time. (v. 40)

Perhaps Moses' most important teachings concerning the land can be found in Deuteronomy 8–9, which summarize what God had done for Israel from Egypt until then. Above all, the chapters remind Israel to be humble when it comes to the land. The land and its wealth are gifts to be held with humility.

> Do not say to yourself, "My power and the might of my own hand have gotten me this wealth." But remember the LORD your God, for it is he who gives you power to get wealth, so that he may confirm his covenant that he swore to your ancestors, as he is doing today. If you do forget the LORD your God and follow other gods to serve and worship them, I solemnly warn you today that you shall surely perish. (Deut. 8:17–19)

The severity of these words cannot be missed. Israel cannot be cavalier about its use of the land or its abuse of its inhabitants. This land is not like any other land. The wonder of this land has little to do with its natural beauty or its powerful history. We dare not be romantic or sentimental here. With many Christians I often read Deuteronomy 11:11–12 in this way. "But the land that you are crossing over to occupy is a land of hills and valleys, watered by rain from the sky, a land that the LORD your God looks after. The eyes of the LORD your God are always on it, from the beginning of the year to the end of the year." What does God look for? God looks for holiness and justice among those who possess this land.

WHO REALLY OWNS THE LAND?

God's remarkable interest in the land of Israel/Palestine is easily explained. The Bible teaches that the nation of Israel does not own the land; God does.[12] God's investment in the land did not disappear when the covenant with Israel was written. Since Israel and God would live closely together in covenant relation, God and Israel together would enjoy the land. Leviticus makes this perfectly clear. As the law outlines how to use the land (tenant agreements, farming practices, purchasing land), the Israelites are reminded: "The land shall not be sold in perpetuity, for the land is mine; with me you are but aliens and tenants" (Lev. 25:23). Israel is a tenant in the land, not a landlord. Israel is a renter, a visitor, an alien. The land is "a delightful gift — owned by [God] and leased to Israel in partial fulfillment of His word of promise."[13] Israel must hold this land loosely, because God will always determine the tenure of its occupants.

One of the interesting features of the first six books of the Bible is that the phrase "the land of Israel" is never used. Instead it is called "the land of Canaan." This point is striking when we consider that this land is given to Israel in these books. Thus Genesis 23:2 says, "And Sarah died at Kiriath-arba (that is, Hebron) in the land of Canaan; and Abraham went in to mourn for Sarah and to weep for her."[14] Naming is always significant in the Bible. This title for the land preserves an important reminder that the land has a heritage that is larger than Israel's own history. Its importance is not defined by the new thing God is doing in the covenant with Israel. The land has a life and identity that is independent of Israel.

God's ownership of Israel/Palestine is clarified further through the rituals of Israel's religion.

1. The land was not to be considered private property, but was something distributed by God. Therefore the whole land was divided up by the casting of lots (Num. 26:55) to make way for God's will. The divisions of land were God's decision, not that of the people of Israel.[15] Note that the tribes and

---

12. "Never in Israel's history did she ever own outright the land, earth, or soil in our sense of the word; it was always granted to her by Yahweh [God] as a fief in which she could cultivate and live on it as long as she served him" (Kaiser, *Toward an Old Testament Theology,* 126).

13. Ibid., 127.

14. In the English Bible, "land of Canaan" appears sixty-two times while "land of Israel" appears twenty-nine times.

15. In Exodus 28:30 and Leviticus 8:8 we learn that the priest cast lots with "the Urim and Thummim" that he kept in his vestments. These judgments by lot were considered to be God's commands for his people. On lots, see R. deVaux, *Ancient Israel: Its Life and Institutions,* trans. J. McHugh (New York: McGraw-Hill, 1962), 352ff.; also W. D. Davies, *The Gospel and the Land: Early Christianity and Jewish Territorial Doctrine* (Berkeley: University of California Press, 1974), 27–28.

not individuals were trustees of the land (Num. 36:3; Josh. 17:5).[16] Tribal supervision of land meant that individual ownership was always mediated through some corporate body.

This notion of "loose ownership" is reinforced through the Jubilee year celebrations outlined in Leviticus 25. God's gift of land could not be bought or sold permanently as if the Israelite owner could hand on a deed. Land could never be taken forever. Long-term investments in which wealthy people would develop large estates were impossible. The land was not the occupant's to do with as he or she wished. By God's decree, every fiftieth year the land had to be returned to its original owner. He controlled who would occupy the land.

2. The harvests were understood in light of God's ownership. First things such as crops and firstborn animals belonged to God and were therefore offered to him in sacrifice (Lev. 27:30–33; Deut. 14:22; 26:9–15). These sacrifices represented the entire yield of the land and were a ritual way of acknowledging God's ownership of the whole.

3. The command to "keep the Sabbath" (Exod. 20:8–10) was extended to the land: "When you enter the land that I am giving you, the land shall observe a Sabbath for the LORD" (Lev. 25:2). Some have viewed this ecologically, thinking that productivity would be enhanced by giving the land rest every seventh year, but here the sense is different. The land itself is obligated to keep a Sabbath for the Lord. The land is almost personified as if it too owed worship to God. This emphasis underscores the special relationship the land has with God and, in this case, Israel was to free the land to fulfill its obligation to its creator and owner.

4. The land is often called a place of rest for Israel (Deut. 12:9). But curiously the land is actually called God's resting place (Ps. 95:11; Isa. 66:1). "Resting place" is a technical term used to describe the place where God's presence dwells. In the wilderness wanderings, this place is where God paused (Num. 10:33) or where he dwelt (Ps. 132:8).

5. Naming is significant throughout the Middle East. In the Bible, Israel/Palestine is the place where "God's name dwells" (Deut. 12:11; 14:23). Similarly God "puts his name there" (Deut. 12:5, 21; 14:24) and assures "that his name is there" (1 Kings 8:16, 29). This naming is a mark of ownership indicating that the land is God's own possession.[17]

6. Finally, the land is described as "holy." In Hebrew, the term *holy* has less to do with morality than we think. Land itself cannot have moral

---

16. von Rad, *The Problem of the Hexateuch and Other Essays,* 86.
17. Kaiser, *Toward an Old Testament Theology,* 133–34.

qualities as people can. Holiness (Heb., *qodesh*) means separation: something separated from the common world by its relationship to God is called holy. God dwells in the land, and by virtue of its closeness to him, its character is altered. Other land cannot share this quality. Other land is "unclean land" (Amos 7:17). Thus Numbers 35:34 warns, "You shall not defile the land in which you live, in which I also dwell; for I the LORD dwell among the Israelites." The land reacts violently to defilement ("otherwise the land will vomit you out for defiling it, as it vomited out the nation that was before you," Lev. 18:28) because it has a ritual quality quite separate from the life of Israel. The land lives in close connection to God, and therefore God's attributes radiate through it.[18]

WHO REALLY OWNS THE WATER?

A parallel interest in the Bible is the ownership of water. This aspect too is an intimate part of the "land" promised to Abraham, for this land — which could easily become a desert — must drink water from heaven which God alone can send. Job reminds us that God alone "bestows rain on the earth and sends water upon the countryside" (Job 5:10; cf. 36:26f.). For Israel this rain which fills cistern and well is a gift that (like land) is linked to the covenant. And through the prosperity this heavenly water brings, Israel will be able to share with her neighbors. Listen to the words of Deuteronomy 28:12, "The LORD will open to you his good treasury in the heavens, to give the rain of your land in its season and to bless all the work of your hands; and you shall lend to many nations, but you shall not borrow." During the festival of Tabernacles each autumn when the land is desperate for water, special prayers are offered for rain and water ceremonies occur at the altar in order to urge God to send his gift. Even Jesus knew of these festivals and made an appearance at one in John 7:37. Still today, Arab Muslims in Jordan believe that if rains come during the Jewish festival of Tabernacles, it will be a very good, wet season.

But the opposite is also the case. Covenant disobedience results in drought (Deut. 28:24). In fact, throughout Israel's history, the withdrawal of water resulting in famine was one means that God used to chastise his people (Amos 4:7; Joel 1:10–12). So Haggai announced: "Therefore the heavens above you have withheld the dew, and the earth has withheld its produce"

---

18. Davies, *Gospel and the Land*, 29; also, W. D. Davies, *The Territorial Dimension of Judaism* (Berkeley: University of California Press, 1982), 17–21.

(1:10). The most famous of these pronouncements is perhaps Elijah's promise that neither rain nor dew would fall on Israel until the land was righteous (1 Kings 17:1). Just as covenant sin leads to the loss of land, so too, covenant sin leads to the loss of rain (2 Chron. 6:26f.).

Without water, all land becomes desert. Israel/Palestine is an arid place, and water is a precious commodity. The absence of rainfall leads to drought, which forces people to leave the land (as happened in the days of Joseph). For example, Palestinian agriculture has adapted to this problem by using crops that can survive (olives, grapes, figs, etc.). Israeli agriculture, on the other hand, has developed a large citrus market for European export. A single orange grown in Israel will use up countless times the amount of water needed by equal amounts of grapes.

Therefore I must apply the same standard for water as I do for land. Israel does not own its water. *God owns it.* Water is a heavenly gift to be shared and treasured. It should not be used without thanksgiving. The preservation and protection of water was even known in the Old Testament. Proverbs 5:15 says, "Drink water from *your own* cistern, running water from *your own* well" (emphasis added).

To take water from a neighbor in this country is a serious crime whose scope has changed completely since biblical times. Water — like land — can be stolen. Modern equipment and technology have the capability of depriving some of water in order to lavish others with prosperity. The same prophets who witness and criticize the misuse of land also identify the misuse of its resources.

SUMMARY

When we try to address the question of "Who owns the land?" only one answer seems appropriate: *God owns the land.* When we ask, "Who owns the water?" only one answer fits as well. *God owns the water.* To be sure, the nation of Israel is promised possession of the land as an everlasting gift, but this promise is conditional; it depends on Israel's fidelity to the covenant and its stipulations. The land has a relationship with God too. This land is the land where he lives, and by association with him, it is holy. Thus Israel may possess this promise of residence in the land and still be expelled from it through unfaithfulness.

Israel is a tenant, not an owner: "The land is mine — with me you are but aliens and tenants" (Lev. 25:23). Humility and gratitude and caution should therefore hallmark anyone's residence in the land. As God's tenants, Abraham's descendants are called to reflect God's goodness and thereby bless those who live in community with them. As we shall see, aliens or sojourners (non-Israelites) are protected and respected in this land.

We began this chapter with the account of St. John's Greek Orthodox Hospice in the Christian Quarter of Jerusalem. Does the Bible's promise of land empower men and women to take land unjustly? Does divine privilege mean that fairness may be thrown to the wind? Must the heirs of these promises exemplify goodness as a part of their inheritance? Should they be a blessing so that through them "all the families of the earth shall be blessed"?

As we shall see in the next chapter, Israel's own history tested God's expectations. The Israelites wanted the land but held no regard for the covenant or their relationship with God.

Chapter Five

THE NATION OF ISRAEL
AND THE LAND

When an alien resides with you in your land, you shall not oppress the alien. The alien who resides with you shall be to you as the citizen among you; you shall love the alien as yourself, for you were aliens in the land of Egypt: I am the LORD your God.   —Leviticus 19:33

Then Solomon took a census of all the aliens who were residing in the land of Israel, after the census that his father David had taken; and there were found to be one hundred fifty-three thousand six hundred.   —2 Chronicles 2:17

Beth She'an is one of the most spectacular sites in Israel/Palestine that today is fast becoming one of the greatest archaeological parks in the country. Located on the east end of the Jezreel Valley (and twenty miles south of Tiberius), it was a fortress that protected one of the main access routes into the region. King Saul lost his life in battle here. When he died, his body was hung on the city's walls. Today a tremendous archaeological tell marks the spot, and excavations continue annually.

In New Testament times, Greeks and Romans built a city here. Called Scythopolis, it was a major city, boasting one of the largest theaters, baths, markets, temples, and horse racing tracks in the country. No doubt Jesus passed through its streets as he traveled between Galilee and Jerusalem.

Many of these ancient sites have been occupied for centuries by Palestinian villages whose names still reflect the sounds of its ancient history. Biblical Emmaus, for example, can be found at the village of Imwas west of Jerusalem (note how the two sites sound the same). Bethany, known for the raising of Lazarus, is today called El Azariya, which recalls Lazarus's name. Sepphoris was an Arab village of Saffuriya till it was conquered and became the Israeli settlement of Zippori.

Near the colossal ruins of Beth She'an lived the thriving Arab town of Beisan, whose name likewise recalled this great Old Testament heritage. In

1948, it had an Arab population of 5,180 and a Jewish community of 20.[1] No history of conflict was known between these communities — until 1948.

Na'im Stifan Ateek was eleven years old in 1948.[2] He and his family belonged to the Anglican Christian community in Beisan. Their home was a locus of Christian activity: Bible studies, visiting missionaries, and Sunday school classes met there. His father even helped build an Anglican church for Beisan. In the absence of a resident Anglican pastor (who came from Nazareth once a month for Holy Communion), Na'im's father served as the church's lay reader.

On May 12, 1948 (two days before the state of Israel was declared), Israeli soldiers occupied Beisan. There was no fighting, no resistance, no killing. The town was simply taken over. After searching the homes for weapons and radios, on May 26 they rounded up the leading men of the town to make an important announcement. Everyone would have to leave their homes in a few hours. "If you do not leave, we will have to kill you," they said.

When the people had gathered in the center of town, the soldiers separated the Muslims from the Christians. The Muslims were sent east to Jordan, and the Christians were put on buses and deposited on the outskirts of Nazareth. Within a few hours, Na'im's mother, father, seven sisters, and two brothers were refugees. They had lost everything except the things they could carry. In Nazareth they joined some friends, and seventeen of them lived in two rooms near "Mary's Well." Na'im's father went to work at once helping relief efforts for the countless Christians and Muslims flooding Nazareth daily as refugees.

Ten years later, in 1958, the government permitted many of the Palestinian families to travel for one day without restriction. Na'im's father was eager to bring his children to Beisan so that they could see their "home." The Anglican church had become a storehouse. The Roman Catholic church was a school. The Greek Orthodox church was in ruins. Na'im remembers the moment his father stepped up to the door of his home, the one he had built with his own hands. He wanted to see it one last time. But his request was refused. The new Israeli occupant said, "This is not your house. It is ours."

---

1. F. Jaber, *The Colonization of Palestine* (New York: Americans for Middle East Understanding, 1992), 27.

2. The personal story of Na'im Ateek is told in full in his excellent book *Justice and Only Justice* (Maryknoll, N.Y.: Orbis, 1989), 7–17. In it, Ateek describes the dilemma of being Palestinian, Arab, Christian, and an Israeli citizen. Today Ateek heads Sabeel, an Arab Christian justice ministry in Jerusalem, as a minister in the Anglican church. See the website: *www.sabeel.org.*

I frequently drive through the modern Israeli town of Beth She'an which occupies the land once known as Beisan. I often reflect on the beauty of this place and the historic nature of its setting. Each time I am troubled when I remember that an ancient community — filled with Christians — was uprooted at gunpoint and is now gone.

About eleven miles west of Beisan was another beautiful place called Jezreel (the city from which the valley takes its name). Tucked under the shoulder of Mount Gilboa (an outcropping of Samaria), Jezreel had good land, good water, and excellent access to the all-important Jezreel Valley. Once in the Old Testament, an Israelite king coveted a vineyard in Jezreel in the same manner that Beisan was coveted by the Israelis. In a similar manner, the king took it, and God sent his prophet Elijah to severely rebuke the leader of God's people. In a moment we turn to this story, because it powerfully tells us about land and justice. When land is occupied, does the Bible not respect the rights or honor of the people who have lived there for centuries? When land is occupied by people who are not Jewish, what does God expect?

JOSHUA'S CONQUEST

The book of Joshua is required reading in Israeli schools today. The book holds an important place because in its pages many people think that a precedent can be found for the establishment of Israel as a nation.[3] Once I was having dinner at an evangelical graduate school on Mount Zion in Jerusalem. Speaking with a group of pastors and students, I wondered how we as Christians could explain Israel's taking of land in the "Occupied Territories." I was surprised to hear many of them agree that Joshua's conquest set a legitimate precedent and pattern for the modern day.

The instructions given to Joshua and the people of Israel before they enter the land are quite explicit. Read carefully the words of Moses as he explains what they are to do upon entering Canaan:

> When the LORD your God brings you into the land that you are about to enter and occupy, and he clears away many nations before you — the Hittites, the Girgashites, the Amorites, the Canaanites, the Perizzites, the Hivites, and the Jebusites, seven nations mightier and more numerous than you — and when

---

3. A comprehensive study of Joshua noting its implications for modern Israel has been written by a Palestinian pastor in the Arab Anglican church. See Z. Nassir, "The Israelite Conquest of Palestine: Theological Implications for Claiming a Land" (B.Div. diss., Baptist Theological Seminary, Rüschlikon, Switzerland, 1987). See also A. Rantisi, *Blessed Are the Peacemakers: A Palestinian Christian in the Occupied West Bank* (Grand Rapids, Mich.: Zondervan, 1990), 157ff.

the LORD your God gives them over to you and you defeat them, then you must utterly destroy them. Make no covenant with them and show them no mercy. Do not intermarry with them, giving your daughters to their sons or taking their daughters for your sons, for that would turn away your children from following me, to serve other gods. Then the anger of the LORD would be kindled against you, and he would destroy you quickly. But this is how you must deal with them: break down their altars, smash their pillars, hew down their sacred poles, and burn their idols with fire. For you are a people holy to the LORD your God.... (Deut. 7:1–6)

Paragraphs such as this are troubling. It seems as if Joshua is commanded to pursue a policy of genocide in order to rid Canaan of its inhabitants. How does this compare with God's command elsewhere to value and protect human life? Even Jonah was commanded to preach to the Assyrians (whose life was no better than the Canaanites). But no such suggestion comes in Joshua. This instruction seems to be a cavalier, sweeping disposal of an entire people. Three observations are necessary:

1. The battles in Joshua are aimed at coalitions of kings from the north and the south who realize that their sovereignty over Canaan is in jeopardy. Note Joshua 9:1–2:

Now when all the kings who were beyond the Jordan in the hill country and in the lowland all along the coast of the Great Sea toward Lebanon — the Hittites, the Amorites, the Canaanites, the Perizzites, the Hivites, and the Jebusites — heard of this, they gathered together with one accord to fight Joshua and Israel.

Joshua fights and destroys urban areas that exhibit military resistance to his arrival. The book offers no suggestion that Joshua ever massacres or depopulates large regions that did not join one of these armies. In fact, only three Canaanite cities are burned to the ground: Jericho, Ai, and Hazor. There is no Canaanite Holocaust.

2. Moses' words have in mind the corrupting religious influences of the Canaanites. Note how Deuteronomy 7:5 underscores the obliteration of Canaanite religion: "But this is how you must deal with them: break down their altars, smash their pillars, hew down their sacred poles, and burn their idols with fire." This was a fertility religion devoted to snake worship, the sacrifice of children, and cult prostitution. According to many scholars, the religion had no moral interest at all. The Canaanites were not errant believers in God. Rather their culture had reached the depths of pagan depravity.

3. Joshua treats many of the Canaanites with respect. In Jericho, Rahab was not an Israelite, yet because she aided the spies and feared their God, she was protected and her life was preserved (Josh. 2). Further, even though

Joshua is commanded to make no covenant with these people, he is tricked by the people of Gibeon to make such a pact. Even though Joshua erred, even though the Gibeonites were dishonest, still Joshua keeps his word and preserves the Gibeonites (Josh. 9). In 10:6–8, Joshua even enters a battle to protect them from an attack by a five-king coalition. The significance of this event cannot be missed. Israelites risked their lives to protect Canaanites who were about to be destroyed by hostile armies. If covenants conceived in deception are respected, so too would be covenants conceived in goodwill.

This acceptance of non-Israelites is also seen when Joshua first enters the land, and he requires that the people renew their commitment to the covenant in the central mountains (on the mountains of Ebal and Gerizim, Josh. 8:30–35). The audience participating in this renewal ceremony consisted of Israelites and non-Israelites. Residents who were foreign to Israel's history stood beneath the blessings and curses of the law. This event is surprising if only Israelites were permitted to enjoy this land and God's covenant.

> And afterward [Joshua] read all the words of the law, blessings and curses, according to all that is written in the book of the law. There was not a word of all that Moses commanded that Joshua did not read before all the assembly of Israel, and the women, and the little ones, *and the aliens who resided among them.* (Josh. 8:34–35, emphasis added)

4. Joshua never drives out all of the Canaanites. Joshua 13 lists those areas that remained under Canaanite control. In addition, we know that Jerusalem was never conquered by the tribe of Judah: "But the people of Judah could not drive out the Jebusites, the inhabitants of Jerusalem; so the Jebusites live with the people of Judah in Jerusalem to this day" (Josh. 15:63). Curiously, Joshua 12:10 says clearly that the king of Jerusalem was defeated and his army destroyed when he joined a southern coalition of forces arrayed against Israel (10:3–5, 22–27). And yet the Jebusites who lived in Jerusalem (who were now without military defense) were left alone. Why did Joshua not storm Jerusalem and take it?

To sum up, the portrait given in Joshua is not as uniform as we might think. City-fortresses hostile to Joshua suffer a devastating defeat, but not every Canaanite life is expunged from the land. Indeed, significant areas, particularly in Galilee near Mount Hermon, the coast of Lebanon, and the foothills inhabited by Philistines remain in Canaanite control.

The parallel between Joshua's conquest and the modern Israeli occupation of the land is inappropriate. Joshua's mandate applied to a specific historic period of time when the Canaanites promoted a religion utterly inimical to God's law. Modern Israel/Palestine is populated by many Christians and Muslims who have a deep reverence for the Lord God of Abraham. In fact, Rahab's spiritual disposition was not unlike that of the Palestinians who acknowledge and worship the same God as the Jews but are not Jewish themselves.

CRISIS AMONG THE JUDGES

After Joshua's conquest, the Israelite tribes settle in their designated territories and begin to enjoy the land God had promised to them. However, Judges tells us through a cycle of stories that each generation of people willfully neglects the covenant and then is brought under God's judgment. Judges 3:7–8 is typical:

> The Israelites did what was evil in the sight of the LORD, forgetting the LORD their God, and worshiping the Baals and the Asherahs. Therefore the anger of the LORD was kindled against Israel, and he sold them into the hand of King Cushan-rishathaim of Aram Naharaim; and the Israelites served Cushan-rishathaim eight years.

In response to their prayers for mercy, God raises up a judge (such as Ehud, Deborah, Gideon, or Samson) who leads Israel to victory. This results in a period of national peace in which correct worship is restored (generally for forty years) until the next generation enters the scene.

This much of Judges is well known. However, the book concludes with two troubling stories that serve as a summary of the evil that is growing in the land. The final verse of the book epitomizes Israel's condition: "In those days there was no king in Israel; all the people did what was right in their own eyes" (Judg. 21:25). Judges 17–21 describes the fallenness of the tribes of Dan and Benjamin in parallel terms.

The story of Dan illustrates Israel's *religious* corruption (chaps. 17–18). Dan leaves its territory in the western coastal hills (the Shephelah), travels north through the central mountains of "Samaria," and meets a priestly assistant (a Levite) in Ephraim and offers him a job as tribal priest.[4] They said to him, "Come with us, and be to us a father and a priest." The tribe resettles in the far north near Mount Hermon and there establishes a new religion based on this new priest's idol. Spearheaded by six hundred men of

---

4. Not only was it wrong for the Levite to promote idol worship, but a Levite was never permitted to serve as priest. At this time priestly worship was conducted only at the town of Shiloh in the north central mountains of Israel. Ironically Shiloh is quite near where the Danites recruited the Levite.

Dan, this act is an utter rejection of God's covenant, apostasy and religious corruption in its worst form.

The story of Benjamin illustrates Israel's *moral* corruption (chaps. 19–21). As the final story of Judges, it is meant to shock and sober. Once again a Levite takes center stage. Because his young concubine had fled home to her father in Bethlehem, the Levite goes there to recover her. He then travels with her north, en route no doubt to Shiloh, where he assists the priests. Because nightfall has come, he seeks lodging in Gibeah, a city of the tribe of Benjamin. After an elderly man takes them in, that night men of Gibeah pound on the door. They wish to rape the Levite (19:22). The host offers his virgin daughters instead but to no avail. Then the Levite throws his young concubine out the door, and she is raped by the group of men throughout the night. In the morning the Levite finds her on the doorstep and gives her an order to get up, but she is dead.

He then chops her body into a dozen parts and ships them to each tribe. Outraged by the immorality witnessed in Gibeah, the tribes descend, attacking Benjamin and killing all but six hundred men; and then, lest tribal Benjamin become extinct, they kidnap wives for them at Jabesh-Gilead (after slaughtering the rest of the city) and Shiloh (where God is worshiped). This series of events shows moral anarchy and sexual violence unlike anything witnessed before.[5]

These two parallel stories make an important point.[6] In chapter 3 we learned that God's blessing of land was dependent on fidelity to the covenant. What was implicit in the law, Judges now shows in reality: *sinfulness results in the loss of inheritance.* Dan neglects its promised land in the coastal hills and migrates into apostasy in the far reaches of the north. Tribal Benjamin almost disappears from history because of losing any sense of God's moral commands. Its sin as well as that of the Levite are simply heinous.

Land and righteousness are linked. The book of Judges plays out the theological theme provided in Moses' covenant: fidelity to covenant righteousness is a prerequisite to enjoying the blessings of that covenant. When each generation neglects the covenant, the land is conquered by a foreign power. When a specific tribe offends the covenant, its promises are placed in jeopardy. Joshua had reminded the people that this result would occur. When they first entered

---

5. This story intentionally echoes the account of Lot in Sodom (Gen. 19). There the two visiting angels are threatened with homosexual rape and Lot offers his two daughters. Because of the hostility of Sodom, the angels destroy the city with fire after Lot's family is told to flee.

6. Note their parallels: a Levite, six hundred men, profound sin in the central hill country, and violation of the covenant. Dan was one of Israel's least significant tribes. Benjamin was deemed the most privileged since its forefather (Benjamin) was the youngest and last son of Rachel, Jacob's favored wife.

the land, recall that he gathered them at Mount Ebal and Mount Gerizim and read the law once again aloud. He reminded them that the covenant did not simply bring privilege; it brought expectation. The covenant brought the prospects for both blessing and judgment at the same time.

ISRAEL'S KINGS

Throughout Judges and 1 Samuel, the people of Israel insist on having a king (cf. the offer to Gideon, Judg. 8:22ff.). While they think that this status will enhance their prospects for nationhood, the prophet Samuel warns that just the opposite will happen (1 Sam. 8). To have a human king is to reject God as king, which will lead to neglect of the covenant. Kings, Samuel argues, bring war (vv. 10–12) and taxes (vv. 15–18). They will consume the young who are seduced into serving the "empire" (vv. 13, 16). And, interestingly, they will steal the land (v. 14). Listen to Samuel's words of warning: "He will take the best of your fields and vineyards and olive groves and give them to his attendants." Samuel understands that land is one of the most precious gifts given by God. And when nations experience corruption — which in his view is inevitable — the gift of this land will be abused.

It would be a mistake to think of the nation built by Saul, David, and Solomon as culturally monolithic, as if it were "a Jewish state" in the modern sense. Non-Jews were not marginalized or expelled. On the contrary, "ancient empires were hegemonic, not ethnically exclusive."[7] Different cultures were integrated into the mainstream of national life under the sovereignty of the king and his dominant nation. For instance, in 2 Samuel 4:2–3 we read that two of Saul's military captains were "Be-er'othites." This group was a "foreign" or "alien" tribe, a non-Israelite people living within Saul's kingdom.

This integration of non-Israelites can be seen in King David's case by looking at the different men who populated the ranks of his military officers. Second Samuel 23 (also 1 Chron. 11:10–47) lists the core of David's military organization: three leading "champions" and thirty secondary commanders. In this list, numerous non-Israelites are included from territories conquered by David.[8] Zobah (2 Sam. 23:36) was in the central valley of

---

7. R. Ruether and H. Ruether, *The Wrath of Jonah: The Crisis of Religious Nationalism in the Israeli-Palestinian Conflict* (New York: Harper & Row, 1989), 9.

8. See J. Mauchline, *1 and 2 Samuel,* New Century Bible (London: Oliphants, 1971), 320–21. Note that the young man who mercifully killed the wounded King Saul and brought David Saul's crown was "a resident alien, an Amalekite" (2 Sam. 1:13).

Lebanon, Maacah (v. 34) was a Syrian kingdom above the Golan Heights,[9] and Ammon (v. 37) was on the plateau east of the Jordan River (the capital of modern-day Jordan, Amman, gets its name from this kingdom).[10] The Hittites (v. 39) came from modern-day Turkey in the distant north. Remarkably David's army was thus led by a diversity of men, many of whom were not native Israelites. Using today's geographical terms, he enlisted men from Lebanon, Syria, Jordan, and Turkey, and they were some of his trusted leaders. David's generals and colonels were fully international.

The inclusion of the "alien" or foreigner can be seen in yet another way. Non-Israelites assisted in the construction of the Temple in Jerusalem (1 Chron. 22:2). At one point Solomon took a census of the number of resident aliens in his kingdom and discovered 153,600 of them (2 Chron. 2:17). After King Hezekiah cleansed and restored worship at the Temple following a time of severe disbelief, he called the people to Jerusalem and led them in a Passover festival. Were foreigners invited in? Indeed. "The whole assembly of Judah, the priests and the Levites, and the whole assembly that came out of Israel, and the resident aliens who came out of the land of Israel, and the resident aliens who lived in Judah, rejoiced" (2 Chron. 30:25).

Why did Israel give such respect to these resident aliens? The answer came from Israel's own history. Israel had been alienated once in Egypt. They too had been refugees. The Israelites were commanded to give offerings from their crops to God each year. As they handed the basket of goods to the priest, they were to recite: "A wandering Aramean was my ancestor; he went down into Egypt and lived there as an alien, few in number, and there he became a great nation, mighty and populous" (Deut. 26:5; cf. Ps. 119:19). Because God had been generous with the alien Israel, so too, Israel was obligated to be generous with other foreigners. At the end of his life, when David prayed for Solomon his son, his prayer for Solomon's humility was rooted in this notion: "For we are aliens and transients before you, as were all our ancestors; our days on the earth are like a shadow, and there is no hope" (1 Chron. 29:15).

ALIENS AND SOJOURNERS IN THE LAND

Two themes are beginning to appear. First, Israel's possession of the land is linked to covenant righteousness. Possession of the land is conditioned

---

9. In 2 Samuel 10:6–14, we have an account of mercenaries from Maacah fighting against David and suffering defeat.

10. The Ammonites descended from Lot (Gen. 19:38). Even though the Ammonites did not inherit the land promises (since they did not descend from Abraham), still Deuteronomy 2:19 required that they be treated with honor.

on faithfulness to God. Thus, when David gives advice to his son Solomon before the construction of God's Temple begins, he says, "Now therefore in the sight of all Israel, the assembly of the LORD, and in the hearing of our God, observe and search out all the commandments of the LORD your God; that you may possess this good land, and leave it for an inheritance to your children after you forever" (1 Chron. 28:8). Keeping the land is hinged to keeping the law.

Second, one feature of righteous nationhood is Israel's fair treatment of resident aliens or foreigners — non-Israelites who were in the land before Israel arrived. Rather than being expelled, they are included in the fabric of Israelite society. In fact, Israel's population had a significant non-Israelite minority (over 150,000 people).

Let us take a closer look at the rights of these "aliens" who lived alongside the Israelites. One curiosity of the Bible is that the social fabric of ancient Israel made generous allowances for "the alien (or sojourner), the orphan, and the widow." As non-Israelites, aliens were accorded surprising privileges. They were not pushed to the outskirts of society to make way for a comprehensive Jewish state. Here is a partial list of the benefits for aliens given in the law:

1. *Religious Privileges: Non-Israelites were included in religious ceremony and worship*

- Aliens enjoyed the Sabbath rest and could not be required to work (Exod. 23:12).
- Aliens could participate in all the major festivals in Jerusalem (Num. 9:14); however, in order to participate in the Passover, the alien had to be circumcised (Exod. 12:48).
- Aliens could even make personal sacrifices at the altar for worship (Num. 15:14).
- Access to the holiest ceremonies was not restricted. For instance, when Joshua recommitted Israel to the covenant with God, aliens stood alongside Israelites near the ark (Josh. 8:33).

2. *Social Privileges: Non-Israelites were cared for in "social programs" that assisted the needy*

- The Israelites were commanded not to harvest their fields thoroughly so that aliens, orphans, and widows could take freely what was left (Lev. 19:10; 23:27; Deut. 24:19–21).
- When the tithes were collected (these functioned like modern taxes), the income was also to be distributed to the aliens, orphans, and widows so that their lives could be blessed with material sustenance (Deut. 14:29; 26:12).

- The law protected anyone from falling into permanent slavery through indebtedness. Means of redemption were extended to all, including the alien (Lev. 25:47–50), which protected the social and financial future of the non-Israelite family.

3. *Legal Privileges: Non-Israelites were to have access to the same system of justice enjoyed by the Israelites*

- Israel had a system of "cities of refuge" throughout the land which kept people from being victimized by revenge. The accused could flee there to find protection and justice. Aliens could use these cities without restriction (Num. 35:15; Josh. 20:9).

- Wages had to be fair, and none could be withheld from the alien (Deut. 24:14).

- Similarly, aliens could not be oppressed or discriminated against as if they were not full citizens. Leviticus 19:33–34 is explicit: "When an alien resides with you in your land, you shall not oppress the alien. The alien who resides with you shall be to you as the citizen among you; you shall love the alien as yourself, for you were aliens in the land of Egypt: I am the LORD your God."

- The court system available to Israelites was to be available to aliens. There were not to be two systems of justice (Deut. 1:16; 24:17). Note the tone of Deuteronomy 27:19: "Cursed be anyone who deprives the alien, the orphan, and the widow of justice. All the people shall say, Amen!"

- The Bible repeats numerous times that one law was to be applied to all people. Aliens and Israelites were not to obey different legal codes. No law could bind aliens unless it was also binding on Israelites (Lev. 24:22; Num. 9:14; 15:16, 29).

The resulting conclusion is inescapable. Israel was commanded to create a remarkable society, and one test of its goodness was the way the foreigner, the alien, or the non-Israelite was treated. This land (which belongs to God) would produce a people who were a genuine blessing to their neighbors, who incorporated them into their lives and who invited them into their leadership.

TWO STORIES, TWO KINGS

Respect for anyone who owns land — including the resident alien — and the righteous requirements of possessing the land come together in two important Old Testament stories. In each case, an Israelite desires land. In each case, he has to make a moral choice about how to treat the person who owns it.

In 1 Chronicles 21, King David is instructed to build an altar for God on a small hill just north of David's Jerusalem. This place was going to become the site of Solomon's glorious Temple (1 Chron. 22:1–5), and therefore an angel even points out the exact location (21:18, 20). Thus if the land belongs to God, surely this plot of land is especially his! If David is to be the steward of the whole land, this plot will be at the center of Israel's inheritance. This Temple will be God's own house, the symbolic place of his dwelling with his people.

But one problem comes up. The chosen site is a threshing floor owned by a man named Ornan, a Canaanite resident of pre-Israelite Jerusalem when the city was called "Jebus." Ornan "the Jebusite" is among those people listed in Genesis 15:20–21 whose land would be inherited by Israel. If David, the conqueror of Jebus/Jerusalem, had taken the land unilaterally from Ornan, it would not surprise us. Israel had inherited that threshing floor. But note what happens. Ornan tries to give it to David freely, along with a yoke of oxen for a sacrifice, but the king refuses the gift. "No," David responds; "I will buy them for the full price. I will not take for the LORD what is yours, nor offer burnt offerings that cost me nothing" (1 Chron. 21:24). David then pays six hundred shekels of gold for the site.

This story is interesting because it records that David dealt *justly* with Ornan the Jebusite when trying to obtain land that was precious and valued. If any land was "God's land," it was this threshing floor. Yet David did not take it at "spear point." As champion of God's covenant, David showed justice and righteousness in how he acquired it.

In 1 Kings 21, we find a different sort of story. King Ahab possessed a second palace in the Jezreel Valley not far from the Arab town of Beisan mentioned at the beginning of this chapter. Adjoining the king's property was a beautiful vineyard owned by Naboth, a longtime resident of this land. King Ahab offered to buy the vineyard, but Naboth refused to sell. Money was not the issue; this land had been in Naboth's family for generations. His history and heritage were at stake. For Naboth, this land was sacred and deeply loved. The king even offered Naboth an alternative vineyard somewhere else, but Naboth was not interested.

Ahab's wife, Jezebel, had the perfect solution. Since Naboth would not move, she would have him accused unjustly and then murdered. At a public ceremony, scoundrels hired by Jezebel charge Naboth with cursing both God and the king.

After the elders stone Naboth to death, Ahab quickly moves in and takes possession of the vineyard. But the story does not end here. In the very next paragraph, God calls the prophet Elijah to deliver this message: "Thus says the LORD: Have you killed, and also taken possession? Thus says the LORD: In the place where dogs licked up the blood of Naboth, dogs will also lick up your blood" (1 Kings 21:19). Shortly thereafter, Ahab is killed in battle.

This story is crucial for our study because it shows God's uncompromising concern for justice among his people as they possess the land.[11] Naboth's rights must be protected. When justice is flouted, God's judgment is swift. Na'im Ateek, the Palestinian pastor from Beisan, comments on the Naboth story: "[God's] ethical law, championed by the prophets, operated impartially: every person's rights, property, and very life were under divine protection." Whenever injustice occurred, God intervened to defend the poor, the weak, and the defenseless.[12]

In 1966, an Arab peasant asked an official at the Israel Lands Administration, "How do you deny my right to this land? It is my property. I inherited it from my parents and grandparents, and I have the deed of ownership." The official replied, "Ours is a more impressive deed; we have the deed for the land from Dan [in the far north] to Elat [in the far south]." Another official was paying a peasant a token sale price for his land. Holding the peasant's property deed, the official remarked, "This is not your land; it is ours, and we are paying you 'watchman's wages,' for that is what you are. You have watched our land for two thousand years, and now we are paying your fee. But the land has always been ours."[13]

SUMMARY

The Bible is not ambiguous when it describes how God's people must live when they reside in his land. They must pursue justice and integrity at all costs. Further, the treatment of resident aliens is one test of their national character. To abuse non-Israelites is to neglect God's commitment to the underprivileged and the alien. To live unrighteously is to ignore God's covenant. And to mistreat the alien by taking his land places Israel's inheritance in jeopardy. While the covenant promises to Abraham are forever, those who inherit and enjoy these blessings must live righteously in order to keep them.

We began this chapter looking at the story of the old village of Beisan, known in the Bible as ancient Beth She'an. In the early days of Israel's birth, when Zionism fueled the vision that would shape this country's future, Israeli troops coveted the strategic site of the town. Unlike Ahab's day when

---

11. The story itself has become a model for biblical justice, a key for unlocking the Bible for Palestinian Christians like Na'im Ateek, who once lived in Beisan. For many Palestinian believers, Israel has been guilty of the sin of Ahab. See Ateek's comments, *Justice and Only Justice*, 86–89.

12. Ibid., 88.

13. Report by the attorney Hannah Nakkara in *Al Ittihad*, July 15, 1966. Cited in S. Jiryis, *The Arabs in Israel*, trans. from Arabic by Inea Bushnaq (New York: Monthly Review Press, 1976), 74.

Naboth's vineyard was valued for its good location and remarkable fertility, in the 1940s Israel coveted Beisan for its strategic value. Beisan sat on the main highway connecting the Jordan Valley to inner Galilee and the west. Soon Israeli Highway 71 would be built and a large Arab population was inconvenient. And just as in the days of Ahab, impure motives and military prowess won the day. Beisan was stolen. And over five thousand people lost their homes.

If Elijah had visited the day after Beisan had been "cleansed" of its Palestinians, what would he say? "Thus says the LORD: Have you killed, and also taken possession?" When forgetting how to treat aliens and sojourners, Israel has forgotten its *own* theological history — not simply its biblical history of suffering in Egypt, but its twentieth-century history of suffering in Europe.

God calls Israel to live in the land with righteousness because in its history Israel itself has experienced profound unrighteousness. When Israel refuses to act in this manner, the nation jeopardizes its own claim to life in the land.

Chapter Six

THE PROPHETS
AND THE LAND

For if you truly amend your ways and your doings, if you truly act justly one with another, if you do not oppress the alien, the orphan, and the widow, or shed innocent blood in this place, and if you do not go after other gods to your own hurt, then I well dwell with you in this place, in the land that I gave of old to your ancestors forever and ever.   —Jeremiah 7:5–7

The Palestinian village of Beita (pronounced *beta*) has stood for centuries in a remote section of the hills of Samaria between Jerusalem and biblical Shechem (Nablus today). Electricity came to Beita twenty years ago. Water is still drawn from the village well. Life here is hard.

Nearby is the Israeli settlement of Elon Moreh. Well-scrubbed, beautiful, modern, and heavily guarded, Elon Moreh was built in these hills just a few years ago, much to the dismay of the Arabs who live nearby. The tile roofs and gardens of Elon Moreh make it look like a patch of San Diego lifted from California and set in Israel.

On Friday, April 6, 1988, tragedy struck — the type of tragedy that has been seen countless times in the last fifteen years. It was Passover season, and Israel was celebrating its fortieth anniversary. Sixteen teenagers from Elon Moreh were hiking by Beita with two armed civilian guards.[1] They said they were on a picnic — and so the press reported it — but, as the village *Mukhtar,* or mayor, told me later, "No Israelis come to this little hill for a picnic." He was right. Tension between the village and the settlement had been strong for some time. And Beita was no picnic area.

When the group of eighteen approached the village, one of the guards, Romam Aldubi, age twenty-six, fired his M-16 at a village farmer who was plowing his field. The farmer died within the hour. Another farmer, Taysir Saleh, was called over. When he asked, "What do you want with our village?" he was shot point-blank in the stomach by the same guard with the

---

1. They were required to notify the local army outpost to hike here but did not. The two guards were Romam Aldubi, carrying an M-16 automatic rifle, and Menachem Ilan, who had an Uzi submachine gun.

M-16.[2] When the mother and sister of the first farmer discovered the death of their loved one, they rushed at the Israelis, throwing stones.

Suddenly a mob formed. Arab teenagers from Beita began throwing stones by hand and with slings at the Israeli teenagers. The Arab village men tried to intervene and protect the Israeli teenagers. One girl from Elon Moreh, Rachely Savitiz, later told how an Arab family grabbed her and hid her in their home for protection. As the group neared the village, the two Israeli guards opened fire with their automatic weapons, and bullets flew everywhere. One Arab boy fell dead.[3] Another fled across the field and was killed by a bullet in his back.[4] Two other Arabs were wounded. Then one of the Israeli girls, a fifteen-year-old named Tirza Porat, fell dead from a bullet wound to the head. She was the first Israeli casualty since the Intifada (the Palestinian Uprising) began. No one knew who fired the shot. Aldubi became crazed and wanted to machine-gun the crowd of villagers, but the other Israeli guard stopped him.

Arab villagers grabbed the two armed men to pacify them and took their M-16 rifle and Uzi submachine gun. They removed the ammunition clips and tried to break the guns, slamming them on the ground.[5] Other villagers continued to protect the Israeli teenagers from harm during the melee and transported any who were hurt to a medical facility in Nablus.

Immediately hundreds of Israeli soldiers descended on Beita and sealed it off. Even Arab ambulances from Nablus were not permitted in. House-to-house searches began at once in an attempt to find the murderers of the Israeli girl. The following nine days shocked the Middle East and the world. For three days, Beita earned front-page headlines in the *New York Times*.[6]

Thursday, April 7. Jerusalem Post headlines: "Settler girl stoned to death." Elon Moreh buries Tirza Porat at a nationally watched funeral while hundreds of soldiers chant, "Revenge, revenge. Expel the Arabs." One speaker from Elon Moreh promises to build another settlement near Beita in the dead girl's name. Prime Minister Yitzhak Shamir speaks at the funeral,

---

2. Tasir survived and was extensively interviewed. His testimony (and that of the other Israeli eyewitnesses) was later accepted by the Israeli army as correct. See the *New York Times,* April 9, 1988, A-8.

3. Hatan Fayez Ahmed, age nineteen.

4. Mousa Abu Shalseh, age twenty.

5. The M-16 and Uzi were later returned to the army. The M-16 clip still had six rounds left, which shows the danger of the elder's actions, grabbing a loaded, firing M-16.

6. The following account was carefully compiled from the following news sources, which followed the Beita story daily: *Jerusalem Post* (Israeli), *Al Nahar* (Jerusalem, Palestinian), the *New York Times,* and the services of Reuters and the Associated Press. With a translator I also interviewed the *Mukhtar* (village elder) of Beita, as well as twelve men and one family in the village.

promising that revenge will be had. "God will revenge her blood," he says. Rabbi Chaim Druckman also speaks: "The village of Beita should be wiped from the face of the earth." The minister of justice, Avraham Sharir, recommends that dozens of Beita homes be destroyed and hundreds of the residents be exiled to Lebanon.

That afternoon, helicopters search the hills looking for hiding Arab youths. One is found running and is shot and killed without being identified. The army blows up four Beita homes of Arabs suspected of violence, though no evidence is provided that the inhabitants are guilty. In Hawara village, one mile away from Beita, armed Israeli settlers rampage through the streets, breaking car windshields and windows in homes. The army looks on.

On Thursday evening Israeli television runs lurid photographs of the Israeli girl's body. Public outcry against Beita grows dramatically throughout Israel. Beita becomes a "media event."

Friday, April 8. The Israeli army blows up eight more homes in Beita without conducting any formal trial or investigation. The Israeli army's autopsy says that the bullet that killed the girl was from the same gun that killed the Arab youths on that Wednesday, which suggests that an Israeli guard killed her by accident. Israeli Chief of Staff, General Dan Shomron, astonishes everyone with his remarks: "The Arab residents of Beita had intended no harm to the Elon Moreh hikers." The settlers of Elon Moreh reject this report angrily. Increased Arab demonstrations break out in nearby Nablus, and forty-nine Arab youths are injured.

Israeli soldiers ransack the central hospital in Nablus looking for injured Beita residents. Doctors and nurses are locked in an office, and numerous patients are beaten. The next day, the hospital staff stages a protest.

Saturday, April 9. Fourteen more houses in Beita are marked for demolition. Thirty people have been arrested in connection with Wednesday's incident, but no Israeli settlers have gone into custody. Sixty-five homes in Beita are damaged by soldiers. Since it is the Sabbath, the day is quiet.

Sunday, April 10. Israeli Defense Minister Yitzhak Rabin confirms publicly that the girl died from a gunshot fired by Romam Aldubi, one of the Israeli guards. Aldubi's profile is released. A militant follower of radical Rabbi Meir Kahane, Aldubi had fired on Palestinians at the Balata refugee camp outside Nablus and had been banned from entering Nablus again or serving in the army. Still, he owned an army-issued M-16. Rabin identifies Aldubi as the culprit.

Hours later, the army announces that it plans to expel from the country six Beita youths connected with the incident. They have received no trial.

They will be deposited by helicopter in southern Lebanon, never to return home again.

A high-ranking army officer comes to the village and speaks in confidence with the mayor of Beita. He apologizes secretly for what the army is doing to the village. The homes are being destroyed to appease the outraged Israeli settlers.

Israel's Trade Minister, Ariel Sharon recommends publicly that all Beita residents be expelled and every home in the village be destroyed.

The Israeli Supreme Court bars any further destruction of Beita homes. Israeli newspapers *Ha'Aretz* and *Hadashot* call for a stop to the punishment of Beita. *Hadashot* calls it an attempt to pacify the settlers of Elon Moreh.

Monday, April 11. Israeli Chief of Staff Shomron is criticized by the settlers because he praises the people of Beita for protecting the Elon Moreh teenagers during the conflict. Some in the Israeli Parliament call for his resignation. Still, the army blows up two more homes, destroys Beita's grove of almond trees, and uproots hundreds of its ancient olive trees. No trial has yet been held for anyone in Beita.

The U.N. Security Council adopts a resolution — supported by the United States — condemning Israel's expulsion of Palestinians.

Charles Redman, a spokesman for the U.S. State Department, reiterates the U.S. government's position: deportations violate the Geneva International Human Rights Agreements, which Israel signed.

Tuesday, April 12. U.N. Secretary General Javier Perez de Cuellar publicly criticizes Israeli actions concerning Beita and the deportations. Britain likewise makes a public condemnation. U.S. Ambassador Thomas R. Pickering, speaking at Jerusalem's Hebrew University, complains that Israel cannot continue demolishing homes, deporting Arabs, and failing to provide fair judicial process. Prime Minister Yitzhak Shamir defends the army and warns the Palestinians that more expulsions and demolitions will occur unless they stop their hostilities.

Wednesday, April 13. The army publishes its final report on Beita, admitting that the gunshot killing the girl was indeed fired by an Israeli. Elon Moreh is responsible for the incident. However, the army has no plans to rebuild Beita's destroyed homes.

Tuesday, April 19. At 3:00 p.m., an Israeli helicopter gunship lands in southern Lebanon. Ghassan Ali Ezzat Massri, Mahmoud Yacoub, Musstafa Ayed Hamayel, Najeh Jameel Saada Dweikat, Sari Khaleel Dhaher Hamayel, Ahmad Fawzi Khaled Deek, Omar Muhammad Saud Daoud, and Ibraheem Muhammad Khader are told to get out and never return to Israel/Palestine again. Six of these young men are from Beita. They have never seen the inside of a courtroom. They have never been defended, and they will never return home to their families again. Accused of throwing stones, they are given a life sentence of exile.

When I visited Beita not long after these incidents and was given a tour of the destroyed homes by the village mayor (or *Mukhtar*), I was saddened and angry and depressed. Soldiers had come in the following months and made Beita's men remove the debris of the homes so that the evidence of their destruction would be minimal. As I stood in the rubble of one of the homes, I picked up a piece of plaster with light green paint on it and put it in my pocket. It now sits on a shelf in my office. The artifact is a witness, a record of violence to a people whose story has been forgotten everywhere except among the Palestinians.

The entire Old Testament links justice and the land. We have seen this in the books of law as well as in the history of Israel's kingship. When Joshua first entered the land, he renewed Israel's covenant by designating Mount Ebal and Mount Gerizim as "guardians of the covenant." The mountains would look down on the people and assess if blessings or curses should come to the Israelites.

The same can be found in the prophets. Men like Jeremiah, Amos, Isaiah, and Ezekiel had little patience for a nation that ignored righteousness as it built its empire. Kings who consumed land, who moved landmarks, and who destroyed innocent people and their homes would soon find themselves facing a prophet, just as Ahab faced Elijah. Or they would face God. Even King David, for instance, was told that he was disqualified from building God's holy Temple because he had slaughtered so many people — so many foreigners — in his quest for nationhood (1 Chron. 22:8). *King David had blood on his hands.*

THE LAND AND THE PROPHET

Israel failed to understand that it could not be a nation like other nations. Its kings could not treat the land like other lands. As Walter Brueggemann puts it, this lesson is "a perennial lesson Israel had to learn and to perceive otherwise as a perennial temptation."[7] In fact, the land becomes a sort of prism that reflects the deepest values at work in Israel. The land tempts the corrupt while it encourages the righteous. The corrupt want to consume

---

7. W. Brueggemann, *The Land: Place as Gift, Promise, and Challenge in Biblical Faith* (Philadelphia: Fortress, 1977), 90.

more land for more power and wealth. The righteous employ its bounty to build a better place for all.

As the land stands over against Israel like Mount Ebal towers over Shechem, assessing Israel's life in light of the covenant, so too the prophet plays the same peculiar role. The nation is accountable to external standards. God imposes his will in the land through the prophet. To abuse and ignore the prophet is to work against the covenant and, finally, to lose the land. Kings may not appoint prophets, just as they do not write the laws of the land. Both are called into being by God, and the king and his court must conform to them obediently. This accountability makes Israel a remarkable state, an ideal state in which the imperial authorities are held to some system of justice. In Israel, the king is not supreme; the law is supreme.

When the land is introduced in Deuteronomy, prophets are introduced too: "When you come into the land...the LORD your God will raise up for you a prophet" (Deut. 18:9–15).[8] Likewise the description of prophets follows closely on the description of kings, perhaps because of the threat that kings and their governments pose. The temptation to power and corruption demands the voice of a prophet who can chasten the monarch. Deuteronomy 18:19 says, "Anyone who does not heed the words that the prophet shall speak in my name, I myself will hold accountable."

THE PROPHETS' WARNINGS

The prophets characteristically warned against the aggressive taking of land or the abuse of landowners, which were considered forms of heinous injustice. Note the words of Isaiah and Micah:

> Ah, you who join house to house,
>   who add field to field,
> until there is room for no one but you,
>   and you are left to live alone
>   in the midst of the land! (Isa. 5:8)

> Alas for those who devise wickedness
>   and evil deeds on their beds!
> When the morning dawns, they perform it,
>   because it is in their power.
> They covet fields, and seize them;
>   houses, and take them away;
> they oppress householder and house,
>   people and their inheritance.

---

8. Ibid., 91ff.

> Therefore thus says the LORD:
> Now, I am devising against this family an evil
>   from which you cannot remove your necks;
> and you shall not walk haughtily,
>   for it will be an evil time. (Mic. 2:1–3)

These words compare with the statement of Elijah to King Ahab when the king took the vineyard of Naboth illegally: "Have you killed, and also taken possession?" (1 Kings 21:19). These two offenses — murder and land seizure — would bring about the end of Ahab's reign. His offenses would terminate his privileges in the land. The prophet Elijah guaranteed it.

Virtually every one of the Old Testament prophets echoes the same theme. Reaching back to the covenant land promises and the law, they point to Israel's violation of God's rule and the necessary judgment that will follow. In each case, the land is a vehicle of judgment. God withholds rain (Amos 4:6), sends pestilence (4:10), and impairs the harvest (4:6) in order to discipline his people. The land is the vehicle of disciplining. God's ultimate judgment will be to remove the people entirely from the land.

Speaking to the northern kingdom,[9] Amos identifies the absence of justice in the land and announces the coming anger of God:

> Hear this word, you cows of Bashan
>   who are on Mount Samaria,
> who oppress the poor, who crush the needy,
>   who say to their husbands, "Bring something to drink!"
> The Lord GOD has sworn by his holiness:
>   The time is surely coming upon you,
> when they shall take you away with hooks,
>   even the last of you with fishhooks. (Amos 4:1–2)

Amos says that the coming judgment will result in the loss of land:

> "[Y]our land shall be parceled out by line;
> you yourself shall die in an unclean land,
>   and Israel shall surely go into exile away from its land."
>   (Amos 7:17)

Hosea echoes the same idea. The land will refuse production to the unrighteous, and it will even reject those who abuse it:

> Threshing floor and wine vat shall not feed them,
>   and the new wine shall fail them.
> They shall not remain in the land of the LORD.
>   (Hos. 9:2–3)

---

9. In 931 B.C.E., the tribes in the north broke away from the tribes in the south, causing a civil war in Israel. The prophets direct their chastisements to each sector of the country.

Ultimately exile came in the form of Assyria's swift armies in 722 B.C.E., and the northern kingdom lost its inheritance because it had lost any sense of what it meant to live under God's covenant: "Therefore the LORD was very angry with Israel and removed them out of his sight" (2 Kings 17:18).

The same held true for the southern kingdom with its capital at Jerusalem. Jeremiah records how God viewed his gift of land to Israel.

> I thought
> how I would set you among my children,
>   and give you a pleasant land,
>   the most beautiful heritage of all the nations.
> And I thought you would call me, My Father,
>   and would not turn from following me.
> Instead, as a faithless wife leaves her husband,
>   so you have been faithless to me, O house of Israel,
> says the LORD. (Jer. 3:19–20)

Jeremiah identifies many wrongs and lists them in excruciating detail. Among these he mentions the abuse of the resident aliens who live in the land. If the orphan, the widow, and the alien are abused, God will refuse to dwell with Israel in the land. This judgment does not contradict the eternal promise to Abraham — which Jeremiah acknowledges. It simply means that these Israelites who do such things will lose the privileges of the promise.

> For if you truly amend your ways and your doings, if you truly act justly one with another, if you do not oppress the alien, the orphan, and the widow, or shed innocent blood in this place, and if you do not go after other gods to your own hurt, then I will dwell with you in this place, in the land that I gave of old to your ancestors forever and ever. (Jer. 7:5–7)

Isaiah likewise affirms God's commitment to justice and emphasizes how the land itself will be lost if Israel does not alter its way of life.

> Wash yourselves; make yourselves clean;
>   remove the evil of your doings
>   from before my eyes;
> cease to do evil,
>   learn to do good;
> seek justice,
>   rescue the oppressed,
> defend the orphan,
>   plead for the widow. (Isa. 1:16–17)

Chapters 1–5 form a litany of complaints against the unrighteousness of the people. "Jerusalem has stumbled / and Judah has fallen" (3:8). "They proclaim their sin like Sodom" (3:9). Moral failings stand out. "It is you who have devoured the vineyard; / the spoil of the poor is in your houses" (3:14).

In this setting we find Isaiah's famous "Song of the Vineyard." Isaiah describes the good land as a vineyard tended and loved by God, and yet those whom he planted there (the Israelites) produced wild fruit, wicked fruit, unrighteous fruit that God never planned. God's decision will be to forsake the vineyard altogether:

> Let me sing for my beloved
> > my love-song concerning his vineyard:
> My beloved had a vineyard
> > on a very fertile hill.
> He dug it and cleared it of stones,
> > and planted it with choice vines;
> he built a watchtower in the midst of it,
> > and hewed out a wine vat in it;
> he expected it to yield grapes,
> > but it yielded wild grapes.
>
> And now, inhabitants of Jerusalem
> > and people of Judah,
> judge between me
> > and my vineyard.
> What more was there to do for my vineyard
> > that I have not done in it?
> When I expected it to yield grapes,
> > why did it yield wild grapes?
>
> And now I will tell you
> > what I will do to my vineyard.
> I will remove its hedge,
> > and it shall be devoured;
> I will break down its wall,
> > and it shall be trampled down.
> I will make it a waste;
> > it shall not be pruned or hoed,
> > and it shall be overgrown with briers and thorns;
> I will also command the clouds
> > that they rain no rain upon it.
>
> For the vineyard of the LORD of hosts
> > is the house of Israel,
> and the people of Judah
> > are his pleasant planting;
> he expected justice,
> > but saw bloodshed;
> righteousness,
> > but heard a cry! (Isa. 5:1–7)

Judgment fell upon the southern kingdom in the same manner that it fell upon those in the north. In 586 B.C.E., Babylonian armies swept down from the north, conquered the land, destroyed Jerusalem, and carried the survivors into captivity. The inheritance of Abraham was lost.[10] The prophets simply predicted what the law had promised. Unrighteousness would lead to a loss of land.

Did Israel despair? The laments recorded following the conquest and exile are filled with longings for the land. That God would punish his people was one thing. That he would withhold the ancestral promises was quite another. Psalm 48 records the pride and overconfidence Israel possessed in the land. Since God lives in the walls of Jerusalem (48:3), no foe could dare confront Israel's national ambitions. Psalm 137 describes the shock and grief that swamped the nation when Babylonian infantry demolished these walls. The entire book of Lamentations wrestles with the confusion of the loss of promise. Was God's goodness compromised when he let the land be taken? No, rather Lamentations leads the reader to repentance, forgiveness, and renewal.[11]

THE PROPHETIC HOPE

If, however, possessing the land is tied to Israel's fidelity to the covenant, it is not surprising that when the prophets looked to the future, they predicted a new generation that would embrace the covenant with zeal and reclaim the land at the same time. The prophets did not simply send out a message of despair; they gave encouragement. Someday Jerusalem would be rebuilt by people who were devoted to God and who defended the justice of the covenant in the land.

Each of the prophets who predicted the judgments we have mentioned — Amos, Hosea, Isaiah, and Jeremiah — embraced this hope of restoration.[12] Hosea typically writes:

> On that day I will answer, says the LORD,
> I will answer the heavens
> and they shall answer the earth;
> and the earth shall answer the grain, the wine, and the oil,
> and they shall answer Jezreel;
> and I will sow him for myself in the land.

---

10. For a full description of the Babylonian conquest, see Jeremiah 52 and 2 Kings 24–25.

11. Today the book of Lamentations is read and sung aloud on the ninth of Ab in Israel, the anniversary of the destruction of Jerusalem's Temple in 586 B.C.E.

12. See Amos 9:14–15; Hosea 2:14–23; 11:8–11; Jeremiah 16:15; Isaiah 2:1–5; 9:1–9. Cf. Ezekiel 36–37.

> And I will have pity on Lo-ruhamah,
> and I will say to Lo-ammi, "You are my people";
> and he shall say, "You are my God." (Hos. 2:21–23)

In these words the prophet is predicting a new harmony, not just between God and his people, but between the people and the land. God will replant Israel in the land, and the land will eagerly produce new bounty for its residents.

Of course, these predictions did come true. The Babylonians who exiled Israel were themselves defeated by the Persians, and the Persian king, Cyrus, permitted God's people to return to their land. Another generation in another era followed the leadership of Ezra and Nehemiah, listened to the exhortations of Haggai and Zechariah, and recommitted themselves to the unique society God had envisioned for his people.

Na'im Ateek points out that the return of Israel from Babylon to Canaan is really a "second exodus" that parallels the first return from Egypt to Canaan. The first exodus is filled with negative attitudes toward the native peoples who already lived in the land. They are supposed to be destroyed. Ateek remarks: "The second [exodus] is totally different. One gets the feeling that the returning exiles reflected greater realism. They were much more accepting of the people around them."[13] This assertion is true, yet if we read Ezra and Nehemiah carefully, we see that these people were still rigorous about their faith. Ateek then goes on to cite a crucial prophetic passage that describes this "second return":

> You shall allot it as an inheritance for yourselves and for the aliens who reside among you and have begotten children among you. They shall be to you as citizens of Israel; with you they shall be allotted an inheritance among the tribes of Israel. In whatever tribe aliens reside, there you shall assign them their inheritance, says the Lord GOD. (Ezek. 47:22–23)

As the prophets designed the contours of this future society, interestingly they did not leave out a place for the resident alien, the non-Israelite. When Ezekiel describes the return to the land and its acquisition by the exiles, he specifically says that provision must be made for the non-Israelites within Israel. Note how Ezekiel echoes the words of the law (Lev. 19:34), which tell how aliens are to be treated like "fellow citizens." Aliens must have an inheritance too. When these resident foreigners are abused or defrauded, the postexilic prophets lodge harsh complaints against Israel's leadership. Ezekiel and Malachi address the problem directly:

---

13. N. Ateek, "Power, Justice and the Bible," in *Faith and the Intifada: Palestinian Christian Voices,* ed. N. Adieux, M. Ellis, and R. Ruether (Maryknoll, N.Y.: Orbis, 1992), 111.

Father and mother are treated with contempt in you; the alien residing within you suffers extortion; the orphan and the widow are wronged in you.... The people of the land have practiced extortion and committed robbery; they have oppressed the poor and needy, and have extorted from the alien without redress. (Ezek. 22:7, 29)

Then I will draw near to you for judgment; I will be swift to bear witness against the sorcerers, against the adulterers, against those who swear falsely, against those who oppress the hired workers in their wages, the widow and the orphan, against those who thrust aside the alien, and do not fear me, says the LORD of hosts. (Mal. 3:5)

Zechariah identifies this problem of righteousness too, but he repeats the law, the old warnings about injustice and consequences (7:10) as if to say, "Remember, the covenant and its expectations have not disappeared."

ISRAEL'S PROPHETIC VOICES TODAY

Are there no voices that have seen this behavior, this sinfulness, and resisted? Are there no Jewish voices that desire to be heard? No prophets in the land? While few of the Israeli groups that decry these abuses would list themselves as prophets, still their voices are prophetic and courageous. In summer 2002, sixty thousand Israelis marched on Tel Aviv calling for the government to stop the abuses in the Occupied Territories. Buses were organized and departed from sixty-five locations throughout Israel. Over fourteen hundred police guarded the event. Sponsored by Israel's "Peace Coalition," the assembled army met in Rabin Square — dedicated to one of Israel's great peacemakers — and listened to leader after leader call for justice in the land.

Who are these groups? The leading organizer of such gatherings is Peace Now, a group formed by 348 Israeli military officers in 1978.[14] Today its rallies will commonly draw hundreds of thousands of Israelis into the streets. One of its chief activities is "Settlement Watch," in which they catalogue and monitor the development of illegal settlements throughout the Occupied Territories. But Israel's Peace Coalition includes a host of affiliate organizations: Meretz, Labour Doves, The Kibbutz Artzi Movement, Hashomer Hatzair, Netivot Shalom, The Bereaved Parents Forum, The Green Line, Women in Black, The Democratic Choice, Gush Shalom, Rabbis Against Home Demolitions, Coalition of Women for Just Peace, and Taayush.

Perhaps the most courageous development on the Israeli scene has been the large numbers of decorated military soldiers who today are refusing to

---

14. For the Israeli website: *www.peacenow.org.il/English.asp*. The American organization is *www.peacenow.org*.

serve in the West Bank or Gaza. Their slogan is that they have embraced "The Courage to Refuse," and their public statement — signed at great personal risk — reads as follows:

> We, reserve combat officers and soldiers of the Israel Defense Forces, who were raised upon the principles of Zionism, sacrifice and giving to the people of Israel and to the State of Israel, who have always served in the front lines, and who were the first to carry out any mission, light or heavy, in order to protect the State of Israel and strengthen it.
>
> We, combat officers and soldiers who have served the State of Israel for long weeks every year, in spite of the dear cost to our personal lives, have been on reserve duty all over the Occupied Territories, and were issued commands and directives that had nothing to do with the security of our country, and that had the sole purpose of perpetuating our control over the Palestinian people. We, whose eyes have seen the bloody toll this Occupation exacts from both sides.
>
> We, who sensed how the commands issued to us in the Territories, destroy all the values we had absorbed while growing up in this country.
>
> We, who understand now that the price of Occupation is the loss of IDF's human character and the corruption of the entire Israeli society.
>
> We, who know that the Territories are not Israel, and that all settlements are bound to be evacuated in the end.
>
> We hereby declare that we shall not continue to fight this War of the Settlements.
>
> We shall not continue to fight beyond the 1967 borders in order to dominate, expel, starve and humiliate an entire people.
>
> We hereby declare that we shall continue serving in the Israel Defense Forces in any mission that serves Israel's defense.
>
> The missions of occupation and oppression do not serve this purpose — and we shall take no part in them.

Israel is unsure what to do with these men and women. They are telling the public what really happens when they serve as occupiers, and about five hundred of them have even published their stories on the web.[15] They are arguing that their orders sending them into the territories are "illegal commands," and therefore they are not obligated to obey the orders. Captain Haim Weiss from the Israeli tank corps is one such "refusenik," who wrote the following to his commanding officer:

> The current situation leaves me no choice but to refuse. The citizen's conscience provides a critical foundation for the checks and balances inherent in a democracy. Israel has done more than grant citizens full rights to protest against injustices. By including the concept of "a clearly illegal command" in the code of military law, it has obliged its soldiers to refuse to carry out orders that are immoral or opposed to the values on which a democracy is based.

15. See *www.seruv.org.il/defaulteng.asp* for an English version.

As I see it, this concept means that when a soldier is issued with a command opposed to his moral values, he must refuse to obey it, report the event, and ensure that such orders will not be repeated. A soldier who does not do so cannot escape being held morally responsible by claiming that he only carried out orders, but can expect to be tried for his actions. This law indicates that the military and the state see the soldier as an autonomous moral being, who must carry out commands only if they pass his moral scrutiny.

In addition to public humiliation, the Israeli military has now begun to imprison these soldiers for their refusal to serve, and the website (see above p. 106, n. 15) is calling for the public to write the commanders of their prisons.

Finally, today we are hearing from orthodox Jewish leaders who have grave misgivings about the theological legitimacy of the modern state of Israel. Most of these orthodox Israelis will not serve in the military, but more significantly, today they are writing books and articles undermining the spiritual legitimacy of the country. A quick search on the Internet for "Anti-Zionism" will bring a host of these groups to the surface. These organizations include articulate rabbis who belong to a long tradition of intellectuals and who see the modern state of Israel as compromising the essential commitments of Judaism. One prominent site belonging to Neturei Karta is run by Rabbi Chaim Tzvi Freimann, who writes:

> We are opposed to the ideology of Zionism, a recent innovation, which seeks to force the end of exile. Our banishment from the Holy Land will end miraculously at a time when all mankind will unite in the brotherly service of the Creator.
>
> In addition to condemning the central heresy of Zionism, we also reject its policy of aggression against all peoples. Today this cruelty manifests itself primarily in the brutal treatment of the Palestinian people. We proclaim that this inhuman policy is in violation of the Torah.[16]

Rabbi Dovid Weiss, speaking at the U.N. Human Rights Commission in Durban, South Africa (August 28, 2001), took the extreme position that the only avenue to peace was the dissolution of the Israeli state altogether.

> Zionist assertions to having solved the "Jewish question" by "ending exile" have proven a dismal failure. If anything, the Zionist's claim to having created a safe haven for Jewry is patently false. The truth is that Israel today, whether governed by "doves" or "hawks" is the most dangerous place in the world for Jews. Such was to be expected, as Israel's very creation was an act of defiance against the Creator's guidelines.
>
> Our position is the only one offering a real alternative to the status quo. Anti-Zionist Jews believe that the one path to peace in the Middle East,

---

16. *www.netureikarta.org.*

the only means for Jews to fulfill their proper role in exile and the only
path demonstrating justice and kindness towards the Palestinians, is the total
dismantling of the Israeli state. Only then, with sovereignty transferred to
Palestinian rule, will a true peace be attained.[17]

This resistance to the Israeli policies of occupation today is born out of
a genuine fear that if the present situation continues, Israel may no longer
be a viable country. Noam Livne, a soldier refusing to fight, describes his
fear: "Israel today is rapidly, vigorously and arrogantly approaching its end.
To me, the possibility that the State of Israel will exist in another 30 years
seems to be fantasy. We have felt this way for some time, we speak about it
occasionally in passing, but we never speak about the subject in depth. The
general feeling is that every possible conflict in the country has worsened."[18]

"POST-ZIONIST" SCHOLARS IN ISRAEL

Since the late 1980s, an entirely new generation of Jewish scholars in Israel
has revisited Israel's history and debunked the most "sacred truths" of Zionism. The Israeli press has popularized this movement as *post-Zionist* and it
is a subject of discussion throughout the Israeli public.[19]

The traditional heroic telling of the founding and expansion of Israel had
been challenged by Palestinian scholars since 1948 — but following the 1967
war, increasing numbers of Israeli scholars questioned the moral justification
of what the country had done and investigated closely the causes and out-
comes of Israel's wars. Finally the Israeli war in Lebanon in 1982 inspired
novelists, filmmakers, musicians, journalists, and artists to join the ranks of
these critics who were challenging the moral underpinnings of the state.

These scholars began to rewrite Israeli history, viewing it from the vantage
of the Palestinian experience. Israel was no longer seen as a "victim" of Arab
aggression but, instead, Zionism was explained as a "victimizing" colonial
movement. For many young Israelis, this voice had never been heard, and
it resonated with a deeply rooted skepticism about the heroic refugee/settler
story they had been told since childhood.

What are some of the fundamental myths this movement challenges?
First, the account of 1948 had always been told as a story of ill-equipped
Holocaust survivors facing a hostile British government and a united Arab

---

17. See *www.netureikarta.org/speech29aug01.htm.*
18. See *www.seruv.org.il/Signers/34_1_Eng.htm.*
19. U. Ram, *The Changing Agenda of Israeli Sociology: Theory, Ideology and Identity*
(Albany: State University of New York Press, 1995); I. Pappé, "The Post-Zionist Discourse
in Israel: 1990–2001," *Holy Land Studies* [Sheffield] 1, no. 1 (2002): 9–35.

world preparing to annihilate them. "The victory [of 1948] was miraculous and was won by the ingenuity of David Ben-Gurion and the heroism of the soldiers on the ground."[20] Research had always known about the non-combat nature of Palestinian society and that most Palestinians had fled during the war rather than fight. But if this were true, what became of the heroic Israeli story? Simply put, scholars were refuting the myth that Israel was in danger of annihilation on the verge of the 1948 war. The Israeli army was superior in every respect and knew it — and the fragmented Arab resistance crumbled rapidly.

The second fundamental myth challenged by these scholars is the voluntary exodus of the Palestinians. Israel (as the story goes) was a people without a land entering a land without a people, and the Arabs who were there in western Israel relocated to the West Bank following 1948. Scholars have unmasked this myth too. Israeli historians now talk about the mass and planned expulsion of the Palestinians, an early form of "ethnic cleansing." The most troubling national confession has been the destruction of at least four hundred Palestinian villages, the ruin of dozens of Arab urban neighborhoods, and several massacres that would motivate the Arab population to flee.

This reassessment of Israel's founding has continued to analyze and critique its other military campaigns as well, particularly the war of 1967, the occupation of southern Lebanon in 1982, and the present military occupation of the West Bank and Gaza. Sociologists have candidly asked if Israel should be called "an apartheid state" (linking the fate of Palestinians with that of North African Jews), and political scientists such as Benny Morris have analyzed Israeli political decisions arguing that Israel is an "active" rather than a "reactive" player in regional politics.[21] Many observers have linked Israel's present behavior to past wars and begun to assess the country as a "militaristic society."[22]

Popular culture has now reflected this trend as well. Jewish poetry, fiction, and theater each have reflected these concerns. Even Arab poetry and literature have now made their way into Israeli society through the work of Jewish translators who want these voices heard. Social critics note how in the last twenty years Arab music (such as Um Kulthum and Ra'i) has entered the Israeli mainstream. All this activity signals a society that intuits

---

20. Pappé, "The Post-Zionist Discourse in Israel," 13.

21. B. Morris, *Israel's Border Wars: Arab Infiltration, Israeli Retaliation, and the Countdown to the Suez War* (Oxford: Clarendon, 1993).

22. S. Carmi and H. Rosenfeld, "The Emergence of Nationalistic Militarism in Israel," *International Journal of Politics, Culture and Society* 3, no. 1 (1989): 5–49.

the desire to move, to hear another view, to engage Arab society. One Jewish writer has even analyzed how the Arab is typically presented in traditional Israeli theater: as a shallow, one-dimensional figure toward whom characters usually display hatred, fear, and hostility.[23] This analysis expresses an emerging national cultural self-examination and criticism.

This sentiment has not been embraced by everyone, however, particularly since the outbreak of violence in 2000. Resistance within the Israeli academy has been firm as well. In 1998, an M.A. student at the University of Haifa completed a well-researched thesis that uncovered an Israeli atrocity in the Arab village of Tantura during May 22–23, 1948, in which Israeli soldiers massacred 250 Arabs. He interviewed Jews and Arabs who claimed to be eyewitnesses and published the results in 2000. The Israeli army unit that committed the crime sued Katz, and today the case is still pending in court. Ilan Pappé teaches in the political science department of that university, has examined the thesis carefully and affirmed its truthfulness. According to Pappé, the affair has created a tremendous legal and academic storm in Israel.[24]

SUMMARY

The Old Testament is consistent when it comes to the land and the covenant. The prophets affirmed what the law had always said: the land of Israel/Palestine cannot become the secular possession of some secular state. This land is unlike any other land. "The eyes of the LORD your God are always on it" (Deut. 11:12). The land itself holds Israel to covenant standards of justice. Likewise the prophets hold Israel to this same standard. When this standard is violated, judgment is sure to result.

I began this chapter by retelling the tragic story of the Palestinian village of Beita. If this were a random act of violence perpetrated by individuals — such acts are common both by Israelis and by Palestinians — then it would somehow be easier to accept, as one more example of the inexcusable violence that torments this land. What makes this episode so troubling is that the systems of Israeli justice refused to work in behalf of "the alien, the widow, and the orphan." Leading Israeli politicians, statesmen, and military officers encouraged a cycle of abuse that the world community has judged to be heinous.

---

23. D. Orian, *The Arab in Israeli Theater* (in Hebrew) (Tel Aviv: Or-Am, 1995), as noted by Pappé, "Post-Zionist Discourse in Israel," 20–21.

24. I. Pappé, "The Tantura Case in Israel: The Katz Research and Trial," *Journal of Palestine Studies* 30, no. 3 (2001): 19–39; also Pappé, "Post-Zionist Discourse in Israel," 32.

Today the pattern of abuse (although hidden) continues. Since 1948, hundreds of villages have been completely destroyed. In more recent years (since 1987), Israel has demolished over twenty-six hundred homes making thousands of people homeless.

What then of God's covenant with modern-day Israel? Does Israel still live under the constraints of covenant justice? If Israel makes a biblical claim to the land, Israel must necessarily also live a biblical life, a life that resonates with the goodness God intended to create in his land.

Chapter Seven

JERUSALEM

He who has not seen Jerusalem in her splendor has never seen a desirable city in his life. He who has not seen the Temple in its full construction has never seen a glorious building in his life.　　　　—Babylonian Talmud, Sukkah 41b

When God created the world, he had ten measures of beauty to distribute. Nine he gave to Jerusalem, one he gave to the rest of the world. God also distributed ten measures of sorrow. Nine he gave to Jerusalem, one he gave to the rest of the world.　　　　—Jewish Proverb

For the sake of Zion I will not be silent, for the sake of Jerusalem, I will not be still....For Jerusalem has stumbled, and Judah has fallen; because their speech and their deeds are against the LORD, defying his glorious presence.
　　　　—Isaiah 62:1; 3:8

No single city can arouse the level of wonder and mystery, inspiration and hope as does the city of Jerusalem. The walls of the Old City, the majesty of its medieval gates, the glistening Dome of the Rock, its ancient history and turbulent present — these things continue to draw us to this place. When Jesus' disciples first came to the city and saw its renovations under Herod the Great, they could not help but exclaim, "Look, Teacher! What wonderful stones and what wonderful buildings!" (Mark 13:1). The Bible even urges us to pray for and love this city: "Pray for the peace of Jerusalem! May they prosper who love you! Peace be within your walls, and security within your towers! For the sake of the house of the LORD our God, I will seek your good" (Ps. 122:6, 9).

But as the prophets knew, "seeking the good" of Jerusalem also meant watching the character of its life. "O Jerusalem," Jeremiah cries, "who will turn aside to ask about your welfare?" (Jer. 15:5). In the history of Israel — past and present — Jerusalem has always been at the center of Jewish life. This city hosted the Temple of God built by Solomon, so one might say "God has an address on earth."[1] On the other hand, when Israel neglected the covenant and pursued other gods, the trouble could always be traced

---

1. A. Heschel, *Israel, an Echo of Eternity* (New York: Farrar, Straus, and Giroux, 1969), 209.

to Jerusalem — where religious and political corruption might begin, where holiness might be lost, and the rest of the nation led astray.

Today Jerusalem is likewise at the center of the struggle between Arab and Jew. Israel is eager for the rest of the world to recognize the city as its "eternal capital." While Israeli government buildings are located in West Jerusalem, most international embassies are still in Tel Aviv because Palestinians likewise have an ancient heritage and attachment to Jerusalem. Arabs call the city "Al Quds" (the Holy). In Islam, Jerusalem is the third most holy city (after Mecca and Medina). Among Middle Eastern Christians, churches in Jerusalem are the most holy on earth and a place of regular festival worship.

In the recent Camp David II discussions (July 2000), both sides wanted Jerusalem to be their capital. A Palestinian state, argued Yasir Arafat, must have its center in East Jerusalem. And the Jewish capital, urged Ehud Barak, will always be found in West Jerusalem. Not surprisingly in 1947 when the United Nations considered partitioning this country, they wanted to place Jerusalem under international control. Following the war of 1948, this dream faded quickly. Jerusalem was promptly divided — east and west — the Israelis taking the west, the Jordanians taking the east. Not until 1967, when Israel captured the entire city, was Jerusalem unified.

We need some historical perspective on this great city in order to understand the dimensions of the problems facing it. As the Jewish proverb says, Jerusalem is perhaps the most beautiful city on earth, and it also bears more suffering than any other.

A BRIEF HISTORY

Jerusalem in the Bible

Centuries before the Israelites entered Canaan under Joshua's leadership, Jerusalem was called "Jebus" and was occupied by a people called the "Jebusites."[2] Joshua never conquered this city (Josh 15:63; Judg. 1:21), and it remained outside Israelite control until the reign of King David hundreds of years later. Jerusalem therefore had a non-Israelite history that lasted for almost a thousand years before the coming of Israel.

David's conquest of Jebus (2 Sam. 5:6–10) was strategic. Not only was the city centrally located between the tribes of Judah and Benjamin (thereby avoiding intertribal conflict), but it was easily fortified, had its own water source, and rested on hills along the central mountains of the country. David built his palace there (2 Sam. 5:11) and eventually brought the Ark of the

---

2. Archaeological evidence points to the occupation of Jebus as early as 2000 B.C.E.

Covenant to the city (2 Sam. 6:12–19). David purchased the land on the north side of the city, which eventually would be the site where Solomon built the Temple (1 Chron. 22:1–5). This land originally belonged to Ornan the Jebusite, who used it as a threshing floor; David acquired the land for six hundred shekels of gold (1 Chron. 21:25).

Solomon not only built an impressive Temple in Jerusalem (1 Kings 6) but he also constructed an impressive palace complex (1 Kings 7:1–8). Soon the city was refurbished with a new wall. Here we glimpse the first bit of trouble. Solomon spent thirteen years building his palace and eleven on the Temple, and the king's palace was even larger than God's house.[3] No doubt political interests were already asserting themselves as Solomon's quest for empire began to change the character of the country. Solomon's wealth and power soon disappeared at his death, however, when the kingdom split, north and south, in a devastating civil war. Jerusalem continued to serve as capital of the south and hosted the line of David, while the north promoted the older patriarchal region around Hebron.

Jerusalem continued to stand for about four hundred years as the southern capital until 587 B.C.E. when Babylonian armies under Nebuchadnezzar laid waste the entire region, carrying survivors to Babylon as slave/exiles (2 Kings 25; Jer. 52). The Temple was burned down, and its holy objects were likely carried off by the conquering armies.[4] When the exiles were permitted to return, Jerusalem lay in ruins (539 B.C.E.). Many Jews remained in Babylon, but those families who returned struggled to return the city to its former glory. This reclamation took generations, and not until almost one hundred years later did Ezra lead the rebuilding of the Temple (Ezra 6) and Nehemiah led the reconstruction of the walls (Neh. 1–6). Nevertheless, Jerusalem was only a fraction of the city it had once been under the Judean kings.

Note that during this period, Jerusalem could be either a force for unity or a catalyst for division.[5] David wisely understood that Jerusalem had the capacity to bring dramatic unity to the country, but the city would also become the focal point of any conflict that might arise. When the kingdom was feeling the pressures of its diversity (north and south), Jerusalem was the fissure, the point at which the country broke in two.

---

3. The Temple: sixty-by-thirty cubits, thirty cubits high. The palace: one hundred-by-fifty cubits, thirty cubits high.

4. Some believe that the ark and many of the Temple treasures were hidden or carried away by the priests, which has led to immense speculation concerning the location of these items. Most scholars believe that they were carried to Babylon.

5. G. McConville, "Jerusalem in the Old Testament," in *Jerusalem Past and Present in the Purposes of God*, ed. P. W. L. Walker (Cambridge: Tyndale House, 1992), 25.

The Jerusalem of Ezra and Nehemiah continued to live in its diminished glory until the conquests of Alexander the Great in 333 B.C.E. The city was not destroyed but rapidly began to assimilate the Greek influences that came for two hundred years. Jewish resistance to Greek domination sparked a revolt in the 160s, and by the 140s Jerusalem was once again in Jewish hands, although this control was short-lived. About eighty years of inner turmoil could not return the city to Solomon's prestige, and in 63 B.C.E. Jerusalem was once again conquered by Pompey's Roman army. So the city remained: dominated by Roman soldiers right through the New Testament period. Herod the Great (37–4 B.C.E.) completely rebuilt the city beginning in 20 B.C.E. and made the Temple into a true example of monumental architecture that was not completed for eighty years. Sadly, within ten years of its completion, Roman armies ended a Jewish revolt and completely destroyed Jerusalem, burning everything to the ground in 70 C.E.

After the war, Jerusalem was in such ruins that even the Sanhedrin never returned, moving instead to Galilee. Attempts at rebuilding the city were futile, and revolt against Rome still simmered in the country. In 132 C.E., Roman armies attacked again and not only reconquered Jerusalem (135) but expelled the Jews, not permitting them to return to their holy city.

To sum up, Jerusalem had a lengthy non-Jewish history before its capture by King David. Furthermore, the city was conquered and destroyed within seven hundred years: once in 587 B.C.E. and once in 70 C.E. In each case, the destruction and exile were interpreted as a judgment by God. The Old Testament makes this point clear (2 Chron. 36:15f.), but Jesus also emphasizes this judgment in his parable of the vineyard and the tenants (Matt. 21:33–44). Following the Roman expulsion of Jews from Jerusalem in 135 C.E., Jewish control over the city did not exist for over eighteen hundred years. Only a small minority of Jews lived in Jerusalem, and they had little or no influence on its government.

Medieval Jerusalem

In 135, the Roman Emperor Hadrian renamed Jerusalem ("Aelia Capitolina") and gave the city the basic design we see today.[6] Hadrian's line of walls follow those of Herod in many places and today is close to the wall line of the Old City. Roman armies were garrisoned here (the Tenth Legion), and eight hundred retired soldiers were given land in order to

---

6. For example, the Damascus Gate, which opens to a plaza then divides east to the Temple area or west into the Christian Quarter (to the "cardo"), was designed at this time.

repopulate the city. But the historical record falls silent until the fourth century, when suddenly Christian interest — thanks to the converted Roman Emperor Constantine — brings pilgrims to the city. Jerusalem quickly saw remarkable rebuilding efforts as Christian investment refurbished the walls, built churches (such as the Holy Sepulchre), and renewed the city entirely. "Byzantine" Jerusalem lived for three hundred years under Christian leadership and became a leading voice in the growth of the worldwide church, sending its bishop to all of the major church councils. Even maps published in this period showed Jerusalem as the center of the earth. Arab Christians, who had been in the country for centuries, were assimilated into Greek culture but retained their Middle East identity.

All of this manner of activity changed in the seventh century. In 638, Omar Ibn Khattab, the leader of Muslim armies, took Jerusalem in his conquest of the Middle East and began a 450-year Muslim reign that did not end until the eleventh-century Crusades. Omar did not destroy the city or harm its residents, but he was amazed at the beauty of Jerusalem's churches and the contrasting filth and debris at the site of Judaism's Temple. But Muslim buildings — such as the Dome of the Rock (691) — put a Muslim stamp on the city and in particular on the Temple Mount. A traveler in 670 tells how this mount was refurbished and how Jews were permitted to visit there. Mosques were built and the city's walls were renewed. But Christianity among Jerusalem's residents continued to flourish in the city, even though many were converted to Islam and Arabic language and culture assimilated everyone.[7]

When the hostile caliph (or ruler) Hakim destroyed many churches in 1009 (including the Church of the Holy Sepulchre), a new incentive for European Crusades was found. The European siege in 1099 was brutal. Arab Muslims were slaughtered alongside Arab Christians and Jews — each labeled "infidels." Rapid Crusader development of the city continued until 1187 when the Arab warrior Saladin expelled them. But war continued to toss the city back and forth for decades until 1249 when Arab armies secured it from the Europeans. For almost three hundred years, Arab control (from Damascus and then Cairo) brought stability. At this time, large Islamic institutions grew and Jerusalem became a city that drew religious leaders from throughout the Islamic world.

Jerusalem was conquered once again in 1517 by Turkish (or Ottoman) armies. One of its first rulers, Sulayman the Magnificent (who ruled from

---

7. See A. Wessels, *Arab and Christian? The Christians of the Middle East* (Kampen, Netherlands: Kok, 1995).

Constantinople) built the Jerusalem we see today. From the Damascus Gate to Jerusalem's walls, from the many fountains in the city to pools and aqueducts, Sulayman's engineers gave Jerusalem a newfound glory. The population doubled in fifty years and agricultural works were developed. Christians and Jews enjoyed genuine freedoms in this period, although they had to pay taxes not levied on Muslims. Jerusalem was no longer neglected and enjoyed a prominence that would last until 1917.

Keep in mind that Jerusalem was a very small city during this period and not anything like we see today. Residents remained inside the walled city, and development on Jerusalem's surrounding hills was minimal. This type of settlement was simply a natural pattern in the medieval world where city walls provided security and protection. Monasteries built nearby constructed their own elaborate defensive walls, and Arab villages that were unprotected lived with great risk.

The Twentieth Century

After World War I, the Turkish alliance with Germany meant that the close of the war witnessed the dismantling of the Ottoman Empire. From 1917 until 1948, Britain controlled all of Palestine, but as we have already seen, British rule following World War II became impossible. Regional Arab leaders, now free from the Turkish yoke, dreamed of nationhood, which clashed directly with incoming Jewish refugees from Europe. The U.N. plan for the division of the country recommended that Jerusalem be an international city so that everyone's competing claims could be respected. Jerusalem grew dramatically from 1917 to 1948, and the era saw construction around the perimeter of the city for a variety of communities.

Following the War of Independence in 1948, Jerusalem became a flash point of conflict. About eighty thousand in the west fled east as fighting intensified over control of the city. When a cease-fire was reached, East Jerusalem remained in Jordanian hands; Palestinians there automatically became citizens of Jordan. Jews in the Old City (the Jewish Quarter) fled west as their neighborhood was virtually destroyed. West Jerusalem was Jewish, and Arab homes there — evacuated during the war — were taken and given to new, incoming Jewish residents. Israel declared Jerusalem its capital in 1949.

Not until 1967 did the Israeli conquest of the West Bank bring the entire city under Jewish rule. Israelis immediately removed all walls, barriers, and obstacles that had gone up over nineteen years of division. Jews returned to the Jewish Quarter of the Old City, the area west of the Temple Mount (the "Wailing" or "Western" Wall) was cleared of poor Arab homes, and a worship area built. Israel announced that all Muslims and Christians would always have access to all worship sites. The city also grew. Before 1967, the population of the city was about 264,000 (75 percent Jews, 25 percent Arabs). By 1980, the population was 407,000 (72 percent Jews, 28 percent Arabs). By 1999, the city had grown to 634,000 (68 percent Jews, 32 percent Arabs).[8]

Implications

The history of Jerusalem has an importance that we easily miss. Today in Jerusalem we often hear that the city has been the "eternal capital" of the Jewish people. This argument is employed to buttress Israeli claims to complete sovereignty, but a brief historical survey unveils some surprising facts that now need to be digested in simplified form. Recently the world was asked by Israel to celebrate the three thousandth anniversary of King David's capture of the city — as if no intervening history took place. Scholars throughout the world were deeply offended, and the celebration — aimed particularly at tourism — quietly failed.

If we merely catalogue the number of years that Israel has had autonomous political control of the city since, say, 2000 B.C.E., we can find only five hundred such years.[9] But this tally would be unfair since Jewish life has thrived in Jerusalem during periods when foreign armies dominated it. Therefore let me ask a different question: *How can we catalogue those centuries when Jewish cultural life was dominant in Jerusalem?* The result of this survey will place in perspective the rival Arab/Jewish claims to the city. The most generous possible estimates are shown in the chart on the following page.

The result of this sort of chart is important. Even if we eliminate the Canaanite occupation of ancient Jebus — even if we do not consider the period when Christian influence was dominant (either in the Byzantine or the Crusader periods) — Israel's historic claim on Jerusalem is only a small portion of this history. Arab claims to Jerusalem are significant. Indeed a small Jewish community existed in the city for the last three thousand years, but the same claim can be made for the Arab community. *For the last two thousand years, Judaism has dominated Jerusalem for only two hundred years.*[10]

---

8. Today Jerusalem's rate of growth is 15 percent per year. These numbers are available from the Jerusalem Municipality website: *www.jerusalem.muni.il/english/cap/toshavim.htm# Distribution.*

9. About four hundred years under the monarchy, eighty years under the Maccabean rulers, and thirty-six years since 1967.

10. I cannot emphasize enough how offensive this sort of chart will be to some readers. The ongoing "Jewish" history of Jerusalem is a sacred theme in Israel today.

Canaanite Cultural Dominance • Beginning in about 1500 B.C.E. (though likely earlier)	500 years
Jewish-Israelite Cultural Dominance • Davidic monarchy, 500 years • Exile to the Roman expulsion, 700 years • Modern occupation since 1967, 36 years	1236 years
Christian Cultural Dominance • From Constantinian Jerusalem to Muslim conquest, 300 years • Crusader Jerusalem, 100 years	400 years
Arab/Turkish Cultural Dominance • From Omar to the Crusades, 470 years • From Saladin to the fall of the Ottomans, 730 years	1200 years

THE MODERN PROBLEM

Following the conquest of Jerusalem (and the West Bank) in 1967, Israel annexed the city and attached forty-four square miles of land to it. This land was taken not from areas traditionally considered "Jerusalem" at all, but rather from twenty-eight Arab villages whose land was coveted. The present fight over the ownership of Jerusalem has little to do with its original parameters, but concerns villages like Beit Hanina and Um Tuba and Beit Jala, places about which the average Israeli has never heard. In a single day, Israel tripled the size of Jerusalem. Before the war of 1967, West Jerusalem consisted of 23 square miles of land and Arab East Jerusalem had 3.7 square miles of land. After the annexation, Jerusalem was suddenly 71 square miles.

The problem arises of how to identify the many Arabs living within the new limits of Jerusalem. Unlike the Arabs in Bethlehem who are in "occupied territory" and *outside* Israel (but nevertheless controlled by the Israeli army), Jerusalem's Palestinians live *within* Israel. Arab residents of East Jerusalem may apply for Israeli citizenship (after meeting stringent conditions) and are entitled to certain social benefits denied to other Palestinians in the West Bank. Most Palestinians, however, have refused citizenship and remain "residents." But this leads to a host of questions: If these people are not Israelis, what are they? Where do they belong? To whom do they belong? Is their future in jeopardy?

Land Confiscation for Settlements

One of the major concerns of Israel since 1967 is keeping a Jewish majority in Jerusalem. Housing quotas have little to do with urban planning, but rather work to encourage Arabs to leave the city. In 1999, high ranking advisors to Jerusalem's former mayor, Teddy Kollek, disclosed that his government held a private target of limiting the Arab population at 28.8 percent.[11] They commented, "Allowing too many new homes in Arab neighborhoods would mean too many Arab residents in the city — this has been the essence of the municipality and government policy." The reason this goal is important is so that no one can challenge Israeli ownership over greater Jerusalem in the future.

This strategy has taken a number of forms. Limits are placed on Arab construction. From 1990 to 1997, 18,443 Jewish homes were built. In the same period, only 1,484 Arab homes were built. This discrepancy is not due to a lack of funding on the part of the Arabs, but rather from strict limits on Arab neighborhood growth and the nationalizing of Arab land for Jewish use. Today in Arab East Jerusalem, 43,000 Jewish homes are standing entirely on expropriated land. In the same area there are only 28,000 Arab homes, which leads to massive overcrowding among Palestinians. One-fourth of all Arab homes in the city are extremely overcrowded.[12] By some estimates, 35 percent of East Jerusalem has been confiscated for Jewish development (and 90 percent of this land was privately owned by Palestinians).[13]

The frequent visitor to Jerusalem today will be astounded at the growth in housing around the city. The city has been encircled with developments and settlements so that its perimeter cannot be negotiated in future peace talks. According to official documents from the Municipality of Jerusalem, the city is planning for a "massive" building push that will bring 95,000 additional housing units into the city's *Jewish* neighborhoods.[14] But this construction is only possible when new land is acquired.

Let's look at one example. If you drive south of Jerusalem toward Bethlehem, to your left (east) just past the Gilo turnoff there is a prominent hill. Once covered with trees, today it is covered with high-rise buildings. Israelis call it "Har Homa," but the ancient Arabic name is "Jabal Abu Ghaneim." This privately owned land was expropriated by the government and is being developed by Makor Urban Development Company. Makor is planning to build eighty-two hundred residential units, three hotels, a golf course, shopping malls, and a high-tech industry center for an estimated $1.5 billion.

11. "Ruthless Quota System for Arabs," *Jerusalem Post,* May 10, 1999; see A. S. Cheshin, B. Hutman, and A. Melamed, *Separate and Unequal: The Inside Story of Israeli Rule in East Jerusalem* (Cambridge, Mass.: Harvard University Press, 1999).

12. "Injustice in the Holy City," *B'Tselem Journal* (December 1999): 4. Twenty-three percent of all Arabs in Jerusalem live with over three people per room. Only 2 percent of Jews live like this.

13. "Israel and the Occupied Territories," *Amnesty International Report* 15–55–99 (December 1999): 19.

14. *www.jerusalem.muni.il/english/cap/toshavim.htm#Distribution* [see page 5].

When construction began, Arabs from nearby Beit Sahour and Bethlehem were outraged since much of this land belonged to these communities. But Har Homa is going forward, closing the final "corridor" south of Jerusalem and completing the Israeli developments that surround the city for Jewish residences.

The expropriation of land is even true of embassy properties. Currently the U.S. government keeps its embassy in Tel Aviv because it does not want to recognize Israel's claim on Jerusalem. However, a parcel of land in West Jerusalem is leased to the United States for future construction if the embassy moves. Dr. Walid Khalidi, a Palestinian historian, pursued a three-year study showing that even this land was illegally acquired by Israel from its owners. If the U.S. embassy is built there, it will be standing on stolen Palestinian land, land belonging (in some cases) to Arabs who are American citizens.[15]

Home Demolitions

Since 1967, Israel has worked to change the ethnic character of Jerusalem. Government officials have discussed and implemented racial quotas in order to ensure a large Jewish majority. As the population density of Palestinians in the city increases, Arabs face impossible decisions. If they reside outside the city limits, they will lose their "residency" card to return for employment. If they try to build on family-owned land, they are not given building permits. From 1967 until 1999, only 2,950 permits were given to Arabs — and so they build (on their own land!) anyway. Soon the bulldozers come. Illegal Jewish construction takes place in Jerusalem as well, but in this case the land is often not owned by the builder. Palestinians are responsible for about 20 percent of illegal construction, yet 60 percent of demolitions are carried out against them. Since 1987, Israel has demolished 284 Arab homes in East Jerusalem, leaving many people homeless. Today as many as 12,000 Arab homes may be under demolition orders.[16] Since the current conflicts began in September 2000, Israel has increased the demolition program, destroying more than 500 houses.

The case of Fu'ad Khader is telling. Khader's house was "legal" for tax purposes since he had been paying property taxes for eight years. Yet his family was growing, his children were married, and they had nowhere to go. If they moved outside the city limits, they would lose their jobs and Fu'ad would not see his grandchildren. So he worked with a neighborhood

---

15. The American Committee on Jerusalem, Press Release, March 9, 2000.
16. "Israel and the Occupied Territories," 22.

committee which understood that the city would permit an extension on his house. But he was wrong.

> In 1992 I finished building a house on my land in the Taber neighborhood of Beit Hanina in Jerusalem, and my three daughters Sarah, Najwa, and Faiza moved in with their husbands and children. On November 25, 1999, I was at my home in Atarot at 7:30 a.m. when my daughter Sarah called me. She was crying on the phone and nearly hysterical and told me, "Father come quick and save us. The army wants to destroy our house."
>
> When I reached the house I approached the Interior Ministry representative who had the demolition order and I told him about our agreement. After this we would not build any more and they would not demolish while the residents prepared a zoning plan. I pleaded with him not to harm the house.
>
> While I was talking to him, police officers emptied out the house and threw out everything that was inside: furniture and possessions were thrown out and most items were damaged or broken. The bulldozer started to demolish the house right in front of our eyes.
>
> The winter is coming. It is already very cold to live in the two tents we erected on the site of the demolished house. So we stay in the tents by day and at night we divide up the family.
>
> What am I supposed to do? They wouldn't give me a permit and they don't take care of my housing needs and when we build houses for ourselves, they come and demolish them.[17]

Residency Rights/Expulsions

If Fu'ad Khader decided to move his family outside the city limits of Jerusalem, he would lose his "residency" rights permanently. He could not return to Jerusalem again. Jerusalem Arabs must carry a special "blue" residency card that is precious to them because it permits them to live in the city. However, from 1967 until 1998 over 6,000 of these cards have been confiscated under various pretexts and the families left with an illegal status in Jerusalem. Since 1996, Palestinians have to legally show that East Jerusalem is their "center of life." Living outside or working outside will immediately jeopardize this status. Since 1996, an *average* of 700 people have been expelled per year on this basis. In 1998 alone, 788 Jerusalem ID cards were canceled.

The result of the Israeli policy is that many Palestinians, forced to leave the city in order to find housing, now live in constant fear of being "found out." They may live, say, in Ramallah, but work in Jerusalem. If they are caught at a checkpoint, though, their blue card may be lost and they will be expelled.

---

17. "Injustice in the Holy City," 7.

Infrastructure and Services

Visitors to Jerusalem are often amazed at the difference in the quality of life found around the city. Tour guides generally keep their guests away from the Arab neighborhoods because, by American standards, they seem run down and even dangerous. Little municipal investment occurs in these neighborhoods despite the fact that their residents pay taxes like anyone else. Some numbers: If we look at the Jerusalem Municipal Development Budget for 1999, we find the entire story. The total budget for the city was $103 million, and yet only $9.7 million was spent on Arab neighborhoods. Under "town beautification," $4.4 million was spent in Jewish areas, $0.5 million went to Arab areas. For Jewish "neighborhood renewal," $1.5 million was spent, while no investment went to Arab areas. Public transportation investment was sixteen times greater in Jewish areas ($49 million vs. $2.9 million).

The little things add up too. Jewish Jerusalem has 36 swimming pools and 531 sports facilities. Arab Jerusalem has no pools and 33 sports facilities. Libraries? Two for Arabs, 26 for Israelis. Parks? Twenty-nine in East Jerusalem, 1,079 in Jewish West Jerusalem. Is it any wonder that the regions of the city look different? Sarah Shartal, an Israeli writing in the *Toronto Star,* says it poignantly:

> Inside our country we have always divided our citizens by race. It's written into our identity cards. Jewish Israelis have more legal rights than Arab Israelis with respect to where they can live and work. Although we're taxed equally, we spend more on Jewish schoolchildren than on Arab children. In Jewish towns and cities, we built better housing, better roads, better community centres and better social services. I grew up loving my country and now I am ashamed.[18]

Take a walk outside the Damascus Gate up the Nablus Road, where Palestinians must go in order to renew their ID, obtain a birth certificate, or change their address. On an average day, ninety-five people will be standing in line between 8 and 10 a.m. A wait of six or seven hours is not uncommon. Gideon Levy, an editorial writer for the newspaper *Ha'aretz,* describes it harshly: "In the queue at the East Jerusalem Ministry of the Interior, pregnant women faint. Old men are pushed and collapse, infants scream for hours in the burning sun. This is how Israel treats the Palestinian residents of its united capital."[19] In West Jerusalem, no one waits outside. A cafeteria, a drinking fountain, and access for strollers and wheelchairs are available. East Jerusalem has none of these.

---

18. *Toronto Star,* October 18, 2000, A35.
19. *Ha'aretz,* May 7, 1999.

Access to Jerusalem

While many of us have traveled to Jerusalem as tourists and pilgrims, walking freely through the markets and visiting Jerusalem's great churches, Christians living just a few miles from these places have never seen them. From the beginning of Israel's occupation of Jerusalem, assurances were given that access to the city's holy sites would remain unrestricted, but this has not happened.

How remarkable to meet a Bethlehem Christian who has never seen Jerusalem when the city is only a fifteen-minute car drive north! For the Catholic and Orthodox traditions, coming, say, to the Church of the Holy Sepulchre is not something casual; the visit is a deeply significant part of their lives. Easter festivities such as the "Ceremony of Holy Fire" at this church is an ancient, treasured tradition for all of these Christians. In order to enter Jerusalem to worship, Palestinians in the West Bank and Gaza must request a permit, which can be rejected without explanation and without an opportunity to appeal. Why is this done? Israel argues that such action is necessary to combat terrorism.

But access to Jerusalem has other dimensions as well. Much of Palestinian national life takes place there and the restrictions on travel harshly limit opportunities to visit important cultural and educational institutions. For example, the two best hospitals for Palestinians are in East Jerusalem (Al Moqassed Hospital and Augusta Victora). If a family needs advanced care for premature infants, pediatric surgery, or intensive cardiac care, these facilities are the only real options. But if they live in Hebron and the situation is an emergency, they have a crisis.

When violence breaks out in the West Bank, Israel enforces a complete "closure" on Jerusalem. West Bank Palestinians who otherwise have a permit to enter the city (for work) are prohibited entry. Closures can go on for days and weeks, sorely crippling the earnings of families.

A quick look at a map shows that Jerusalem also becomes a geographical obstacle for Palestinians. To the north is Ramallah, a prospering Arab city. To the south is historic Bethlehem and further south is the large city of Hebron. However, how can a family with relatives drive from Ramallah to Bethlehem *without* driving through Jerusalem? Israel does not permit informal "transit" through Jerusalem and has not built a road that will link the regions, even though settler bypass roads weave through the entire countryside. Palestinians therefore must drive into the eastern desert, skirting Jerusalem on very dangerous roads for a journey that takes four times longer.

Another feature of the landscape are the Israeli roadblocks that now are as commonplace in the country as intersections. Many people have given up getting to Jerusalem, and now they can barely move out of their villages. Vehicles and pedestrians are stopped whenever they try to move from one area to the next. By 2001, Israel had posted ninety-seven military checkpoints in the West Bank and thirty-two checkpoints in Gaza.[20] One *New York Times* reporter records spending five hours trying to travel from Nablus to Ramallah, a mere distance of twenty-five miles.

Theological Reflection

When the biblical prophets spoke to Jerusalem, what vision did they bring? Jeremiah and Isaiah saw a city that would reflect the righteousness of God so profoundly that the world would give glory to God.

> This is what the LORD says: "Let not the wise man boast of his wisdom or the strong man boast of his strength or the rich man boast of his riches, but let him who boasts boast about this: that he understands and knows me, that I am the LORD, who exercises kindness, justice and righteousness on earth, for in these I delight," declares the LORD. (Jer. 9:23–24)

God delights in kindness, justice, and righteousness. Jeremiah eagerly brought these words to Jerusalem. The prophet Micah was no different. The test of godliness is summed up easily: What is good? What does the Lord require of us? "To do justice, and to love kindness, and to walk humbly with your God" (Mic. 6:8).

When Isaiah dreamed of the quality of life God's people would build in the world, he dreamed of Jerusalem as a city that would care for the poor, the captive, the prisoner. He dreamed of a city that would comfort all who mourn, a city that would "provide for those who grieve in Zion — to bestow on them a crown of beauty instead of ashes, the oil of gladness instead of mourning, and a garment of praise instead of a spirit of despair" (Isa. 61:1–2). *Who in Jerusalem today offers oil of gladness and a crown of beauty that will vanquish despair?*

Jesus gathers up these very words from Isaiah and echoes them in his first sermon in Nazareth. His mission too is one of healing for those whom the powerful forces of the day have trampled. "The Spirit of the Lord is on me, because he has anointed me to preach good news to the poor. He has sent me to proclaim freedom for the prisoners and recovery of sight for the blind,

---

20. C. Haberman, "Palestinian's Daily Chore, A Dirty Obstacle Course," *New York Times,* August 21, 2001.

to release the oppressed, to proclaim the year of the Lord's favor" (Luke 4:18–19). On Palm Sunday, when Jesus entered Jerusalem during his final week, he rode a donkey across the Mount of Olives. Crowds were cheering. Palms were waving. But Jesus stopped when he saw Jerusalem and he wept over it, saying, "If you, even you, had only known on this day what would bring you peace — but now it is hidden from your eyes" (Luke 19:41–42).[21]

Jesus thought of his people as "cities of light" set on top of hills. No doubt he had in mind the many Galilee towns and villages — like Sepphoris or Gamla — which stood prominently on hilltops. Cities like these cannot be hid, and they become a point of navigation for travelers who are charting unfamiliar terrain. I am confident that Jesus would say the same about Jerusalem. Here too is a city upon a hill that is striking in its prominence. It too could be a city of light, a city that leads the land in the ways of peace. The prophet Zechariah held just this vision. He envisions a time when God will return to Zion, to Jerusalem, and the result will be breathtaking:

> This is what the LORD says: "I will return to Zion and dwell in Jerusalem. Then Jerusalem will be called the City of Truth, and the mountain of the LORD Almighty will be called the Holy Mountain. Once again men and women of ripe old age will sit in the streets of Jerusalem, each with cane in hand because of his age. The city streets will be filled with boys and girls playing there." (Zech. 8:3–5)

ADDENDUM

Many Christians have spent their lives working in Jerusalem, striving for this vision of Zechariah. Dr. Kenneth E. Bailey is a longtime friend who has served the Middle East from Egypt to Lebanon since he was young. Fluent in Arabic, Dr. Bailey has taught in Beirut and Jerusalem for many years. He is also a sought-after lecturer around the world who can provide profound insight into the Middle East. A prolific writer of books, articles, plays, and poetry, Bailey offers his vision for Jerusalem:

> RESURRECTION. ODE ON A BURNING TANK
> THE HOLY LANDS, OCTOBER 1973
>
> I am a voice,
>   the voice of spilt blood
>   crying from the land

---

21. Today on the Mount of Olives, the Franciscan church, Dominus Flevit ["the Lord wept"], is built on this site to commemorate the event. The original chapel was built in 1881, and the new church, reproducing the outline of a seventh-century chapel, was built in 1955.

The life is in the blood
  and for years my blood flowed in the veins of a young man.
    My voice was heard through his voice
    and my life was his life.

Then our volcano erupted
  and for a series of numbing days
    all human voices were silenced
      amid the roar of the heavy guns,
      the harsh clank of tank tracks,
      the bone-jarring shudder of sonic booms,
        as gladiators with million-dollar swords
        killed each other high in the sky.

Then suddenly — suddenly
  there was the swish of a rocket launcher —
  a dirty yellow flash —
  and all hell roared.
The clanking of the great tracks stopped.
  My young man staggered screaming from his inferno,
  his body twitched and flopped in the sand

And I was spilt into the earth —
  into the holy earth
    of the Holy Land.

The battle moved on.
  The wounded vehicles burned,
    scorched,
      and cooled.

The "meat wagons" carried the bodies away as
  the chill of the desert night
  settled on ridge and dune,
And I stiffened and blackened in the sand.

And then — and then
As the timeless silence
  of the now scarred desert returned,
there — there congealed in the land,
  the land of prophet, priest, and king —
I heard a voice —
  a voice from an ageless age,
  a voice from other blood
    once shed violently in the land.

The voice told me this ancient story;
  precious blood intoned this ancient tale.

"A certain man had two sons.
　One was rich and the other was poor.
　　The rich son had no children
　　while the poor son was blessed with many sons and daughters.

In time the father fell ill.
　He was sure he would not live through the week
　so on Saturday he called his sons to his side
　　and gave each of them half of the land as their inheritance.
　　Then he died.

Before sundown the sons buried their father with respect
　as custom required.

That night the rich son could not sleep.
　He said to himself,
　　'What my father did was *not just.*
　　I am rich, my brother is poor.
　　I have bread enough to spare,
　　　while my brother's children eat one day
　　　and trust God for the next.
　I must move the landmark which our father has set
　　in the middle of the land
　　so that my brother will have the greater share.
　Ah — but he must not see me.
　If he sees me he will be shamed.
　I must arise early in the morning before it is dawn
　　and move the landmark!'
　With this he fell asleep
　　and his sleep was secure and peaceful.

Meanwhile, the poor brother could not sleep.
　As he lay restless on his bed he said to himself,
　　'What my father did was *not just.*
　　Here I am surrounded by the joy of my many sons
　　　and many daughters,
　while my brother daily faces the shame
　　of having no sons to carry on his name
　　and no daughters to comfort him in his old age.
He should have the land of our fathers.
　Perhaps this will in part compensate him
　for his indescribable poverty.
Ah — but if I give it to him he will be shamed.
I must awake early in the morning before it is dawn
　and move the landmark which our father has set!'
With this he went to sleep
　and his sleep was secure and peaceful.

On the first day of the week —
   very early in the morning,
   a long time before it was day,
the two brothers met at the ancient land marker.
   They fell with tears into each other's arms.
   And on that spot was built the city of Jerusalem."

Chapter Eight

MODERN ISRAEL
IN THE LAND

The State of Israel! My eyes filled with tears, and my hands shook. We had done it. We had brought the Jewish state into existence — and I, Golda Mabovitch Meyerson, had lived to see the day. Whatever happened now, whatever price any of us would have to pay for it, we had re-created the Jewish national home. The long exile was over.   — G. Meir[1]

It should be clear that there is no room for both peoples to live in this country.... If the Arabs leave, it is a large and open country; if they stay, it is small and poor. Up to this point, Zionists have been content to "buy land," but this is no way to establish a country for the Jews. A nation is created in one move...and in that case, there is no alternative to moving the Arabs to the neighboring countries, moving them all, except, perhaps, those living in Bethlehem, Nazareth, and the Old City of Jerusalem. Not one village, not one tribe must remain. They must be moved to Iraq, Syria, or even Transjordan.
                                                                 — Joseph Weitz[2]

Of the many books published about Israel and the Middle East, two provide unexpected insights. They are written by two Jewish intellectuals from utterly different backgrounds — and completely different generations.

The first is Golda Meir's autobiography, *My Life,* published in 1975.[3] Golda Meir was born into a poor Russian family and named "Goldie Mabovitch. Only later in 1956 did she "Hebraize" her name to Golda Meir. Her family emigrated to Milwaukee, Wisconsin, in 1906 when she was just a little girl. She grew up to be a passionate worker in Zionist organizations, and she and her husband moved to a kibbutz in Galilee in 1921. From her position as a specialist in chicken raising, she became an executive member of the Jewish Administrative Agency under British rule. In 1948, she was

---

1. G. Meir, *My Life* (New York: Putnam, 1975), 226.
2. J. Weitz, *Diaries and Letters to the Children* (Tel Aviv: n.p., 1965), 2:181.
3. See also R. Slater, *Golda, the Uncrowned Queen of Israel: A Pictorial Biography* (New York: Jonathan David, 1981). Another fascinating story of personal experiences, though written with a much harsher tone, is that of Menachem Begin (Israel's sixth prime minister, 1977–83), *The Revolt* (Los Angeles: Nash, 1972). This is Begin's account published originally in 1948, describing events leading up to the birth of modern Israel.

130

one of the signers of Israel's Proclamation of Independence and the same year was appointed to be Israel's first ambassador to Moscow. From 1949 until 1974, she served in Israel's Parliament (the Knesset). Serving first as minister of labor (1949), she then became foreign minister (1956), and in 1969 she was elected Israel's fourth prime minister. Leading her fledgling country with vigor and tenacity (foreign diplomats often received memos: "Watch out for Golda"),[4] she served with distinction until 1974, becoming known throughout the world as one of Israel's most distinguished leaders and thinkers. When she died in 1978, doctors discovered that for twelve years she had even been suffering from leukemia.

Within the pages of Golda Meir's warm and personal story, I glimpsed a view of Israel that is crucial for any student of the Middle East. She knew the persecutions and discriminations of Europe and America, and she dreamed about a Jewish homeland where anti-Semitism would no longer torment her people. She had witnessed the era of German Nazism, which murdered six million of her people. As a leader in Tel Aviv, she worked to rescue her people by smuggling Jews out of Europe after World War II and buying black-market weapons through secret channels. She fought with the British, argued with the Arabs, and cut deals with American Jewish leadership. She made frequent trips to America, raising millions of dollars for her country's economy and learning the critical role the United States would play in Israel's future.

In Golda Meir's mind, the state of Israel was the historical result of centuries of anti-Semitism now wed to a vision, a Zionist vision, for a Jewish homeland. Golda Meir embraced the idea of a state where democracy, diversity, and tolerance would characterize the land. As she expected, she found herself bruised and embittered by Arab politicians who had no interest in a Jewish state in their corner of the world. Nevertheless, her ideals, shaped in no small part by her biblical and Jewish traditions, remained until her retirement.

The second remarkable book is Thomas Friedman's *From Beirut to Jerusalem*.[5] Friedman was born in Minneapolis in 1953 to a liberal Jewish family

---

4. Before the war of 1948, Golda Meir negotiated extensively with King Abdullah of Jordan, trying to keep his country neutral before the upcoming war. In this capacity, she traveled in disguise to Jordan, wearing Arab dress and accompanied by an unarmed translator. Abdullah had never negotiated face to face with an Israeli like Meir. In fact, he had never met a woman diplomat in the Middle East before. Courage, cleverness, and unyielding debate were typical of this remarkable woman.

5. T. L. Friedman, *From Beirut to Jerusalem* (New York: Doubleday, 1989). Friedman has been the recipient of numerous awards in journalism and is a columnist for the *New York Times*.

("I was a three-day-a-year Jew—twice on the New Year [Rosh Hashanah] and once on the Day of Atonement [Yom Kippur]").[6] From 1979 until 1983, he worked in Beirut, Lebanon, as a reporter for UPI and later for the *New York Times,* winning the Pulitzer Prize for his coverage of the Israeli invasion of 1982. From 1984 until 1988, he wrote for the *Times* in Jerusalem, winning another Pulitzer for his outstanding work.

Friedman's passionate, intuitive, often-humorous narrative is filled with anecdotes as he describes nine years of his travels and research. But visible between the lines is his disillusionment. In fact, when he crossed from Lebanon to Israel in 1984, he found that the chaos on both sides of the border was similar. In Beirut, terrorists had blown his apartment sky-high while he was en route home one afternoon. In Jerusalem, the demolition of his ideals was just as great.

Friedman found a country that could not decide if it was going to be a free and open democracy or an exclusive Jewish state. The former would open its doors to the Palestinians. The latter would close them. Israel had to decide. Living within its borders were over a million Arabs, wondering since 1967 what their fate would be. Full citizens with the Israelis? Free to create their own homeland? Or hostages being neither let in nor let out?

Golda Meir came to Israel/Palestine with a vision shaped by her rich Jewish traditions and a firsthand experience with persecution. Quickly she found the vision being compromised as she played high-stakes politics with her Arab neighbors. Friedman came to Israel/Palestine hoping to find something secular, something democratic that stood out in the bitter world of Mediterranean politics. "Israelis," he learned, "cannot decide what their nation should stand for not only politically . . . but also spiritually."[7]

Meir and Friedman represent the two levels of disappointment that many of us feel as we visit and study the modern state of Israel. By comparison with other states in the Middle East, Israel is an exemplar of moderation, civility, and freedom. When the Syrian city of Hama (population 180,000) defied the rule of the late President Hafez Assad, he solved the problem cleanly. At 1:00 a.m. on Tuesday, February 2, 1982, he surrounded the town with tanks and artillery and leveled the place. Assad heard little dissent. Israel has not participated in this sort of wholesale massacre.

Yet when we look at the traditions that have shaped this country, when we look at the caliber of its leadership, we expect more. Israel is not to be compared with the tribal regimes that run Lebanon, Syria, and Iraq. Israel

---

6. Ibid., 4.
7. Ibid., 284.

seeks to be compared with the Western democracies that have shaped its political worldview. Moreover, Israel invites comparison with the biblical model of nationhood because it claims that this heritage has empowered it to inherit the land.

MODERN ISRAEL AND BIBLICAL ISRAEL

The first question Christians have to answer is whether or not modern Israel corresponds to biblical Israel described in our Scriptures. Is this a revival of the Israelite nation, a resuscitation of the kingdom whose heritage extends back to King David, King Solomon, and King Rehoboam?

From the Israeli point of view, the answer does not take a moment's hesitation. The earliest Zionists (from Weizmann to Ben-Gurion to Meir) all interpreted their work as restoring a biblical tradition even though they had secularized that tradition completely.[8] For this reason, then, Israelis insist on calling the West Bank "Judea and Samaria." These biblical names are used to make theological and historical claim on the land. Each year, the Jewish Passover service reminds worshipers to dream about "next year in Jerusalem." This liturgy has kept biblical Jerusalem in the hearts and minds of Jewish families for centuries. Likewise, to see Jews praying at the "Western Wall" (formerly the "Wailing Wall") is deeply moving. This mammoth section of limestone is a sought-after place of prayer because of its historic connection with the past: the remaining section of the last Jewish Temple. Even army officers take their oath of office lined up on the tarmac in front of it.

Many Western Christians have likewise been eager to see in Israel a fulfillment of the prophecies that mention God's people returning to their land. This desire was clear even in the nineteenth century when Zionists began to first lobby for returning to the land. For instance, William Blackstone in 1891 presented a petition signed by five hundred clergy urging that Palestine be given to the Jews. Later that year he wrote:

> No other people can boast of such high authority for the title to their earthly inheritance. It is rooted in the Holy Word, which all Christian nations receive as the foundation of their religion, and the rule of their practice. Does not the present dire extremity of Israel, and the quickening of their national sentiment,

---

8. But we must be clear that in no way were the earliest Zionists "religious." The biblical traditions were mere metaphors. The "New Israeli" or "New Jew," as they called these early pioneers, was a secular, cultural Jew. On the final evening editing the constitution of the country, its writers debated if they should include the name of "God" in its language.

and the expression of Gentile sympathy, and the providential openings toward the land, all point to the uplifted hand of God?[9]

When Israel declared its nationhood in 1948, countless writers rushed to their Bibles seeking an answer to the question of Israel and prophecy. For example, in 1958, A. W. Kac (a Jewish physician) published a full-fledged academic study entitled: *The Rebirth of the State of Israel, Is It of God or of Men?*[10] In the 1960s, this interest grew dramatically with the writing of scholars like John Walvoord, who proclaimed confidently that the rebirth of Israel was indeed a fulfillment of prophecy and a signal that the second coming of Jesus Christ was near.[11]

Following the Israeli victory of 1967, interest in Israel was meteoric. In 1970 Hal Lindsey published *The Late Great Planet Earth,* and although hardly well-reasoned or researched, the book caught the interest of Christians everywhere. Since 1970, it has sold 25 million copies.[12] Lindsey reached the same audience in 1981 with *The 1980s: Countdown to Armageddon.*[13] This little book was on the *New York Times* best-seller list for more than six months. Since then, Lindsey's pen has not rested. *Prophetical Walk through the Holy Land* (1983); *Israel and the Last Days* (1991); *The Final Battle* (1995); *Planet Earth — 2000 A.D.: Will Mankind Survive?* (1996); *Apocalypse Code* (1997); *Planet Earth, The Final Chapter* (1998); *Facing Millennium Midnight* (1999); and *The Promise of Bible Prophecy* (2000) each echo the same themes.[14]

The linchpin in all of these writings is that modern Israel has indeed resumed the life of ancient Israel, that a direct line may be drawn between the biblical nation and the Israeli government in Jerusalem today. Calling the rebirth of Israel the "fuse of Armageddon," Lindsey spoke for countless others when he said:

---

9. W. Blackstone, "May the United States Intercede for the Jews?" *Our Day* 8 (October 1898): 46.

10. London: Marshall, Morgan & Scott, 1958.

11. Walvoord's three earliest books are *Israel in Prophecy* (1962), *The Church in Prophecy* (1964), and *The Nations in Prophecy* (1967). These volumes are currently bound together as *The Nations, Israel, and The Church in Prophecy* (Grand Rapids, Mich.: Zondervan, 1988). Similarly, see W. M. Smith, *Israeli/Arab Conflict and the Bible* (Glendale, Calif.: Regal/Gospel Light, 1967).

12. H. Lindsey (with C. C. Carlson), *The Late Great Planet Earth* (Grand Rapids, Mich.: Zondervan, 1970). See also the excellent critique of T. Boersma, *Is the Bible a Jigsaw Puzzle? An Evaluation of Hal Lindsey's Writings* (St. Catherine's, Ont.: Paideia Press, 1978).

13. New York: Bantam, 1981.

14. For a critique of this perspective, see D. Wagner, *Anxious for Armageddon: A Call to Partnership for Middle Eastern and Western Christians* (Scottdale, Pa.: Herald Press, 1995); and G. Halsell, *Forcing God's Hand: Why Millions Pray for a Quick Rapture and Destruction of Planet Earth* (Washington, D.C.: Crossroads, 1999).

With the Jewish nation reborn in the land of Palestine, ancient Jerusalem is once again under total Jewish control for the first time in 2600 years, and talk of rebuilding the great Temple, the most important prophetic sign of Jesus Christ's soon coming is before us. This has now set the stage for the other predicted signs to develop in history. It is like the key piece of a jigsaw puzzle being found and then having the many adjacent pieces rapidly fall into place.[15]

Most Christians have responded to this outlook by weighing the prophecies studied by Walvoord, Lindsey, and others. Many have disagreed vigorously with their conclusions, but their question is different from mine. Rather than wondering if Israel is fulfilling prophecy, I am willing to grant their premise for the moment and ask a more fundamental question. *Assuming for now that such continuity exists between the Old Testament and the twenty-first century, how does Israel's national life compare with the life of God's people outlined in the Bible?* If Israel qualifies prophetically, does Israel also qualify ethically and morally to be God's people in the land?

This question was the standard that the prophets (like Amos and Isaiah) used when they assessed Israel's fidelity to the covenant. As we have seen, the prophets and the land itself have specific expectations about life and nationhood. When these standards were ignored, the right to possess the land was called into question. Paul reflects these same sentiments in Romans 2. Taking the voice of Isaiah, the apostle chastises Israel for living a life that dishonors God. "The name of God is blasphemed among the Gentiles because of you" (Isa. 52:5; Rom. 2:24). Unrighteous behavior can invalidate a person's claim to being God's people (Rom. 2:25–29).

MODERN ISRAEL AND BIBLICAL NATIONHOOD

Conservative Christians have been reluctant to open the question of Israel's behavior and its claims to being a nation of God's chosen people. But once a sensitive, reasonable person discovers just a handful of facts about Israel, the country can never be seen the same again. Most of us will say, "This can't be true" and hope to deny it. I have felt this way more than once. The situation is much too painful to describe but too important to ignore. Today a whole body of responsible, academic study has laid bare the character of the Israeli state. In addition, Christians and non-Christians alike have collected an overwhelming record of personal stories of Palestinians. Today, because of the Internet, stories and photographs abound on websites dedicated to uncovering untold suffering. These stories are endless and parallel what the

---

15. *Late Great Planet Earth*, 58.

academic record proves. *Most troubling of all, we are simply not being told about this record in our churches.*

I am convinced that if the prophets of the Old Testament were to visit Tel Aviv or Jerusalem today, their words would be harsh and unremitting. Strangely enough, just as in the Bible, their authority would likely go unrecognized, and like Jeremiah, they would be imprisoned by the Israeli Defense Forces as a security risk.

What are the deepest problems that trouble the modern state of Israel and contradict its claim to biblical nationhood?

An Exclusivist State

A fundamental problem is found in the character of Israel as a state in the first place. Some of the earliest Zionists seemed to have a vision of a nation that would be free and open to all peoples. Ben-Gurion, Israel's first prime minister, repeated this desire often. In 1946, before Israel was founded, he said to British and American leaders:

> We will have to treat our Arabs and other non-Jewish neighbors on the basis of absolute equality as if they were Jews, but make every effort that they should preserve their Arab characteristics, their language, their Arab culture, their Arab religion, their Arab way of life, while making every effort to make all the citizens of the country equal civilly, socially, economically, politically, intellectually and gradually raise the standard of life of everyone, Jew and others.[16]

The problem with Ben-Gurion, however, is that what he said in public was not what he felt in private. That same year he said, "When we say 'Jewish independence' or 'a Jewish state,' we mean Jewish country, Jewish soil, we mean Jewish labor, we mean Jewish economy, Jewish agriculture, Jewish industry, Jewish sea."[17] This comment reflects the spirit of the earliest Zionists like Theodor Herzl, who believed that the removal of Arabs bodily from Palestine was a part of the Zionist plan "to spirit the penniless population across the frontier."[18] But this view did not exist only at the turn of the twentieth century. In 1989, Benjamin Netanyahu (prime minister from 1996 to 1999) was speaking at Bar Ilan University following the brutal

---

16. *The Jewish Case: Before the Anglo-American Committee of Inquiry on Palestine as Presented by the Jewish Agency for Palestine* (Jerusalem: Jewish Agency for Palestine, 1947), 71, as cited in R. Ruether and H. Ruether, *Wrath of Jonah: The Crisis of Religious Nationalism in the Israeli-Palestinian Conflict* (New York: Harper & Row, 1989), 132 n. 5.

17. *The Jewish Case: Before the Anglo-American Committee of Inquiry on Palestine as Presented by the Jewish Agency for Palestine* (Jerusalem: Jewish Agency for Palestine, 1946), 66.

18. *The Diaries of Theodor Herzl*, ed. M. Lowenthan (New York: Dial Press, 1956), 188 (June 12, 1895, entry). He went on to say that this "process of expropriation and the removal of the poor must be carried out discreetly and circumspectly."

Chinese repression of demonstrations in Tiananmen Square. His viewpoint: "Israel should have exploited the repression of the demonstrations in China, when world attention focused on that country, to carry out mass expulsions among the Arabs of the [occupied] territories."[19]

Ben-Gurion's promise of a nation built on "equal civility" never materialized. Israel is a nation that excludes non-Jews by design. Imagine if Holland declared that it was a country built exclusively for white, Dutch Protestant Christians. Others could live there, but they could not form nationwide political parties, travel freely, receive equal wages, cultivate an independent culture, or have access to the systems of justice and politics like white, Dutch Protestants. We would be outraged. As happened in South Africa, the world would be severe in its judgment. Denis Goldberg, a Jew, was imprisoned in South Africa in 1985 for trying to overthrow the apartheid systems there. He was released by Israeli intercessions but refused to move to Israel. His reason: "I see many similarities in the oppression of blacks in South Africa and of Palestinians." He moved to London. In fact, Nobel laureate Archbishop Desmond Tutu visited Jerusalem at Christmas in 1989 and remarked, "I am a black South African, and if I were to change the names, a description of what is happening in the Gaza Strip and the West Bank could describe events in South Africa."

A recent study conducted by Hebrew University, Jerusalem, analyzed how Palestinians are presented in Israeli newspapers. The results were astounding, though not surprising among communications experts who study media treatment of minorities. Little coverage of Arabs appears, and the content is negative. About 2 percent of articles published in Hebrew newspapers is about Arabs. Most reports covered stories of "disorder" and arrests, never Arab cultural events, elections, or routine news. On TV, only ninety news stories were found in four years, which is one every sixteen days. When the study focused on a specific annual conflict ("Land Day"[20]), they learned that Jewish voices (and reporters) always interpreted what the Arabs were doing. No Arabs are represented in leading roles in the Jewish press. The U.S. equivalent would be covering a race riot in Philadelphia, showing film of blacks looting and being arrested, and only having white police interpret every scene.[21]

---

19. The Israeli journal *Hotam,* November 24, 1989.

20. This annual protest among Palestinians is rooted in events that took place on March 30, 1976, when six Arab citizens of Israel were killed in a fight over the government confiscation of their land. Each year, the Israeli government prepares for violence.

21. G. Wolfsfeld, E. Avraham, and I. Aburaiya, "When Prophecy Fails Every Year: Israeli Press Coverage of the Arab Minority's Land Day Protests," Paper presented to the 48th Annual Conference of the International Communication Association, July 1998, Jerusalem.

Israel makes every attempt to place Palestinians on the margins of society.[22] Here, though, we have to distinguish carefully between Palestinians who live within Israel's 1967 borders and those who live in the Occupied West Bank. Within Israel, the Arab population makes up about 20 percent (or 1.2 million), but they are barely represented in the government.[23]

Israel's government is much like the Parliament system of Great Britain. Political parties (of which there are many) enlist voters, and coalitions are formed among parties to gain a majority in the Knesset, a 120-seat Parliament. Individuals do not vote for candidates; rather political office is decided through party representation. For many years no nationwide Palestinian political party *that includes the Occupied Territories* has been permitted into the system, so Arabs hold only a few Knesset seats (merely 7 percent).[24] This statistic is remarkable when we remember that 20 percent of pre-1967 Israel is Arab. If I include the populations of the West Bank and Gaza — whose destinies are controlled by decisions made in this government — Palestinians make up 40 percent of Israel/Palestine but barely have a voice in the government. These people in Gaza and the West Bank have never been permitted to vote in Israeli elections. This concern is answered today by new elections in these regions for Palestinian regional leaders — but this fledgling government barely holds any power to rule and holds only those privileges that Israel doles out. Yasir Arafat's airplane cannot even take off from Gaza airport without Israeli permission.

Discrimination

Throughout the Intifada uprising from 1987 to 1992, Arab self-identity was so repressed that even showing the four colors of the Palestinian flag in art (green, white, black, and red) could lead to arrest. I knew Palestinian women who would sew these flags and hide them under their beds in defiance. West Bank Palestinians could not travel, build a house, obtain a job, or dig a well in their backyard without hard-won permission.

In this period, Israel also employed a system for identifying and limiting the movements of its people through its licensing of automobiles. License plates were all color coded: yellow for Israelis, white for Gaza, blue for the

---

22. See the comprehensive studies of I. Lustick, *Arabs in the Jewish State: Israel's Control of a National Minority* (Austin: University of Texas Press, 1980).

23. I am using the following figures for Israel's population based on 1999 figures published by the U.S. government [see the C.I.A. factbook: *www.odci.gov/cia/publications/factbook*]. Israel: 5.7 million with 166,000 settlers on the West Bank, 19,000 on the Golan Heights, 6,000 settlers in Gaza, and 176,000 in East Jerusalem. The West Bank: 1.6 million Arabs. Gaza: 1.1 million.

24. N. Qurah, "The Arabs in Israel Since 1948," *Zionism and Racism* (Tripoli: n.p., 1977), 94-96.

West Bank, and green for taxis and service vehicles. West Bank licenses in this era also had a letter before the seven numbers that told the police the city or village the car came from.[25] If a "West Bank" car was seen in pre-1967 Israel, say, in Tel Aviv, it would be stopped by the police or army. I asked a well-known architect in Ramallah, Saleem Zaru, if he ever took his kids to Tel Aviv to the zoo. His answer was telling. Even if he had the travel papers, the harassment because of his license plate would be very upsetting to the whole family. We might note, though, that yellow "Israeli" plates may travel anywhere in the country.

Today the license plate system is being replaced by new Palestinian plates for Arabs in the Occupied Territories. But again, while "yellow" Israeli plates may move anywhere, a family with Palestinian plates in Bethlehem cannot drive to Jerusalem without special permission. Nevertheless, other systems are in place to identify the population. Driver's licenses and ID cards indicate if the driver is Jewish or Arab.[26]

When Palestinians are stopped on the street by soldiers, their ID cards are always checked. Each card has a computer number, which a soldier reads over a radio to a computer operator. This massive data base has much information about Palestinians. If the Arab is not carrying a card or leaves it at home, he can be arrested. If an ID from Gaza shows up in Jerusalem and the Arab has no written permission, he or she is taken into custody. A friend of mine from Ramallah went to West Jerusalem to see a dentist. As she walked down the street, off-duty soldiers stopped her and demanded her card "since she looked Arab." Card checking is a regular form of Israeli intimidation.

Essentially Palestinians within Israel's borders cannot enter the main systems of Israeli society. The major labor organizations, political parties, and even the military are all off-limits. Only 4 percent of Israeli university students are Arab because all entrance exams must be taken in Hebrew, and much admission discrimination takes place. Further, qualifying Arab students often find that their tuition is not waived, and thus they are economically excluded. On the West Bank, Arab universities, which are poorly funded, are viewed as politically suspicious. During periods of turmoil, they have been closed down by the military. Over 1 million people live in Gaza. About eight thousand of these are students attending two universities in

---

25. For instance, Hebrew R [resh] on white background is Ramallah, H is Hebron, B is Bethlehem. A yellow background indicates a village near these towns: a yellow R is a village near Ramallah, etc.

26. In fact, Jews renew their licenses on the fifteenth of the month, non-Jews on the first.

Gaza, which offer very limited curricula. About thirteen hundred Gaza students are enrolled in West Bank universities, but a new law in January 1996 forbade these students from traveling out of Gaza to their schools. Further, an Arab university does not even exist within the pre-1967 borders of Israel. This environment is creating an entire generation of Palestinians who have become a migrant labor force in low-paying sectors of society: construction, agriculture, and public services (e.g., restaurant workers).

Sometimes the foreigner misses the subtleties of discrimination. Since 1949, Israel has offered special benefits to people who have served in the military, including school, housing, welfare and job entitlements.[27] However, Palestinians are restricted from joining (for obvious reasons), and thus a whole network of financial benefits are denied to them. But *Jews* who are exempt from military service nevertheless gain these same benefits (thanks to a revised law in 1970). Arabs who are exempt because of their race are not included under this law.

West Bank residents who hold work permits in Jerusalem must leave the city by nightfall. In the early 1990s, an administrator of a Christian school in the West Bank once had to stay the night at a colleague's home in Jerusalem because he missed his ride. At 2:00 a.m., the army arrived and took him away since he possessed the wrong ID card. He spent five months in a Hebron prison without ever going to court. Then he was expelled from the country for two years. In order to avoid exile to Lebanon, he went to school in Cairo for the duration of the punishment.

Citizenship is a telltale sign of membership in any nation. The Law of Return (1950) declares that every Jew in the world has the right to immigrate to Israel and claim automatic citizenship and social privileges.[28] Not only is this situation a remarkable statement about Israeli life, but it affects others who have lived on the land for centuries, have fled during war, and are eager to return. Even the United Nations has affirmed the rights of these people to go home.[29] Palestinians whose homes are still in Israel, whose families have lived in the land for centuries, are denied reentry. They languish in camps surrounding Israel's borders or on the West Bank while Jewish newcomers occupy their homes.

---

27. The "Discharged Soldiers Act" of 1949.

28. Jewishness, though, has been carefully defined by Israel's Orthodox rabbis. They exclude illegitimate children of Jewish parents, children with a Jewish father but whose mother became a Christian, and Jewish believers in Jesus. Technically, a Jewish person who was an atheist would qualify as a Jew and be able to claim citizenship. See S. Z. Abramov, "Who Is a Jew?" in S. Z. Abramov, *Perpetual Dilemma: Jewish Religion in the Jewish State* (Cranbury, N.J.: Associated University Press, 1976), 270–320.

29. United Nations General Resolution #194, December 11, 1948.

Any country that de facto excludes a segment of its society from its national benefits on the basis of race can hardly qualify as democratic. For this reason, on November 10, 1975, the United Nations declared that Zionism should be considered racism — a political philosophy that excludes others based on race, history, and creed.[30] Even Israeli civil rights groups say the same. In 1998, the Association for Civil Rights in Israel accused the government of race-based discrimination and "creating a threatening atmosphere that makes violations of human rights more acceptable."[31] A special U.N. investigation in Geneva studied a report recently that uncovered seventeen Israeli laws in which racially based discrimination was explicit.[32]

Some writers sincerely believe that the treatment of Palestinians in Israel is a form of apartheid.[33] Allegra Pacheco, a Brooklyn-born daughter of traditional Jews, defends Palestinians in Israeli courts because of how deeply Israeli discrimination offends her. Since coming from America, her opinions have become razor sharp: "A *Jewish* state can never be democratic for all its citizens; it's only a democracy for Jews."[34]

Israel's character stands in stark contrast to the biblical model we have studied in the previous chapters. In the Old Testament, the place of the resident alien (the non-Israelite) was assured. He was not denied access to the primary forms of national expression: the Temple, the justice system, or the military. Therefore Israel's exclusivism must answer the demands of covenant justice so clearly outlined in the Bible.

Stealing Land

Land ownership has been the darkest side of Israeli history since 1948. While the Israelis purchased land on which to build their settlements and cities, these transactions barely account for the land to which Israel lays claim today. Both Turkish and British administrations respected the "public properties" and open lands around Arab villages. These lands were collectively owned and reserved for village growth and pasturage. Village elders knew precisely where boundaries should be drawn and in many cases had these lines recorded by Turks. However, Israeli law has defined this land as state

---

30. U.N. Resolution #3379 (November 10, 1975). The full text and background can be found in *Zionism and Racism, Proceedings of an International Symposium* (Tripoli: n.p., 1977). The U.N., under strong pressure from the United States, removed this decision in 1991.

31. "ACRI Blasts 'Official' Racism Against Arabs," *Jerusalem Post,* July 2, 1998.

32. "Two Views of Israeli Racism Before U.N. Committee," *Ha'Aretz,* March 4, 1998.

33. J. H. Davis, *The Evasive Peace* (New York: New World Press, 1968), 115. Davis worked for many years in the Middle East with the U.N. Relief & Works Agency (UNRWA). See also U. Davis, *Israel: An Apartheid State* (London: Zed Books, 1987).

34. *Jerusalem Post Magazine,* March 6, 1998.

property (under the control of "The Jewish National Fund" or transferred to the "Jewish Agency") and it may be used only by Jews. Villages are thus denied room to grow. If land is uncultivated, Israel nationalizes it (often after the Arab farmers have been prohibited from entering it). Sometimes the property is taken as "a security zone" or as "needed public property." Palestinian claims to land ownership are aggressively fought in court by government attorneys. If modern documentation cannot be shown, the case is lost, since evidence from before the Israeli occupation is rejected. Some deeds dating back to the Turkish period are generally refused by the court. Other Arab families simply do not possess modern documentation — especially those families in rural peasant villages. Furthermore, since 1967, Israeli law has prohibited West Bank Palestinians from registering their land.

The worst cases of land confiscation are found in the Occupied Territories of Gaza and the West Bank. Land is often closed off, the water rights are removed, and then the land is declared abandoned and quickly nationalized. In areas where new Israeli settlements have depleted water tables, Arabs have asked for permits for new wells, which are generally denied, leaving the Arabs without water.[35] In the Occupied Territories, Israeli land records are kept secret so that Palestinians cannot contest them.[36] Today, according to the field office of World Vision Jerusalem, 70 percent of the West Bank's land has been confiscated by Israel and 43 percent of Gaza has been taken. In 1997 alone, over six thousand acres of Palestinian land was taken in Jerusalem and the West Bank. During the first eighteen months of Ariel Sharon's rule, forty-four completely illegal "hilltop" settlements — often consisting of a trailer and a tent — have been built and left unchallenged in the West Bank.[37]

Stealing Water

We have already seen how Israel has built its nation by conquest and the appropriation of other people's land. This activity has created millions of refugees. The same is true of water management.

Today, modern Israelis and Palestinians rarely wait for rain to fill their cisterns. Water is taken from the Sea of Galilee and moved down the coast in the national water carrier. In the central mountains, water sources generally come from two subterranean aquifers that serve both the Palestinian West Bank and Israel. Whoever controls access to these water sources certainly

---

35. From 1967 to 1983, only five permits for new wells were granted to Palestinians. Raja Shehadeh, *Occupier's Law: Israel and the West Bank* (Washington, D.C.: Institute for Palestinian Studies, 1985), 153–54.

36. Ibid., 39–40, as cited in R. Ruether and H. Ruether, *Wrath of Jonah,* 156 n. 55.

37. U. Schmetzer, "In Israel Some Are Unsettled by Hilltop Outposts," *Chicago Tribune,* July 26, 2002, 3.

controls life in this region. As with the use of land, this control becomes a test of righteousness for people who live in the Middle East.

One of the most active Israeli advocacy groups is B'Tselem, also known as the Israeli Information Center for Human Rights.[38] B'Tselem gives the following report: Since 1967, severe water shortages have become commonplace throughout Palestine because the Israeli water authority (Mekorot) drastically cuts water allocated to Palestinian towns and villages. For example, the average Israeli consumes 348 liters of water per day while the average Palestinian is given 70.[39] That is, Jews use five times more water per person than Arabs. In the West Bank the discrepancy is worse. Israel reserves 80 percent of the water in these areas for its own use while 20 percent goes to Palestinians. If these Arabs need more water, they must pay four times the usual price for it. Every settler receives nine times more water than the West Bank Palestinian.[40]

How does this happen? Over 150 villages representing 215,000 people are not connected to any water network and so must purchase their water from high-priced dealers with trucks. In addition, some cities in the West Bank must rotate water supply by areas in order to distribute the little water available, particularly during the summer. In Yatta, for example, the village is divided into fourteen sectors, each sector receiving water once every forty-five days for two to three days. Finally, while Israeli settlers are permitted to drill deep wells into the aquifer and through their heavy use lower the water table, the old wells in the villages cannot be deepened. Nor can new wells be dug. Eventually villages run dry. In Bethlehem where 180,000 Palestinians live, the demand is for 18,000 cubic meters per day, but the supply given is no more than 8,000. Hebron's 300,000 people need 25,000 cubic meters per day, but they are given 5,500 cubic meters instead.

When Arab families find themselves without water for their homes or fields, they sometimes tap into the settler water system pipes illegally. When this pilferage happens in the West Bank, the army comes and generally confiscates or destroys the entire irrigation system in the fields, thus leaving the farmer destitute. Sometimes this "illegal" use of water leads to the demolition of the home.

God owns this water, this holy water in the Holy Land. When the water is held selfishly, misused so that others suffer, the same judgment given by Elijah surely would come again to the land. In 1998, the Israeli newspaper

---

38. See their website: *www.btselem.org*.
39. This figure takes into account industrial, agricultural, and personal use.
40. M. Raheb, *I Am a Palestinian Christian* (Minneapolis: Fortress, 1995), 48.

Ha'aretz reported that during the summer five hundred thousand Palestinians — about a third of the population — went without water for two entire months.[41] Isa Atallah, head of the Palestine Water Authority in Hebron, remarked, "It is really frustrating when your children are going thirsty and you see the settlers next door watering their gardens and swimming in their pools."[42]

The Destruction of Villages

In addition to the confiscation of "public" lands and the unjust distribution of water, Israel has witnessed the military occupation of entire villages, the removal of their residents, and the destruction of their homes. Occasionally Israeli settlers move into them, but generally they have been blown up or bulldozed. Hundreds and hundreds of villages have suffered this fate. According to some, almost five hundred Arab villages have disappeared since 1948.[43] And Arab historians are telling the story. In 1992 a stunning book was published as a testimony to this now-destroyed village life. *Lest the Civilized World Forget: The Colonization of Palestine* is a record of 394 of these villages meticulously researched by Jamil Fayez, a Palestinian physician in North Carolina. Following a summary of the "myths" surrounding the disappearance of these villages, Fayez goes on to list their names — one at a time — providing a sort of litany for the dead.[44] Typical records read like this:

> 57. AL KHAESAH located 24.8 miles NNE of Safad. Population: 1,840. Obliterated in 1948, with the Jewish settlement of QIRYAT SHEMONA built on its 2,820 acres.

> 107. AL RAMLAH located 12.5 miles SE of Jaffa. Population: 16,380. Occupied in 1948. Most of its inhabitants were forcefully evicted, while a few

41. "Water Crisis in the Occupied Territories," *Ha'aretz,* July 27, 1998; cf. "Water Shortage in the Territories," *Ha'Aretz,* August 20, 1998; and J. Isaac, *A Sober Approach to the Water Crisis in the Middle East, A UNESCO Symposium* (Jerusalem: Applied Research Institute, 1995).

42. "Controlling Thirst in the West Bank," *Holy Land Briefing* 2, World Vision Church Relations, Jerusalem, 1998.

43. Cf. I. Shahak, "Arab Villages Destroyed in Israel: A Report," in *Documents from Israel, 1967–1973: Readings for a Critique of Zionism,* ed. U. Davis and N. Mezvinsky (London: Ithaca Press, 1975), 47; also S. Jiryis, *The Arabs in Israel* (New York: Monthly Review Press, 1976). The authoritative resource is W. Khalidi, *All That Remains: The Palestinian Villages Occupied and Depopulated by Israel in 1948* (Washington, D.C.: Institute for Palestine Studies, 1992). Today, the remaining Arab villages in pre-1967 Israel lack most basic services. See their association on the web: *www.assoc40.org.*

44. *Lest the Civilized World Forget: The Colonization of Palestine* (New York: Americans for Middle East Understanding, 1992); the AMEU is located at 475 Riverside Drive, Room 241, New York, NY 10115. (212) 870-2053; Fax: (212) 870-2050.

hundred remained. The town, renamed RAMLA, was taken over by Jewish immigrants who stole and occupied the houses of the Palestinians. In time they confiscated an additional 442 acres of surrounding lands and gardens.

244. IKRET located NE of Acre near the Lebanese border. Population of 500 Palestinians, all Maronite Christians, who were forced to evacuate their village in 1948. All the village buildings were blown up on Christmas day, 1952, and all its 6,181 acres were stolen.

These three stories are just a sample from the pages and pages that fill the book and help explain why there are over 3 million Palestinian refugees in the world. Today, with the Internet, refugee organizations are publishing their stories rapidly. Another thorough list (complete with photos and maps) can be found at *www.alnakba.org*. The list reminds me of the Israeli shrine for the Holocaust, Yad Vashem, near Mount Herzl in West Jerusalem. Here records are kept for destroyed Jewish villages in places like Poland. The litany is the same. A litany for the dead. Yet it seems that no one has learned from history.

Sometimes the best approach is simply to hear the story of one such village attack. At 7:15 a.m. on July 13, 1948, Israeli soldiers began entering homes in Lydda, a village near Tel Aviv. Audeh Rantisi, then a young man, tells what happened. "I was eleven at the time. I heard the soldiers say in English, 'Leave your house open and go outside.'" Audeh's father took his family out and headed toward their church (since they were Christians) but in town, soldiers directed them east to the mountains. Panic hit the large mass of people now standing on the road when they learned that 136 Muslim men had just been machine-gunned after they had been forced into the village's Dahmash mosque. The soldiers did not let the mass of people use the road, but forced them over rough terrain during a sweltering one-hundred-degree day. Women in heavy Palestinian dresses stumbled carrying children and what few things they could gather in the minutes they were given to leave. Audeh's father carried his key — which he would never use again. And he left behind his generations-old olive oil soap business. One Israeli soldier from Kibbutz Ein Harod remembered what he saw: "slow-shuffling columns" of people leaving in their wake "utensils and furniture and in the end, bodies of men, women and children, scattered along the way" who died from exhaustion, dehydration and disease.[45]

Soldiers fired overhead as the crowd cried and screamed. Planes buzzed the long lines of refugees. At a checkpoint, blankets were spread on the

---

45. B. Morris, *The Birth of the Palestinian Refugee Problem, 1947–1949* (Cambridge: Cambridge University Press, 1987), 210. Morris is an Israeli historian.

ground and soldiers ordered everyone to give up their valuables (money, wristwatches, jewelry). A young man — just married — named Amin Han-han was carrying a small container with some money which he refused to give up. He was shot point blank and fell into his new bride's arms. Audeh writes, "It was the first time I had ever seen one human being kill another. I was so shocked and afraid. It happened so fast, so casually. I remember feeling I wanted to throw up."

Soldiers on horseback now pushed the thousands of villagers up the rocky mountain on a trek that would cover thirty miles. Bullets whistled overhead, and Audeh remembers one just missing him and exploding in the neck of his donkey. On the third day, the sun took its toll. Many died, especially the pregnant women. There was no water and many expired from dehydration. Their bodies were wrapped and left under trees. Most tragic were the many young children left behind who could not withstand the heat and lack of water.[46] At the village of Jimzu where there were two wells, soldiers stood in circles urinating in them but the people drank anyway.

But at the end of this day, the crowd met a road going to the city of Ramallah. Arab trucks from this large town arrived to help and people were packed on board and driven further into the mountains to start their lives as refugees, joining more than seven hundred thousand people who had lost their homes during Israel's 1948 war.

Not long after 1967, Audeh had an opportunity to revisit Lydda for the first time to see his childhood home. Jewish families had taken it and he noticed a young boy playing in the yard. Audeh approached him. "How long have you lived in this house?" he asked. "I was born here," the boy replied. "Me too," Audeh said. "This is my father's house."[47]

The Bible is crystal clear about theft and in particular about the theft of land. This act is the sin of Ahab and Jezebel. The prophets (such as Elijah) were swift to pronounce judgment on governments that practiced national theft. People who own land — Jew or Gentile — must have their rights protected, or the occupier will find God to be his opponent.

---

46. "Countless children died outright of thirst." I. Abu-Lughod, *The Transformation of Palestine* (Evanston, Ill.: Northwestern University Press: 1971), 149.

47. Audeh Rantisi's story can be found in his book *Blessed Are the Peacemakers: A Palestinian Christian in the Occupied West Bank* (Grand Rapids, Mich.: Zondervan, 1990). For these years, see pp. 23–39. A short form of his story (and that of Charles Amash) can be found in *The Link* 33, no. 3 (July 2000): 3–10. See also M. C. King, *The Palestinians and the Churches*, vol. 1: 1948–1956 (Geneva: World Council of Churches, 1981). A similar view is available from J. Glubb, a British general who worked in Palestine at the time. See *A Soldier among the Arabs* (New York: Harper, 1957).

The Demolition of Homes

The most important story to emerge since 1987 is the "ethnic cleansing" of the West Bank through the demolition of Palestinian homes. Following the war of 1948, Israel was keen to destroy villages and move their populations into the mountains or out of the country. But once the mountains were occupied in 1967, their settlement by Jews meant dealing with the inconvenience of Arab homes where settlements and roads would be built. Since 1987, Israel has demolished over 2,200 Palestinian homes.[48] Some put the number at 2,650. The result? Home demolitions have produced 16,700 homeless people, 7,300 of whom are children. Still more remarkable is that in the five years following the 1993 Oslo Accords — in which genuine overtures to peace were offered — Israel demolished 96 homes in Arab East Jerusalem and 566 homes in the West Bank. Many think that the Israeli governments of Benjamin Netanyahu and Ehud Barak intentionally deceived the Western media by promising to limit settlements and bring peace while quietly accelerating the growth of settlements.[49]

Today the advent of the Internet has meant that such acts of violence can be published immediately. Of course, this reporting has been done in great detail by Palestinians,[50] and in some cases one can feel the anger and fury simply by reading a web page. But a growing body of Israelis are also deeply offended by this violence and work to end it. Two deserve mention. B'Tselem was founded in 1989 and is known as the "Israeli Center for Human Rights in the Occupied Territories." B'Tselem even won the Carter Center award for human rights work. Here Israeli attorneys, journalists, academics, and prominent Knesset members work to document human rights violations in the West Bank and educate the Israeli public about what is happening. Their website is a goldmine of information.[51] B'Tselem provides annual figures on house demolitions year by year. The figures on the following page combine houses demolished when there was no permit and when there was a permit to build. The table also combines demolitions in East Jerusalem with those in the West Bank.

The scope of this violence is difficult to comprehend. In 2001, the Israeli army completely destroyed 30 homes in East Jerusalem and another 67 homes in the West Bank. These homes were built on the owners' property

---

48. Amnesty International counts 7,000 Palestinian homes destroyed since 1967, but figures from this earlier period are less reliable.

49. *The Palestinian Center for Human Rights, Annual Report 1999*, 2.

50. For an excellent directory of Palestinian websites, see *www.geocities.com/SouthBeach/Lagoon/8522/palestine.html#1* and the guide produced by Bir Zeit University in the West Bank: *www.birzeit.edu/links/index.html*.

51. *www.btselem.org*.

Year	Home Demolitions, East Jerusalem and West Bank
1987	104
1988	548
1989	491
1990	209
1991	273
1992	168
1993	112
1994	149
1995	68
1996	168
1997	255
1998	180
1999	39
2000	9
2001	105
2002	33

but did not have building permits. Israeli also destroyed as a punitive measure 8 homes which were built legally. In addition, since 1987 Israel has also "sealed" 296 homes, forbidding their residents to live in them. In the June 1, 1998, newspaper *Ha'Aretz*, Gideon Levy referred to the Israelis who do this as "the high priests of calamity." These home destructions and sealings result in families going homeless or living in tents.

A more activist group is *Gush Shalom*, founded in 1992 by Uri Avnery.[52] This group of Jewish and Arab intellectuals has staged massive protests in Israel, lobbied the Israeli Parliament aggressively, and brought a new awareness to the Israeli public about home demolitions. In addition to historical and statistical information, their website provides photographs and descriptions of house demolitions. The accounts make for troubling reading.[53] But these Jewish groups — such as the Jewish Peace Fellowship — are growing rapidly because of an increasing sense of outrage from the Israeli public.[54]

More than statistics, these numbers represent families. In 1997, the four members of Ahmad Isma'il's family were living in one room of his father's

---

52. *www.gush-shalom.org.*
53. *www.gush-shalom.org/demolition/back.html.*
54. See the partial list at *www.gush-shalom.org/links.html.*

house in the village of Qatana near Ramallah. He had just built a ten-thousand-dollar home on family property and it was ready for his family: walls, floors, roof, doors, and windows were finished. On July 31, 1997, Israeli bulldozers destroyed it because he did not have a building permit (which the government refused to provide). Within view of his home, however, Israeli settlements were growing daily.

In order to control population growth in valuable areas, to punish politically active families, and to take land for settlement growth, Palestinians are commonly denied the right to build on their land. This is remarkable when one calculates the differences in population density in Israel/Palestine. Housing density among Palestinians is twice that of Jews (2.2 persons per room to 1.1). In East Jerusalem, 60 percent of the Arab population lives in housing density of 2 per room (for Jews it is 13 percent). Twenty-seven percent of Arabs live in housing with more than 3 per room, compared with 2.4 percent of Jews. New housing goes up for Jews regularly in Jerusalem. But today according to Amnesty International, *ten thousand Arab homes in East Jerusalem — one-third of the Palestinian population — are threatened by demolition orders.*

What does a demolition feel like? In 1998, the Israeli peace activist Gila Svirsky had the privilege of seeing one. She was riding a bus sponsored by "The Israeli Committee Against Home Demolitions," which had passengers from a number of peace groups (Gush Shalom, Peace Now, Rabbis for Human Rights, etc.) as well as a minister of the Israeli Parliament. Getting a glimpse of a demolition is rare since they happen swiftly to avoid protests, but a cell phone alerted them to bulldozers moving not far away.

In 1967, refugees from Jerusalem's Old City fled to a small, unpaved village called 'Anata in the countryside east of Jerusalem. Since they were not permitted to go home, these "internal" refugees built new houses on the fringe of the desert and began a new life. As Gila's bus rounded the corner the bulldozer was already tearing through a hillside house belonging to Salim and Ajrabiyeh al-Shawamreh and their six children. The passengers jumped out but were held back by heavily armed soldiers. Gila's account:

> There we stood on the side of the hill and watched with an unbearable sense of helplessness as the "civil" administration's bulldozer took the house apart wall by wall. He drove through the front garden with a profusion of flowers and a lemon tree and slammed the front door as if he were God Almighty. Backing away, he slammed again until the entire front was shattered and dangling from metal rods. Then he came from every side, slamming and crashing his shovel against the walls. Finally he lifted off the roof, barely suspended, and sent it

crashing below. When he was done, he went around the back of the house and crashed through all the fruit trees, including a small olive stand.[55]

Gila and the others confronted the soldiers. "How can you sleep at night?" Every single soldier said the same thing: "This is legal; we are only following orders." The answer was an echo of other soldiers, in other decades from other countries who committed atrocities. Gila soon found herself hugging a fourteen-year-old girl named Lena who watched her father's home demolished this day. She wept uncontrollably. Villagers began throwing rocks at the bulldozer and the soldiers opened fire with their rifles. No one was hurt. Gila and the others collected olive branches to take home, "crushed," as she says, "by power run amuck."

The demolition became well-publicized (thanks to the activists), and its story was reported on CNN. An Israeli official's explanation: "They built too close to a settler bypass road." But the road was almost a half mile away.

Christians and Jews alike (over seventy of them now) joined the village in rebuilding the home — now all of it illegal. Even the news media set up cameras wondering when the soldiers would return. For three days they worked. Then at 5 a.m. on a Monday morning, soldiers appeared and surrounded the building project. Soon a bulldozer crested the hill and flattened their efforts, this time destroying most of the trees and even the tent the family used.

Ironically the demolition came on the day after the Jewish holiday Tisha B'Av, which mourns the Roman destruction of the Jewish Temple in Jerusalem in 70 C.E..

What does a demolition look like from the inside? The case of Salim Isma'il al-Shawamreh provides the picture we need. Amnesty International supplies his story:[56]

The family of Salim Isma'il al-Shawamreh came from the Old City to Shu'fat refugee camp in 1967, after the Israeli occupation of the West Bank. Salim had five brothers and five sisters, and the whole family lived in a twenty-by-thirteen- foot room. In 1980 Salim al-Shawamreh went to Saudi Arabia and worked as an engineer for eight years. There he saved enough money to buy a plot of land in 'Anata village two kilometers away, where he planned to build a house for his family.

From 1990 he sought and failed to gain building permission; the Israeli Civil Administration said that the land was not in the area zoned for development in 'Anata's village plan. Eventually, in 1994, he gave up and built

---

55. Distributed by World Vision, Jerusalem. *Reflection Report 27*, August 3, 1998.
56. *www.amnesty.org/ailib/aipub/1999/MDE/51505999.htm.*

a home without a permit on the plot and lived there with his wife, four daughters, and two sons. It was, he says "a good life."

Then, on July 9, 1998, "I was sitting to take lunch and I went out and the whole area was surrounded by soldiers, there were more than two hundred. They said, 'This is not your home, you have fifteen minutes to take out your belongings.' " It took eight hours to demolish the house, during which time Salim telephoned Israeli peace groups. A number of Israelis, including members of the Israeli Parliament, joined the protest. The Israeli Defense Force used rubber-coated metal bullets, truncheons, and tear gas to clear the area, injuring seven people, including two women.

The al-Shawamreh family decided immediately to rebuild their house. They rapidly built a frame house and held a party, dancing in celebration, on August 2, 1998. At 4 a.m. the next day they opened their eyes to the sight, once again, of a hillside swarming with Israeli soldiers. The soldiers pulled down their tent, destroyed their water tank, ripped out the electric cables, and pulled out the fruit trees they had planted on the hill side.

The Civil Administration was questioned as to the necessity of this demolition by the Israeli press and gave contradictory replies — at one time saying that two signatures were missing from the ownership documents, at another that the land was zoned for agricultural use, at another that the hill slope was too steep to build a house, and at another that the house was near a bypass road. The next year, 1999, it was decided to challenge the demolition by building a third time. Volunteers from the Israeli Committee against House Demolitions and the Peace Now movement joined in every Friday, and by November 1999 the house was nearly completed.

Human Rights Abuses

A friend whom I'll call Karen, an American Christian worker, was walking through Jerusalem's Old City not long ago. As she exited the Damascus Gate, she saw something stunning. Three soldiers were beating a young boy. Karen's habit in such situations — which are common — is to intervene. "Why are you beating this boy? Could you please stop so we can talk?" They paused while one soldier kept his boot on the boy's neck as he spoke. "He didn't obey us." Reinforcements arrived quickly, and the beating continued until blood flowed freely from the boy's swollen face. The crowd of Arabs screamed loudly and soldiers fired weapons into the air to disperse them. Soldiers grabbed the boy, dragged him out of the Damascus Gate and into a waiting military van.

Karen returned the next day to talk with shopkeepers to get the story. The boy was beaten because he could not produce his identity papers. When he arrived at the police station he was beaten further, then sent home, placed under house arrest for six weeks, and told if he was seen on the street, he would go to prison. Arab children are required to carry ID cards when they turn sixteen. This boy was fourteen.

Arrests and beatings have become commonplace in Israel. According to reliable Israeli sources, each year one thousand to fifteen hundred Palestinians are interrogated by the Shin Bet (security service), and 58 percent of them are subjected to interrogation that employs torture.[57] We have to let statistics like this sink in.

This aspect of life in Israel is perhaps the most disturbing — if village and home destruction were not bad enough. Human rights abuses are so acute in this country that human rights organizations led by both Arabs and Jews have grown rapidly. Most abuses can be organized into the following categories.

Closures. When there is conflict in regions of the West Bank or Gaza, Israel places entire villages under "curfew," not permitting movement. In 1998, there were twenty-one of these days, and in 1999, there were thirteen. But in areas where there has been crises with settlers, Palestinians are placed under curfew while settlers are not. Today, since the conflicts of the so-called "Second Intifada," Israel has kept large areas of the West Bank under sustained closure. Recently (July 2002), Bethlehem's population was under "house arrest" for four straight weeks. The psychological burden this condition places on families is stupefying. Children cannot go outside and small Arab homes become prisons crowded with extended families. Many families do not let their children go near windows for fear that they will be shot. Within days, anger and depression become regular features of life.

An example: Hebron is a city of thirty thousand Arabs, and in the center of town live four hundred of Israel's most aggressive settlers who are guarded by twelve hundred soldiers (three soldiers for each settler!). On February 25, 1994, Baruch Goldstein, a settler from Brooklyn, New York, entered the large mosque in Hebron during Muslim prayer. Dressed in his military reserve uniform and using his government-issued automatic rifle, he killed over twenty-nine Palestinians as they prayed. Arab men finally stopped him and killed him with a fire extinguisher. Today Goldstein is viewed by the settlers as a martyr and hero.

Immediately after the shooting, the Arabs of Hebron were placed under a forty-day curfew — but no curfew was placed on the settlers. Imagine the effect of such an action on businesses and families. The curfew was so severe

---

57. *Ha'Aretz*, December 10, 1998.

that more men died trying to get to the hospital than died in the shooting itself. Soldiers at roadblocks enforced the curfew despite the wounds of the victims.

Within the year, the army brought in bulldozers, closed the Arab markets around the mosque, and destroyed many of the shops. Immediately, new settlement buildings were built where the market had been and more Israeli settlers moved in.

Curfews are inflexible. Since 1995, over ten infants have died because mothers were not permitted to take their children for medical care. Listen to the words of Shireen Tawfiq Al-Haddad, a mother in Hebron:

> On Saturday, August 22, 1998, at about 2:00 p.m., I was changing the diapers of the triplets who were born to me on May 12. When I turned to Qussai, the third baby, I saw that he had thrown up and his responses were not alert. He was breathing but weak. My neighbor, Um Abed, suggested I take him to the hospital.
>
> I immediately rushed out of the house with the child. Opposite our house there were two Israeli jeeps full of soldiers. I went over to them and told them that my son was ill and that I wanted to take him to the hospital. The soldiers told me they had no orders to let me through and that I couldn't go out because there was a curfew in our neighborhood. After I waited an hour, I left the soldiers, went around behind them to another street where I stopped a local car that was passing by. The driver stopped and took me and my son to the hospital.
>
> At the hospital my son Qussai was pronounced dead. He was three months and ten days old. They wrote that the cause of death was acute pneumonia. We went home to wash the baby and put him in a shroud.[58]

Immigration/Reunification. Immigration laws in most countries of the world, including Israel, permit close family members to reunite with the citizens of their country and gain permanent status. Thus if an Israeli marries an American while in college in Boston, she can bring her new husband to Israel and he can become a citizen. In regions where there has been war and the movement of refugees, this problem becomes acute. Families may be separated and suddenly find themselves on opposite sides of fences. On the Israel-Lebanon border, for example, families daily meet to speak through the fence, holding up newborn babies for grandparents to see. Even weddings have taken place along the fence so that other relatives can participate "through the barbed wire."

Israel does not, however, recognize family reunification for Palestinians in the Occupied Territories. Over ten thousand Palestinians live separated from spouses and children. Israel has a quota for these permits, and today

---

58. *B'Tselem Quarterly for Human Rights in the Occupied Territories* (December 1998): 26.

over thirteen thousand requests are pending. At the current quota rate, these requests (even if approved) will not be granted until 2006. In fact, Israel's high court of justice has accepted the government's position that Palestinian petitioners in the West Bank and Gaza have no "right" to family reunification.

This problem is aggravated by "right of return" laws. Anyone claiming Jewish heritage can apply for citizenship to Israel, move to the country, and begin receiving public aid and benefits. But Palestinians whose homes still stand in the country, whose family can trace its heritage back hundreds of years, who languish in refugee camps just across the border, are not permitted to return to their homes and families.

Arrest/Detention. Suspected of political activity or crime, Palestinians are commonly arrested and detained without trial. To be in areas of East Jerusalem or the West Bank and witness Palestinians being taken away by jeep is not uncommon. From 1987 until 1998, Israel issued 20,000 detention orders, which placed over 5,000 people in prison for up to five years each. Looking at the number of detainees year by year gives perspective to the problem: In 1996, Israel held 267 people in detention; in 1997, 354; in 1998, 82. Osama Jamil Barham, for example, was arrested in 1993 and remained in prison for five years without having any charges pressed against him. No trial. No defense. But he was one of the lucky ones. Dr. Anat Matar, a philosophy professor in Tel Aviv, "adopted him" and along with her two children wrote him and became an advocate for his release. Just imagine if your spouse was picked up by the police one day and disappeared for five years.

When these cases do go to trial, defending the accused becomes virtually impossible. In fact, I don't know whether to laugh or weep when reading a transcript from a military trial. The defense cannot hear the evidence in order to fight it. In 1994, Hasan Fataftah was asking for release from detention with his lawyer, the well-known Leah Tsemel. A partial transcript:

Tsemel: What are the suspicions against him?

Prosecutor: That's in the classified information.

Tsemel: Why was his detention requested?

Prosecutor: In the classified.

Tsemel: I request you give some answer.

Prosecutor: I can't detail more than what's written in the order.

Tsemel: How many pieces of information were brought before the [military] commander? How many events?

Prosecutor: In the classified.

Tsemel: I request the gentleman to answer.

Prosecutor: Less than 100, more than 50.

Tsemel: Are we talking about violent or military activity?

Prosecutor: I can't respond.

Tsemel: Are there pieces of information about conducting or planning [violent activity]?

Prosecutor: I will not answer that because it implicates the sources of information.

Tsemel: Why was the detainee detained?

Prosecutor: Because the accumulation of NSM [negative security material] allowed the order.[59]

Israeli women attorneys are the best-known among advocates in these military courts. Women like Allegra Pacheco, Felicia Langer, Lea Tsemel, Tamar Peleg, and Lynda Brayer work alongside Palestinian attorneys in some of Israel's hardest cases. Pacheco, thirty-four, grew up in New York in a Jewish family and graduated from Columbia University law school. In 1988, Lea Tsemel (in the above transcript) sponsored her for a three-month internship. Pacheco comments, "I was inspired by her. I decided I wanted to do what she does." She worked in New York and Washington for a few years but was shocked into action by Baruch Goldstein's 1994 massacre in Hebron (described earlier). In one try she passed the Israeli bar exam and that same year gained Israeli citizenship. Her busy office in Bethlehem welcomes Palestinians who are at their wits end and who cannot pay a high-profile lawyer.[60]

Prison and Torture. Throughout the First Intifada from 1987 until 1992 the number of prisoners in Israeli prisons was staggering. Arabs were imprisoned for everything from stone throwing to failing to carry an ID card. Six months imprisonment without trial was commonplace, and no prisoner had access to the normal systems of Israeli justice. Military courts — which kept charges and evidence classified — issued judgments without public review.

But perhaps the worst aspect of the imprisonments has been the torture experienced by Palestinians while in captivity. While Israel adamantly

---

59. *B'Tselem Quarterly for Human Rights in the Occupied Territories* (December 1998): 14–15.
60. "Woman on the Edge," *Jerusalem Post Magazine,* March 6, 1998, 16–18.

denied that such practices did take place, on February 11, 2000, the government made an astounding public admission that this was indeed the practice from 1988 to 1992. The report was written in 1997 and held back for three years because of its explosive implications. Common practices included beatings, hanging prisoners upside down, sleep deprivation, food deprivation, restricted toilet use, suffocation, "the cupboard,"[61] electric shock, burning, violent shaking, painful postures, and covering their heads with filthy sacks. At desert prisons in the south (such as Ansar), captives were made to sit unclothed in the sun tied to a stake.[62]

"Shabah" is well known in the prisons. Here the prisoner is made to sit with a sack on his head in a small child's chair. The front legs of the chair are shortened, making it hard to balance. Hands are crossed and tied behind the back (behind the chair) and legs are shackled. Both ankle and wrist shackles cut through the skin. 'Abd a-Rahman Khader al Ahmar was "interrogated" for fifty-three days without trial. Released in 1998, he later described his experience with Israeli police who used *Shabah:*

> Twice I fainted from being shaken. Sometimes they would shake me three or four times a day. When I fainted, they revived me and there was someone there — maybe a medic. They took a short break and then they started using various methods again. Almost everyday I underwent shaking. Your body is finished, destroyed. Your whole body hurts. Your head aches and its impossible to think for lack of sleep. You feel dizzy. Everyone thinks about what is important to them in this situation. As far as morale goes, I felt fine, I felt that I was managing to withstand all these things and that I wasn't letting them win. After about a week or ten days I began to feel really sick. I began to vomit. At first they said they weren't worried about my condition but only that the floor was getting dirty. I also vomited in court. I vomited for two years.

In September 1999, the Israeli High Court of Justice ruled that torture (or "extreme pressure") may not be used on any prisoners. But as recent reports from Amnesty International indicate, this ruling has not been enforced. Since September 1999, eight Palestinians citizens have been "extrajudicially" killed because of beatings and excessive force.[63] They were killed while under police custody.

Deportation. Israel is one of the only democracies in the world to deport residents outside its borders as a punitive measure: taking accused persons

---

61. The prisoner is placed alone in a one-meter-by-one-meter wooden cell that is completely dark; he is handcuffed, with a sack over the head. Light and air come in only under the door. This continues for days while the prisoner hears screams and threatening sounds.

62. For a comprehensive list of types of torture, see *www.alhaq.org/frames_issues.html.*

63. See the Amnesty report:
www.web.amnesty.org/web/ar2000web.nsf/reg/27f43cfc8a8247df802568f2005a7622.

by bus or helicopter and carrying them across the border (often Lebanon) and depositing them there — never to return. This practice is strictly against international law (Art. 49, Geneva Convention) and because of international pressure, Israel stopped the practice in 1992. But what has happened to, say, young men who have been permanently banished to the dangerous hills of Lebanon when their home is in Jerusalem?

A quick glance at the numbers of deportations is telling. From 1967 until 1986, Israel deported 993 Palestinian prisoners. They were simply dumped in the hills of Lebanon. During the Intifada (1987–92), Israel deported 529. The most heinous example of this came in the mass deportation of December 16, 1992. Buses carried 415 Palestinians blindfolded and handcuffed into southern Lebanon. All information about it was censored from the press. Nevertheless news reached the media, and despite attorneys' pleas, Israel's High Court of Justice sustained the decision to take the men north. On December 18 the U.N. Security Council unanimously adopted a resolution (799) condemning the action based on Geneva Convention rules.

Violence in the Streets. On Sunday night, June 29, 1998, Muhammad Khalil a-Dabai, twenty-three, was in his bedroom asleep in the Shuafat refugee camp. Suddenly he awoke to see fifteen soldiers with two dogs surrounding his bed. He screamed, "What are you doing in my bedroom?" His account:

> My wife was very frightened, she is only 16 and a half. They said they had a search warrant, and they started to search. In fact, they didn't search, they just took everything, every dress or shirt in the closet, and put it next to the dog's nose so it could smell it. We were married 20 days ago and we bought a new living room set 12 days ago. They demolished it. In the end they told me: You're under arrest. They took me and held me under interrogation until the following afternoon. They did not torture me physically. In the interrogation they claimed I had weapons and the next day took me to court and extended my remand for eight days. After eight days I was released on bail of 1,000 shekels [$250]. In fact, they had nothing to prove against me but they caused me huge damages, they came into the bedroom where I was with my bride, and that is contrary to all custom. This is a great injury.[64]

From 1987 until mid-1998, 1,648 people have been killed in Israel/ Palestine: 1,463 Palestinians, 178 Israelis (mostly settlers), and 7 foreign citizens. This land witnesses breathtaking violence on both sides of its struggle, but these numbers make clear that the ratio (8:1) is unbalanced. Of these deaths, three hundred were Palestinian children under the age of seventeen. Four similar Israeli children died.

---

64. *B'Tselem Quarterly for Human Rights in the Occupied Territories* (December 1998): 19.

One of the most distressing studies I have seen was published in 1988 by Al Haq (in Ramallah), a Palestinian human rights organization.[65] The study is called *Punishing a Nation: Human Rights Violations During the Palestinian Uprising, December 1987 to December 1988*.[66] The volume itemizes Israel's record of abuse and torture among the Palestinians both in and outside of prison. During the Intifada, the army had cannons that shot gravel and glass at crowds. Fortunately this machine has been retired.

Still today the army fires so-called "rubber bullets" at youths throwing stones.[67] These projectiles are rubber-coated steel bullets that have little to do with "rubber." In fact, referring to them as "rubber" is one of the world's great euphemisms. The Palestine Red Crescent Society can even provide excellent photographs of these on the web.[68] The army has strict rules on their use: they cannot be used under forty meters from the target and must be aimed at the legs, but in the mind of the soldier, "rubber" bullets can be fired indiscriminately (as the injury record shows). In Israel, the rubber bullet has become a standard tool for dispersing demonstrations. Between 1987 and 1998, fifty-eight Palestinians were killed by rubber bullets — twenty-eight of them children, most under thirteen years old. And hundreds — too many to count — have been injured. To date, only three soldiers who killed with rubber have gone to trial, and of these only one received a censure in his personal file. Make no mistake. Rubber bullets are deadly fire.[69]

Concentrated tear gas is also used, and its strength is so toxic that its use is illegal in the United States. In fact the Israeli supplier, the Pennsylvania company TransTechnology, clearly prints on each can that it may not be used in enclosed places, but these instructions are ignored.[70] Its repeated use in alleys and buildings has killed many and led countless mothers to

---

65. *www.alhaq.org*.

66. The volume is carefully organized with well-documented cases of abuses. Chapters include "Use of Torture" (chap. 1), "Obstruction of Medical Treatment" (chap. 2), "Settler Use of Excessive Force" (chap. 3), "Methods of Punishment" (chap. 4), "Curfews" (chap. 5), "The Administration of Justice" (chap. 6), "Economic Sanctions" (chap. 7), "Repression of Education" (chap. 8), and "Repression of Organizational Activity" (chap. 9). See also Amnesty International's *Israel and the Occupied Territories: The Military Justice System in the Occupied Territories: Detention, Interrogation and Trial Procedures* (July 1991).

67. The army used soft rubber bullets first in 1989 but they proved ineffective. Plastic was used, but they were too dangerous. In 1990, rubber bullets with steel centers were introduced and continue in service today. "B'Tselem Report: 'Rubber Bullet's Fatal," *Ha'Aretz*, December 6, 1998. See also J. Mahoney, "Israel's Anti-Civilian Weapons," *The Link* 34, no. 1 (January–March 2001): 2–13.

68. *www.palestinercs.org/bullet_types_images.htm*.

69. "As Euphemisms Go, 'Rubber Bullets' is a Killer," *Ha'aretz*, December 13, 1998.

70. For information on Israel's use of tear gas, see the Palestinian Red Crescent Society's website: *www.palestinercs.org*.

miscarry their unborn children. On May 23, 1999, Israelis from the settlement of Kiryat Sefer took over a sizable portion of land belonging to the neighboring Arab village of Dir Kadis. Bulldozers began cutting hills fifty meters from the village, and Dir Kadis's residents came out protesting since they owned title to the land. When they tried to stop the bulldozers, the army intervened, shooting tear gas at the Arabs. Sa'ida Haddad fled into her home and soldiers fired gas through the window. Sa'ida was in her fifth month of pregnancy; when she arrived at the hospital along with many village children, she miscarried.[71]

Let us look at a case study. In 1980, sixteen-year-old Tariq Shumali was accused of throwing a stone at an Israeli vehicle near his home in Beit Sahour. He was beaten so badly that he had to be hospitalized for internal kidney hemorrhaging. No other family members had done anything wrong, nor was anyone given a trial or defense. Yet the boy's father was jailed, his sister was fired from her job as a teacher, the family home was sealed off by soldiers, and the family was deported to an abandoned refugee camp in Jericho, where they lived in a mud-brick hut. The army wanted to make the family an example to the rest of the town.[72]

Time magazine, in its August 31, 1992, issue printed a report of Israeli undercover violence on the West Bank.[73] Military commandos (special units called *sayarot*) dressed like Palestinians infiltrate village homes and assassinate Arab activists. In August, Munir Jaradat, age eighteen, was found in the village of Silat al Harithiya and accused of belonging to "the Red Eagles," a violent Palestinian organization. There was no arrest, no trial. Munir was shot dead on the spot.

Leading Israeli legislators have been outraged by these death squads. Israeli Education Minister Shulamit Aloni said she was opposed "to 18 and nineteen-year-old boys [in the army] passing judgment on Palestinians and then carrying out death sentences against them."[74] B'Tselem says that only half of the Arabs killed by the commandos are even armed. In one well-publicized incident, Rashid Ghanim, twenty-three, was playing soccer near his home. Four commandos rushed him and shot the unarmed man in cold blood.

---

71. Reported by Gush Shalom and the Other Israel at *msanews.mynet.net/MSANEWS/199811/19981130.12.html*. During the Intifada in December 1987, the United States rushed 150,000 canisters of this banned gas to Israel from a plant in Saltsburg, Pennsylvania.

72. C. Chapman, *Whose Promised Land?* (Herts, Eng.: Lion, 1983), 179.

73. "Deadly Force. How Israeli Commandos Are Waging an Undercover War in the Occupied Territories," *Time*, August 31, 1992, 49–50.

74. Ibid.

In 1992, a Gaza mental health survey was conducted to measure the results of violence-related trauma to children: Out of an estimated 150,000 children (aged eight to fifteen) in Gaza, more than 63,000 had been beaten by soldiers, 7,000 had suffered fractures from those beatings, 35,000 had been struck with some form of Israeli military ammunition, and more than 130,000 had suffered the effects of toxic tear gas five times more concentrated than any tear gas used in the United States.[75]

Numbers like this must be placed in perspective. If the same ratios were applied to the United States (where 53 percent of the population is under age seventeen), the following statistics would result: Over five years, 5,460,000 of the youth would be shot at, beaten, or teargassed by foreign soldiers. The scenario is staggering. Case studies are in such abundance from every source that few deny them anymore

Take one horrific case published by the Swedish Save the Children Fund. The incident is summarized by J. A. Graff, whose Canadian publication, *Palestinian Children and Israeli State Violence,* chronicles 138 case studies of military violence to children.

> On February 10, 1989, [four-year-old] Ali aimed his toy gun and made click-ing noises at a passing Israeli patrol. He was playing near his house in Jabalya refugee camp (Gaza). Seeing this, three soldiers raced over. One grabbed the toy and stomped on it, and then grabbed Ali's right hand as another solider held the child from behind. The third soldier "began to pound Ali's out-stretched arm with his wooden truncheon. The soldier holding Ali's arm out slapped him hard across the face over and over again." Neighbors tried to intervene but were prevented by the rest of the patrol. The soldiers "contin-ued slapping his face and pounding his arm with the truncheon until the arm broke." Then another soldier "lifted Ali high into the air and dashed him to the pavement. Just as he hit the ground, the soldier who had been slapping his face struck him on the left shoulder with the butt of his rifle.... When the three soldiers finished with Ali, they rejoined the patrol and continued down the street."[76]

Today this cycle of violence is continuing. Each year when Israel cele-brates its national independence day on May 14, Palestinians recognize their own holiday called the "Nakbah" — which means "the calamity." While Israelis dance and sing songs of freedom, Palestinians sing songs of captiv-ity and march in the streets, and conflict often results. One can see lines

---

75. J. A. Graff, "An Open Letter to Mrs. Clinton," *The Link* 26, no. 2 (May–June 1993): 3.
76. Ibid. Quotations are from the Swedish report. See Graff's full treatment, *Palestinian Children and Israeli State Violence* (Toronto: Near East Cultural and Education Foundation of Canada, 1991).

of refugees marching, say, from Nazareth to their lost village of Saffuriya, now occupied by Jews and renamed Tzipori. On May 14, Saffuriya/Tzipori is surrounded by soldiers in case violence exists.

On May 14, 2000, such violence erupted throughout the country. Palestinians, exhausted by seven years of fruitless peace talks (since the Oslo Accords, 1993), took to the streets. The result? Over four hundred young Palestinians were hospitalized through shootings and seven were dead. And later that same year, even worse conflicts erupted leaving hundreds of Palestinians dead. But this time, Israelis decided to retaliate with breathtaking force. Field-grade weapons were turned on the cities and villages of Palestine in response to demonstrations. A pastor who works in Bethlehem wrote to me via e-mail saying, "My God, we're under siege. No one under forty has seen anything like this." He described tanks and helicopter gunships firing into residential centers of Christian Palestinian villages such as Beit Sahour and Beit Jalla. In such conflicts, the children always suffer most.

Recently Bethlehem was under siege for weeks. A pastor in the Bethlehem Lutheran Christmas Church, Mitri Raheb, recently told me a typical story: A Christian family in his church was asleep when they were awakened by the thud of helicopter rotors. Suddenly a missile ripped through their home, and the family with their young children ran screaming into their olive orchards. A five-year-old girl named Alice hid behind olive trees as the Apache lifted over the burning house and chased the children with floodlights for ten minutes. Rev. Raheb fears that Alice's trauma may never go away. She is haunted by nightmares. To date, four Christian families in Mitri's church have lost their homes to Israeli terror.

I have interviewed victims, I have read innumerable first-person reports, I have talked with pastors whose teenagers have been arrested and tortured without reason, and I have witnessed unprovoked violence myself in Israel. That the cycle of violence continues in this land is no wonder. The biblical prophets would not be amused.

Am I a stakeholder in this problem? Indeed. As a Christian, I feel the obligation of standing with others who are likewise Christian. Likewise I feel the obligation to speak out when injustice hurts people, any people, whom God loves. But I am already a stakeholder as an American. When American tax dollars supply Israel with $3.5 billion per year in aid—that's over five hundred dollars per person in Israel coming from our U.S. taxes—I am contributing directly to the welfare and the life of Israel. Over the last seven years, the United States has sold over $7.4 billion in arms to Israel. That is staggering. The missile and the Apache attack helicopter that destroyed Alice's home were made in America.

Perhaps the most troubling and the most obvious problem is that Israel is holding almost 3 million people — the population of the West Bank and the Gaza Strip — captive. Much like the "townships" of South Africa, the residents of these places have severe restrictions on their freedom.

Israel captured these areas in 1967 but has not dealt with the problem of their populations. Limited sovereignty has been given to the Palestinian Authority (the P.A.) in a select number of cities, but vast areas remain under military control. Many of these towns still pay taxes which finance their occupation armies and do not bring the social services Israeli towns enjoy. One village outside Bethlehem (Beit Sahour) refused to pay its taxes in the late 1980s, arguing, as a man there told me, "It is the American principle. No taxation without representation." The village of Beit Sahour suffered severely for the tax rebellion but has been visited and honored by Desmond Tutu and Jimmy Carter for its peaceful efforts.

While peace conferences continue, these people languish without hope. Around Jerusalem and across the Occupied Territories, Arabs watch in vain as new Israeli settlements are built weekly, as new roads are cut into the hillsides, securing Israel's grip on the land. The Palestinians feel despair and a fueling of the flames of radicalism.

But let's be clear. This sort of terror is tearing as well at the Israeli soul. The Jewish tradition which understands justice and suffering knows in its heart that something is wrong. As I have noted, Israeli peace groups are growing, Israeli lawyers who oppose the government defend Palestinians, some soldiers have refused to serve in the Occupied Territories, and the Israeli public is almost divided evenly on whether to give the Palestinians what they need. One evangelical friend of mine was driving away from his home in Jerusalem recently when he was stopped by a roadblock. He was offended by soldiers in his neighborhood, stopping vehicles, talking through his car window with a machine gun pointing at them. "Please take your machine gun away from my family while you are talking to us," he said. The young soldier answered plaintively, "I am more upset with this gun than you are. You might be surprised."

Religious Compromise

Israel functions like a secular state where biblical allusions are used to define and clarify national history. Ultraconservative Jews do live there, but they by no means make up the majority. Many are critical of the lack of faith in their own country. Some harshly critical rabbis even call for the dismantling of the Israeli state (as a quick search on the web under "Jews against Zionism" reveals). In Israel, Jewishness has to do with culture, not necessarily with personal spiritual devotion. As one Israeli leader told me in 1992, fewer than 30 percent of Israelis are actually practicing their religion. Thus the state recognizes citizenship applications of Jews even if they claim to be atheists. Atheism does not invalidate one's Judaism.[77]

This observation is legitimate because, as we have seen, possession of the land is tied to obedience to the covenant. God's people cannot make a religious claim to the land without exhibiting religious devotion to the covenant. I am not talking here about the reconstruction of the Temple and the revival of its sacrificial ceremonies. I am describing a quality of spirituality, a deep interpretation of life and God's relation to national history. A secular outlook has taken over Israel, and many of us would be hard pressed to distinguish this nation from another secular state.

What We Are Not Being Told

Sadly we are not being told about the relationship between modern-day Israel and the land. We are not being told that Israel is taking land in spite of the just complaints of the families living on the land. Israel is committing the sin of Ahab.

Christian pastors throughout the Middle East are trying to be heard. Some have written books telling their stories.[78] Many have traveled to the United States and Europe speaking out in conferences, seeking support from churches and mission agencies. These voices of these credible men and women are just now being heard as evangelical publishers have published their stories. They are courageous people of God whose anguished reports deserve an audience. Every refugee camp and village in Israel/Palestine is filled with stories of families who fled and then found new barbed wire keeping them from going home. When Christians in the West discover these stories, when congregations meet these pastors, their hearts are moved. Since 1995 many American churches — from Houston to Washington, D.C. — have established "sister" relations with Palestinian congregations to support them and hear their stories.

As Christians we need to take a closer look at the character of Israel. If Israel's appeal to nationhood, to possessing the land, is buttressed by an

---

77. Studies of the complex relation between politics and religion in Israel are abundant. See C. S. Liebman and E. Don-Yehiya, *Religion and Politics in Israel* (Bloomington: University of Indiana Press, 1984); idem, *Civil Religion in Israel: Traditional Judaism and Political Culture in the Jewish State* (Berkeley: University of California Press, 1983); Abramov, *Perpetual Dilemma.*

78. E. Chacour, *Blood Brothers* (Old Tappan, N.J.: Revell, 1984); Rantisi, *Blessed Are the Peacemakers;* E. Chacour, *We Belong to the Land: The Story of a Palestinian Israeli Who Lives for Peace and Reconciliation* (New York: Harper & Row, 1990); M. Raheb, *I Am a Palestinian Christian* (Minneapolis: Fortress, 1995).

appeal to biblical promise, then its record of national life must be open to inspection. If the link to the biblical promise is the basis of Israeli nationhood, then modern Israel must be judged by the standards that the prophets applied to biblical Israel. Today Palestinian Christian leaders in the land, Christian relief agencies (evangelical and mainline), and secular agencies (such as the Red Cross, the United Nations, and Amnesty International) all offer the same complaint: Israel is not promoting justice.

The very Scriptures in which Israel has anchored its hope are the Scriptures that judge Israel today. Jesus was outraged by the complacency and belligerence of Jewish leaders who condemned him. They appealed to their Scriptures to justify their privileged position as God's people to reject what God was saying to them through Jesus. "Do not think that I shall accuse you to the Father; it is Moses who accuses you, on whom you set your hope" (John 5:45). *The same Bible that bears the promises of God likewise bears the expectations of God.* When these expectations are ignored, when righteousness is thrown to the wind, the prophetic voice cannot be silenced: God's displeasure will be stirred and his judgment will be swift.

In spring 2001, the director of World Vision/Jerusalem was visiting Hebron with his staff and there overheard a tour given to Canadian Jews by local Jewish settlers. With a sweep of her hand, the tour host said, "Be confident that it may take time but we will evict all these Arabs...slowly, slowly we will build on the blood of the Jews." When the World Vision staff engaged the group and challenged the fairness of their views, one Canadian responded, "God gave us this land...we are chosen, it is ours, and if we have to kill twice as many Palestinian animals as we have already we will do it." The WV staff responded: "But doesn't the Bible say that the 'chosen people' are chosen for service and obedience to help the poor and needy — like it says in Isaiah 41:17?" The Canadian then screamed, "That is not in my Bible! It must be only in yours."[79]

---

79. *World Vision Reflection 59,* July 6, 2001, "That Is Not in My Bible."

Part Three

THE NEW TESTAMENT
AND THE LAND

Chapter Nine

JESUS AND
THE EARLY CHRISTIANS

I am a Palestinian [Christian] living under Israeli occupation. My captor daily seeks ways to make life harder for me. He encircles my people with barbed wire; he builds walls around us, and his army sets many boundaries around us. He succeeds in keeping thousands of us in camps and prisons. Yet despite all these efforts, he has not succeeded in taking my dreams from me. I have a dream that one day I will wake up and see two equal peoples living next to each other, coexisting in the land of Palestine, stretching from the Mediterranean to the Jordan.   — Rev. Mitri Raheb, Bethlehem Pastor

After his assistant had served us Arabic coffee, I asked Father George Makhlouf a question sure to make him uncomfortable. "How can you argue with the Israeli claim to own this land since God gave it to the Jews in the Old Testament? Israeli Jews have inherited the promises to Abraham, have they not?" Father George (as he is called) is no stranger to such questions. As parish priest of St. George's Greek Orthodox Church in Ramallah, he has been fielding them for years. "The church," he began, "has inherited the promises of Israel. The church is actually the new Israel. What Abraham was promised, Christians now possess because they are Abraham's true spiritual children just as the New Testament teaches."[1]

In Father George's view, what I have written so far would have only marginal value for Christian thought. We cannot read the Old Testament and talk about its application today as if the New Testament had never been written. The New Testament announces a new covenant filled with new promises. In some cases, it neglects older promises; in some cases, it refashions them, making them spiritual gifts that were barely anticipated by their original recipients such as Abraham. For example, the book of Hebrews says that Abraham — who received the promise of land and entered it — *never really received what was promised,* but looked on it from afar since the true promise was not in the land itself (Heb. 11:8–16). The New

---

1. Personal interview, March 23, 1992.

Testament goes even further, also identifying Christian believers as the true children of Abraham. In other words, Christians are the heirs of Abraham's original promises, continuing the lineage of those who — like Abraham — believe in faith.

The Greek Orthodox tradition of Father George has been consistent in defending this view throughout the centuries. From the earliest years, the Middle Eastern churches have claimed the promises of the Old Testament for their own.[2] This concept shows up in Orthodox icons. Churches display beautiful pictures (or icons) of Old Testament stories whose truths have now been swept up by the Christian tradition and "baptized" with new meaning. Father George's sanctuary in the Old Quarter of Ramallah is a case in point.

"THE LAND" IN THE FIRST CENTURY

One of the surprising things about the New Testament is that it never refers to the land promises of Abraham directly. This silence is peculiar, especially when we recall how many times the Old Testament mentions this theme. According to Walter Brueggemann, the theme of "the land" is "the most important theme in biblical theology."[3] But in the New Testament we struggle to find even a handful of references. Was "land" an interest of Jesus? Did Paul reflect on the nation of Israel and the identity of the church? If Christians are "children of Abraham," do they inherit Abraham's promises?

The first question we must ask is whether or not the people of Israel were talking about the land in Jesus' day, whether they were as interested in the land promises of Abraham in this later period as they were in the Old Testament. And if there is interest, we need to probe the silence of the New Testament. Does the New Testament neglect this theme intentionally? Is its silence theologically significant?

The premier study of this subject of "land" in the New Testament belongs to W. D. Davies.[4] Davies makes clear that the rabbis in the New Testament

---

2. See P. Richardson, *Israel in the Apostolic Church* (Cambridge: Cambridge University Press, 1969), 1–32.

3. W. Brueggemann, *The Land: Place as Gift, Promise and Challenge in Biblical Faith* (Philadelphia: Fortress, 1977; 2d ed. 2002), cited in P. Walker, "An Interpretation of the Land in the New Testament," in *The Bible and the Land: An Encounter,* ed. L. Loden, P. Walker, and M. Wood (Jerusalem: Musalaha, 2000), 108.

4. See W. D. Davies, *The Gospel and the Land: Early Christianity and Jewish Territorial Doctrine* (Berkeley: University of California Press, 1974), and *The Territorial Dimension of Judaism* (Berkeley: University of California Press, 1982; reprinted with a symposium and further reflections, Minneapolis: Fortress, 1991). For a dialogue between Palestinian Christians and Messianic Jews, see Loden, Walker, and Wood, eds., *The Bible and the Land.* Also see P. Johnston and P. Walker, eds., *The Land of Promise: Biblical, Theological, and Contemporary Perspectives* (Downers Grove, Ill.: InterVarsity Press, 2000).

era did indeed have an ardent interest in the "land." Writings from this period refer to "the Holy Land," frequently describing it as "a goodly land" and "a land which is in thy sight the most precious of all lands." The land of Israel/Palestine is "extensive and beautiful," "pleasant and glorious," and promised for those who are faithful to God.[5] This devotion increased when the people considered how they lived under the heel of the Roman army and were not free to enjoy the bounty of the land as God had planned. In describing the work of the coming Messiah, the first-century Psalms of Solomon says,

> And he shall gather together a holy people whom he will lead in righteousness;
> And he shall distribute them according to their tribes *upon the land*
> And the alien and the foreigner will no longer live with them. (17:26–28, emphasis added)

The rabbis could not separate Israel, God, and the land. Possessing the land of Israel/Palestine was intrinsic to being Jewish. The land was the place of God's revelation and the principal place where he could be known. The volume of oral laws from this period — the Mishnah — devotes fully 35 percent of its pages to issues connected with the land. The Mishnah acknowledges that even the laws recorded in the Old Testament Scriptures presupposed residence in the land: agricultural tithes applied to produce grown in the land; cities of refuge crucial for civil law could be built only in the land. Listen to the words of the Mishnah itself:

> There are ten degrees of holiness. The Land of Israel is holier than any other land. Wherein lies its holiness? In that from it they may bring [the offerings of] the sheaf, the first fruits, and the two loaves, which they may not bring from any other land. (*Kiddushin* 1:9f.)

The centrality of the land is clear even in the prayers of the Jews in this period. The so-called "Eighteen Benedictions" were recited three times each day as an expression of daily piety. Note how Benedictions 14, 16, and 18 emphasize that devotion to the land of Israel and the city of Jerusalem is necessary for faith.

> *Benediction 14.* Be merciful, O Lord our God, in Thy great mercy towards Israel Thy people, and towards Jerusalem Thy city, and towards Zion, the abiding place of Thy glory, and towards Thy temple and Thy habitation, and towards the kingdom of the house of David, Thy righteous anointed one. Blessed art Thou, O Lord God of David, the builder of Jerusalem.

---

5. Davies, *Territorial Dimension of Judaism*, reprint ed., 19.

Benediction 16. Accept us, O Lord our God, and dwell in Zion; and may Thy servants serve thee in Jerusalem. Blessed art Thou, O Lord, whom in reverent fear we worship.

Benediction 18. Bestow Thy peace upon Israel Thy people and upon Thy city and upon Thine inheritance, and bless us, all of us together. Blessed art Thou, O Lord, who makes peace.

In one Jewish commentary on Numbers 34:2, we read reflections on saying blessings during meals.

Of all the blessings there is none more precious than the one, "For the land and for the food." For our Rabbis have said that any one who does not mention in the grace after meals the blessing, "for the land and for the food," has not fulfilled his duty. The Holy One, blessed be He, said, "The Land of Israel is more precious to me than everything."[6]

The preciousness of the land to Israel is illustrated in one more way. Ezekiel taught that the land of Israel was at the center of the earth (38:12; 5:5), and so Jewish writings can describe a journey to Jerusalem as a journey to the center of the world (Ethiopic Enoch 26:1). Another writing even refers to Mt. Zion as "the center of the earth's navel" (Jubilees 8:19)! The framework is clear: Israel is the center of the world, Jerusalem is the center of Israel, and the Temple is at the center of Jerusalem. Even Jews living outside Israel (in the Diaspora) sought to be buried in the land: it was like being buried on an altar of atonement.[7]

The question of land and inheritance — indeed, the question of Israel's political future in the land of Abraham — was as deeply debated in the first century as it is today. This fact explains the number of uprisings that took place during this era when passionate Jewish believers fought to eliminate the oppressive yoke of Roman control. The importance of land and inheritance also explains the zealous interest in the Messiah who would come to restore the land to its rightful heirs.

After Jerusalem was destroyed by Rome in 70 c.e., this Jewish devotion increased as writers described longingly the way life had been before the war. The loss of the land in the destruction of Jerusalem was so acute that the event was acknowledged each year by three weeks of fasting, which concluded on the ninth of Ab, the fifth month of the Jewish calendar.[8]

---

6. Num. Rabbah 23:7 on Numbers 34:2, cited in Davies, *The Gospel and the Land*, 68.

7. M. Wilson, *Our Father Abraham: Jewish Roots of the Christian Faith* (Grand Rapids, Mich.: Eerdmans, 1989), 260. This burial tradition explains the tremendous number of Jewish graves all around the east side of Jerusalem.

8. Today the "Ninth of Ab" is still celebrated in Israel. On that evening, Israel recalls the destruction of Jerusalem both by the Babylonians (586 B.C.E.) and by the Romans (70 C.E.). Jews customarily read the book of Lamentations aloud that night as a feature of their devotions.

JESUS
AND THE LAND

We have to keep this first-century background in mind when we open our Gospels. The notion of messiahship and land were intimately linked. Jesus was not immune to these pressures. Any "messiah" who was uninterested in these issues or who seemed ignorant of them would be dismissed quickly by the public. When Jesus was once asked if tax payments to Caesar were lawful, it was *not* an innocent question. The query likely referred to a tax revolt that would signal his resistance to the Roman occupation of the land. Refusal to pay taxes meant *resistance*. And of course, Jesus refused to join their ranks (Mark 12:14–17).

Jesus had to be cautious with the subject of land because it was loaded with politically explosive ideas. Following the feeding of the five thousand, we learn that the zeal of the crowds became dangerous and many wanted to come and make him "king by force" (John 6:15). What were they thinking? Do they see Jesus as the inspiration for their political aspirations? As a revolutionary leader? As a rival to Rome? As the Messiah who will remove Roman control from the land? The feeding re-created the great manna miracle of Moses — who foreshadowed the coming Messiah (Deut. 18:15–22). And if Jesus was a messiah *like Moses,* he too would lead his people to their promised land. The scene is so inflammatory that Jesus must flee into the mountains.

Later, when Jesus arrives in Jerusalem, even his closest followers get caught up in this zeal. They are wondering if Jesus' arrival will in some manner be the catalyst that will bring God's powerful kingdom to earth. Luke tells us, "He was near Jerusalem and the people thought that the kingdom of God was going to appear *at once*" (19:11).

If talk about claiming the land was central to Jewish consciousness, certainly Jesus gives us some hints, some suggestion that he understand the debates of his day. He too could read the Old Testament. He understood the land promises of Abraham. Did he not believe them?

Jesus and Jerusalem

Jewish interest in the land was paralleled by Jewish interest in Jerusalem. This was the city of God, now trampled down by Roman troops. But even the city of Jerusalem gets minimal attention from Jesus. He fails to revere Jerusalem or pray for it like the rabbis of his era. He does not base his ministry out of Jerusalem. For him, Galilee "of the Gentiles" is a place of faith, while Jerusalem is the city that kills the prophets and the Messiah (Matt. 21:33–41; 23:37–39).[9]

Jesus reveals his glory for the first time in Galilee (Mark 1:14–15; John 2:1–11). Following the crucifixion, the disciples are even directed to go to Galilee to witness the risen Lord (Mark 16:7). In a culture that is keenly devoted to Jerusalem, this is highly unusual. In Jesus' prayers and in his teachings about prayer, he does not include the land of Israel or the city of Jerusalem once, which runs counter to the "absorbed centrality of Jerusalem as the scene of revelation and redemption" in Jewish thought."[10] Judaism taught that Jerusalem would be the center stage for the Messiah, the city that would herald his coming and work. Jesus will have little to do with it.

In what was one of Jesus' most astonishing deeds, when he arrived at Jerusalem during his final Passover, he entered the Temple declaring the bankruptcy of its rituals and "cleansed" it. "You have made it a den of robbers," he announced (Mark 11:17). Furthermore, in what was perhaps one of his most astounding statements, Jesus even announced the doom — not the glory — of Jerusalem when Roman armies would come and utterly destroy it (Luke 21:20). What kind of messiah was this? Did not the age-old passions of land and city run in his veins? Did he not understand that without Jerusalem, Jewish identity would be diminished? *How can a man claim to be the Messiah but not support a national dream to reclaim the promises of Abraham?*

Here we have our first hint. Jesus is challenging the status quo of what Israel thought was important. His messiahship would not be defined by the agendas that spring from Jerusalem or its political aspirants. The link between faith in God and the possession of city and land are now under scrutiny. Israel had linked political nationhood with covenant blessing, and Jesus stood ready to question their assumptions. In Jesus' teachings, something new was afoot.

Jesus, Prophecy, and the Kingdom of God

Jesus' emphasis on the kingdom of God gave him every opportunity to talk about land and inheritance, but he refused. *The kingdom of Israel did not capture his interest.* He preferred to talk about the "kingdom of God" or the "kingdom of heaven." He would not define the Messiah as one who would remove Israel from Roman rule and build a new nation. After his death, his

---

9. This motif is especially clear as in Matthew and Mark. See Davies, *Gospel and the Land*, 221–43. See also P. Walker, *Jesus and the Holy City: New Testament Perspectives on Jerusalem* (Grand Rapids, Mich.: Eerdmans, 1996).

10. Ibid., 234.

followers despaired that he did not "redeem Israel" (Luke 24:21). Even after Jesus' resurrection, his disciples asked, "Lord, is this the time when you will restore the kingdom to Israel?" (Acts 1:6). Their minds were on political restoration, but for Jesus, God's kingdom was fundamentally God's reign over the lives of men and women — not an empire, not a political kingdom with borders and armies.[11] The kingdom was fundamentally a spiritual idea, a spiritual experience that transcended any particular place or time or land. People who took pride in their possession of land or city as the trophy of their spirituality would find themselves in opposition to Jesus' message.

On the one hand, Jesus' words reflect those of the Old Testament prophets when he says that people who possess the land must exhibit righteousness or else they will lose their gift. This teaching is quite clear, for instance, in Mark 12:1–11, where Jesus tells the parable of the vineyard. Thanks to Isaiah, "the vineyard" was a well-known metaphor for the land of Israel (Isa. 5:1–7). The land of Israel is like a vineyard cultivated by God, and God's people consist of vines, lifted from the oppression of Egypt and planted carefully in God's field (Ps. 80:8, 14).

But in his parable Jesus describes residents of this vineyard who reject and kill God's messengers. This prophetic warning is right out of Jeremiah or Isaiah. Rather than fruit that is a blessing to God — to coin Isaiah's imagery — these residents have produced wild grapes, grapes not worthy of the vinedresser. When these people witness the arrival of the vineyard owner's son, they say something remarkable: "This is the heir; come, let us kill him, and the *inheritance* will be ours" (Mark 12:7). *Inheritance!* No single term points more directly to the land of Abraham's promise.

When they kill the son, the owner of the vineyard (God) makes a judgment: "What then will the owner of the vineyard do? He will come and destroy the tenants and give the vineyard to others" (Mark 12:9). Matthew's account of the same parable makes the climax even more severe: "He will put those wretches to a miserable death, and lease the vineyard to other tenants who will give him the produce at the harvest time" (Matt. 21:41). Not surprisingly, after Jesus gives this conclusion, the Jewish leadership tries to arrest him.[12]

But note that Jesus goes one step beyond the Old Testament prophets. He says that *new* tenants, *new* occupants, will gain the vineyard. New residents

---

11. This point has been outlined brilliantly in a little-known book by N. W. Lund, *Israel och Församlingen* (trans. from Swedish by J. Eldon Johnson in his dissertation, "The Pauline Concept of Israel and the Church" [Chicago: North Park Theological Seminary, 1960]).

12. A similar theme of a fruitless vineyard is found in Luke 13:6–9, where the same suggestion is given: the absence of fruit brings swift judgment.

will come to the land of Israel. In his book *The Land,* Walter Brueggemann finds Jesus' teaching about "reversal" at work here. In the economy of Jesus' kingdom, those who weep shall rejoice, those who want to be first must become last, those who grasp at life will lose it — and those who grasp onto the land as if it were their property will find it going to others.[13] This theme of "inversion" (rich becoming poor, blind gaining sight, proud becoming humble, etc.) is at the heart of Jesus' gospel. "Graspers of land" will suddenly find themselves at a loss.[14] And who shall inherit "the earth"? Not those who demand it, but those who are empty, those who choose not to use power (Matt. 5:5).

Consider Jesus' own landless condition. In the culture of the Middle East, the possession of land and the claim to heritage through property were crucial values. But Jesus was without land, without home. In Matthew 8:20, Jesus responds to a disciple by saying, "Foxes have holes, and birds of the air have nests; but the Son of Man has nowhere to lay his head." Landlessness was a part of Jesus' own life. Nowhere does Jesus promise that the possession of land is a by-product of membership in his kingdom.

The one time Jesus refers directly to the land is found in the Sermon on the Mount. "Blessed are the meek, for they shall inherit the *earth.*" The Greek term translated "earth" can easily refer to "the land" (Gk. *ge,* Matt. 2:6). Jesus is likely echoing Psalm 37:11 where the reference is clearly to the land of inheritance.[15] The key here is that Jesus is redefining who obtains the land: not people who are ethnically Jewish, who fight for land, or who claim some ancestral right, but those who are humble.

On another occasion a man comes to Jesus with a complaint, "Teacher, bid my brother divide the *inheritance* with me" (Luke 12:13–15). In response, Jesus points him away from such arguments. Membership in Jesus' kingdom does not consist of grasping after such "inheritances." Is this too an allusion to the land of inheritance?

John's Gospel

If Matthew, Mark, and Luke show us teachings of Jesus that challenge the security of holding on to land in Jewish religion, John introduces us to yet another approach to the question. In this Gospel, Jesus spiritualizes the promise of land, but here we have to be careful with our language. Jesus does not devalue "the material world" as if only spiritual realities were

---

13. W. Brueggemann, *The Land,* 172–73.
14. Ibid., 171.
15. In the Greek Septuagint (see Ps. 36:11), the noun for "land" is the same as Matthew 5:5, *ge.*

important. This approach would deny the world itself that God created — to which Jesus in the flesh belongs. In this Gospel, Jesus takes a different view: *Jesus himself becomes the locus of holy space.* The aim of the old covenant was the land of promise; now the aim is Jesus Christ, who walked in the land.

This teaching is made clear in all of the passages where Jesus is compared with the religious benefits of the land. For example, the Temple in Jerusalem is found to be lacking in comparison with Jesus, whose body itself is "a temple" (2:21–22). Holy places like Bethel (where Jacob saw his vision) are surpassed by this Jesus upon whom "angels of God ascend and descend" (1:51). Jacob's well in Samaria offers no drink like Jesus' living water (4:10). The pool at Bethesda in Jerusalem cannot compare with Jesus, the one who truly heals (5:1–9). Sacred sites now fade in comparison with Jesus, who offers what the site only suggests.

In Jesus' conversation with the woman of Samaria, she attempts to divert his moral probing by referring to the Samaritan ancestral mountain. "Our fathers worshiped on this mountain, but you Jews claim that the place where we must worship is in Jerusalem" (John 4:20). She is pointing to Mt. Gerizim, the rival location to Jerusalem not far from Shechem. But Jesus' response is telling. He does not respond as a rabbi would, pointing to God's Temple in Jerusalem and how its sanctity supersedes anything else in Samaria. "Believe me," Jesus says, "a time is coming when you will worship the Father neither on this mountain nor in Jerusalem." Again and again Jesus is willing to upset cherished Jewish symbols. As Peter Walker writes, "He seemed to be working with a whole new concept of Israel — an 'Israel' no longer defined by the ancestral boundary-markers."[16]

When she points to her "holy mountain" (Mount Gerizim) and compares it with Jerusalem (another Jewish "holy mountain"), Jesus negates both. The most holy place of all, Jerusalem, is set aside for true worship generated by the Spirit. Jesus is redefining the place of promise where God will meet his people.

John's contribution is quite simple. Jesus is a new Moses (1:17) who can even duplicate and surpass Moses' feeding miracle of the wilderness (6:1–34). Just as Moses was leading the people of Israel to their promised land, so too, Jesus leads God's people. But now we learn that Jesus himself is in reality that which the land had offered only in form. To grasp after land is like grasping after bread — when all along we should discover that Jesus is "the bread of life" (6:35).

---

16. Walker, "An Interpretation of the Land in the New Testament," 129.

The drama of salvation in the Old Testament centers around the acquisition and the keeping of Abraham's land of promise. Curiously, this promise of a place, a home, is echoed in Jesus' words in John 14. Jesus goes ahead of us "to prepare a place for us," and he explains that this place will be among the many "rooms" (Gk. *mone*) in his Father's house. This word *room* was commonly used in Judaism to refer to the place of promise, namely the land of Israel. In John 14, however, the "place" is defined again and again until we learn that it is actually the indwelling of Father, Son, and Spirit in the believer's life: "we will come to him and make our home [*mone*] with him" (14:23). Once again, Jesus is pointing to a higher gift, a different promise, which fulfills and replaces the need for land.

We have already learned how the vineyard was a prominent symbol for the land of Israel. In the Gospel of John, the vineyard appears in a unique passage in chap. 15 when Jesus is in the Upper Room on Passover night. Here residence in the vineyard of God is measured by one thing: Are we connected to the Vine? No longer are God's people known as vines living in God's vineyard (Isa. 5). No longer is the land the central reference point, serving as a source of life and hope and future. "The crux for John 15 is that Jesus is changing the place of rootedness for Israel."[17]

The commonplace prophetic metaphor (the land as vineyard, the people of Israel as vines) now undergoes a dramatic shift. God's vineyard, the land of Israel, now only has one vine, Jesus. The people of Israel cannot claim to be planted as vines in the land; they cannot be rooted in the vineyard unless first they are grafted into Jesus. Branches that attempt living in the land, the vineyard, which refuse to be attached to Jesus will be cast out and burned (15:6). What has Jesus done? He has forever changed the *place* of God among men and women. Jesus is the source, the locale where divine life may be appropriated.

Putting it in more technical terms, John translates the promise of land and place into the reality of Jesus. To use the words of W. D. Davies, John shows Jesus *displacing* holy space.[18] John "christifies" holy space.[19] Christ is the reality behind all earthbound promises. When John writes that "we beheld his glory," he is attributing the glory of God to the presence of Jesus, a glory that could be found only in the land, in Jerusalem, and particularly, the Temple. When John says that "the word became flesh and dwelt among

---

17. G. Burge, "Territorial Religion and the Vineyard of John 15," in *Jesus of Nazareth Lord and Christ: Essays on the Historical Jesus and New Testament Christology,* ed. J. Green and M. Turner (Grand Rapids, Mich.: Eerdmans, 1994), 393.

18. Davies, *Gospel and the Land,* 316–18.

19. Ibid., 368.

us" he uses a special term: *dwelt* is the same word for tabernacle throughout the Old Testament.[20] In effect, Jesus is the new place of God's dwelling.

To sum up, we observe a cycle of responses to the question of land: (1) land is rejected as the aim of faith; (2) land is *spiritualized* as meaning something else; (3) the promise is *historicized* in Jesus, a man who lives in the land; (4) the promise is *sacramentalized* — that is, as a sacrament bears testimony to things beyond what we see and touch (without denying these properties), so too Jesus' "landness" (his physicality) is a reality, but believers are urged to push further, to find the "living water" and "bread of life" that he offers.[21]

JESUS AND THE PEOPLE OF GOD

Jesus' criticism of the theological status quo in Judaism can be seen in yet one more way. Not only did he reject those people who would strive after the material benefits of their faith (e.g., land), but he also announced that his kingdom would give birth to a new following, a new people, a fulfillment of the Israelite community sought in the Old Testament. Selecting twelve apostles was his first signal that now a restoration of the twelve tribes of Israel was at hand. Yet, this group was a new community, a messianic community, whose *heritage* would stretch back to Abraham, Isaac, and Jacob, but whose *identity* now would be found in Jesus Christ. Just as Jesus uprooted the assumption that locale (the land, Jerusalem) was a sacred premise in God's plans, once again he implies that religious heritage or even ethnicity does not necessarily make exclusive claims on God. The benefits of God's blessing will be shared by those men and women living in concert with his dawning kingdom.

Jesus did not come to start a new movement outside of Judaism. He did not wish to compete with Judaism. He came in full submission to Jewish faith: he obeyed the law, observed the festivals, and respected temple worship. He was an Israelite *par excellence*. However, many in Israel rejected both Jesus and his kingdom, and as a result, he predicted judgment on the land and the scattering of Israel.[22]

---

20. John was written in Greek, and the Hebrew Old Testament was translated into Greek (called the Septuagint). The Greek word *skene* is the word used both in the Septuagint and in John for "tabernacle."

21. Davies, *Gospel and the Land*, 367.

22. "The Jewish nation which rejected the offer of the Kingdom of God [was] therefore set aside as the people of God and is to be replaced by a new people." G. Ladd, *The Presence of the Future* (Grand Rapids, Mich.: Eerdmans, 1974), 249.

Initially these new people were not Gentiles, however. They were Jews who responded in faith and formed the nucleus of Jesus' earliest followers. God's plan for Israel was that those who accepted the Messiah became the new Israel. "Jesus' disciples are...the people of the Kingdom, the true Israel."[23] For this reason, the Gospels are filled with so much imagery from Israel's nationhood: Jesus is a new Moses, he inaugurates a new exodus, and his twelve apostles symbolize the twelve tribes. His new covenant stands in contrast to the covenant of Sinai.[24]

Did God therefore reject his people, the descendants of Abraham, Isaac, and Jacob? Not at all. The concept that explains this notion of Jesus' disciples as the true Israel in continuity with Judaism comes from the Old Testament theme of "the believing remnant." During times of faithlessness in Israel's history, God had a "faithful remnant" of people who did not fall away. These believers who did not succumb to Canaanite or Egyptian religion were "the true Israel."[25]

Jesus' followers, therefore, represent Israel's remnant. They are at the center of God's new effort in the world. And if this is the case, they are heirs to the promises God has always extended to his faithful followers.

THE EARLIEST CHRISTIANS

Two seminal ideas spring from the teaching of Jesus and no doubt took hold in the thinking of the earliest Christians. First, the *spiritual attachment* to Jerusalem and the land of Israel was eroding. The domain of God's activity had undergone a dramatic shift — no longer focused on the territorial dimensions of Israel's identity, but now focused entirely on Christ, in whom the promises of the covenant are fulfilled. Second, the *spiritual identity* of God's people is being redefined as the messianic community that follows Jesus Christ. No longer is lineage through Abraham a sufficient argument for spiritual security. John the Baptist spares no words for his views: "For I tell you, God is able from these stones to raise up children to Abraham" (Luke 3:8). Failure to believe in Jesus introduces a crisis for Judaism. The children of Abraham may be defined along spiritual lines, not by means of ethnicity and history.

---

23. Ibid., 250.

24. Students of Matthew commonly locate in this Gospel hints that Jesus is a new Moses inaugurating a new Torah or law that fulfills and surpasses that found in the Old Testament.

25. For a full explanation of the remnant and Jesus' kingdom, see Ladd, *Presence of the Future*, 250–52. Note how in John 8, for instance, Jesus questions whether or not someone is *truly* a child of Abraham if he seeks to kill him (8:39–47). In some fashion, therefore, heritage from Abraham may be jeopardized. Divine status is not a question of bloodline but of faith.

The Book of Hebrews

The convergence of these two themes appears most clearly in the book of Hebrews, where the Christian walk assimilates the metaphor of the Israelite journey through the wilderness. However, the new goal of the believer is no long "promised land" but eternal life with Christ. Nowhere is this alignment clearer than in Hebrews 3–4. In these chapters, Christian discipleship is compared with Moses and Joshua leading Israel through the wilderness. For them, the promised rest was the land of Canaan. Hebrews now uses this story to describe the "promised rest" extended to Christians. Land is spiritualized, to be sure, but that the writer of this book employed such a powerful Jewish theme is interesting. Whatever the "land" meant in the Old Testament, whatever the promise contained, this now belonged to Christians. Hence, a "central symbol for the promise of the gospel is land."[26] But now this *land* has undergone a thoroughgoing revision of meaning.

Perhaps the most dramatic redefinition of "land" is found in Hebrews 11. Echoing the story of Genesis, this chapter reminds us how Abraham was called to depart from his homeland in order to inherit a new land God had promised. Hebrews 11:8 makes it clear that this reference is to the land of Israel/Palestine (known then as Canaan). *But remarkably we learn that this land was not really the place of God's promise.* The land was a metaphor, a symbol of a greater place beyond the soil of Canaan.

> By faith he [Abraham] stayed for a time in the land he had been promised, as in a foreign land, living in tents, as did Isaac and Jacob, who were heirs with him of the same promise. For he looked forward to the city that has foundations, whose architect and builder is God. (Heb. 11:9–10)

As we know, Abraham settled in the promised land, and God's promise to him was seemingly fulfilled. But then we read in 11:13 just the opposite: "All of these died in faith *without having received the promises,* but from a distance they saw and greeted them" [emphasis added]. Abraham's *true promise* was not the physical land, but a higher promise that went beyond mere land. The book of Hebrews says that Abraham and his descendants

> confessed that they were strangers and foreigners on the earth, for people who speak in this way make it clear that they are seeking a homeland. If they had been thinking of the land that they had left behind, they would have had opportunity to return. But as it is, they desire a better country, that is, a heavenly one. Therefore God is not ashamed to be called their God; indeed, he has prepared a city for them. (Heb. 11:13–16)

---

26. Brueggemann, *The Land,* 179.

Therefore, Hebrews tells us, God's intentions went far beyond the land. The "city" God has prepared for them is not Jerusalem. We might say that in this passage the land is being spiritualized, viewed as a vehicle to something else. The promise to Abraham is actually fulfilled in heaven.

What would the implications be of a first-century Christian holding this point of view? Certainly this outlook would be at odds with the many nationalistic causes within the country as well as with the territorial commitments of Judaism known throughout the first century.

The Book of Acts

As the messianic community of Christians began to live out their lives following Jesus' ascension, they were forced to reflect on these earth-shaking ideas that originated with Jesus. What about the *territorial* dimension of God's people? Is God's "land" now something wider, something greater than the land of Israel, bounded by the Jordan River and the Mediterranean Sea? And what about the *ethnic* aspects of God's people? Is the concept of "God's people" also something wider, something that reaches beyond the ethnic confines of Judaism?

If these two ideas are pursued, what does it mean for the mission of the church? Could God's people include Gentile believers who do not need to embrace the particularities of Jewish custom and tradition? And could God's "land" now encompass the entire earth since his interests are not limited to the national perimeters of historic Judaism? Jesus' final charge to them in Acts 1:8 makes this clear: their mission is to go beyond Israel and Jerusalem, even to "the end of the earth."

These ideas came alive for the early church when Greek-speaking Jews entered its ranks. So-called "Hellenistic Jews" who lived outside Israel were open to the larger Mediterranean world. Many did not speak Hebrew. In fact, most had lost Hebrew altogether and could speak only Greek. Few were willing to view Israel/Palestine as the only place of residence appropriate for a Jew. They did not adhere to the Jewish nationalism of the day and were quick to be free of it.

Stephen was one of the Hellenistic Jews who embraced faith in Christ in Jerusalem. In Acts 7 he gives the longest speech in the book of Acts, defending his "openness" against harsh criticisms from Jerusalem's leadership. What Stephen says in this speech is vitally important because its implications made it possible for the church to embrace its world mission. In fact, Stephen, reflecting on the wider vision of Jesus and the world, gave the church its "theology of the world." What Stephen said was so revolutionary, so upsetting, that it cost him his life. Acts tells us, "When [the leaders] heard this, they were furious and gnashed their teeth at him" (7:54). But Stephen persisted and the anger of his audience grew. "At this they covered their ears and, yelling at the top of their voices, they all rushed at him, dragged him out of the city and began to stone him" (7:57).

What did Stephen say that was so upsetting? In a word, Stephen was challenging the pillars on which first-century Judaism has been built. Among these, he described how the land of Israel was not the sacred domain of revelation Judaism thought. He outlined how God had spoken in other foreign lands, such as Mesopotamia (Abraham) and Egypt (Joseph, Moses). From this point, he concludes that God's work is not limited to the land of Israel/Palestine alone. God is not confined to the geography of Israel's land. *Stephen challenges the Jewish assumption that the land is integral to the plan of God.* He critiques the wedding of nation and religion that had run rampant in first-century Judaism and fueled hostilities not just with Rome, but with any believer who refused to put land at the center of his or her faith.

In fact, Stephen's wisdom, his creative openness, led the early church to cross the cultural boundaries erected in that day. Mission could now go forward to lands never dreamed possible. Stephen's disciple, Philip, led a mission to Samaria, and Peter ends up in Caesarea, the center of the Roman occupation, converting a military officer, Cornelius. Before long, a church is flourishing in Antioch in the far north, a wealthy gentile city that could even rival Rome in its paganism.

The territorial limits of Israel/Palestine did not exhaust God's agenda for humanity, which was no longer the goal of the spiritual life, but the springboard, the launching place for mission.

The great story that Acts unfolds, however, is the conversion and mission of Paul, whose meeting with Christ had shattered his Jewish preconceptions about God and the world. Paul would become the premier missionary to the Gentiles — a fate no respectable rabbi would ever embrace — and his life would lead him to lands beyond the scope of the promised land of Abraham.

The Apostle Paul

Paul is particularly interesting because he is Jewish. Despite his upbringing outside of Israel in Tarsus, Paul was deeply proud of his Jewish heritage. He tells the Galatians, for example, "how in the practice of our national religion I was outstripping many of my Jewish contemporaries in my boundless devotion to the traditions of my ancestors" (Gal. 1:14 NEB). His pride in his lineage shows up again and again: "circumcised on the eighth day, of the people of Israel, of the tribe of Benjamin, a Hebrew born of Hebrews; as to the law, a Pharisee..." (Phil. 3:4f.; cf. 2 Cor. 11:22; Rom. 11:1f.). Paul eventually moved to Jerusalem and was educated under some of the city's greatest scholars. Therefore we can be sure that Paul felt the full force of the doctrine of the land as it was expressed among his friends. This land of Israel was promised to Abraham — and Abraham's descendants were sole heirs to it.[27]

Of course, Paul's conversion on the Damascus Road completely shattered his theological framework. His commission to go to the Gentiles and his eventual commitment to lands outside of Israel forced him to rethink God's purposes. Does not ethnic lineage bring ancestral privilege? Does not possession of and residence in "the land" bring special blessing?

The first thing we notice is that Paul rarely refers to Jerusalem or the land of Israel. We find no recital of the history of salvation anchoring God's work in Israel. In Romans 9:4, for instance, when Paul lists the blessings that accrue to Jews, he oddly does not mention the land as one of these. At no time does he point to Jerusalem or the Temple as the spiritual focus of the Christian.

However, when Paul refers to Abraham, particularly in Romans and Galatians, he does something unexpected. In popular Jewish thought, Abraham was the great father of Judaism and descent from him conferred salvation.[28] Likewise possessing this lineage made one heir to the land. Referring to the "promises of Abraham" signals immediately that one is talking about land and inheritance. But what would Paul do with his gentile believers who lived outside the land, believers in Antioch or Galatia or Ephesus? Further, what was the ongoing status of Jews who did not believe in Jesus? Did they still possess the promises?

Paul's interest in Abraham in Romans 4 and Galatians 3 completely neglects God's pledge of land, which is surprising in a spiritual climate that saw "land" as intimately attached to spiritual heritage. For Paul, the value of Abraham is that here we find a man who received God's promise, responded in faith, was justified, and then became the father of *many* nations. Paul explains how through Abraham "all the families of the earth shall be blessed" (Gen. 12:3; Gal. 3:8). The blessing of Abraham *to all* is important. Abraham can become the father of many nations because when Gentiles share in Abraham's faith, he becomes their father too (Rom. 4:16). Physical lineage, therefore, has been spiritualized into a lineage based on faith. The "land of Israel" is likewise spiritualized now to include the entire world.

---

27. Davies, *The Gospel and the Land,* 166.
28. Ibid., 168–70.

If believing Christians are indeed children of Abraham through faith, then they are also Abraham's heirs. Listen to Paul's words directly:

> For the promise that he would inherit the world did not come to Abraham or to his descendants through the law but through the righteousness of faith. If it is the adherents of the law who are to be the heirs, faith is null and the promise is void. (Rom. 4:13–14)

> ...and if [we are] children, then heirs, heirs of God and joint heirs with Christ — if, in fact, we suffer with him so that we may also be glorified with him. (Rom. 8:17)

> ...that in Christ Jesus the blessing of Abraham might come to the Gentiles, so that we might receive the promise of the Spirit through faith.... For if the inheritance comes from the law, it no longer comes from the promise; but God granted it to Abraham through the promise. (Gal. 3:14, 18)

The reverse of this argument can be found in Romans 2:25–29. Religious ritual or heritage does *not* determine spiritual privilege: "A person is a Jew who is one inwardly, and real circumcision is a matter of the heart — it is spiritual and not literal" (2:29). For Paul, this perspective opens the way for Gentiles to stand before God with Jews and have equal status. The key determinant is faith in Christ. Qualifying is not a matter of ritual or bloodline.[29]

But in Galatians, Paul does something else that is interesting. In Galatians 3:15–18, Paul makes a very subtle, but very important, suggestion. The ancient promises were made, he says, to Abraham and to "his offspring." Using a style of rabbinic argument less familiar to us today, Paul stresses that "offspring" is singular, not plural: "It does not say, 'And to offsprings,' as of many; but it says, 'And to your offspring,' that is, to one person, who is Christ" (Gal. 3:16). Hence, Christ is the *true recipient* of Abraham's blessings, and if we are "in Christ," we are heirs both of Christ and of Abraham simultaneously. Christ is thus "the Seed of Abraham par excellence and all who are in him are equally Abraham's sons."[30] Brueggemann comments: "It is central to Paul's argument that the promise endures.

---

29. H. Ridderbos outlines Paul's use of names for the church, thereby making the case that Paul believes that "the church is the continuation and fulfillment of the historical people of God that in Abraham God chose to himself from all peoples and to which he bound himself by making the covenant and the promises." *Paul: An Outline of His Theology* (Grand Rapids, Mich.: Eerdmans, 1975), 327.

30. D. Guthrie, *Galatians*, New Century Bible (London: Oliphants, 1974), 102. Similarly, see J. Schniewind and G. Friedrich, "Christ Is the True Heir of the Promise, of the Universal Inheritance, and Determines the Fellow-heirs," *Theological Dictionary of the New Testament*, 10 vols. (Grand Rapids, Mich.: Eerdmans, 1964–76), 2:583, cited in R. Y. K. Fung, *The Epistle to the Galatians* (Grand Rapids, Mich.: Eerdmans, 1988), 156.

The heirs in Christ are not heirs to a new promise, but the one which abides, and that is centrally land."[31]

But we would be wrong to argue that in Paul's mind Christians now can make a territorial claim on the land. Indeed, the believing remnant of Israel, joined by believing Gentiles, make up the messianic community who are now Abraham's children — but the promise and gift of Abraham is now to be found in Christ. Paul treats the land the same way he treats the law in Galatians. The law was provisional (3:19f.) and preparatory until the grace of God could be seen in Christ (3:24). Davies argues, Paul's "silence [about the land] points not merely to the absence of a conscious concern with it, but to his deliberate rejection of it. His interpretation of the promise is *a-territorial*."[32] Paul's logic forces him to "de-territorialize" the promises of Abraham so that Abraham's new children might find their fulfillment of the promise "in Christ." Paul then thinks of the messianic community as having no territorial attachment, but rather having its only attachment to Christ. Davies concludes:

> Salvation was not now bound to the Jewish people centered in the land and living according to the Law: it was "located" not in a place, but in persons in whom grace and faith had their writ. By personalizing the promise "in Christ" Paul universalized it. For Paul, Christ had gathered up the promise into the singularity of his own person. In this way, "the territory" promised was transformed into and fulfilled by the life in Christ. In the christological logic of Paul, the land, like the Law, particular and provisional, had become irrelevant.[33]

This universal blessing that messianic believers can now take to the entire world explains the remarkable statement Paul makes in Romans 4:13: "The promise to Abraham and his descendants, that they should *inherit the world,* did not come through the law but through the righteousness of faith" (emphasis added). Of course, Abraham's promise originally referred to the land of Israel. But in Paul's day, Jewish writers expanded this promise thinking that God has in fact given the Jews the entire world (4 Ezra 6:59). *But Paul now upends their logic.* The divine purposes of God through Abraham, the "seed" through which blessing comes is Jesus Christ. He alone would be the blessing for "all nations," and in this respect his descendants "in faith" would carry this blessing to the world.

Therefore we can see two seminal ideas that originated with Jesus now coming to full force in the thought of Paul. The ancestry of Abraham has

---

31. Brueggemann, *The Land,* 178.
32. Davies, *The Gospel and the Land,* 179.
33. Ibid.

been redefined. The messianic community may be rightly called the "Israel of God" — as Paul does in Galatians 6:16. And the promise of land has been reinterpreted. No longer will God's purposes by defined by the territorial aspirations of Judaism. God's plan embraces a vision for all nations throughout the world. The dividing wall that kept Jews and Gentiles apart in the Temple now is torn down (Eph. 2:11–22), but this may also include the geographic separation, the territorial rivalry between those in "the land" and those outside. Christ's church no longer considers these lines of demarcation any more than it considers the dividing lines between slaves and free, male and female, Jew and Gentile (Gal. 3:28).

Other writers made the same point. Peter, for instance, writes his first letter to Christians who live throughout the Mediterranean world (1 Pet. 1:1). But then he addresses these Christians using language taken directly from the Old Testament for Israel:

> But you are a chosen race, a royal priesthood, a holy nation, God's own people, in order that you may proclaim the mighty acts of him who called you out of darkness into his marvelous light.
>
> Once you were not a people, but now you are God's people; once you had not received mercy, but now you have received mercy. (1 Pet. 2:9–10)

Clearly these verses draw on titles from the book of Exodus (19:6; 23:22). They are a conscious attempt to designate the church as a new people of God.[34] As Peter Richardson writes, "The Church has taken over the inheritance of Israel (1 Pet. 1:4)."[35] James does the same thing when he refers to the church as "the twelve tribes [of Israel]" (James 1:1).[36]

Romans 9–11, Paul's Provision for Israel

If the church has indeed become the people of God, the new Israel, what happens to Israel "outside of Christ"? Paul explains his view of unbelieving Israel in Romans 9–11. These chapters are critical for us since this is the one place where the church and unbelieving Israel are contrasted directly.

First, Paul affirms that God has not rejected Israel, because he himself is an Israelite and so are other Jewish Christians like him. Drawing again on the Old Testament notion of a remnant, Paul argues that Christian believers are the new remnant in God's working: "So too at the present time there is a remnant, chosen by grace" (Rom. 11:5).[37] Thus in 11:1 when Paul thinks

---

34. Ibid., 173.

35. Ibid., 174.

36. This is likewise done in Revelation 21:9–14, where the church bears the names of both the apostles and the tribes of Israel.

37. Paul illustrates this notion of the remnant using Elijah's story from 1 Kings 19. See Romans 9:6–11 and 9:27.

about the question, "Has God rejected his people?" he replies emphatically, "By no means!" The key is in 11:2, "God has not rejected his people whom he foreknew." The remnant is the body of believers within Israel who have kept faith with the covenant and God's purposes, and God knows who they are. Therefore God has been faithful to his covenant people because these people are found now within the church. *Israel in Christ* is now heir to the great covenant history of the Old Testament.[38]

Is this remnant simply Jewish Christians? Not at all. In 9:25–26, Paul cites Hosea's reference to Gentiles: "And in the very place where it was said to them, 'You are not my people,' *there*[39] they shall be called children of the living God." Where was this proclamation given? Jerusalem. God's holy city is the place where the church — filled with Jews and Gentiles — as the remnant, the body of believers predicted by Hosea, will be announced fulfilling God's purposes.

Second, Paul develops the picture of an olive tree as an image of God's people in history, with many branches and, thus, many people. Paul says that unbelieving Israel is like a branch broken off from the trunk of this tree. That is, unbelieving Israel has been rejected (11:15) and "broken off" (11:20) so that gentile believers might be "grafted in" (11:17–19). "God's people" (the tree trunk) is a wider concept than just Israel alone. Unbelief and sinfulness have led to many being "broken off" throughout the years. But even though there have been these periods of judgment, God has never forsaken the "trunk," his people, in history.

Third, the basis of Israel's failure is at the center of Paul's understanding of righteousness. Paul's own religious merits were of no use to him (Phil. 3:4–9). Judaism has the same problem. Merit with God cannot be found in something we can offer, something we conjure up out of our history or religion. God's righteousness works from our emptiness and thus is known to us as grace. If this is true, then Jews and Gentiles are equals (11:32), and Judaism cannot claim any historic privileges any more than Paul could. One cannot demand the promises of God — much less the land — based on religious privilege.[40] Paul writes about Israel:

38. H. L. Ellison, *The Mystery of Israel: An Exposition of Romans 9–11* (Grand Rapids, Mich.: Eerdmans, 1966), 73–76.

39. Paul inserts the Greek word "there" (*ekei*) to the Hosea citation to underscore the place of this new identity for Gentiles. The place will be within Israel itself. See J. Munck, *Christ and Israel: An Interpretation of Romans 9–11* (Philadelphia: Fortress, 1967), 12, 72–73.

40. E. Käsemann, "Paul and Israel," in *New Testament Questions of Today* (Philadelphia: Fortress, 1969), 184. "For since Easter it has become clear that God's dealings are with all people and that Israel's election in days of yore points forward beyond Israel into that comprehensive history which began with Adam. There is no privilege in the face of God's omnipotence" (185).

I can testify that they have a zeal for God, but it is not enlightened. For, being ignorant of the righteousness that comes from God, and seeking to establish their own, they have not submitted to God's righteousness. For Christ is the end of the law so that there may be righteousness for everyone who believes. (Rom. 10:2–4)

Finally, Paul retains a special place for unbelieving Israel even though they are "broken off" from God's people. During the present time, Israel has become "hardened" (11:25), but in the future, after the Gentiles have been "grafted in," all Israel will be saved once more (11:26–27). Paul thus anticipates a future redemption in the plan of God that will include the Jewish people who originally rejected Christ. Israel might be reattached in the present era, but this can happen only through belief in Jesus (11:23). For the most part, Paul's hope for Israel is future, at the end of time.[41]

But more must be said. If Judaism remains — even in its brokenness — a people with a unique future, a people still to be redeemed, then it follows that they currently have a place of honor even in their unbelief. Note Paul's words in Romans 11:28–29: "As regards the gospel they are enemies of God for your sake; but as regards election they are beloved, for the sake of their ancestors; for the gifts and the calling of God are irrevocable."

Paul freely admits that Judaism now stands opposed to the gospel. Judaism is hostile to God's new purposes in Christ. Judaism has rejected the new covenant. Nevertheless, even in this disobedience, these broken branches still possess an incomparable place in history. Unbelieving Judaism is beloved, just as exiled Judaism was beloved in the Old Testament. Judaism holds an enduring role. For the sake of their history, for the sake of the promises made to their ancestors, God will retain a place for Jews in history. In their present condition of unbelief, they deserve honor. And when they accept Christ, be it now or in the future, their brokenness will be restored. Paul enjoys drawing out the metaphor of the olive tree to its limit. God is eager to see "these natural branches" grafted back in place. "For if you have been cut from what is by nature a wild olive tree and grafted, contrary to nature, into a cultivated olive tree, how much more will these natural branches be grafted back into their own olive tree" (Rom. 11:24).

Let us sum up. Few passages of Paul's writings have been more difficult than Romans 9–11. Interpreters are sharply divided in their understanding of Paul's double message: On the one hand, Israel has fallen and the church has assumed its privileges. On the other hand, Paul still holds out an ongoing

---

41. G. E. Ladd, *A Theology of the New Testament* (Grand Rapids, Mich.: Eerdmans, 1974), 561–63.

place for Israel both in the present and in the future. Some Christians think that unbelieving Israel still lives today as heirs to Abraham's promises, that Christ's new covenant did not bring about an epoch-changing shift among God's people. But as we have seen, this view neglects much of Paul's teaching in Galatians and Romans about Christians as Abraham's heirs.

Still other Christians reject Israel altogether, making no allowances for the promises God made throughout the Scriptures, but Paul would find this view equally unsatisfying. As he says in Romans 11:29, "the gifts and the calling of God are irrevocable."

I prefer a middle position that harmonizes Paul's double commitment. Israel has fallen and has been utterly disobedient. Christians have been grafted into their place. Indeed, Christians are the heirs of Abraham. And yet fallen Israel in its unbelief remains unique, honored, and beloved because of God's commitment to Israel's ancestors. Things have not changed. As God says through Isaiah, "I held out my hands all day long to a rebellious people" (Isa. 65:2). Yet Israel's obstinacy did not end God's affection for his people. The same is true today.[42]

Conclusion

Father George of Ramallah would tell us that the question "Who owns the land?" is not so simple. The answer is not just a matter of pointing to the promises of Abraham, identifying modern Israel as heirs to those promises, and then theologically justifying the Israeli claim to land. On the contrary, Christian theology demands that the true recipients of these promises will be found in the Christian church. Perhaps the church alone receives these promises! Christian theology must at least take into account the new covenant of Christ and its implications for Israel.

Romans 11 clearly makes the point that unbelieving Israel still holds a place of honor. These "enemies of the gospel" are beloved, but this does not mean that Israel still holds a solitary place in relation to Abraham's promises. According to Christian teaching, Israel cannot make an exclusive claim to the land as if the new covenant had never happened. In fact, the New Testament refers to previous covenants as "obsolete" and "vanishing away" (Heb. 8:13).[43] Nor can Christians simply move from Abraham's promises

---

42. This fact of Israel's beloved place should challenge even the slightest hint of anti-Semitism in the church.

43. Hebrews makes this theme abundantly clear. See Hebrews 7:18, 19: "There is, on the one hand, the abrogation of an earlier commandment because it was weak and ineffectual (for the law made nothing perfect); there is, on the other hand, the introduction of a better hope, through which we approach God." Similarly Hebrews 9:15 explains the new covenant with reference to "a former covenant." The surpassing glory of the new covenant completely

in Genesis directly to modern Israel, skipping entirely what the New Testament says concerning Abraham's heritage. According to the New Testament, Christians are children of Abraham because this heritage is acquired by faith, not by lineage. In Christ, the promises of God are theirs.

SUMMARY

Imagine the implications that come with this result! Jewish settlers cannot eject Christian residents from Jerusalem saying, "The land is ours according to the Bible." Any Christian that would support the logic of this argument is mistaken. If the Scriptures are to speak in full, the *Christian* Scriptures should be part of the conversation as well.

We also saw that the New Testament goes a long way toward spiritualizing the nature of these promises. That is, the Israelite endeavor to acquire land and forge a nation takes on a different shape in the new covenant of Christ. God's people no longer are called to build an empire based on the books of Genesis or Joshua. The Israeli attempt to take land and forge a nation is religiously misdirected. God's people are called to infiltrate the empires of the world, bringing the gospel of Jesus Christ to all, regardless of history, race, or religious persuasion.

---

replaces that of the old covenant. Hebrews likely has in mind thoughts originally penned in Jeremiah 31 on God's coming covenant.

Chapter Ten

THE PALESTINIAN CHURCH

Is there such a thing as a Christian Palestinian or a Palestinian Christian? I was born in Bethlehem on June 26, 1962, into a family that took root in this city a very long time ago. The Raheb family has lived in and around Bethlehem for centuries.
— Rev. Mitri Raheb, Bethlehem

The central problem we face as Christian Arabs is exactly this trap: we have been defined by others, by Westerners. Our voice was never sought, was never heard, and was never articulated. We have been denied the value of our experience and robbed of our voice and sense of self-worth. The challenge we face is how to make our voices heard, our conceptions and practices articulated.
— Munir Fasheh, Bir Zeit

The cover of David Dolan's book on the Middle East is a telling portrayal of how we have come to view the problem of Israel/Palestine.[1] Its artwork shows two fists fiercely crashing across a map of the region. One fist has a star of David emblazoned on its wrist. The other shows the crescent of Islam tattooed prominently in red. What the artist omitted unveils a deeper neglect and misunderstanding not only in Dolan's book, but throughout our churches. No cross appears among the religious symbols of the Middle East. Contrary to what Dolan would have us believe, the conflict in Israel/Palestine is not between Judaism and Islam. It is among brothers, tribes we might say, whose struggle is comprehensive and includes culture, nationalism, and religion.

Not all Arabs are Muslim. The Middle East Council of Churches believes that about 15 million Arab Christians are living between Algeria and Iran.[2] Lebanon and Syria together have 2.5 million Arab Christians. Jordan has two hundred thousand. Iraq: 1 million. Egypt has about 10 million Christians. An entire valley in West Syria is called "the Christian Valley" due to the dozens and dozens of Christian villages populating it. Because of the holy sites in Israel/Palestine, that an ancient Christian community has existed

---

1. D. Dolan, *Holy War for the Promised Land: Israel's Struggle to Survive in the Muslim Middle East* (Nashville: Nelson, 1991).
2. See the MECC website: *www.mecchurches.org*.

there from the earliest centuries of the church should not be surprising. Of a worldwide Palestinian population of over 5 million, almost 8 percent, or about four hundred thousand people, are Christians.[3] But many of these are scattered throughout the world. Today more Bethlehem Christians are living in Chile and Brazil than in Bethlehem itself.

How many Arab Christians are still living in Israel/Palestine? Salim Munayer, dean of Bethlehem Bible College, notes that within the borders of pre-1967 Israel, about 107,000 Palestinian Arabs are Christians; they are found chiefly in Galilee.[4] In the West Bank, there are approximately 7,000 to 9,000 Christians and another 7,000 in Jerusalem. Thus in Israel/Palestine altogether, most observers believe there are about 125,000 Palestinian Christians.[5] Thus, among Palestinians in the country today, roughly 4 percent of the Arab population is Christian, 96 percent is Muslim. Now, the number of Christians is shrinking. Because of economic stress and persecution, Arab Christians have found ways to emigrate at an astonishing rate. Over 400,000 Palestinian Christians live outside the country today.

The diversity of the Christian church in Israel/Palestine is also surprising. Greek Catholic (Melkite) Christians are the largest group with about 50,000 members. In Syria and Lebanon, their numbers are even larger. One of the most ancient communities is the Orthodox in all its varieties with about 35,000 people. This community today has almost a hundred churches throughout the country and forty monasteries — seventeen of which can be found in the Old City of Jerusalem. Here we find Armenian, Coptic, Ethiopian, Greek, Romanian, Russian, and Syrian Orthodox believers.

There are also Roman Catholics (known as "Latins"), Anglicans or Episcopalians, Baptists, Pentecostals, and many other groups. Catholics (in the five rites represented here) host 120 churches. Baptist life is well represented, with about 1,200 Baptists who worship in twenty-one churches around the country. For instance, there are nine churches in Galilee, two in Jerusalem, and one each in Bethlehem, Haifa, and Petah Tikvah. Some independent Bible churches with "seeker" strategies for outreach are present. Nazareth is home to an evangelical Bible school for correspondence study that distributes more than eight hundred Arabic New Testaments every year.[6] The

---

3. N. Ateek, *Justice and Only Justice* (Maryknoll, N.Y.: Orbis, 1989), 4.

4. S. Munayer, "Arab Palestinian Christians in the Holy Land," unpublished paper printed in Jerusalem. His statistics were taken from *The Statistical Abstract of Israel 1990* (no. 41), Central Bureau of Statistics, Israel.

5. P. Brierley, ed., *The World Handbook of Churches* (London, 1997) gives similar statistics. Among the "trinitarian" churches, 180,000 would identify themselves as Christians and about 104,000 are active in a place of worship.

6. Emmaus Bible School, George Khalil, director, Box 240, Nazareth 16101, Israel.

small village of Tur'an north of Nazareth is a good example of this diversity. Rev. Suhail Ramadan pastors the local Baptist church there and works alongside one Melkite Catholic church and one Orthodox church. Of the village's 10,000 people, 30 percent are Christian, while all others are Muslim.

These facts surprise many American tourists as well as Israelis. Over 250 Christian churches exist in Israel/Palestine, but this figure may even be too small. Many towns have house churches that cannot be recorded. Once when I was explaining this to a group of Jewish settlers on the West Bank, they blinked and accused me of being in error. "Palestinians are Muslims — or else they are not Palestinians! Maybe these Arabs are from the West!" they said. Nothing could be further from the truth. A continuous Arab Christian population has lived in Palestine for almost two thousand years.

Most Palestinian Christians reside in the cities of Bethlehem, Jerusalem, Ramallah, and Nazareth, which have sizable Christian populations and strong churches. But villages such as Beit Jala, Beit Sahour, and Bir Zeit also have strong Christian communities.

Others are in predominantly Muslim cities like Nablus. Father Yousef Sa'adeh pastors his Greek-Catholic (Melkite) congregation in Nablus, where each Sunday 50 people gather for worship. Nablus has about 120,000 residents, but no more than 750 are Christians and most live in small villages surrounding the city.

Christian villages can also be found. The city of Jenin (near Nablus) consists of about eighty villages. Zababdeh is one of a handful of villages in the mix that has three Christian communities: Protestant, Roman Catholic, and Greek Orthodox. Of Zababdeh's three thousand residents, almost half are Christians. Today you can visit Christian Zababdeh thanks to the website of two Presbyterian missionaries there (Marthame and Elizabeth Sanders).[7] Beit Sahour, a town outside of Bethlehem, is host to the famed biblical "Shepherd's Fields." More than 10,000 people, most of whom are Christians, live there. These people have a voice that the West has yet to hear.

The pastors of Palestinian churches minister to people who face the daily struggle of military occupation and who live with feelings of anger, resentment, powerlessness, and despair. Nadia Abboushi is a mother and a musician in Ramallah where she attends the Anglican church. "I never realized life could be so difficult," she says. "There is constant stress; constant agony. Raising children takes thought, maturity, and political awareness. I tell them that this situation is abnormal — life is not like this. But they ask, 'What is normal?'" On Easter day, 1991, her sixteen-year-old son was shot

---

7. Go to *www.fpc-wilmette.org/sanders/index.html*.

at and arrested by the Israeli army while he was walking to his relatives' home in town. After paying a $250 fine, he was freed, but the wound of the unjust episode still haunts the family.

FIVE CONCERNS OF PALESTINIAN CHRISTIANS

Palestinian Christians face formidable challenges as they work to understand their own identity in the Middle East. One pastor in Bethlehem asked me, "How do you lead a youth group when two of its leading members have been tortured in Israeli prison camps?" Christian high school students must learn to make suffering a part of their discipleship — a type of discipleship described throughout the New Testament. In the recent (2002) occupation of Bethlehem, the leading Lutheran church there was attacked by soldiers, its many doors destroyed and its offices looted and ruined. The full story of this church's suffering is available now, thanks to the Lutheran bishop in the region (on the web).[8]

Even using the Bible in their church has become a hurdle. Na'im Ateek, a Jerusalem pastor, remarks, "Western Christians and many religious Jews were using the same Bible as we, but claiming to take from it a revelation from God that justified the conquest of our land and the extermination of our people."[9] Ateek is right. If the Bible is used as a vehicle of death and destruction by those who rule — if it is the Bible that kills you — making it a source of light and life in congregational life becomes hard. One Christian leader in Jerusalem recently made the point plainly to me: "I have no use for the Old Testament," she commented. In her mind, it is the written mandate used by Israel to conquer her.

The struggle to use the Bible was made clear to me in 1992 when I spent a night at Settlement Beth El north of Jerusalem and in the evening joined a discussion group with Jewish settlers who seemed for the most part to be from New York. For them, Israel's treatment of the Arabs was biblically justified as a form of conquest. They defended intelligently the notion of a state with unequal citizens. One man remarked, "Arabs are different than us, do not possess inalienable rights, and should always be second-class citizens." (The exchange reminded me of a conversation I once had with an Australian who was talking about Aborigines who still lived in the bush.) The key here is that today this claim is being made for *theological* reasons. Israeli "apartheid" is being anchored in the Bible, which is deeply troubling

---

8. See *www.churchworldservice.org/Reports2002/middle_east/luth-christmas-church.html*.
9. Ateek, *Justice and Only Justice*, 3.

to everyone who uses the Scriptures in the Middle East and deeply troubling for Christian churches.

Four major concerns can be heard from Bethlehem to Nazareth among the Palestinian Christians. And one more concern is now just being felt in the last ten years. As an American believer I cannot help but pause and listen. These people are my brothers and sisters in Christ. They are the ones whose ancestors nurtured Christian faith as it was first preached centuries ago. To them I am indebted for my own faith.

A PLEA FOR VISIBILITY AND FELLOWSHIP

Munir Fasheh, a professor of education at Bir Zeit University in Ramallah, has made the case that Palestinian Christians are invisible to us.[10] Fasheh is probably correct. When tourists and pilgrims visit the Holy Land, they frequently show surprise when meeting Arab Christians. "When did you become a Christian?" is a question that Palestinian Christians hear regularly, and it wounds them deeply. The question presupposes that Arabs are anything but Christians — Muslims most likely — and that some Western evangelist brought them salvation.[11] Each summer my own college sends fifty college students to Israel to explore the land and its people. They return often after five weeks without having met a single Arab on a personal level, and rarely will they "find" the Palestinian Christians. Leaders in Jerusalem sometimes warn them about the dangers of the Old City or the risks of entering Bethlehem. And as a result, a residual fear settles on the group, an anxiety not unlike that felt by white Americans who have never entered an African American neighborhood and met its people.

Only the courageous seem to step out of such a mind-set and break free. Once I led such a group in Israel/Palestine and a few of my students wanted to know how to leave the tourist trail and meet Palestinian Muslims. Three of them sat under the trees near the Dome of the Rock reading books. Soon children engaged them and next they found themselves playing soccer. And next they were having dinner with a family in the Muslim Quarter of the Old City. Today they will tell you it was the most electrifying evening of the summer. On another occasion I took twenty-five students to Bethlehem in order to join a youth group in an Arab Lutheran church. That evening we played games, sang songs, learned to dance Arab dances, and ate sweet baklawa.

---

10. N. Adieux, M. Ellis, and R. Ruether, eds., *Faith and the Intifada: Palestinian Christian Voices* (Maryknoll, N.Y.: Orbis, 1992), 61–63.

11. See the remarkable stories of J. and M. Hefley, *Arabs, Christians and Jews: They Want Peace Now!* (Plainfield, N.J.: Logos, 1978), 25–37.

Then they moved into small groups, sitting on rooftop patios over Bethlehem discussing the struggles of being a Christian in Palestine or America. Those students told me that they would never be the same.

But perhaps most troubling is the treatment given to Arab Christians by evangelicals from the West who ought to know better. In May 1990 I interviewed Mr. Johann Lückhoff, the director of the International Christian Embassy in West Jerusalem. When I asked him about the Palestinian Christians, his answer was to the point: "They're not really Christians anyway. Christianity for Arabs is just a political commitment."[12] Obviously he had never prayed or worshiped with any of the thousands of Christians in this land. I revisited the so-called embassy in June 2000, and this time was struck by its plush estate, security fences, and the bodyguard parked at the gate. I asked Mr. Lückhoff similar questions and his views had not changed. For him, Arab Christians compromise their Christianity regularly when they embrace any of the Palestinian causes. "Promoting the restoration of Israel is the first sign of Arab spirituality," Lückhoff told me.

To be sure, as an American evangelical I have to avoid weighing a Middle Easterner's faith in my cultural or spiritual terms. His or her faith is shaped differently than mine. James Stamoolis has written in detail about how we misunderstand these "ancient churches."[13] The Eastern churches did not inherit the contributions of Augustine or Aquinas or Luther that have shaped our Western faith. Theirs is a different history equal to ours in every way. When an Arab Melkite Orthodox grandmother from Nazareth says that Christ is her only hope each day, I will not be cynical about her faith. I am not called to be her judge simply because she prefers incense to the hymns of Isaac Watts.

In March 1992, I interviewed a leading administrator working at the International Christian Embassy. When asked about Arab Christians, his first response was telling: "But are they really born-again Christians?" His implication was clearly that they were not. I further asked how I could tell if someone was "Filled with the Spirit" in this culture. He replied, "The first fruit of the Spirit here is a love for Israel and the Jewish people." Never before have I heard such an unwillingness to listen for the integrity of someone else's faith in different cultural terms.

---

12. Personal interview, May 29, 1990. In an interview with *Cornerstone* magazine, Jan Willem van Der Hoeven at the embassy stereotyped all Palestinians as "evil, knife-wielding terrorists." *Cornerstone* 21, no. 100 (1992): 24.

13. J. J. Stamoolis, *Easter Orthodox Mission Theology Today,* American Society of Missiology Series, no. 10 (Maryknoll, N.Y.: Orbis, 1986).

Palestinian Christians want us to embrace them as equals and invite them into fellowship. They want their Christian life to be acknowledged and respected, but they are not waiting for our acknowledgment to in some way make their faith authentic. Their Christian tradition has a life and validity apart from Western recognition. Arab Christians have been living in the Middle East for two thousand years and have survived more oppression and grief than we can imagine. They wish to be received with the honor befitting the churches that gave the West its Christianity. Father Majdi al-Siryani, a Catholic priest working in the village of Beit Sahour, urges us to remember that over the centuries these churches have survived worse circumstances than we see today. "We are strong and courageous. Do not pity us. Stand with us."

A CRY FOR JUSTICE

Christ Evangelical Church in Nazareth is one of the most beautiful Anglican churches in the country. Behind the altar at the front is an Arabic inscription that has served as the motto of the church since its founding in 1871. Nazareth is the city where Jesus not only grew up, but where he announced his ministry and messiahship. This announcement is found in Luke 4:18–19:

> "The Spirit of the Lord is upon me,
>   because he has anointed me
>   to bring good news to the poor.
> He has sent me to proclaim release to the captives
>   and recovery of sight to the blind,
>   to let the oppressed go free,
> to proclaim the year of the Lord's favor."

Today this text has a profound meaning for Palestinian Christians. Once Rev. Zahi Nassir stood in the apse of this church and explained its verses to me. He likes to quote them since, he laughed, Jesus uttered them not far from where we stood! Few churches can make such a claim. The words tell Zahi about Jesus' sense of mission. Jesus had the poor, the captive, the blind, and the oppressed on his mind. I worshiped one Sunday at this Palestinian church and thought about these words as the congregation sang Charles Wesley's hymn "Love Divine, All Loves Excelling" in Arabic translation. The hymn echoes the vision of the verse: that God's salvation would be complete, not just securing our eternal destiny but also giving us a life graced with deliverance from *all* evil and suffering.

Most Palestinian pastors take these verses from Luke 4 seriously. For them the problem of living in a country where discrimination runs rampant, where government policy is overtly unfair, and where the systems of justice are often not available has shaped their ministry. When a family's land is confiscated, when a parish home is blown up without a good reason, or when a member of the youth group disappears into the Israeli military prison system, life cannot go on as before.

Palestinian Christians are looking to us for support. They claim that they are reliving for the first time in history the conditions of the first-century church, in which a Christian minority is suffering under the rule of a Jewish majority. We in the West are the Christians of the Diaspora, or dispersion, and our support is needed. In the very same way, on his third missionary tour, the apostle Paul gathered the support of the Greek Christians for the Middle Eastern church, which was sorely oppressed (see 1 Cor. 16:1–4; 2 Cor. 8:1–15; 2 Thess. 2:13–16).

If one Bible passage has become pivotal to the Palestinian Christian experience, it is the story of Ahab and the vineyard of Naboth from 1 Kings 21 (discussed earlier in chapter 5). This passage is pivotal because it addresses the most profound injustice of all: the theft of land. Israel's excuses of national security, expediency, and primary domain are all compared with Ahab's plot to steal Naboth's vineyard. This biblical touchstone is dear to the Palestinian heart. I can barely count the number of times I have listened to Palestinian leaders use this story as a description of their own experience.

Another important story is that of Zacchaeus in Luke 19.[14] Zacchaeus had been a dishonest tax collector, cheating the people of their livelihoods. Jesus announced that salvation had come to Zacchaeus's house. Jesus had seen evidence of Zacchaeus's new moral life: the thief had been restoring all that he had stolen and giving added compensation besides. This story is extremely important for Palestinians. Proof of godly righteousness is seen in repentance and restoration of things stolen. Israel is stealing the land and the livelihoods of many of its people.

In Nazareth, the reality of land loss is at the forefront of everyone's thinking. Nazareth is at the bottom of a "bowl" in the mountains of Galilee. In 1948, Nazareth had 3,336 acres with a population of 15,000 people. The population today has risen to 56,000, and the land of the Arab city has been reduced to 1,668 acres.[15] Almost 50 percent of the town has been taken. The southeastern hills of Nazareth (called "Nazareth Elite") has all been

---

14. Explained to me by Dr. Mitri Raheb, professor of Church History, Bethlehem Bible College, March 31, 1992.

15. See Arab Nazareth's fascinating website at *www.nazareth.muni.il.*

confiscated for Israeli development. Modern homes and a fabulous shopping mall now tower over the ancient biblical city. Prominent Arab Christian families still own their useless property deeds and forever live looking up at their lost land.

A HISTORIC CLAIM TO RESIDENCE

Rev. Riah Abu El-Assal, the Anglican bishop of Jerusalem at St. George's Cathedral, despairs when he hears arguments for land ownership based on Jewish claims coming from the Bible. He feels that American Christians are often given the following scenario, which is one of the great myths of the Middle East: The Jews owned the land throughout the Old Testament era, were exiled by the Romans in 70 C.E., and in their absence, Arabs moved into the region sometime in the seventh century under the inspiration of Muhammad. Now the Arab interlude is over. The Jews have come home — and therefore the Arab residents with no historic tenure cannot make historic claims to land and residence.

El-Assal, however, once taught Islamic history and is today an important Palestinian Christian leader. He has given a great deal of thought about the historic relationship between "Arabs" and "Jews." He makes two points. First, "Arab" is a racial designation of people throughout the Middle East. And Arab "Jews" were commonplace in antiquity.[16] These people were racially Arab yet embraced Judaism. Even in the Old Testament, the incorporation of such non-Jews into Israel was common. Jethro was a Midianite (neighbors to the Arabs), and his daughter became Moses' wife (Exod. 2:15, 22). We would be hard-pressed to distinguish Jethro from any other Middle Easterner today. In fact, Judaism reached India (as did Christianity) via Arabia, where Arab Jews lived and traveled. When Israel was exiled in 70 C.E., Jews fled to these Arab Jewish communities in Arabia, Iraq, Egypt, and the Persian Gulf.[17] Therefore Arabs were well-acquainted with Judaism, and many of them were Jewish believers throughout the Middle East.

El-Assal's second and most important point is that Arab Jews were among those converted to Christ in the earliest church. Acts 2:11 specif-

---

16. Remember that Jews and Arabs are racially *both* Semites or descendants of Shem, Noah's son. It is a misnomer, therefore, to say that an Arab is "anti-Semitic."

17. When Muhammad came to the scene six hundred years later, Medina's largest tribe was Jewish. Muhammad originally told his followers to pray in the direction of Jerusalem! But because the early church in Arabia would not incorporate his reforms and accept his leadership, Islam was born. Hence, according to El-Assal, early Christianity bears some responsibility for the rise of the Islamic faith.

ically includes such Arabs as among those converted on Pentecost. "This is my lineage," he asserts. "I came from Arab Jews who accepted faith in Christ. I was not an observer at someone else's festival at Pentecost. It was my festival too." Early historians tell us that Thomas carried the gospel to the Arab tribes. Then, as so often happened in the Middle East, entire tribes were converted to Christ once the tribal chieftain took on the faith. "Many became priests and bishops, and some are named among the saints of the church.... hundreds of them were martyred in the cause of the Christian faith."[18]

Most recently Kenneth Cragg, a scholar of Islamics and Middle Eastern history, has published a definitive book, *The Arab Christian: A History of the Middle East*. Cragg supplies ample evidence — from the visits of church dignitaries who met Arab Christians to ancient Arab Christian poetry — to show the existence of an indigenous church in the region from the very earliest periods of church history.[19] He provocatively suggests that in no small measure the abstract, hellenized character of third- and fourth-century Christianity failed to win Arab culture universally. Rather than letting an indigenous form of faith emerge, Byzantine Christianity imposed foreign expectations on Arabs, virtually driving them to formulate an "Arab religion" supremely promoted by Muhammad in the seventh century.[20]

My point is this: If land promises come to Judaism by virtue of tenure in the land and biblical promise, Arabs who embraced Judaism gain these promises as well, and their faith in Jesus does not invalidate their claim to Jewish ancestry. If we ask, Where did the Arab Christians come from? the answer clearly begins with the Day of Pentecost. Hence Arabs are not "latecomers" to the scene in Israel/Palestine even though over the centuries their culture has absorbed cultural features of Islam. Jewish-Christian communities grew, and Arab Jews were in their ranks. These Arabs embraced Judaism and then converted to Christ. At the same time, Arabs living in and around Israel were likewise converted probably in the first generation of the church.

---

18. R. Abu El-Assal, "The Identity of the Palestinian Christian in Israel," in *Faith and the Intifada*, 78–79.

19. K. Cragg, *The Arab Christian: A History of the Middle East* (Louisville: Westminster/ John Knox, 1991), 31–51; cf. J. Trimingham, *Christianity Among the Arabs in Pre-Islamic Times* (New York: Longman, 1979). Irfan Shahid has completed a series of academic studies outlining Arab life in the pre-Islamic centuries. See his *Rome and the Arabs in the Third Century* (Washington, D.C.: Dumbarton Oaks, 1980), *Byzantium and the Arabs in the Fourth Century* (Washington, D.C.: Dumbarton Oaks, 1984), and *Byzantium and the Arabs in the Fifth Century* (Washington, D.C.: Dumbarton Oaks, 1990).

20. Another topic beyond the scope of this book would explore how the decisions of the early ecumenical councils (in particular, Chalcedon in 451) further alienated regional expressions of Christian faith.

These people were among the very earliest Christian communities we know, and they have been living in the Middle East continually ever since.[21]

A DISAPPEARING CHURCH

The situation among the Palestinian Christians is becoming so critical that a virtual exodus of people is leaving the country. Bishop Ignatius IV calls it "the emptying of Christianity from the Middle East.[22] Recently I shared a meal with an Arab Christian family in the West Bank who outlined how each of their college-educated children had emigrated to the United States. With tears they explained, "What could we do? There are no jobs for them here. No hope for a marriage and a home. Of course we love our land, but how much longer can we take this tension?" I asked them if they would like their grandchildren to come "home" to see this land. Their eyes lit up. "Yes. We will never leave. We will die here. And we want our American families to love it as much as we do."

Today Christian leaders speak frequently of "the museumification" of the church. Soon the living church of Israel/Palestine may be gone, with only museum-like buildings left for Christian tourists. A "custodial" community will exist, simply preserving access to the holy sites under the jurisdiction of the Israeli government.

It is helpful to put some numbers on this phenomenon. In 1922, Jerusalem had 28,607 residents, of whom 51 percent (or 14,699) were Christians. In 1978, the Israeli Bureau of Statistics counted only 10,191 Christians — fewer than 10 percent of the Arab population. Most recent estimates are that only 5,000 Christians live in the city, or fewer than 4 percent of the Arab population.

The same is true of traditionally Christian Arab cities such as Bethlehem and Ramallah. So many Palestinian Christians have left that towns in which Christians were once as many as 75 percent of the population now have Christian populations of 30 percent or less. Today there are more Palestinian Christians in Detroit, Michigan, and Jacksonville, Florida, than in Bethlehem.

Frustration with the devastated Palestinian economy, anger with the lack of freedom, and hopelessness about the future have led many to simply leave for destinations such as Canada, the United States, South America, and Australia. Pastors in Palestinian churches constantly see their ambitious

---

21. The view outlined in these paragraphs is hotly disputed, particularly among the Christian Zionists in Israel. See C. Wagner. "The Palestinization of Jesus," *Dispatch from Jerusalem* 17, no. 1 (1992): 1.

22. Ibid., 43.

young men and women leave, and they wonder about the fate of the next generation of leadership. Unless innovative solutions are found both here and abroad, we may witness the "emptying" of Christianity from the Holy Land for the first time in two thousand years.

MESSIANIC JUDAISM

In the last ten years, Palestinian Christian leaders (particularly Protestants) have explored new supportive relations with another group of Christians in the country, the Messianic Jews. These people are believers in Jesus — Christians — who live in Israel and preserve in their worship those Jewish cultural features common among Israelis. But should there be no bridge of faith, no common mission, between Arab and Jewish believers? It is something to note when Akiba Cohen, a Jewish Christian teacher, lectures at the Arab Bethlehem Bible College. Or when Salim Munayer, dean of that college, leads Messianic Jewish and Arab Christian teenagers on camping trips into the southern desert to work on reconciliation and fellowship.[23] In the wake of breathtaking conflicts in the streets, Salim gave this report of such a trip:

> Relationships were deeply forged between Arab and Jewish brothers that will serve the Body and our communities well in the dark days ahead. Prayer and testimony in the desert setting touch the lives of our hosts, the Bedouin and our own, as the Spirit of the Messiah moved among us.[24]

In March 1997, I had the privilege of leading a two-day workshop near Bethlehem for a mixed group of Jewish and Arab pastors. After watching hours of intense discussion between them, I clearly perceived that they had so much in common, yet the gulf between them would take great effort to bridge.

While Messianic Judaism is a strong and well-organized movement in the United States,[25] only recently has it grown in Israel into a noticeable voice in Israeli society. Today according to a 1999 study, about six thousand believers worship in eighty-one messianic congregations in Israel.[26] Sixty-nine congregations have their own facilities and twelve are house groups. Sometimes these groups are sophisticated ministries such as Roeh Yisrael

---

23. This is the ministry of Musalaha based in Jerusalem. See *www.musalaha.org*.

24. E-mail correspondence, October 11, 2000.

25. For a good overview, see the website of the *Messianic Jewish Alliance of America*, *www.mjaa.org*, or one ministry, *Jews for Jesus*, at *www.jewsforjesus.com*.

26. K. Kjaer-Hansen and B. F. Skjott, *Facts and Myths About the Messianic Congregations in Israel* (Jerusalem: United Christian Council in Israel, 1999).

(Shepherd of Israel) in central Jerusalem, led by Joseph Shulam. Not only do they have seventy adult members (and sometimes a hundred in worship) but they have a Bible school, the Netivvyah Instruction Ministry. Sometimes the groups may be like the Modi'in congregation, which formed in 1998 when a handful of families began meeting on Tuesday nights. Today they have twenty-six members.

Messianic Judaism was a fledgling movement twenty years ago, and growth has come about only recently. Fifty-seven of these congregations were founded since 1990 — and of these, twenty-five speak Russian. This fact offers a clue to what has happened. The sizable movement of Russian Jews to Israel became a great opportunity for evangelism and growth. An Arab friend in a north Galilee town discovered in the last ten years that his area was bringing in hundreds of Russian Jewish families who had a marginal commitment to Jewish faith. His small evangelical church in the mountains of Galilee is now brimming with them.[27]

Conversations between Arab and Jewish Christians can be difficult since the messianic community struggles with its own identity. On the one hand, it wants to embrace a courageous faith in Christ. On the other hand, it does not want to sever its cultural ties to Judaism and Israel. For instance, these communities do not want to be called "churches" and their members dislike the name "Christians." Only one of them will use a cross in its worship space, nor will they use the Lord's Prayer. But because of the dominant Jewish culture around them, they shy away from using terms like "rabbi" or "synagogue." Nevertheless they celebrate the Jewish festivals (but not all celebrate Christian ones) and decorate their halls with Jewish symbols such as shofar horns, menorahs, the star of David, and the Israeli flag. Hebrew is spoken freely (though frequently English translation is available) and culturally any Israeli Jew would feel at home.

But many Orthodox Jews dislike the presence of these congregations immensely. In the Orthodox Jewish press, they are commonly grouped with Jehovah's Witnesses and Mormons and viewed as one more cult group. Posters protesting their presence often appear on streets and, in extreme cases, their buildings are firebombed. When I visited the leaders of Roeh Yisrael in 2001, I was amazed to see their security precautions, from door locks to bars on every window. One week after I left, Orthodox Jews attacked their building, defacing their worship hall and setting fire to their expensive Torah scrolls. According to messianic leaders, they are living in a setting exactly

---

27. The same phenomenon has occurred with Ethiopian Jews. In Jaffa, for example, one can visit the large Ethiopian Jewish Messianic Congregation.

parallel to that of the first-century church in Judea: they are believers who must struggle within a majority Jewish world.

Because it frames its theology with reference to its Jewish context, this movement will embrace positions that might seem surprising — and which present a hurdle to Arab Christians who have embraced the historic creeds of the church. For example, the divinity of Jesus (which leads to belief in the Trinity) is an open question for some.[28] Likewise these communities are often kosher (observing dietary laws) and have novel interpretations of Acts 10. They also believe that circumcision, while unnecessary for Gentiles, is still a Jewish-Christian obligation. This belief represents a departure from historic understandings of, say, Galatians and Acts 15. But, they argue, early in its history the church forced Jewish believers to become culturally gentile, and today they are reclaiming that lost heritage.

But perhaps the most significant impediment to Arab-Jewish solidarity in these communities is the Messianic Jewish commitment to Israeli nationalism. While few will refer to eschatology or Israel in doctrinal statements, fidelity to Israeli nationhood is a clear sign of fidelity to "Jewishness" in this country, which explains why American Messianic congregations commonly raise money for Israel. Messianic Jews in Israel face an impossible challenge: how can I express solidarity with my Arab brothers and sisters in Christ when I feel the pull *as a Jew* to support this Jewish nation? As Arab/Jewish tensions increase in the country, this tension increases among these believers. The cultural pressure in Israel to separate from Arabs and succumb to stereotypes is enormous. For Messianic Jews to align themselves publicly will come at a cost.

But the same can be said for Arab Christians. For them to meet publicly with Jewish believers, for two pastors — one Arab and one Jewish — to work together means crossing a huge political and cultural divide. Will an Arab congregation drive into Israel and step into a Messianic congregation for fellowship? Will a Jewish congregation enter the West Bank and stand with Arab Christians, showing solidarity in their struggle for justice? Each move comes with an unpredictable consequence.

SUMMARY

As Christians look at the complex problems of Israel/Palestine, we have apparently neglected an entire community who look to us for support and

---

28. In this case, Christology follows a model of Jesus as "prophet" or "messianic messenger." He still plays an important messianic role, but does not have to be ontologically "one" with the Father.

fellowship. We have been eager to support Israel's life and future, but in doing so we have neglected Christ's ancient church in the cities of his birth, childhood, and ministry. For instance, tourists visit Nazareth for such a brief period that their buses remain lined up on the main street in front of the Church of the Annunciation, and they might as well keep their motors running. Tour guides keep the visit short: thirty minutes for the Catholic church and thirty minutes for the bathroom and shopping. That's it! The Nazareth Christians are wounded by the "sixty-minute visit" in which the "living stones" of Christ's living church are overlooked.

Worse yet, Christians in Israel/Palestine are suffering. Particularly in the West Bank and Gaza (but also elsewhere) they are discriminated against, oppressed, and imprisoned in their own country. During the Intifada the leaders of Jerusalem's churches sought to make a joint pronouncement to declare January 24–31, 1988, a "week of prayer" for peace and justice. As incredible as it sounds, Israeli censors forbade the churches from publishing their statement in the Israeli or Arab media.[29]

In another incident, in May 1988, the Jerusalem Baptist Church called Rev. Alex Awad to be its pastor. He had no criminal or political record, he was a pacifist, and he had excellent American academic credentials and held a sterling record as a faculty member at Bethlehem Bible College. Yet the Israelis found "visa irregularities" in his case in order to stop his ministry and he was forced to leave the country. Thankfully "Rev. Alex" has now been permitted to return after years in exile and today pastors a growing Baptist church in East Jerusalem.

American Christians should stand in solidarity with the church of the Middle East. The time has come for us to embrace and support Palestinian Christians in their desperate struggle for survival. They are our brothers and sisters in Christ.

---

29. D. Wagner, "Holy Land Christians and Survival," in *Faith and the Intifada*, 48. Wagner's copy of the prayer was sent out of the country illegally to him by fax.

Chapter Eleven

LIVING STONES
IN THE LAND

Four years after our flight from Lydda I dedicated my life to the service of Jesus Christ. Like me and my fellow refugees, Jesus had lived in adverse circumstances, often with only a stone for a pillow. They tortured and killed him in Jerusalem, only ten miles from Ramallah, my new home. He was the victim of terrible indignities. Nevertheless, Jesus prayed on behalf of those who engineered his death, "Father, forgive them...." Can I do less?

— Audeh Rantisi, Ramallah

I struggle, wondering how best to describe the vitality and wonder of the Palestinian Christians. I could do it statistically, reporting that about 125,000 Palestinian Christians live in Israel/Palestine and over 400,000 more live outside of the country.[1] I would prefer to take you with me to an Arabic worship service near Bethlehem.

In the village of Beit Sahour, just east of Bethlehem, is a splendid church rarely visited by Western Christians: the Latin Parish of Beit Sahour led now by Father Majdi al-Siryani. Its sparkling sanctuary is filled by 9:00 a.m. with about a hundred Palestinian families and their children. My last visit to the church was on Pentecost Sunday, June 11, 2000, when fifty Christians from First Presbyterian Church, Houston, were in attendance. What a remarkable scene! Fifty Presbyterians were joining in worship with hundreds of Palestinian Catholics — and together they were confirming a pledge made a year before to become sister churches, supporting each other in their missions. Father Majdi had preached in Houston the previous year, and now both pastors were sharing the pulpit in Beit Sahour.

An Arab church elder read from Acts 2, describing events that took place merely a handful of miles from the church's front door. Then both pastors —

---

1. According to *The Statistical Abstract of Israel 1998*, at the close of 1996 there were 123,400 Arab Christians in the country. The estimate for the size of the Palestinian "diaspora" comes from Mitri Raheb (whose profile is given below). He estimates that about 320,000 Palestinian Christians are living outside Israel/Palestine.

Father Majdi and Rev. Victor Pentz — spoke to their people about the miraculous unity that occurred on Pentecost Sunday when Christians from utterly different national backgrounds decided to embrace their unity in Christ as more important than their cultural differences. Then Majdi reminded us of something I had forgotten. Arabs were present on that first Pentecost Sunday in Jerusalem (Acts 2:11). Luke tells us that among the many people in Peter's audience were Parthians, Phrygians, Medes, Elamites, *and Arabs* who were dazzled by this outpouring of the Holy Spirit. Many of these Arabs embraced Jesus as Messiah and had brought their faith to the villages and towns around Jerusalem, which was the birth of the Arab church. Christians had been living in the valleys of Beit Sahour for two thousand years, since Peter gave his first great Pentecost sermon. I remember looking at some of these Arab families while Majdi spoke about their ancient Christian heritage. I feel fortunate to trace my spiritual ancestry back a number of generations. These people were able to point — with pride — to a spiritual ancestry that preceded the Crusades, an ancestry that even went back to the beginning of the church itself.

Following worship we met in the fellowship hall for Arabic coffee and then — as often happens — we were escorted to family homes for expansive lunches. Despite failures in language, despite misconnections between our two cultures, stories about home and children and our churches seemed to bridge wide gulfs. Arab hospitality is famous, and following an exchange of gifts and photographs we departed, knowing that we had experienced something unique, something remarkable. A five-year-old Palestinian girl gave me a hand-carved olive wood crucifix, which today hangs in one of my daughter's bedrooms.

To sing hymns with an Arabic tempo, to kneel in communion with Palestinians, to have the words "This is my body, broken for you" spoken in Arabic by the priest, and then to learn over coffee about profound struggle — I would offer these experiences to any who would know the Palestinian Christians. As pilgrims and tourists, we often enter this land to see archaeological stones. The churches of the Holy Land would have us come see them too, the *living stones of the land,* as they like to be described.

LIVING STONES

For American Christians, the most compelling reason to stand in unity with the Palestinian church comes from meeting Palestinian Christians themselves. Some are preserving ancient Eastern rites, which I barely understand.

Some have deep and vibrant testimonies that put to shame the weak-kneed Christianity that so often inhabits Western churches. Some fit our Western Christian mold perfectly, such as Yohanna Katanacho. Yohanna (or "John") graduated from Wheaton College in 1997 and then went on to Trinity Evangelical Divinity School, where he earned a master's degree. He then began a ministry for IFES (International Fellowship of Evangelical Students) and led one of the most interesting churches in the Old City of Jerusalem. Standing amid five-hundred-year-old walls in a transformed apartment is a growing house church aimed at young people in the Christian quarter of the Old City. Most nights every week, a worship band leads over fifty Arab youth in worship, and Yohanna would teach them from the Bible. To walk the lanes of the Old City with Yohanna gives a glimpse into his parish. Arabs I once thought of as shopkeepers and faceless laborers suddenly greeted him, disclosing that they were Christians of the Old City. At the time of this writing (2002), Yohanna (and his wife, Dina) have moved to Deerfield, Illinois, where he has begun Ph.D. studies in theology at Trinity Evangelical Divinity School. He was awarded a full scholarship under the "John Stott" scholars program and will return to the Arab world as a leading theologian.

Israel/Palestine is home to ancient churches whose style of worship has been shaped by two thousand years of history and whose mission has been molded by years of oppression. For these Christians, their faith has been tested and honed through centuries of struggle. Countless centuries living under Muslim rule has forced them to redefine what being a Christian in the world means. One priest refers to them as "churches of the cross," meaning that, like Jesus, they have taken on suffering as a daily walk. For more than four hundred years, the Ottoman Empire would not even let them ring their church bells. I wish I had been there at the close of World War I when the Ottoman world collapsed, and for a series of ear-numbing days, the ancient church bells of Jerusalem made up for four centuries of silence. To be sure, these churches are not perfect. Critics point to examples of worldliness and compromise and internal controversies, but no church in the world is perfect, much less ours.

The following is a sample list of Palestinian Christians — living stones — in Israel/Palestine. Countless more names could be added. Some are heroic in faith, others are quiet believers. Some have suffered so profoundly that their faith has been shaken to its core, and they would hesitate to be listed in these pages. Here I offer them as an introduction, an invitation, to meet more of the thousands of Arab Christians just like them.

Nora Kort, Jerusalem

For more years than she can count, Nora Kort's family lived on a famous hill just west of Jerusalem's Old City. Her grandparents would stand in their orchards and could gaze at the city's famed Jaffa Gate. They were an old "Jerusalemite" family known since the nineteenth century, and by the 1940s they owned about forty-eight acres of land. They were also strong Christians. Her grandfather had a dream long before Nora was born that

God wanted him to build a church for this area. He did. He used all of his savings, raised money from friends in Russia, and constructed it in the lowest level of his home. He then entrusted it to the Orthodox Church of Jerusalem. For years, Arab Christians outside the city walls worshiped here at "St. George's Church."

In 1948, war erupted and some of Israel's most vicious fighters (the Stern Gang and the Hagganah) charged over the hill. Fighting was

fierce, and Nora's parents fled into Jerusalem's walled city. Her aunt refused to go — but was forced to — and so she ran through the house, gathered up precious heirlooms, and hid them in a nearby cave. Jewish neighbors — friends for many years — pledged to guard the house and keep the cave a secret.

When a lull in the fighting occurred, Nora's uncle would sneak out of Jerusalem in order to collect what things he could, despite the danger. The hill had become a no-man's land. Many friends had been killed already. Nora's immediate family settled into a single room in the Old City and waited, but the family house was slipping from their hands. Jewish settlers occupied it and the Korts would never own it again.

Nora was born not long after the war, and she grew up hearing about her family's heritage. Her father would daily walk Jerusalem's walls, looking west, trying to see his ancestral home. But from 1947 until 1967, he could not walk the half mile to his front door. When Israel occupied all of Jerusalem in 1967 and the borders moved, Nora's father made his first trip home and even opened his old front door with his own key. He was met by a Jewish family from Yemin who refused him entry. His caves and their treasures were gone, leveled by bulldozers. He picked one pomegranate from one of his own trees and his heart broke. For the next twenty-five years, he walked to the house weekly, standing at its gates, hoping to look in. When he died in 1994, he uttered his last words to his daughter "Nora, do not forget."

Nora's first visit to the house came in 1995. The house had been turned into "The Zionist Confederation House," and she was invited to attend a conference that was being broadcast for Israeli TV. Soon she was sitting in her family's living room. She will tell you, "At that moment, my father's voice came alive." She wanted to tell him, "I have not forgotten." So she raised her hand after the speakers were finished and explained, "I am a Palestinian. Do you know that you are sitting in my father's house?" There was dead silence. The TV cameras zoomed in. Nora inquired about her mother's piano — an heirloom she longed to see and hear — and the manager of the house spoke up, admitting she knew of it. But when Nora returned a week later to see it, the piano had disappeared. Quietly an elderly rabbi and his wife approached her in tears. They knew her family, they knew the history, they knew the betrayal.

I visited "Confederation House" recently. It is behind the King David Hotel and enjoys one of Jerusalem's most spectacular views.[2] The house has a modern restaurant inside as well as ample facilities for conferences. I asked one of the attendants about the history of the house and whether Arabs had ever lived there. He said he doubted it. A brochure gave me the answer. It claimed that the house — called St. George's house — had been a base for Arab terrorists, and after having been conquered by Israeli freedom fighters, it had been renovated in 1984. But of course, none of this story was true.

Nora is today one of Jerusalem's most vigorous social workers. She serves the Arab Orthodox Society (founded in 1926), which ministers to the city's poor and ill, bringing medical care, counseling services, and aid. In 1991, she was instrumental in beginning the Melia Art and Training Center inside the Old City. Here eight staff members work with five hundred Palestinian women, training them in the art of Arab embroidery that is then sold to tourists at the Melia Outlet (just inside New Gate). Ninety percent of the money goes to poor Arab families; in 1999 alone, over sixty-seven thousand dollars went to poor women. Then, in 1996, she opened the Bint El Balad Café ("the country daughter"), which again employed more women and let still others bring traditional foods from their homes for sale.[3] Profits return to the villages and the Old City for families in need.

---

2. Confederation can be found by following a lane east from Hamelech David Street adjacent to the King David Hotel. At the end of the lane, climb the hill to the right.

3. To find the Bint El Balad, enter the Old City through New Gate and it will be just a few doors in on your left.

"God is working here," Nora says. "I can see his hands in great ways. He is here. Sometimes I dream — like my grandfather — I dream that this area of Jerusalem will become a cultural center for our people." Nora has also written, "I believe that God is especially close to those who are oppressed. God hears their cry and resolves to set them free. God is father of all but in particular father and defender of those who are oppressed and treated unjustly. This is and has been my mission and my commitment."[4]

Bishara Awad, Bethlehem

Early in the twentieth century, Bishara Awad's grandfather had been the governor of the ancient city of Jaffa on Israel's coast.[5] In fact, the Awad family had been there so long that they possessed church records letting them trace their Christian history back five hundred years in that city.

The family moved to Jerusalem in the 1930s, which is where Bishara was born. When the war of 1948 broke out, the fighting around their home — just north of the Damascus Gate — was severe. No one could walk outside. Then one terrible day, Bishara's father was shot standing on his front porch. As bullets flew, his mother dragged her husband inside and soon he was dead. That night, nine-year-old Bishara helped bury his father in the garden of their home. And at the close of the war, the Awad family joined the ranks of the seven hundred thousand refugees who had lost everything.

Unable to support her seven children, Bishara's mother placed them in an orphanage where Bishara spent the next twelve years. Through his active participation in Sunday school, he became a Christian. In his own words, "I gave my life to God and decided to follow him." When he was a teenager, a generous American sponsor paid for his tuition to attend a Christian school. Another miracle came in 1961 when the dean of an American college was coming through Jerusalem. He liked Bishara, and before Bishara knew it, the young teen had a four-year scholarship to Dakota Wesleyan University

---

4. N. Kort, "God Hears the Cry of My People," in *Faith and the Intifada: Palestinian Christian Voices*, ed. N. Ateek, N. Ellis, and R. Ruether (Maryknoll, N.Y.: Orbis, 1992), 125.

5. Today the bust of "Eskander Awad" can still be seen in Jaffa.

in Mitchell, South Dakota. In 1967 when war broke out again, he was pro-hibited from returning home, but his application for American citizenship was successful. With a U.S. passport, Bishara could return to Jerusalem as a missionary with the Mennonite Central Committee. From 1972 until 1981, he led a boys' home in Beit Jala, a Christian village west of Bethlehem. In those years, God gave Bishara a vision that exceeded his wildest imagining. Christian Palestinians were leaving the country in record numbers. At the turn of the century, 17 percent of the population was Christian; in 1999, 4 percent. To help stem the tide, Bishara founded Bethlehem Bible College in 1979 with only ten students to help equip believers to remain in their home-land to minister to their people. Today over 250 students have graduated from BBC — the only Arabic-speaking Bible college in the country.

The story of BBC is a legacy of God's faithfulness to a small Arabic evangelical presence. The buildings the BBC occupies today on Bethlehem's Hebron Road are extremely valuable and yet their $1.8 million was raised among local and Western Christians. Today the college has a new twenty-one-thousand-volume library, a guest house, a counseling center, six full-time (and six part-time) faculty, and a school choir that frequently tours the world.[6]

Emil Salayta, Bir Zeit

Among Arab pastors in Palestine, Father Emil's story is fascinating. First, he is not Palestinian, but belongs to a Christian Bedouin tribe from south-ern Jordan. These Arab tribes still migrate through the desert today, but in this case, Emil's family settled down in the Christian town of Madaba near Mount Nebo (where Moses died). This fact alone is astonishing. Christianity spread very early to the deserts of Arabia, and a number of these tribes were converted over fifteen hundred years ago.[7] Archaeological records even iden-tify the Christian town of Madaba as early as the fourth century. In mosaics it is called "the beloved of Christ."

Emil attended a Catholic school in Madaba, and then in 1976 when he was twelve, he decided to begin study for the priesthood. He traveled to Palestine to attend seminary in the village of Beit Jala outside Bethlehem. Emil was ordained in 1989 and began work as a young teacher in regional schools.

---

6. For a quick introduction to BBC, visit their website at *www.BethlehemBibleCollege.edu*. In August 2000, BBC earned a full accreditation with the Middle East Association of Theological Education.

7. Bir Zeit's associate priest is also Bedouin. Father Iyad Twal is a twenty-five-year-old recent ordinand from the Jordanian tribe of the Al-Auzaizat. His family likewise settled in Madaba.

When Emil came to the village of Bir Zeit in 1993, he found a church with little vision and a great deal of despair. But within months, the church knew that Emil was about to bring explosive energy to the ministry. Their first clue was that this twenty-nine-year-old priest did not wear a cassock  around town. Bir Zeit is a village of 3,000 people fifteen miles north of Jerusalem that is strongly Christian (950 are Catholic, 500 Orthodox, 50 Anglican). In addition, the well-known Bir Zeit University — which brings 4,000 students to the town — is located there.[8] But in 1993, Bir Zeit was reeling from the conflicts of the Intifada (1987–93). Emil also noted that Palestinian Christians were rapidly leaving the village because of the recent wars and economic frustration. For instance, 5,000 of the village's Christians were already living in the United States, and today Bir Zeit even has its own website to keep them connected.[9] Few Christians could be found between the ages of twenty-five and forty. These people who had left were often the ambitious and the educated — young men and women who had graduated from the prestigious university and who could supply a future to the parish.

Emil became convinced that working for the social welfare of his people was equally important to their spiritual welfare. He took on a leadership role for all of the Catholic schools in Jordan, Cyprus, and Israel/Palestine — 43 schools, 18,000 students, and 1,200 staff. He also studied his own village and learned that the lack of affordable housing contributed to young families leaving. Terrible unemployment (about 30 percent throughout the West Bank) and Israeli limitations on village growth were pushing young families away. Therefore, in 1996, he launched the "Living Stones" ministry, an ambitious project that would build forty-six full-size apartments on land donated by the parish and financed in part by the Spanish government.[10] Soon $2,170,000 was raised and World Vision contributed another $500,000. I was there the day the keys were handed out (June 10, 2000). Newly married couples and young men waiting to get engaged received their

---

8. See the website for the university, *www.birzeit.edu.*

9. See *www.birzeitsociety.org.*

10. These homes are like European "flats" or American "condominiums," each the size of a moderate-sized Western home.

keys and joined in with hundreds and hundreds of Christians who celebrated in the streets. But that is not all. "Living Stones" also launched ministries for the elderly, job training for the young, and aid services for the poor. Thanks to Emil, the newly built Latin high school in Bir Zeit is the only Palestinian school that requires its students to study Hebrew. His students even are pen pals with Israeli children across the country.

World Vision continues to work with the church through its contributions to the Latin schools in the area. Nearly a thousand children have been sponsored in Arab villages throughout the West Bank, and another four hundred have been sponsored in Bir Zeit alone. In 1995, National Presbyterian Church, Washington, D.C., built a partnership with Father Emil's parish and helped contribute to the housing project. Already over a hundred Christians from Washington have visited the village. Lynne Farris, formerly their assistant pastor, commented recently, "The partnership has meant a great deal to us because we have been able to develop new friendships with our brothers and sisters in the West Bank. I never had a Palestinian friend before I met Father Emil, and now I have many from this beautiful part of God's family."

Father Emil has moved to Rome, where he is now pursuing doctoral studies in theology. The legacy of his work continues, and the church in Bir Zeit is now led by an equally creative and passionate priest, Father Iyad Twal.

Cedar Duaybis, Jerusalem

When the 1948 war erupted, Cedar Duaybis was a girl of twelve. Her family hoped to ride out the war at home in the port city of Haifa, but when they learned of the massacres of Arabs in villages like Deir Yassin, they fled. "Haifa was on fire and so were our hearts," she will tell you. Near their home, barrels of dynamite were rolled down their hilly street and many were getting killed. Cedar remembers lying on the floor of a truck, face down, as bullets tore through its thin shell. Finally they made their way into the hills of Galilee and arrived as refugees in Nazareth.

While their fate was grim, 80 percent of the Christians of Haifa fled to Lebanon and assumed they would come home. But Israeli military fences would keep them out for the rest of their lives. From that time on, the Duaybis family would travel to the Lebanese border to look through those fences and call out words of affection to uncles and aunts they would never embrace again.

Cedar's life in Nazareth was difficult, but this had little to do with the secondhand clothes she remembers so well. By the age of fourteen at the time of her confirmation in the Anglican church, this bright, thoughtful girl had reached a crisis of faith. The world seemed to be rejoicing that the State of Israel was born — Christians from America were citing prophecies and calling it God's handiwork — and yet Cedar had seen only death and

devastation coming from the Israeli soldiers. If the God of the Bible had done this, if the God of Israel was also her God, how was she to believe in him? Perhaps such a God who kills people at whim does not deserve faith.

The inner struggle for faith was a part of each night's conversation at home. Cedar's mother, Genevieve, submitted to this history, accepting the catastrophe as God's will. Her father, Fu'ad, refused. For him, God was a God of love, and these horrors had nothing to do with his will. Fu'ad argued passionately that injustice had to be resisted. Soon Cedar's father abandoned the church. "If this is Christianity — to accept oppression — then Palestinians cannot be Christians." The Old Testament had become a weapon of war. The conquest stories of Joshua were now conquest stories about the Palestinians. The internal conflict in Cedar's young heart spun out of control.

Since many pastors had been lost during the war, priests came from Jordan to lend a hand. At twenty-three, Cedar fell in love with one such man, an Anglican priest from Jordan who had volunteered to help the needy church of Palestine. But she also wondered if his counsel, his faith, could help resolve the struggle that had never been resolved in her own heart. She missed the hymns of the church. She missed its fellowship and knew that the confusion and anger harbored inside were destroying her. And yet she was angered at the silence of the church as it offered no answers, no resolution to the problem of suffering and oppression. When the young couple wed in 1959, Cedar found that her inner tensions only increased. How could she be a pastor's wife when so many grave doubts about God haunted her? Young women were looking to her for inspiration, but her life was desperately empty and she could tell no one.

One of her husband's closest friends was a fellow Anglican priest named Na'im Ateek. Na'im would eventually become the pastor of the Arabic-speaking congregation at Jerusalem's prestigious St. George's Cathedral, and it was Na'im's thoughtful, well-integrated faith that saved one young woman from abandoning hers. Na'im preached that God was committed to justice — not conquest — and that in the present era, he was not *necessarily* on the side of Israel. As a Christian intellectual, Na'im was taking a stand — confronting the enemy, resisting the oppressor from his pulpit.[11] Cedar listened to him and was awed. Here was a new way to read the Bible. In its pages she found glimpses of hope she never had before. The Palestinians were not the new Canaanites, targeted for conquest. They were not godless pagans, doomed before Joshua's sword. As God's prophets stood against ancient Israel, so too they would stand against modern Israel. For the first time since her childhood, Cedar found a place where she could stand *and still be a Christian.*

As Cedar's ministry unfolded, her heart was touched by the suffering of the Palestinian women who had lost husbands and sons. Through the YWCA she worked tirelessly in programs bringing them assistance. But she worried most about the children. She writes, "Perhaps the most agonizing experiences Palestinian mothers face is to watch the dehumanizing effect of repression and prolonged deprivation on the children, to watch helplessly as they become hardened and radicalized or lose their faith. While other kids are spending their time in sports and hobbies, our children are withering away in prison."[12]

Cedar continues to serve the Palestinian church today in Jerusalem, and she has joined ranks with Na'im Ateek's ministry called "Sabeel" (which in Arabic means "the way" or a "spring of water"). Working as a Christian advocate for Palestinian rights, Cedar is a seasoned intellectual whose faith now runs deep and her commitments unflinching. Her desire is for her people to

> discover the liberating power of Christ, who, by living in our midst, gave us a model for life. He revealed to us what it means to be truly alive. He came that we may have life in all its fullness, something we cannot achieve when others around us are denied life. He showed us that being fully alive means being fully involved. For a Christian, it becomes a matter of duty, an obligation, and not just a matter of choice, to stand for justice.[13]

---

11. Na'im Ateek wrote many of these thoughts while studying at Berkeley, and they were later published in the courageous book *Justice and Only Justice: A Palestinian Theology of Liberation* (Maryknoll, N.Y.: Orbis, 1989). He eventually left St. George's Cathedral and began Sabeel, a center for the Christian study of justice and liberation. See their website at *www.sabeel.org.*

12. "Women, Faith, and the Intifada," in *Faith and the Intifada*, ed. Ateek, Ellis, and Ruether, 120.

13. Ibid., 121.

Mitri Raheb, Bethlehem

As a Christian intellectual, Mitri Raheb's Ph.D. from Marburg University (Germany) and the caliber of his professorial work stand up to international standards of scholarship.[14] He has not only taught church history at Bethlehem Bible College, but he also pastors the Evangelical Lutheran Christmas Church in Bethlehem (founded in 1854). There each Sunday, about fifty-five families gather for worship and forty children study in Sunday school. But in addition, Mitri's energies are devoted to the International Center of Bethlehem (Dar al-Nadwa).[15] A sorely neglected nineteenth-century building had been used first for refugees in 1948 and then it became a part of the church's school in the 1970s. In 1992, the building was converted to a guest house (The Abu Jubran Guest House), and in 1995 further work created the International Center, which serves more than twenty thousand people annually.

Here there is an array of programs that enhance Palestinian Christian life in Bethlehem: youth festivals, art shows, public lectures, conferences, alternative tourism, training of Palestinian tour guides, and Internet clubs just begin the list. According to Mitri, 2 million tourists come to the Holy Land every year, over 85 percent of whom are Christians. During their visits, they spend less than two hours in the West Bank. Today a creative church tour could reside in Bethlehem at the International Center and skip the hotel, participate in local activities, and genuinely meet the Palestinian Christians of Bethlehem.

In 1995, Mitri published his courageous account of life within the Christian Arab minority in his important book *I Am a Palestinian Christian* (Minneapolis: Fortress, 1995). The book presents an incisive analysis of life under occupation, his struggles as a pastor, and his reading of the Bible which challenges many assumptions popularly held in Israel.

Mitri likes to explain that his Christian family can chronicle its presence in Bethlehem as far back as a thousand years. "Raheb" means "monk" in Arabic, and one valley near Bethlehem bearing this name was owned by

---

14. Mitri's doctoral dissertation on the Palestinian Lutheran Church in Jordan was published in Germany in 1990 by Gütersloh.

15. See the center's website: *www.annadwa.org*. Dar al-Nadwa literally means "house of worldwide encounter."

his ancestors. But the history goes back even further. Five Jewish-Christian families (whom Mitri can name) lived in Bethlehem just after the New Testament was written, and they are the great, great ancestors of Christianity in this city. Remarkably these families are still in Bethlehem to this day. Other Christians came later — especially with the Crusades — but the Raheb family reaches back to the earliest believing communities of Christendom. As heir to the faith of these earliest "Jewish-Christian" believers in the Holy Land, Mitri is amazed by people who would deny his identity and history.

A few moments with Mitri, however, and one comes to the certain conclusion that he is living with his people in the midst of their suffering. In a recent conversation with Mitri, I inquired about the sorts of things he has experienced as a pastor. He told me about two elders, ages thirty-five and forty-five, who each spent twenty-one months in prison without being formally charged. Their families — without incomes — have suffered terribly. He also will tell you about the Daher family, whose vineyard about seven miles south of Bethlehem has been under threat of confiscation by the Israelis because it was "uncultivated." The Daher family had purchased the land a hundred years ago when they migrated from Lebanon and invested their savings. The vineyard had been a famously rich one, but for many years the Israelis had restricted water distribution in Bethlehem, and the Daher vineyard was in trouble. The real reason for the confiscation, though, was simple: the Daher vineyard occupied a lovely hilltop surrounded by three Israeli settlements. It was a thorn in the side of large Jewish organizations (the Amana Movement of Gush Emunim, the Ha'oved HaLeumi Party) that wanted to consolidate Jewish control over this area.

When the Daher family came to Mitri with the military confiscation order, Mitri was barely surprised. The situation was a perfect repeat of the biblical story of Ahab and Naboth's vineyard in 1 Kings 21. Corrupt Israeli leaders twisted justice in order to steal land. Mitri's church decided to fight back. Committees were set up to prevent the loss of land. One committee, headed by an attorney, worked on an appeal. Another committee obtained tractors to immediately re-plow the land. A third committee quickly obtained plants to renew the fields: they collected seventeen hundred young cabbage plants, two hundred olive trees, and more than a thousand almond and plum trees. A fourth committee worked on media relations and when word got out, Christians, Muslims, Americans, and Europeans could be seen in the Daher family vineyard planting trees.

Is this the role of a pastor? Is this Mitri's calling? Is this Christian ministry — to mobilize a congregation in order to save the homes of its member believers?

Today the Daher family farm still stands, but it experiences regular threats. Incredibly their land has now been adopted by international legal communities based in Geneva, Switzerland, which are viewing this as a test case of Israeli justice. Physical threats and acts of violence have also come against the Dahers, but they have stood firm. Settlers tried to bulldoze a road through the middle of these vineyards claiming the need for safe transit, but this ploy failed as well. In 1999, I had the privilege of standing with the young men of this family on the highest point of their lands. The cave where their grandfather lived while he tilled the land for the first time stood behind us. But there — looming to the west — was an incredible sight. A settlement, pristine and modern, with every sign of rapid growth — a new suburb for Jerusalem — hovered on the edge of Daher's land. One son pointed to the edge of his land in a nearby valley. We squinted to see in the distance. Bulldozers were scraping away at the perimeter of the farm and in many cases crossing the valley, defiantly eroding the boundary this family defends. These facts provide the incredible "cutting edge" issues of Mitri's pastorate.

Perhaps the most powerful moment I have ever had with Mitri Raheb came when he unfolded an old letter from his wallet, so brittle that the paper crackled. The letter was written by a young man who was a leader in Mitri's youth group while the young man was imprisoned some years back in Ansar III, an army prison famous for torture. The smuggled note is clearly sacred script for Mitri. He explained that it was a "letter of faith written under imprisonment — much like the letters of the New Testament." In the letter, the boy described the awesome physical torture he endures. He calls his prison "the slaughterhouse." Then he goes on to interpret Isaiah 53 as an explanation of his suffering. But these aspects of the correspondence are not the most remarkable. The bulk of the letter consists of five suggestions on how Mitri might improve the youth group. In the midst of his profound suffering, the young man has the needs of the church on his mind. I couldn't help but think of Paul in Philippians 2. When he was imprisoned, wondering about his own martyrdom, he is concerned with the well-being of the church he has left behind.

Mitri wonders if any pastor can be equipped for this sort of calling. But clearly God has given this pastor gifts not listed in any seminary catalog. "Living in this situation makes you mature," he says. "Either you emigrate from this place — or you stay and witness the righteousness of God at work."

Jonathan Khuttab, Jerusalem

The challenge that confronts most Christian professionals in Israel/Palestine is how they might employ their expertise in order to assist the struggle of the Palestinian people in practical ways. Physicians might serve those who cannot pay or might volunteer in impoverished areas. Educators and social workers (such as Nora Kort) sometimes work among urban poor or in refugee camps. As an internationally respected attorney, Jonathan Khuttab has confronted the Israeli occupation in the courts and in the press.

Jonathan received his B.A. degree at the evangelical Messiah College in Pennsylvania in 1973 and obtained a doctorate in law from the University of Virginia in 1977. Then for two years (until 1979), he practiced law in New York, becoming a member of the New York bar. In 1980, he returned to Israel/Palestine, joined the Israeli bar, and began studying Hebrew. He is one of the most respected attorneys in Jerusalem today. His understanding of the political crisis of his country is so keen that he frequently appears in interviews on CBS, ABC, NBC, and CNN. He has appeared more than once with Ted Koppel on ABC's *Nightline*.

In addition to his law practice and his active involvement at St. George's Anglican Church in East Jerusalem, Jonathan founded two organizations that today stand for justice in Palestine. The first, Al Haq (in Arabic, *The Truth*) is a human rights research and publications organization that today is the West Bank affiliate of the Geneva-based *International Commission of Jurists*. Al Haq's many employees compile courtroom-quality documentation of human rights abuses throughout Israel, the West Bank, and Gaza. Its support comes through major grants from Western churches, the Ford Foundation, and many other sources. Al Haq even provided the first public law library in the West Bank, and its list of publications offers an impressive record of Israel's treatment of the Palestinians since 1948. International law students come here as interns from throughout the world to see firsthand how to work in the trenches of international justice.[16]

Jonathan's second and newest endeavor is called the Mandela Institute, through which he is working for the care of needy Palestinian political prisoners, their civil rights, their medical needs, and any basic provisions for their comfort (such as warm clothes and blankets in winter). Mandela even

---

16. See the website: *www.alhaq.org*. Al Haq supplies a comprehensive list of links that address the problem of human rights in the Middle East. See *www.alhaq.org/frames_links.html*.

supplies paper and books, but above all, it works for visitation rights so that families may see their imprisoned sons and fathers regularly. Visitation is always a problem, and generally attorneys and pastors are denied access to those in their care. Jonathan is working to change this.[17]

In 1992, I asked Jonathan why he started these programs. His answer: "Christians should have the Lordship of Christ throughout their lives."[18] For him, social needs and political justice are included as well. "Attitudes toward our enemies, toward suffering, toward the world — these should all be addressed by our Christianity."

Jonathan exemplifies the ultimate expression of the committed Christian layperson. He is a high-profile change agent in his community who has brought professional expertise and Christian compassion together. The week I visited him, he was running to and from the Augusta Victoria Hospital in Jerusalem. A team of American surgeons from Norfolk, Virginia's "Operation Smile" was doing free cleft lip/palate surgeries for poor Arab families. Typically, Jonathan was the head of the local committee sponsoring them. He could frequently be heard standing in the hospital halls, translating Arabic and English for frightened Palestinian families as surgeons explained the progress of their children.

Jad Isaac, Beit Sahour

When the Intifada began, the Christian village of Beit Sahour outside Bethlehem suddenly found itself in the spotlight. Palestinians everywhere decided to "disengage" from the Israeli economy, which meant refusing to purchase even Israeli agricultural products. In 1988, Jad Isaac was an associate professor of plant physiology at Bethlehem University.[19] He and a group of his friends all loved gardening and used their professional expertise to teach their neighbors how to build small family "plots" (of two hundred square meters) that would intensively raise enough food (vegetables, fruit, and livestock) to support one family. Virtually overnight almost ten thousand Arabs were buying gardening products from "The Shed" — an outlet for seeds brought up from Jericho. Charitable contributions subsidized the seeds, giving even the poor an opportunity to build gardens. In March 1988 alone, two hundred thousand seedlings — tomato, eggplant, pepper, cauliflower, and lettuce — were distributed along with a thousand fruit trees, four thousand chickens, eight lambs, pesticides, drip irrigation equipment, and farming

---

17. See the website: *www.mandela.org*.
18. Personal interview, April 4, 1992.
19. Isaac earned his master's degree from Rutgers University and his Ph.D. from the University of East Anglia in the United Kingdom.

gear. The *Jerusalem Post* called the work "a quiet kind of uprising." Journalists flocked to the village — as did Palestinians from all over the West Bank. Soon "Intifada gardens" were spreading from home to home like wildfire.

That is, until June 1988. Citing "state security," the Israeli army closed everything down in Beit Sahour. But Jad knew that it was coming. This form

of resistance was incredibly successful, and the international press loved it. His picture appeared in newspapers from the *Washington Post* to the *Manchester Guardian*. From May 17 until June 5, Jad was arrested daily by the army — generally at night. Harassment continued for the leadership committee until finally The Shed had to close. Then on July 8, 1988, Jad was arrested and taken for five months to the dreaded Ansar III prison camp, but his garden network did not stop. Underground suppliers continued providing seeds to families as the resistance continued. And Israeli pressure mounted. In 1989, the Israeli's punished the village by "emptying" the town for forty-five days, confiscating all household appliances as payment for back taxes.

Jad speaks haltingly about the experience of being in prison. Its scars still haunt him. Being a strong leader, he quickly found himself in charge of the prison pharmacy. He studied Hebrew and taught fellow prisoners ecology, economics, politics, and English. He even taught the structure of DNA by using bread-bag wires as models. Academic papers were penned on the inside of wrappers from cigarette boxes.

"For the first time," Jad said, "I understood suffering." He experienced torture and food deprivation and extreme fatigue. He lost weight dramatically. On August 17 of that year, he watched three Palestinians shot dead by their Israeli guards when they refused to build a prison fence. When he describes the event, his voice still shakes with anger.

In fact, righteous anger floods Jad's soul. He feels profound disillusionment with his Greek Orthodox tradition, which, he feels, has not taken a sufficiently active role in promoting the needs of the poor. Human values and human dignity are at the core of his Christian upbringing, and the church has failed to defend them.

Today Jad is no longer at Bethlehem University. He is the director of Applied Research Institute, an agricultural research group in Jerusalem.[20] Here scientists like Jad are studying the environmental issues of Palestine, resource issues, water distribution and quality, as well as producing satellite-quality maps of land use (which track Israeli confiscation and misuse of land). He is still active in promoting peace and justice. He helped found the Rapprochement Centre in Beit Sahour, where young Palestinians and Israelis can meet on neutral turf and talk about their differences, but Jad does not attend church. The Christian church will have no credibility for him until it courageously confronts the pain and injustices of his homeland.

Salim Munayer, Bethlehem, Jerusalem

One might think of Salim Munayer as a "second generation" refugee. Born seven years after his family's tragic losses, he has now established a successful career and come to terms with Israeli occupation. Salim's parents lived in

Lod (or Lydda) until April 1948 when the first Israeli attack came.[21] Moshe Dayan (later to be Israel's defense and foreign minister) led the siege at the head of an armored column. Israeli historians describe him as driving "full speed into Lydda, shooting up the town, and creating confusion and terror among the population."[22] An eyewitness from the *Chicago Sun-Times* was there and reported on the "blitz tactics" of Dayan. "Practically everything in their way died. Riddled corpses lay by the roadside." Another reporter talks about corpses of Arab women, men, and children strewn about in the wake of the ruthlessly brilliant charge."[23] On that day, over 250 residents of Lydda were killed. And once the town was emptied, unrestrained looting by soldiers began. Israeli troops carried away eighteen hundred truckloads of Arab property — everything from agricultural equipment to a button factory. Seven thousand retail shops were emptied as well as five

---

20. See the website: *www.arij.org.*
21. The siege of Lod took place throughout the summer of 1948. See the eyewitness account of Audeh Rantisi provided in chapter 8.
22. D. Neff, "Expulsion of the Palestinians, Lydda and Ramleh in 1948," *The Washington Report on Middle East Affairs* (July–August 1994): 72.
23. Ibid.

hundred workshops.[24] One of the leading participants of the attack, Joseph ben Eleazer, later became a Christian — and at the end of his life seeking forgiveness was paramount in his heart.

The Munayers were the largest Greek Orthodox family in Lod. In the chaos of the siege, their home was occupied as a military headquarters and later became the city hall. When Salim was born in 1955, his world was filled with the tensions of occupation and the reality of being a minority in a majority-Israeli state. His parents remained in Lod and worked to integrate him quickly into this new situation, eventually obtaining Israeli citizenship for the family. Salim grew up bilingual, even attending a Jewish high school. After graduation from the Israeli Tel Aviv University, he attended Pepperdine University in California for one year and later enrolled in Fuller Seminary's School of World Missions. His English now proficient, he recently completed a Ph.D. at Oxford in social psychology on "The Ethnic Identity of Palestinian Arab Christian Adolescents in Israel" — an apt description of his own childhood.

When Salim began teaching at Bethlehem Bible College in 1985, he was amazed at the different life lived by his fellow Arabs under military occupation. Then in 1987 the Intifada exploded all around him, and at once the crisis of the occupation was squarely in his life. In 1989 when he became the school's academic dean, Salim says he experienced an "awakening" as he witnessed the destructive climate of occupation.

In this context, God used Salim's talent as a bridge-builder. He understood the cry for justice among his Palestinian people — and he understood the fear deeply ingrained in the Jewish heart. Salim realized that without excellent communication, no relationship between Jews and Arabs was possible, and without a relationship, the future was doomed. Salim thus began the ministry of Musalaha (or "reconciliation") in 1990.[25] When relationships form in a context of conflict, Salim believes we dehumanize our enemy and make understanding impossible. Arabs will stereotype Jews and Jews will stereotype Arabs. The only hope is to form new contexts, new settings where new understanding can be formed. Salim is convinced that openness will be found chiefly among the young whose hearts are still permeable. These young men and women have never had a serious conversation with someone from "the other side."

Among other activities, Musalaha sponsors desert encounters for Messianic Jews and Arab Christians. Imagine thirty young people (ages fourteen

---

24. Ibid., citing A. R. Norton, *The Washington Post*, March 1, 1988.
25. See the website *www.musalaha.org.*

to eighteen) with fifteen camels trekking through the desert for five days, with the first hurdle being how one Arab and one Jew decides who will ride and who will walk. Mealtime and evening programs discuss "desert stories" from the Bible, devotionals about reconciliation, and personal sharing. After the trek, aggressive follow-up and continued contact take place "across" the Arab/Jewish divide. In the last ten years, Musalaha has led about fifteen hundred people on these reconciliation treks.

Today Salim continues to serve as the dean of BBC while he directs the work of Musalaha. World Vision has now joined Musalaha in partnership, as have many American churches. The ministry of Salim is growing. For example, in August 2000, some of the young adults in Musalaha traveled north to Galilee to pick up recent refugees from Lebanon (displaced by the Israeli pullout). Their dream was to visit holy sites in Jerusalem for the first time — and that dream was realized. For two days they walked and worshiped in Jerusalem, the Mount of Olives, and Bethlehem. They also met their first Messianic Jews, a truly amazing experience for them. Musalaha now sponsors theological conferences, women's conferences and publishes books,[26] and leads thought-provoking trips. Imagine traveling with a mixed bus of Arabs and Jews to Yad Vashem, the Jewish Holocaust Memorial in West Jerusalem. Then, in the same day, imagine the same group going to Deir Yassin where once in 1948 a Jewish militant group brought another massacre on a small Arab village.

Maroun Laham, Beit Jala

Sometimes a turning point comes to your life at the point of a gun. In 1974, two years after Maroun Laham became a Catholic priest, he was traveling in Lebanon outside Tripoli, not long after the outbreak of the Lebanese civil war when atrocities had become commonplace between Muslim and Christian militias. Recently numerous Muslims had been murdered near Tripoli, and as Maroun's bus left the city it was hijacked by Muslim fighters. Thirteen Christians were found on board, and they were escorted off and told they would be shot in revenge for the earlier Muslim deaths. Maroun was a young priest — only twenty-two — and he was facing near-certain death. He remembers privately giving absolution to the entire group, waiting for the machine-gun fire to begin. But miraculously his captors decided to set them free.

---

26. See L. Loden, P. Walker, and M. Wood, eds., *The Bible and the Land: An Encounter* (Jerusalem: Musalaha, 2000). Here Arab Christians and Messianic Jews wrestle with the land promises of the Bible from their differing perspectives. For copies, e-mail: *musalaha@netvision.net.il.*

The Laham family lost their home in 1948 following Israel's war of independence. They were given fifteen days to leave the country, and so his father led his family to Lebanon and then on to Jordan as refugees. At twelve, after many years in public schools, Maroun was invited by his church to consider  the priesthood as a vocation. He accepted and came to the Latin Seminary in the village of Beit Jala, next door to Bethlehem. After his graduation in 1972, Maroun served parishes throughout Jordan and the Gulf. But the patriarch in Jerusalem saw his potential for academic study, and from 1988 to 1992 he earned a Ph.D. at the Vatican's Pontifical Lateran University in Rome. Since then he has been the director of Catholic schools in Jordan, Israel/Palestine, and Cyprus (1992) and today serves as the rector of the Beit Jala's Catholic seminary (since 1994). The school is a huge facility, with eighty-seven full-time students. In fact, it is the only Catholic seminary between Pakistan and Italy for training priests.

Maroun is a true intellectual and represents an impressive lineup of Arab Catholic leaders that brings remarkable academic prowess to ministry in Israel/Palestine. Out of eighty-four priests serving in the region, thirty have earned Ph.D.'s, and Jerusalem's Latin Patriarch Michel Sabbah wants that figure to grow. Anyone wishing to hear a mature analysis of the crisis of the Palestinian church from a Christian perspective would do well to listen to Father Maroun and his many Catholic colleagues.

About 80 percent of the people in Beit Jala are Christians: six thousand of them are Orthodox and a thousand of them Catholic. Very few are Protestants. Maroun sees the Arab church entering a difficult time. Families are leaving (because of political strife and economic hardship) and conflicts still flare up, but he is philosophical. The church in the Holy Land has always absorbed suffering; since the day of Pentecost, it has only been free for two hundred years. One of his chief worries centers not on Israel but on Muslim-Christian relations (an echo perhaps of the trauma in Lebanon in 1974). Muslim and Christian politicians and academics understand and respect each other. The problem exists at the level of the "street," among average families with minimal education. At this level, the Muslim majority views the Arab Christian as "less than Arab," as linked suspiciously to the West — and to Israel. This perception gives many Arab Christians considerable fear as they live alongside their Muslim neighbors.

Much of this misunderstanding is the responsibility of leaders in churches and mosques who need to dispel stereotypes, Maroun argues. Both communities need to eliminate negative religious stereotyping. Until this is done, community will be limited community. Recently Maroun was driving south from Nablus on Highway 60. He picked up a hitchhiker along the way who was impressed to meet his first priest. "Have you ever heard of Christians?" Maroun asked. "Not really," came the reply. "I think they worship a piece of wood, don't they?"

Majdi al-Siryani, Beit Sahour

We have seen that pastors in Palestine struggle with the problem of violence in their communities, especially when they have faced it directly. When Majdi al-Siryani joined his first church, its leadership was deeply political, having been shaped in large measure by the uprising in the early 1990s.

Many of his leaders had been imprisoned and tortured. One week the church decided to support a public protest — a strike — to resist the Israeli occupation. But Israeli soldiers intervened and this young priest found himself swimming in water deeper than he imagined. An Israeli soldier (an American) saw him in the crowd and hit him with the butt of his rifle. Majdi was shocked. He had never been hit before. Impulsively he slapped the soldier back and both young men stood speechless, wondering what would happen next. Quickly two soldiers joined them and Majdi was interrogated by the three aggressively, but he was not harmed. As a priest, he knew he was using his clerical identity and its privileges to defy his attackers.

Or another occasion, in 1998 Majdi was traveling through the Bethlehem checkpoint and was outraged as he watched two soldiers abusing hundreds of Palestinian workers. Again he stepped forward, weaving his way through the crowd wearing the protective garb of the priesthood, and he spoke directly to them. "You cannot treat these people like cattle. Stop it." In 1999, he was at the same checkpoint on his way to a movie, and at the guardhouse an Arab man was shot in the head and paralyzed because of the bullet wound. When Majdi tells these stories his anger begins to boil. He still knows the paralyzed man. He describes, further, two Arab men shot at Rachel's Tomb (near the same checkpoint) in May 2000. They were reaching for a cigarette to give to a soldier and the gesture was misunderstood. Not one of these episodes made it into the Western press.

Like Emil Salayta in Bir Zeit, Majdi al-Siryani comes from one of the many Bedouin Christian tribes that for centuries roamed the deserts of modern-day Jordan — Bedouin such as the Azezat people, a tribe consisting of over five thousand Catholics. Majdi also has a connection with Father Maroun in Beit Jala. Born in 1961, Majdi was young and impulsive when he came into ministry in 1986, and Maroun became his mentor, guiding his ministry from its earliest days at the Beit Jala seminary. The Latin leadership wisely spotted Majdi's talents and in the early 1990s sent him to Rome to complete a Ph.D. He spent seven years in Italy studying civil and canon (or church) law as it applied to the status of Jerusalem.[27]

Majdi's impeccable English comes from an early pastoral assignment he accepted to the United States. For three years he was the pastor of an Arab congregation in Pomona, California, and there gained an understanding not only of American Christian perspectives on his world, but the view of his home from the West. Majdi today is the priest of the Catholic church in Beit Sahour, a village east of Bethlehem. The church is just like any in America with one signal difference: its placement lives in a village that has seen more harsh military measures — and exhibited more resistance — than any other.

Should a Christian resist when oppressed? Is nonviolent resistance acceptable? Majdi is clear that nonviolent resistance to oppression should always be the Christian's first choice, but the chief problem is that Arab culture does not know how to do it, nor does it recognize the power of nonviolent strategies. He points out that Jesus "confronted" the Pharisees calling them a host of offensive names (Matt. 23). Jesus also refused to cooperate with the authorities and on one occasion deliberately created a public disturbance (Matt. 21:12–17). Majdi at times clearly despairs at the failure of resistance, and he wonders if nonviolence requires a degree of social power before it is successful.

Majdi's church in Beit Sahour now enjoys a partnership with First Presbyterian Church in Houston, yet he wonders what this relationship will mean. Is it simply about missions funding and gifts? He is wary. "The poor need gifts — and we are not poor. No one starves here. We are not peasants. We are hibernating and need no pity. Our churches have great dignity." When

---

27. This work was completed at the Pontifica Universitas Lateranensis, Rome.

wealthy Americans appear in his church and their visit results in cash gifts, he fears the corrosive effects of such gestures on his people. It can become a form of patronage. Recently his church collected twelve hundred dollars to send to Ethiopia, and this is an expected aspect of his people's renewal. His Palestinian congregation must address stewardship issues as well.

Najeeb Yousef Rizik

In Nazareth, most tourists have an opportunity to visit "Mary's Well," located below the Greek Orthodox church in the center of town. What they may not know, however, is that this well is surrounded by a thriving

Arab congregation. Each Sunday about three hundred people are in worship between 8:30 and 11:15 a.m., and not just the elderly. Elementary school kids can be seen in every corner, and high school–age students gather in groups. Young families are commonplace. The elderly have a daily program — and a huge, newly refurbished fellowship hall for social programs. In fact, when I have taken students to Galilee to work on archaeological digs, I have brought them to the church on Saturday night where they can meet almost fifty young Arab Christian youth (ages fifteen to twenty-five) who make this their regular meeting place.

Najeeb Rizik is the president of this growing congregation called The Nazareth Orthodox Annunciation Church, and he represents a common profile among Palestinian Christian leaders. Because of a lack of educational opportunities, Najeeb studied in the United States (in Texas). His professional training came from Arkansas State University, where he was licensed in pharmacology, but he and his wife found that they loved the Southwest and remained there for eighteen years. Not long ago, Najeeb brought his family back to Nazareth to return to his roots — and to help where he could. Despite the strife and hardship, he will tell you that he loves Palestine. Despite the occasional protests of his children, he is here to stay. Today Najeeb owns a successful pharmacy in Tur'an, a village just north of Nazareth.

But in addition to returning to Nazareth with American business ideas (sale flyers now appear in the Tur'an postal system!) and an eloquent mastery of English, he has also returned with Western models of evangelical ministry in his mind. For instance, in the summer of 1999 he helped begin an Awana ministry at the church. On the first day they had 40 kids, and by day three the number had climbed to 120. His vision today includes building a school with a distinctive Christian curriculum. His church has even been instrumental networking all of the Orthodox youth groups around the country so that Orthodox Christians, say, in Nazareth, may meet and encourage Christian youth in Bethlehem.

But Najeeb's church also tells another story little-known among visitors to Israel. While the Catholic Church has worked hard to develop Arab leadership within its ranks — Emil, Majdi, and Maroun being three excellent examples — the Greek Orthodox Church is mired in a sorely contested struggle. Orthodox priests tend to be Greek while their congregations are entirely Arab; according to many, this difference has limited the success of the churches. Until the sixteenth century, the patriarch of the Orthodox church in Jerusalem had always been Arab, but for four hundred years it has been controlled by Greece. The current patriarch in Jerusalem, Diodoros, came to the country when he was sixteen and today is eighty. While his investment in the country is impressive, Arab Orthodox still feel a growing rift. "We must Arabize our church," argues Najeeb, "so that Arab leadership will carry on our ministries." But the Greek leadership resists. Najeeb repeatedly asks his bishop to send Bible teachers to work with his youth, but none come. In Jerusalem, the one bishop who is Arab — Attallah Hanna — is frequently the object of scorn and controversy.

Worse yet, the Greek Orthodox Church here is troubled by financial scandal. The church owns literally millions of dollars of property in Israel/ Palestine — much of it located in the most valued areas of Jerusalem — and today the Greek leadership is liquidating it for incredible sums of money. But here is the key: this money is moving to Greece and not returning to the ministries of the local Arab church. The sale of even small parcels of Jerusalem land could completely refurbish a church school or medical clinic in a Palestinian town. The patriarch's office began leasing land in the British era for either 49- or 99-year contracts. In June 2000, the patriarch negotiated an unparalleled 999-year lease with Jewish land developers for the Rehavia district of Jerusalem near the Israeli Parliament, the Knesset. The sum? Twenty million dollars. Incredibly, the money was paid (a phalanx of Israeli lawyers were in attendance) and the patriarch denies it ever happened! The twenty million dollars has disappeared.[28]

---

28. This scandal, not reported in the Western press, was outlined to me by Mr. Uri Mor, director, Israeli Ministry for Religious Affairs, Department of Christian Communities. Interview, June 13, 2000.

Najeeb despairs. He fears that ministries with so much potential may begin to flounder. His own daughters have even begun to attend the Baptist church in Nazareth, and he wonders. Should he personally enter the ministry to bring new hope to his church?

Elias Chacour

"Abuna" (Arabic: "Father") Chacour is a well-known Palestinian Christian leader thanks to his two popular books, *Blood Brothers* (1984) and *We Belong to the Land* (1990).[29] His ancestry goes back many generations to the

village of Biram in northern Galilee. Biram was an entirely Christian village for generations. In 1948 when Abuna was eight, Israeli soldiers tricked the villagers, telling them of an impending attack and massacre. The soldiers told them to flee and even provided a written guarantee of return. After two weeks living in caves and groves of olive trees, the people returned to find their homes ransacked and their food supply gone. Soldiers rounded up the village men at gunpoint and drove them away toward eastern borders while the elderly, the women, and the children were left to fend for themselves. Chacour's mother took the young family to the village of Jish while his father and his oldest brothers disappeared for two months. They walked through Jordan, Syria, and Lebanon and slipped back into Galilee to be reunited with their family. They were the lucky ones.

But Biram was to be no more. In 1950, the Israeli Supreme Court ruled in favor of the village and demanded the return of the people but months later in 1951 army bulldozers leveled it. Today Abuna Chacour occasionally visits it, climbing over housing stones and the broken church that served as the center of village life, and he visits the crumbling cemetery where his ancestry rests. Many of the original residents of Biram still come for picnics and are even still buried here when they die. "We cannot live in Biram," one said, "only die here."

Eventually, after six years of study in Paris, Chacour was ordained into the ministry of the Melkite church, a communion of Christians going back

---

29. Chacour is also known for his three nominations to receive the Nobel Peace Prize in 1986, 1989, and 1994.

to the eleventh century.[30] Called by some the Greek Catholic Church, today its liturgies are the same as the Greek Orthodox with one difference: it has remained in communion with Rome. Galilee alone has thirty-five parishes and twenty-five priests. In August 1965, the newly ordained "Abuna Chacour" had been assigned to serve the Galilee village of Ibiliin not far from the Israeli city of Haifa, and he is still there to this day.

Not only was the church of Ibiliin in a shambles (it had even been looted), but the community was utterly despairing. The young priest threw himself into the work despite discouragement and countless setbacks. Abuna quickly recognized that one of the critical needs of the young people was education. With tensions mounting between Arabs and Jews in the 1970s and 1980s, opportunities for Arab youth were limited. Therefore the Ibiliin church opened a high school in 1982 with four teachers and 80 students, and by 1990 it was enrolling 1,300 students. Today its diplomas are recognized by Israeli universities throughout the country. In 1994, the Ibiliin church opened its first scholastic year at the college level with 100 students, and today they enroll 750. Even the Israeli government has been quick to recognize the excellence of their work. Their college of education received awards from the Israelis every year since 1997, and today the engineering school even receives government subsidy.

Chacour's vision is to create a Christian educational setting that is second to none. Though its mission springs from Christian conviction, it opens its doors to everyone. Over 54 percent of the students in Ibiliin are Muslim. Thirteen Jewish students are enrolled in the college. Among the faculty, 68 percent are Christian, 25 percent are Muslim, and 7 percent are Jewish. The college has now become a regional center for continuing professional development for teachers in Galilee. Their annual conference enrolled 240 teachers in 1998, 680 teachers in 1999, and in 2000 850 teachers attended.

The situation has not always been easy. Chacour is a bold and sometimes outrageous "prophet" for his causes. Whether he is being searched at the airport for passage out of the country (an experience common to all Arabs) or speaking up for justice in programs filmed by the BBC, Chacour's voice is penetrating and incisive, echoing the sharpness of an Amos or a Jeremiah. When he first began building his schools, the Israeli government refused to give him a building permit. After months of arguing turned into years, he built anyway and defied the government to tear it down. He enlisted the Western media to watch, and evangelical organizations such as World

---

30. In the eleventh century, these Christians remained loyal to the king of Constantinople when it once allied itself with the pope in Rome. The Arabic name "Malech" means "royalist," referring to this allegiance, and is the source of the name Melkite.

Vision quickly came to his side. As Chacour built, the Israelis threatened to destroy — until Abuna came on a plan.

In 1992, he was visiting Washington, D.C., and he told his driver to take him to the home of Secretary of State James Baker. He knocked on the door and there met Baker's wife, Susan. He asked for help and wondered if she and Mr. Baker would visit his village on their next trip to Israel. As outspoken Christians, the Bakers took his plea to heart. And at the end of his tenure in Washington, James Baker called in a personal favor from Shimon Perez, the Israeli prime minister. Perez became Chacour's "ambassador" in Jerusalem and permits and accreditation came swiftly. Today the Mar Elias College is fully accredited by the Ministry of Education.[31]

---

31. Chacour has also been the recipient of numerous awards. In 1994, he won the World Methodist Peace Award in Rio de Janeiro. In 2001 (February), he won the Niwano Peace Prize in Tokyo.

Chapter Twelve

EVANGELICALS
AND THE LAND

I feel that the destiny of the State of Israel is without question the most crucial international matter facing the world today. I believe that the people of Israel have not only a theological but also a historical and legal right to the land. I personally am Zionist, having gained that perspective from my belief in the Old Testament scriptures. — Jerry Falwell[1]

Assuming the validity of the ancient Promise of the Land and acknowledging Israel's security needs, are these enough to justify taking land that has been occupied by the Arabs for hundreds of years, or taking land that was 100 percent Arab in population? Do those factors justify flouting the principles of justice and mercy? — Wesley G. Pippert[2]

Since the beginning of the Second Intifada in September 2000, evangelicals have once again focused on developments in Israel. Some communities — called Christian Zionists — mobilized their numbers and viewed American support for Israel as a test of spiritual faithfulness. Other evangelicals expressed grave concern about Israel's excesses and began a vocal call for justice in the Holy Land. In this chapter we need to explore how evangelicals view Israel and why.

On October 6, 2002, the CBS news magazine *60 Minutes* offered a lengthy study of evangelicals, calling it "Zion's Christian Soldiers." While Israel was laying siege to Arafat's compound in Ramallah — one week after the International Christian Embassy had brought over five thousand Christians to celebrate Israel's statehood in Jerusalem — CBS decided to pay a visit to prominent Zionists and visit Israel during a major Christian Zionist celebration. One prominent figure was the well-known Baptist pastor Jerry Falwell. Claiming to speak for 70 million American evangelicals, Falwell urged that "the Bible belt in America was Israel's only safety belt today." When President George W. Bush called for Israeli restraint against the Pales-

---

1. Cited in M. Simon, *Jerry Falwell and the Jews* (New York: Jonathan David, 1984), 62.
2. W. G. Pippert, *Land of Promise, Land of Strife* (Waco, Tex.: Word, 1988), 124.

tinians, Falwell successfully delivered a hundred thousand e-mails to the White House saying that "nothing will bring the wrath of the American people down on a government quicker than abandoning Israel." Suddenly Bush's criticism of Israeli violence fell silent. For Falwell, Christians must stand with the Jews in obedience to the Bible and sustain the struggle against the followers of Muhammad — whom Falwell called a "terrorist."

In the same program, Kay Arthur, founder of Precept Ministries (Chattanooga, Tennessee) and frequent host of tours to Israel, likewise saw political support for Israel as a critical aspect of Christian faithfulness. But she went further. Any peacemaking with Palestinians, in her view, was a sin. When Rabin, for example, worked out the Oslo Peace Accords with Arafat "he was going against the word of God." And, according to Arthur, "God stopped it." CBS pressed further and unmasked Arthur's political/ theological conclusion: the assassination of Rabin came about by the will of God because "God did not want the Oslo Accord to go through."

This trenchant support for Israel among Christian Zionists is stronger today than ever before. A quick look at a few current websites gives the picture quickly: "Christian Action for Israel," "Christian Friends of Israel," "Stand for Israel," "The International Christian Embassy," and "Bridges for Peace" each represents grass-roots organizations that mobilize conservative Christians to support Israel politically. In a recent poll conducted by evangelical Ralph Reed and Rabbi Yechiel Eckstein, 62 percent of "conservative Protestants" expressed strong support for Israel. Among evangelical "men," the percentage rose to 77 percent.[3]

This trend of strong evangelical support for Israel has now been going on for over ten years. The headlines of the *Jerusalem Post* for Monday, March 23, 1992, announced boldly, "American Evangelicals Pledge Support." On Sunday (the day before), more than eight hundred American evangelicals attended the International Christian Prayer Breakfast in Jerusalem ostensibly to "pray for the peace of Jerusalem" as commanded in Psalm 122. But as so often happens in Israel, religion and politics became one. With Jerusalem's mayor, Teddy Kollek, joining him at the platform, Prime Minister Yitzhak Shamir spoke to the crowd and received three standing ovations. His speech was interrupted countless times by applause. Pastors, businesspersons, and politicians were all there affirming their support for Israel as evangelicals.

---

3. *www.standforisrael.org/index.cfm?FuseAction=PressReleases.Home&PressRelease_id =3.*

But the agenda was more strategic. In an American election year when Israel's request for a $10 billion loan guarantee was being debated, the conference brochure made their purposes explicit: "We Christians call upon our Bible-believing brothers and sisters to re-examine their political support and not vote for any presidential candidate, prime minister, or other politician whose policy concerning Israel would be contrary to the mandates of God."

After the breakfast, everyone was asked to walk to Jerusalem's Western Wall, where speakers urged the crowd to vote only for those candidates who would support the loan guarantees and to defeat any presidential candidate who would offer land or autonomy to the Palestinians.

As the *Jerusalem Post* reporter listened to it, this plea represented the voice of America's 80 million evangelicals speaking.

On the next day, the organizers of the breakfast launched a Bible-reading marathon on the Mount of Olives. Nine hundred people each read fifteen to thirty minutes to complete the entire Bible. It was a "prophetic event," they announced, fulfilling Isaiah 2: "The word of God shall go forth out of Jerusalem." Again the Israelis looked on, took notes, and witnessed more evidence of American evangelicals standing in solidarity with Israel's national purposes.

Today that same link between evangelicals and Israel continues. Ralph Reed, for example, once worked to become the self-appointed spokesperson of evangelical Christians in Washington, D.C., and recently launched his campaign "Stand for Israel" with Rabbi Yechiel Eckstein. Their goal is explicit. Reed declares: "The Stand for Israel campaign will begin immediately with a goal of mobilizing 100,000 churches and an estimated one million Christians in the United States to express solidarity with the State of Israel."[4]

A curious fact of history is that original support for Israel's nationhood in the 1940s and 1950s came from liberal Protestant Christians in the United States.[5] After witnessing the tragedy of the Jewish Holocaust, supporting a people seeking a refuge from persecution made sense. In fact, in 1939 when 83 percent of the American population opposed the admission of European refugees (including Jews), the Presbyterian Church petitioned the government aggressively to let them in. In May 1939, the General Assembly condemned Nazism, committed itself to rescuing European Jewry, and vowed to fight against anti-Semitism in the United States. In 1940, the

---

4. See their website: *www.standforisrael.org*. Today Ralph Reed is the chairman of the Republican Party in Georgia.

5. R. Ruether and H. Ruether, *The Wrath of Jonah: The Crisis of Religious Nationalism in the Israeli-Palestinian Conflict* (New York: Harper & Row, 1989), 173.

General Assembly even urged congregations to give sanctuary to fleeing refugees.

But these same mainline Protestant churches began to express outspoken criticism after Israel's 1967 war. Israel's expansionist policies and abuses to Palestinians seemed to be an affront to the very values Judaism sought and could not find in Europe. Today Presbyterians, Methodists, Episcopalians, and others have lodged harsh complaints. Publications such as *The Link* (published by Americans for Middle East Understanding) often host authors from these churches who write critical essays on Israel.[6] For instance, the January–March 1992 issue devoted eleven pages to Paul Hopkins, secretary for the Middle East (Presbyterian Church, U.S.A.) from 1980 to 1985. When Hopkins began to speak out about Palestinian concerns based on his own numerous experiences, he was charged with being "anti-Semitic." This lengthy essay was his defense.

Since 1967, evangelicals have taken the forefront in support of Israel. Yet the same shift I described among mainline churches is now at work even within this community. Evangelicals in surprising numbers are "crossing the line" and witnessing firsthand the nature of life in the West Bank. Palestinian pastors are writing and speaking, and in the last few years, their voices have been heard.

THE BASIS OF EVANGELICAL SUPPORT FOR ISRAEL

To be fair, the vast majority of evangelicals instinctively believe that vigorous support for Israel is the only appropriate response to the conflicts in the Middle East. Their stance has little to do with history, less to do with politics. Evangelical commitment to Israel is grounded in sincere Christian conviction. The average believer sitting in the pew is persuaded that such support is God's will: the Jews are God's people, and they are returning to the land God promised to them. As someone said to me recently, "You just can't get around it. The Jews are chosen. And this means they get special treatment."

Because evangelicals have always had a passionate commitment to theology and the Bible, two theological themes that come from the Scriptures have influenced their view.

---

6. For information about *The Link,* write: Americans for Middle East Understanding, Inc., Room 241, 475 Riverside, Drive, New York, NY 10115, or visit their website: *www.ameu.org.* "AMEU" likewise offers many books for sale about the Israelis and Palestinians. Virtually all of their publications have a decidedly pro-Palestinian slant.

Dispensationalism

First, many evangelicals are *dispensationalists*. Even those who do not use this title or understand it still follow an informal dispensational theology when they study the Scriptures. They divide biblical history into a number of historic periods (such as the era before the fall of Adam, the period after the giving of the Law, and the "dispensation" of the church age). Dispensationalists examine each period, carefully studying the methods of God's efforts among his people. Many are familiar with *The Scofield Reference Bible,* which applies the dispensational scheme in comments throughout the text of the Scriptures. If their pastors have studied at seminaries such as Dallas or Talbot, they may well have heard this perspective from the pulpit.

Most dispensationalists distinguish God's program for the church from God's program for Israel. As Charles Ryrie, a noted dispensationalist, puts it, "The church did not begin in the Old Testament but on the day of Pentecost, and the church is not presently fulfilling promises made to Israel in the Old Testament that have not yet been fulfilled."[7] The church is thus a separate entity from Israel, living on a parallel track, possessing a different covenant. Therefore no interference occurs between the biblical Israelites and modern Israel. A straight line can be drawn between them, and the Christian church will not merge with Israel until the end of the age.

The conclusion of this point of view is simple: If the church does not supplant Israel and if Christians are not the new children of Abraham (as we suggested earlier), then the promises of Abraham appropriately belong to modern Israel even today. Authors will frequently presuppose this deduction when they describe the building of the state of Israel. Listen, for instance, to the words of John Walvoord of Dallas Seminary: "The repossession of a portion of their ancient land by the new state of Israel is especially striking because of the promise given by God to Abraham of perpetual title to the land between Egypt and the Euphrates."[8]

Walvoord clearly believes that the politics of modern-day Israel are a continuation of the politics of Old Testament Israel. Israel's modern national agenda is now a renewal of the kingdom agenda known from the time of Joshua, Saul, and Solomon. The taking of land is justified for biblical reasons.

But other interpreters disagree heartily. Their view is that God has worked consistently with people throughout biblical history, and the people of God

---

7. C. C. Ryrie, "Dispensation, Dispensationalism," in *The Evangelical Dictionary of Theology,* ed. W. Elwell (Grand Rapids, Mich.: Baker, 1984), 322.

8. J. Walvoord, *The Nations: Israel and the Church in Prophecy,* three volumes in one (Grand Rapids, Mich.: Zondervan, 1988), 2:25.

form a continuity from Adam and Noah to the early church. There are not today two people of God with different programs. In each era, God has presented himself in the same way, and those who acknowledge his grace in faith are his people. Thus gentile Christians stand on a par with Jewish believers and can read the Old Testament as belonging to them. Moreover, today there are not "two Israels" — a natural Israel (the Jews) and a spiritual Israel (the church). These Christians point to passages such as Ephesians 2:11–17 where Paul affirms that in Christ the former categories of "Jew" and "Gentile" are abolished since now in Christ God has made a new people, "making the former two one." Hear Paul's words directly:

> Therefore, remember that formerly you who are Gentiles by birth and called "uncircumcised" by those who call themselves "the circumcision" (that done in the body by the hands of men) — remember that at that time you were separate from Christ, excluded from citizenship in Israel and foreigners to the covenants of the promise, without hope and without God in the world. *But now in Christ Jesus* you who once were far away have been brought near through the blood of Christ. For he himself is our peace, who has *made the two one* and has destroyed the barrier, the dividing wall of hostility, by abolishing in his flesh the law with its commandments and regulations. His purpose was to create in himself *one new man out of the two,* thus making peace, and in this one body to reconcile both of them to God through the cross, by which he put to death their hostility. He came and preached peace to you who were far away and peace to those who were near.

Paul here envisions one new entity that does not necessarily obliterate the cultural differences between Jewish Christians and gentile Christians, but it certainly no longer gives pride of place to Jews who reject their Messiah. In this view, God has *one people:* those who follow his Son.

The End Times

An important second dimension to this discussion is that many evangelicals are persuaded that Israel is playing a role in the end times. In 1948 when the fledgling Israeli state was established, prophecy was fulfilled. Listen again to the words of Walvoord:

> Of the many peculiar phenomena which characterize the present generation, few events can claim equal significance as far as Biblical prophecy is concerned with that of the return of Israel to their land. It constitutes a preparation for the end of the age, the setting for the coming of the Lord for His church, and the fulfillment of Israel's prophetic destiny.[9]

---

9. Ibid., 2:26.

One book undoubtedly played a leading role in popularizing this understanding of Middle Eastern history and the Bible. Hal Lindsey's *Late Great Planet Earth* (published in 1970) was a spellbinding description of the fulfillment of prophecy and the imminent end of the world. I still remember reading it for the first time in 1972 while I was living in the Middle East as a college student. I was twenty, and it disturbed me to no end. At least, I reasoned, if the end of the world was coming, I was in the perfect spot to watch it happen. Lindsey's book is still popular today and has sold a record-breaking 25 million copies.[10]

This view is also called "premillennialist" because it designs a special pattern for the unfolding of the end. Before Christ returns to establish a thousand-year reign (the Millennium), certain prophecies must be fulfilled. In other words, a prophetic prelude to Christ's return and rule (hence "premillennialism," or Christ's premillennial return) takes place. Divinely decreed signs will occur, such as earthquakes, famines, wars, the appearance of the Antichrist, and the preaching of the gospel to all nations. Prominent among these signs is the restoration of Israel to the land. This event alone starts the "eschatological time clock" — it lights the fuse that will detonate Armageddon, the great catastrophic war that Christ will end with his second coming. Lindsey calls the restoration of national Israel "the key to the jigsaw puzzle": "With the Jewish nation reborn in the land of Palestine, ancient Jerusalem once again under total Jewish control for the first time in twenty-six hundred years, and talk of rebuilding the great Temple, the most important prophetic sign of Jesus Christ's soon coming is before us."[11]

Together these two themes — a dispensational commitment to Israel's separate existence and an eschatological interest in fulfilled prophecy — have built the bedrock of evangelical attitudes toward the Middle East. Today the best example of this approach can be found in the hugely popular multivolume fictional series *Left Behind* by Tim LaHaye and Jerry Jenkins. To date, this series has sold 50 million copies. Buried in its plot is a framework that buttresses these basic ideas.[12]

---

10. In 1991, I read *The Late Great Planet Earth* carefully with a group of college seniors. They looked up every reference in the Bible and analyzed Lindsey's interpretation. I was surprised when they unanimously told me that it was one of the most unconvincing books they had ever read. As one student put it, "Lindsey simply bends the Scriptures to say what he wants."

11. H. Lindsey (with C. C. Carlson), *The Late Great Planet Earth* (Grand Rapids, Mich.: Zondervan, 1970), 47.

12. This series is published by Tyndale Publishing and has its own website: *www.leftbehind .com*. Its eleventh volume will be published in 2003.

Evangelicals like LaHaye are quick to say that a literal reading of the Bible and a sincere appreciation of the miracle of Israel's restoration in the twentieth century ought to be enough to convince any skeptic. But most important, this commitment should be translated into political support for Israel. Thus on January 27, 1992, a full-page ad in the *Washington Times* announced boldly, "Seventy Million Christians Urge President Bush to Approve Loan Guarantees for Israel." Under the ad, thirty-three Christian leaders listed their names explaining, "We deeply believe in the biblical prophetic vision of the ingathering of exiles to Israel, a miracle we are now seeing fulfilled." Who are the 70 million? The ad is clear: America's evangelicals. Many evangelicals like myself, however, take deep offense at advertisements such as this, which pretend to speak for the entire evangelical community in a secular forum. They do not.

CHRISTIAN ZIONISM

This unqualified endorsement of Israel's politics based on biblical principles has spawned a movement called Christian Zionism, which has utterly wed religious conviction with political realities and interpreted biblical faithfulness in terms of fidelity to Israel's future. The Israeli government loves it. In 1980, Jerry Falwell received from Prime Minister Menachem Begin the Jabotinsky Award for Service to the Cause of Israel. The award did not recognize Falwell's merits as a Christian minister, but his efforts to assist Israel politically. In April 1998, Israel's Prime Minister Benjamin Netanyahu addressed three thousand people at a "Voices United for Israel Conference." Most were evangelicals. Ralph Reed, Jerry Falwell, and Pat Robertson each supported it. As Netanyahu told the conference, "We have no greater friends and allies than the people sitting in this room."[13]

Within months of Benjamin Netanyahu's election (1996), Israel invited seventeen evangelical leaders to Jerusalem to form the Israel Christian Advocacy Council. Together they toured the country and attended a conference in which they pledged support for the agenda of the current government. Don Argue (president of the National Association of Evangelicals), Brandt Gustavson (president of the National Religious Broadcasters), and Donald Wildmon (president of the American Family Association) were a few of the participants. After these leaders signed a written pledge to "never desert Israel," Argue added, "We are a people of the Book first, and Israel is the

13. T. P. Weber, "How Evangelicals Became Israel's Best Friend," *Christianity Today,* October 5, 1998, 38ff.

land of the Book. We represent 49 denominations and some 50,000 congregations and we were taught on our mother's knee to love Israel."[14] In fact, many members of this evangelical council together published a pro-Israel ad in the *New York Times* titled "Christians Call for a United Jerusalem," arguing for Jewish sovereignty over the city (April 10, 1997).

Thus Christian Zionists have a zeal for Israel and are willing to promote more or less political agendas. For example, Pat Robertson's *700 Club* regularly features news stories about Israel and invites Israeli political leaders to appear for interviews. In January 1998, Robertson hosted Benjamin Netanyahu on the *700 Club* and asked him, "What would you like our audience to do?" Netanyahu replied, "I think you are already doing it: letters to the editor, communication with representatives, and support to Israel." This support is generous. The International Fellowship of Christians and Jews, led by Rabbi Yechiel Eckstein of Chicago, coordinates contributions from evangelicals and in 1998 raised $5 million for the United Jewish Appeal for the Israeli government. On February 4, 1998, Pastor John Hagee of Cornerstone Church in San Antonio announced that his church was giving $1 million to Israel.

Therefore it comes as no surprise that numerous organizations have grown up with important offices in Israel: the list includes Bridges for Peace, The International Christian Embassy, Kings Assembly in Jerusalem, Christ Church Jerusalem, Friends of Jerusalem, Christian Friends of Israel, Israel Vistas, Friends of Israel Gospel Ministries, The National Christian Leadership Conference for Israel, and Christians' Israel Public Action Campaign. Together they raise millions of dollars in aid for Israel, sponsor conferences both in the United States and in Israel, distribute vast quantities of literature, and promote tours for Christian pilgrims.[15]

The International Christian Embassy, Jerusalem

Almost every address in Israel can tell a story. If I travel south on David Street in West Jerusalem and enter the so-called "German Colony," I will discover one of Jerusalem's most interesting neighborhoods. I made my third visit to this neighborhood recently, and there at Number 10 Brenner Street found the stately mansion that once belonged to a Palestinian family. In 1948 during Israel's first war, the wealthy and influential Said family (who were Christians) fled Jerusalem for Egypt seeking safety. When they

---

14. See D. Wagner, "Reagan and Begin, Bibi and Jerry: The Theopolitical Alliance of the Likud Party with the American Christian Right," *Arab Studies Quarterly* 20, no. 4 (1998): 8.

15. For a survey see K. Sidey, "For the Love of Zion," *Christianity Today,* March 9, 1992, 46–50.

returned, they discovered that their fully furnished home had been confiscated and eventually given to the well-known philosopher Martin Buber.
When the Said family tried to regain their house, Buber refused them entry
and appeals to the government fell on deaf ears. Eventually the Israeli government gave the house to the government of Chile for their embassy. But
on July 30, 1980, when Israel declared unilateral ownership of Jerusalem,
over a dozen embassies left for Tel Aviv, refusing to support an action that
was widely viewed as illegal. The embassy of Chile then left for Tel Aviv,
but the house did not return to the Palestinian Said family. It was handed
over to a Christian Zionist group promising to deliver evangelical support
to Israel's people.[16] Christians from Europe, South Africa, and the United
States founded the so-called embassy in September that year, which today
claims to represent members from over a hundred countries.

The International Christian Embassy is now the most overt link between
Christian Zionists in the West and the Israeli government. Its mission is
to express to Israel heartfelt support for its life and future, to "comfort
Zion," as Isaiah 40:1 says. In 1999, the embassy director, Johann Lückhoff,
commented in a public speech, "We are here [in Jerusalem] to witness the
miracle of Israel and the restoration of the Jewish people, exactly as it was
spoken by the prophets thousands of years ago."[17] At the same gathering,
the leader of Israel's right-wing Likud party stood with him saying that the
embassy and its programs are "the most wonderful guests" the city has.[18]

Of course, many Christians have taken offense at this, wondering how
this "embassy" can claim to represent Christianity to Israel. Through a variety of programs such as resettling Jews from Ethiopia and Russia and direct
aid to needy families, the embassy has an annual budget of about $8 mil-
lion, half contributed by Americans.[19] They have sixty-five local employees
in Jerusalem and several foreign offices. On a recent visit I asked to see a
current financial report of distributions and was surprised that these are not
made available. In fact, the embassy has never been certified by the widely
respected Evangelical Council for Financial Accountability, which monitors
the financial integrity of 950 of our best ministry organizations.

The embassy's most direct promotion of Christian Zionism is its well-
known Feast of Tabernacles festival, which takes place every autumn. Here

---

16. See their website: *www.intournet.co.il/icej/*.
17. *New York Times,* September 29, 1999.
18. For a study of the connection between the Likud Party and Christian Zionism, see
D. Wagner, "Reagan and Begin, Bibi and Jerry," 33–52.
19. *New York Times,* September 29, 1999. According to Mr. Timothy King, financial
director, Jerusalem office, the embassy distributes about $3.2 million per year in aid.

Christian leaders gather to read papers, network, and promote their agenda of linking the moral and financial support of evangelical churches with the establishment and security of Israel. Oddly, no interest is expressed in supporting the Arab Christian communities within the country.

For nine days during the "feast" over five thousand American Christians from almost a hundred countries come to Israel to tour the country and join in celebrations in Jerusalem. In October 2002 they marched around and through the Old City of Jerusalem along with twelve thousand Israelis, waving flags, singing songs, and celebrating an odd mixture of spiritual zeal and political enthusiasm.[20] At one point, Prime Minister Ariel Sharon addressed the crowd, affirming evangelical support for Israel and calling on America to further aid his country's struggle with the Palestinians.

But we need to be clear that this activity is not simply about worship. Major political leaders always address the crowds. Israel's prime ministers and Jerusalem's mayor, Ehud Olmert, *always* appear and thank the audience for their presence as a symbolic support for the government's vision for the country.[21] At the Tabernacles 2000 ceremony, ultraconservative Likud leader (and current prime minister) Ariel Sharon, the former general who led the siege of Lebanon, was the keynote speaker. His speech represented the perfect wedding of an appeal to the Bible and Zionist politics. But pastors who speak generally sound the same theme: we must believe that the restoration of Israel fulfills biblical prophecies, and the destinies of both nations and people turns on their attitude to this new work of God. As the director of the embassy once told me, "Christians will be judged by how they treat Israel."[22] To neglect Israel and its restoration is to incur judgment and to miss God's blessing in what appears to be "the last days." And — remarkably — even the destiny of the individual Christian will be affected by their view of "restored Israel." The embassy's website declares:

> We believe it is God's desire that Christians across the world be encouraged and inspired to arise to their prophetic role in the restoration of Israel. The Bible says that the destiny of the nations, of Christians and of the Church is linked to the way they respond to this work of restoration.

---

20. One Israeli pundit refers to it as "a Broadway show" or "Saturday Night Live" in Jerusalem (*Jerusalem Post*, October 1, 1999).

21. Transcripts of Tabernacles sermons can be found at the website *www.intournet.co.il/icej/*. When Ehud Barak failed to speak in 1999, it was the first time in twenty years the prime minister had not appeared. While the embassy says the failure resulted from the prime minister's fatigue, the embassy had actually been a vigorous supporter of Barak's political rival, Benjamin Netanyahu, and had been a sharp critic of Barak. Barak no doubt wished to send a message to the embassy.

22. Johann Lückhoff, personal interview, March 30, 1992.

On my visits to the embassy, I have always been impressed with their friendliness and eagerness to enlist my support — and disturbed by their political involvements. Their promotional brochures feature photographs and endorsements from former Prime Ministers Menachem Begin and Yitzhak Shamir and former Jerusalem Mayor Teddy Kollek. Their literature table has sold books and videos produced by the Israeli army. A quick visit to its website shows a host of articles that are filled with raw political views that consistently stereotype Palestinian motives. During the Al-Aqsa Uprising in 2000, the website even published editorials claiming that Arabs sacrifice their own children in street battles. Nothing could be more offensive to Arab families.

And yet in the midst of these efforts, no interest is apparent in carrying on a ministry to Judaism like Paul's — a ministry that proclaims Jesus as Messiah. In fact, the embassy intentionally avoids any discussion of this "divisive subject."[23] On a recent visit, I asked the current chaplain of the embassy, Ed Smelser, why they did not do evangelism among Jews as Paul did. He seemed uncomfortable. It was simply not their mission.

Perhaps the most disconcerting thing about the embassy is its overt antagonism toward the Palestinian people. Its leaders readily deny the validity of Palestinian Christianity and compare the spirit of the Arab resistance movement with the "spirit found in the Holocaust." As one embassy leader said to me during the uprising of last decade: The Intifada was another form of Nazism.[24]

On an earlier occasion, the embassy director stereotyped all Arabs as untrustworthy. My questions pressed the point: "Should we not care for the Palestinian Christian community too?"

The answer was stunning: "They are not really as Christian as you might think." The word *Arab* came out as if it were unclean. "Arabs lie, they cheat in business deals, and they will give you their word one day and then deny it. They don't seem to respect life or truth like anyone else does."

I was stunned at his words. "But don't the Palestinians have rights?" I pressed.

"Sometimes," he said, "you have to keep God's long-term plan in mind. Sometimes particular rights have to be suspended."

I decided to try another approach. "Do you know any moderate Arabs worth listening to?"

He said quickly, "After ten years here, no."

Needless to say, I left the embassy that day deeply troubled.

---

23. Ibid.
24. From interviews with Lückhoff and Jim Schultz at the embassy offices, March 30, 1992.

Bridges for Peace

In the early 1970s, Dr. G. Douglas Young was already heading up the newly opened "Institute of Holy Land Studies" (now Jerusalem University College on Mt. Zion). As a committed Zionist, Young formed a new organization in 1977 that would assist in the establishment of the prophetic return of Jews to the Holy Land. In 1977, he founded a Jerusalem-based ministry that would work side-by-side with Israel in order to facilitate Jewish immigration and the security of the state. He called it "Bridges for Peace."

Today Bridges is led by Clarence Wagner and is the oldest Christian Zionist ministry in Israel.[25] It has an impressive bimonthly newspaper called *Dispatch from Jerusalem* that monitors political and religious developments between the United States and Israel. Its *Update from Jerusalem* is a weekly e-mail informing Christians of current news. And its "Jerusalem Mosaic" is an acclaimed television show on life in Israel.

Bridges for Peace does just what its name implies. It builds bridges, particularly between the Israeli Jewish and American Christian communities. "Operation Ezra" uses cash gifts to help Israel's most needy, including immigrants, the elderly, and Arab believers. "Operation Rescue" helps poor Jews immigrate to Israel from Russia. "Adopt-A-Family" now links 135 immigrant families with American evangelical families for support. Altogether Bridges has about thirty-five agencies that bring aid in some form to needy families and, according to Bernard Resnikoff of the American Jewish Committee, "Bridges for Peace Is One of Israel's Greatest Assets."[26]

Like the Christian Embassy, Bridges is deeply committed to politics. For example, Bridges also sponsors conferences. In November 2002, over two hundred Christians from about ten nations (representing, Bridges says, 50 million Christian Zionists) sponsored a "Solidarity Mission" in Jerusalem "to demonstrate unwavering support for the nation of Israel and the Jewish people worldwide." Here delegates met with government, military, media, and policy leaders to learn more and affirm Christian support for Israeli policies. The Bridges website announces the bold theme of the mission: "Israel Is God's Plan — God Is a Biblical Zionist."

In 1995 when Bethlehem began to celebrate its own "Palestinian" festival, Bridges openly encouraged visiting Christians to avoid the town — to stand against the Palestinian Authority — and instead visit the Jewish community of Efrat nearby.[27] But most important, this organization distributes

---

25. See their website: *www.bridgesforpeace.com.*
26. *Jerusalem Post,* December 22, 1997.
27. Ibid.

information as generously as it distributes food and blankets. Its newsletters (particularly *Dispatch from Jerusalem*) editorialize every aspect of Israel's politics and rarely show sympathy with Palestinian concerns for justice. For instance, the *Dispatch* collects inflammatory quotes from Arab leaders, using them to stereotype Palestinian leadership.[28] It profiles Arabs as aggressive and hostile. The index of articles now available on the web makes breathtaking reading and leaves one wondering how this aspect of its work is a Christian ministry.

Curiously, no planned ministry to Christian Arabs is offered, much less to the Palestinians as a whole. No bridges are being built. American visitors who come to the country through the direction of the Christian Zionist organizations like this can spend weeks in Israel/Palestine and not realize that a whole other community (the Palestinian community) is being overlooked.

Both Bridges and the Embassy are so keen to support Jewish life that they refuse (with veiled embarrassment) to promote evangelism among Jews. This approach (or lack of it) is odd when one remembers that evangelism has been a part of conservative Christianity's mandate for generations. Even Paul would speak of Jesus to his fellow Jews, but Christian Zionists will not because it may risk their status in the country. Such a lacuna in Zionist theology is noticed not merely by other evangelicals, but by Jewish observers describing them, for instance, in the *Jerusalem Post*.[29]

A NEW EVANGELICAL OUTLOOK

Many of us within the evangelical church are offended by Christian Zionism. While we are committed to peace and justice for all parties in Israel/Palestine, we are offended by those people whose faith is consumed by the politics of Israel's restoration. For the Christian Embassy to be called an "embassy" at all is presumptuous. In its literature the "embassy" compares itself with foreign embassies that have "forsaken" Jerusalem and moved to Tel Aviv. Worse still, the "embassy" is courted by leading Israeli politicians, especially in the conservative Likud Party, who see these Christians advancing their political aims. But the "embassy" bears no diplomatic mission for all of the West's churches. It does not come close. No evangelical majority has asked the embassy to represent it.

---

28. *www.bridgesforpeace.com/publications/dispatch/notablequotes/Article-0.html.*
29. "Helping Jews Is Very Christian," *Jerusalem Post,* December 22, 1997.

Christianity Today published a contemporary study of Christian Zionism in its March 9, 1992, issue and there recorded the growing criticisms of the movement from within evangelicalism itself. The question is whether such Zionists represent the spirit of political nationalism more than the Spirit of Christ. The magazine also analyzed the sweeping changes that evangelicals are making in their thinking. Israel must, according to the average believer, stand at the bar of international justice and human rights.

Professor Marvin Wilson is a specialist on Judaism and teaches at Gordon College, an evangelical institution near Boston. His words sum up the new outlook accurately: "The number one obstacle to peace is nationalism, because so often it insists on the denial of the other guy. A biblical view can't be anti-Arab and pro-Israel, or anti-Israel and pro-Arab. God's heart is where justice is."[30]

Numerous evangelical authors have likewise turned their attention to the problem of Israel/Palestine in a new way. As far back as 1970, Frank Epp wrote *Whose Land Is Palestine?*, exploring the political crisis with genuine balance.[31] In 1988, Wesley Pippert, a correspondent for United Press International (and an evangelical Christian), wrote one of the best books yet released on the subject from an evangelical perspective.[32] Even Multnomah Press released a volume that gives genuine respect for Palestinian rights. Its author, Stanley Ellisen, concludes that Israel should be treated like any other secular state in the world, giving it both security considerations and expecting from it appropriate human rights.[33] In 1993, Presbyterian scholar Donald Wagner published his important history of the Palestinian crisis and gave an impassioned plea for evangelicals to shift their commitments.[34] I cannot underscore sufficiently its significance. This attitude is a paradigm shift from what we saw even twenty-five years ago.

Today evangelicals are beginning to experience a change in focus. In a poll conducted by *Christianity Today* in 1992, 39 percent of the magazine's readers said that their view of Israel was "more critical" than before. Eighty-eight percent believe "Christians should hold the State of Israel to the same standard of justice and human rights in its international affairs and internal affairs as any other nation." Convinced that biblical teachings about justice

30. K. Sidey, "For the Love of Zion," *Christianity Today,* March 9, 1992, 50.
31. F. H. Epp, *Whose Land Is Palestine? The Middle East Problem in Perspective* (Grand Rapids, Mich.: Eerdmans, 1970).
32. Pippert, *Land of Promise.*
33. S. A. Ellisen, *Who Owns the Land? The Arab-Israeli Conflict* (Portland, Ore.: Multnomah, 1991).
34. D. E. Wagner, *Anxious for Armageddon: A Call to Partnership for Middle Eastern and Western Christians* (Scottdale, Pa.: Herald, 1995).

are equally important to prophecies of the end, they are looking for new ways to understand God's will in the Middle East.

A quick look at some leading evangelical organizations bears out that these trends are now in the wind.

World Vision International

World Vision is the premier evangelical charitable organization in the world. The sheer scope of its work is astounding. Since its founding in 1950, World Vision has grown into an international presence respected by governments around the globe. In 1999, the group was involved in 103 countries distributing over $407 million. Over 4,500 relief projects worldwide touch approximately 50 million lives.[35] Nothing can compare. Its child sponsorship program is imitated everywhere. As an evangelical ministry, its witness to Jesus Christ has never been compromised. World Vision's mission statement describes its work simply:

> World Vision is an international partnership of Christians whose mission is to follow our Lord and Savior Jesus Christ in working with the poor and oppressed to promote human transformation, seek justice and bear witness to the good news of the Kingdom of God.

World Vision has been active in the Middle East since 1975 and today works in Jordan, Syria, Lebanon, Iraq, and Palestine (Jerusalem, Gaza, and the West Bank). Its work in Palestine is coordinated by its office in East Jerusalem, which employs sixteen Arab staff and three Westerners. Since 1975 World Vision has grown into a significant effort aiding the Palestinian poor at sixty-five development sites benefiting 150,000 people. American families have already "sponsored" 9,000 Palestinian children through this office. The ministry is also investing in the physical needs of the poor. One example: 35 percent of Palestinian children show signs of malnutrition, and World Vision has helped build a network of well-baby clinics throughout the country.

But unlike other Christian charitable organizations that pursue relief work without becoming entangled in local politics, in the last ten years World Vision made two significant decisions. First, it has networked extensively with the local Palestinian churches — the Catholics, Orthodox, Evangelical Lutheran, and Anglican. Through these networks the ministry has decided that if it is committed to improving the lives of the Palestinian communities, it must

---

35. World Vision's excellent website can be found at *www.worldvision.org*. Its international office is located in Monrovia, California. Its domestic ministry office is located near Seattle, Washington.

leverage its influence against systems of injustice that perpetuate suffering. In a word, World Vision has followed the lead of Arab Christian pastors seeing ministry as necessarily confronting injustice. The informal motto of World Vision/Jerusalem — printed even on its T-shirts — is a quote from Pope Paul VI, "If you want peace, work for justice."

But the second decision is more dramatic. The Jerusalem office has become an outspoken, high-profile advocate for human rights in Israel. World Vision assists both Palestinian and Israeli human rights organizations (e.g., Israeli Coalition Against Home Demolitions, Palestinian Land Defense Committee) as well supports advocates who defend families in courts when their land is confiscated or their home is demolished. American pastors who bring visitors to Jerusalem can even contact the office to set up "alternative travel" in order to meet Palestinian Christians and learn about their struggles.[36] They can even supply leaders with "information packets" that offer a wealth of "inside" information about Israel and the Palestinians. The director of the Jerusalem office also publishes a regular e-mail newsletter, which highlights justice issues in the country from an evangelical perspective.

This prophetic advocacy is the result of a change of vision at World Vision. Its leadership not only encourages but expects country directors to prayerfully take strong human rights advocacy stands. This expectation — indeed this requirement — stems from World Vision's holistic view of ministry, which includes the prophetic. The Jerusalem office not only supports efforts listed above, but has invested in reconciliation ministries ("The Palestinian Conflict Resolution Center"), child care centers for Arab children ("Open House"), and even Palestinian-led human rights organizations ("LAW: The Palestinian Society for the Protection of Human Rights").

Why is this significant? World Vision has been working "in the trenches" of this country for years and has felt constrained to make a *political* decision. As *Christians* its leaders feel compelled to confront the overwhelming record of Israeli injustice. Bringing aid to the poor, they argue, is not enough if the source of the suffering stands nearby. Historically, evangelicals have not been inclined to take such a stand. Today it is happening, and World Vision is leading the way.

Christianity Today

If World Vision is our premier charitable organization, *Christianity Today* is certainly the leading magazine of the evangelical church. Founded in 1956 by

---

36. Contact World Vision Jerusalem: Phone: 972.2.6281793 or 972.2.6272065. Fax: 972.2.6264260. Or write: World Vision Jerusalem, Box 51399, Jerusalem, Israel 91190. Or find their location on the World Vision website: *www.worldvision.org*.

Billy Graham, today Christianity Today Inc. boasts eleven publications that reach over 2.5 million readers. Even its website, *www.christianitytoday.com,* is fast becoming an essential tool for pastors and theologians researching trends in the church and its ministries. When a secular newspaper wants to understand what is happening in evangelicalism, *Christianity Today* is its source. When I need to track religious news items in the press, "CT" is an essential guide.

In its editorial policy, CT has worked to be an "equal opportunity critic" when it comes to human rights. Both the Israeli government and the Palestinian Authority have been criticized in its pages for their abuse of citizens' rights. On the fiftieth anniversary of Israel's nationhood, the magazine openly supported an unarmed, independent Palestinian state whose security would be assured by U.N. peacekeepers. The issue's cover story, written by Baptist history professor Timothy Weber, offered a lengthy, incisive explanation of "How Evangelicals Became Israel's Best Friend." Weber exposed the link between dispensationalism and evangelical politics, and underscored how the church has been deeply involved in supporting the Israeli government *because of theological commitments concerning the end times.* Evangelicalism's confidence in interpreting prophecy and its boldness in political advocacy lacks humility, Weber argued.[37]

In a supporting essay in the same issue, Calvin Shenk, a professor at Eastern Mennonite University, asked readers to consider how Jesus would view Jerusalem today. His conclusions were astounding. "Devotion to Jerusalem without righteousness," Shenk wrote, "leads to unholy nationalism." Jesus wept over Jerusalem. Why? Because the city did not understand the things that made for peace (Luke 19:42). No doubt he would invite us to weep as well.

Again, this approach is a signal development for evangelicals. Evangelical scholars are lodging criticisms of Israel's political posture as well as the theological position that has made commitment to those politics inevitable. *Christianity Today* regularly provides updates about the life of the Arab church and even features articles written by Palestinian educators and pastors, such as Bishara Awad, president of Bethlehem Bible College. If trends are signaled by our major print outlets, these shifts in emphasis found at CT are certainly important.

The Center for Middle East Studies, North Park University

Founded in 1891 by Swedish immigrants who set up camp in Chicago, North Park University is today one of the only urban evangelical colleges in

---

37. See *www.christianitytoday.com/ct/8tb/8tb038.html.*

the United States. Only a few remnants of Sweden remain in the neighbor-hood — a gift shop, a restaurant — since new waves of immigrants have moved in and the Swedes moved on. The local elementary school welcomes children who speak over thirty different languages, and in this fascinating ethnic mix is a healthy complement of Arabs and Jews. On Lawrence Avenue you can find "lounges" where men are playing backgammon just like in Ramallah. A Palestinian restaurant and grocery is just blocks from campus, and in the opposite direction are orthodox Jewish schools and synagogues.

In 1989, students and faculty from the university who had traveled to Israel/Palestine were moved by the suffering of its people. They came home and asked North Park's president if they could launch a scholarship program for Palestinian Christians who had no college to attend. He agreed, provided the students figured out how to fly them to America. Within months every-thing was in place, and today North Park's "Palestine Scholarship Program" still offers one "full ride" scholarship per year to an incoming Palestinian Christian, creating a community of Palestinian Christians around the world who have come through the college.

In 1995, North Park opened the "Center for Middle East Studies," which organized classes on the history of the region and sponsored guest lectures.[38] But above all, its mission was to provide "community" for the Arab pop-ulation in Chicago and speak up for justice issues, particularly in Israel. It sponsors trips to Israel/Palestine and has brought a host of important Pales-tinian speakers to campus. In 1996, the Middle East Students Association was formed where Arab students — both Muslim and Christian — would find community and support.

These developments would not be sensational were it not part of a larger picture. The interests of North Park echo those of World Vision and *Christianity Today.* Evangelical leaders are validating the importance of the Middle East and affirming that, as Christians, support of the Palestinian church may be morally necessary.

Other Christian colleges and universities have done the same. A national Christian network of biblically based justice work is called "International Justice Mission."[39] Taylor University in Indiana has now joined this net-work, launching their own "IJM" effort and first on its agenda has been teaching its campus about Israeli injustices. Even the Council for Christian Colleges and Universities based in Washington, D.C. (a coalition of evangel-ical colleges throughout the nation), now has a study center in Cairo where

---

38. For details, see their website: *www.campus.northpark.edu/centers/middle/mesa.html.*
39. See their website: *www.ijm.org.*

students are seeing a very different view of Israel and the Middle East.[40] These actions are all part of a larger trend in which Christian colleges are studying the problems of the Middle East and discovering new solutions.

Evangelicals for Middle East Understanding (EMEU)

In 1985, Dr. Ray Bakke and Dr. Don Wagner traveled to Cyprus, Syria, Jordan, Israel/Palestine, and Egypt on a three-week "listening tour" coordinated by the Middle East Council of Churches.[41] God had put it on their hearts to "hear" the concerns of Arab Christians and to see what American evangelicals could do. Jordan's King Hussein was among the many leaders who amazed them with meetings in which the importance of the Christian communities were affirmed. "Christians are the glue that holds the Middle East together," Hussein remarked. Bakke and Wagner came away with four conclusions: (1) The crisis in the Middle East demands increased moral and spiritual support from Western Christians; (2) Christian Zionists represent a dangerous dynamic in the volatile Middle East as they give unconditional monetary and political support to Israel while ignoring the Arabs; (3) Western Christians know virtually nothing about the rich legacy of Arab history; (4) Western evangelicals are involved in excellent ministries throughout the Middle East. They have demonstrated keen sensitivity to the issues of the region and have begun to form a partnership with Middle Eastern Christians.

Arab Christians asked Bakke and Wagner to help them address these issues in the West. While progress had been made with Catholics and mainline churches, few evangelicals understood the concerns of the Palestinian Christians.

In 1986, twenty-five Christian leaders from the Middle East, North America, and England met under the leadership of John Stott. In addition, representatives from InterVarsity Christian Fellowship, the Middle East Council of Churches, the Lausanne Committee for World Evangelization, the Anglican Church, the National Council of Churches (USA), and many others were present. As a result, Evangelicals for Middle East Understanding was born. Today the group has over eighteen hundred supporters on its mailing list.[42]

---

40. For details, see their website: *www.cccu.org/students/mesp.htm.*

41. The "MECC" is an ecumenical body uniting 8 million Arab Christians worldwide. Its American offices are located at Room 614, 475 Riverside Drive, New York, NY 10115. See their website: *www.mecchurches.org.*

42. See their website: *www.emeu.net.*

EMEU is clear today that the organization is not "anti-Jew" or "against the state of Israel." In the words of Bakke, Christians should not support an intolerable nationalism that oppresses people. EMEU works to inform American Christians within the evangelical camp about the realities of life in Israel/Palestine and the suffering of fellow Christians there. In 1991, its most dramatic meeting took place on the island of Cyprus. One hundred and fifty Christian leaders met for the first time: 90 from the West and 60 from Middle Eastern countries.[43] Representatives from the ancient Middle Eastern churches (Coptic, Melkite, Orthodox, Catholic) joined with more recent Arab denominations (Lutheran, Baptist, Anglican, etc.) to explain the plight of their people and their needs as Christian leaders.

EMEU sponsors a national conference each year in cities like Washington, D.C., Houston, San Francisco, Los Angeles, or Chicago, inviting hundreds of Evangelical leaders and laypersons to hear the stories of Arab Christians. For the hundreds of pastors who have attended, the conference is an unforgettable experience. In addition, EMEU hosts travel and conferences throughout the Middle East. In 2001, the group sent a large delegation to the first-ever Protestant-sponsored gathering of Christian leaders in Baghdad. Then in 2002 it hosted a conference in Beirut attended by 150 people from the United States, Lebanon, Syria, Jordan, Palestine, Iraq, and Egypt.

Alternative Travel

Today "alternative travel" has become a well-organized, sophisticated ministry. Betty Jane Bailey runs the Network for Alternative Travel, whose resources can be accessed on her website.[44] With her guidance, anyone planning a trip to the Holy Land can first locate the Middle East office of their denomination to see what work is going on in the country. Then they can read concrete tips on how to move through the country and how to have a very different "behind the scenes" experience with the Palestinian church.

Is this significant? Fifteen years ago, no one was talking about alternative travel. Today few groups do not consider it. Churches have used Bailey's connections and wisdom to chart new routes through the Holy Land. Christians want to see more than archaeological sites and historic vistas. They want to meet the Christians of the Holy Land.

The same connections are also available through Palestinian Christian organizations in Palestine itself. The International Center of Bethlehem, spon-

---

43. See "The Other Peace Conference," *Christianity Today,* November 11, 1991, 46–48.
44. See *www.holylandalternatives.net.* Bailey has also published a book: Alison Hilliard and Betty Jane Bailey, *Living Stones Pilgrimage with the Christians of the Holy Land* (Notre Dame, Ind.: University of Notre Dame Press, 1999).

sored by the Lutheran Christmas Church, not only has a conference facility and housing, but will facilitate group trips in their "Authentic Tourism" department, whereby visitors can see a different side of Israel/Palestine with Arab Christian guides.[45] No longer do visitors need to be led by preplanned tourist schedules engineered by major tourist companies. Similarly World Vision's Jerusalem office, which is staffed by numerous Palestinian workers, likewise has a desk devoted to helping pastors and leaders build "alternative travel" into their plans.[46]

Church Partnerships

The result of such alternative travel in Israel/Palestine is that American pastors are meeting Arab pastors. American laypersons are meeting Arab laypersons. They are discovering in Christ a unity that was unimagined just ten years ago. When Craig Barnes led his congregation (National Presbyterian, Washington, D.C.) to the Holy Land a few years back, little did he realize that he would become fast friends with Father Emil Salayta of Bir Zeit. Soon his missions pastor, Lynne Faris, was making connections between their congregations so that Christians from each church could visit one another. Today the two congregations enjoy a "sister" relationship for mutual support and encouragement.

Nor did Victor Pentz, formerly pastor at First Presbyterian Church, Houston, expect that his people would form relationships with Arab Christians just outside Bethlehem. Today this evangelical Texas church has a "sister" relation with a congregation in Beit Sahour. The same was true of David Handley (First Presbyterian, Evanston, Illinois) when he visited Bethlehem and met Mitri Raheb's Lutheran congregation.

This trend is growing. Evangelicals have decided to move beyond advocacy and link themselves to specific Christian congregations so that both churches might benefit. In June 2000, when I was attending a celebration of this unity in Bir Zeit with National Presbyterian, I was intrigued to meet a number of pastors in attendance from cities around the country. They were exploring how they might likewise link their congregations to living Christian churches in Palestine.

SIGNS OF CHANGE

The change in evangelical attitudes has even been noted by Middle East "watchers" outside the evangelical mainstream. *The Link* is a quarterly

---

45. See their website: *www.annadwa.org.*
46. For contact information, see "World Vision International" above.

journal published by Americans for Middle East Understanding.[47] Its entire October–November 1992 issue was devoted to a study of changing evangelical attitudes. In an interview in its pages, Dr. John Stott, a leading evangelical spokesperson, was asked, "What is your perspective on Zionism and Christian Zionism?" He replied, "After considerable study, I have concluded that Zionism and especially Christian Zionism are Biblically untenable."[48]

From 1979 to 1981, Christian leaders met regularly in LaGrange, Illinois, to establish a theological consensus on the Israel/Palestine issue. Eventually "The Lagrange Declarations I and II" were endorsed, published in the pages of *Sojourners* magazine, and signed by more than five thousand U.S. Christians.[49] Its signatories came from all parts of the church, including many leading evangelicals: Jim Wallis (*Sojourners*), Nicholas Woltersdorff (Calvin College), Paul Rees (World Vision), John Alexander and Mark Olsen (*The Other Side*), Bill Star (Young Life), Walden Howard (Faith at Work), and Bruce Birch and Dewey Beegle (Wesley Seminary), just to name a few.

The declaration called for a new sensitivity and a new commitment to biblical justice in the Holy Land:

> As believers committed to Christ and his Kingdom, we challenge the popular assumptions about biblical interpretation and the presuppositions of political loyalty held so widely by fellow Christians in their attitudes toward conflict in the Middle East. We address this urgent call to the church of Jesus Christ to hear and heed those voices crying out as bruised reeds for justice in the land where our Lord walked, taught, was crucified, and rose from the dead. We have closed our hearts to these voices and isolated ourselves even from the pleading of low Christians who continue to live in that land.
>
> Forthrightly, we declare our conviction that in the process of establishing the state of Israel, a deep injustice was done to the Palestinian people, confiscating their land and driving many into exile and even death. Moreover, for 13 years, large portions of the Holy Land and its people, including the West Bank of the Jordan River, Gaza, and East Jerusalem, have suffered under foreign military occupation, even as in our Lord's time. . . . We confess our silence, our indifference, our hard-heartedness, and our cowardice, all too often, in the face of these dehumanizing realities.[50]

Evangelicals have also spoken in the political spotlight. In 2002, fifty-eight evangelical leaders wrote to President George W. Bush urging him to pursue a "balanced" policy regarding Israel and claiming that spokespersons

---

47. *The Link,* Room 241, 475 Riverside Drive, New York, NY 10115. Fax: (212) 870-2050.
48. *The Link* (October–November 1992): 7.
49. *Sojourners* (July 1979).
50. See D. Wagner, "Beyond Armageddon," *The Link,* October–November 1992, 7.

such as Jerry Falwell and Pat Robertson do not represent the evangelical majority. The text of the letter was stunning — and was immediately reported by the *Washington Post*. Its text (sent on July 23, 2002) repays careful reading:

Dear Mr. President,

We write as American evangelical Christians concerned for the well-being of all the children of Abraham in the Middle East — Christian, Jewish and Muslim. We urge you to employ an even-handed policy toward Israeli and Palestinian leadership so that this bloody conflict will come to a speedy close and both peoples can live without fear and in a spirit of shalom/salaam.

An even-handed U.S. policy towards Israelis and Palestinians does not give a blank check to either side, nor does it bless violence by either side. An even-handed policy affirms the valid interests of Israelis and Palestinians: both states free, economically viable and secure, with normal relations between Israel and all its Arab neighbors. We commend your stated support for a Palestinian state with 1967 borders, and encourage you to move boldly forward so that the legitimate aspirations of the Palestinian people for their own state may be realized.

We abhor and condemn the suicide bombings of the last 22 months and the failure of the Palestinian Authority in the first year of the intifada to stop the violence against Israeli citizens. We grieve over the loss of life, particularly among children, and the suffering by Israelis and Palestinians. The longer the bloodletting continues, the more difficult it will be for both sides to reconcile with each other.

We urge you to provide the leadership necessary for peacemaking in the Middle East by vigorously opposing injustice, including the continued unlawful and degrading Israeli settlement movement. The theft of Palestinian land and the destruction of Palestinian homes and fields is surely one of the major causes of the strife that has resulted in terrorism and the loss of so many Israeli and Palestinian lives. The continued Israeli military occupation that daily humiliates ordinary Palestinians is also having disastrous effects on the Israeli soul.

Mr. President, the American evangelical community is not a monolithic bloc in full and firm support of present Israeli policy. Significant numbers of American evangelicals reject the way some have distorted biblical passages as their rationale for uncritical support for every policy and action of the Israeli government instead of judging all actions — of both Israelis and Palestinians — on the basis of biblical standards of justice. The great Hebrew prophets, Isaiah and Jeremiah, declared in the Old Testament that God calls all nations and all people to do justice one to another, and to protect the oppressed, the alien, the fatherless and the widow.

Signed,

58 Evangelical Leaders

[The following signed the letter: Fahed Abu-Akel, Moderator, 214th General Assembly, Presbyterian Church (USA), Louisville, KY; James Albrecht, Retired, Regional

Director, Missionary Board of the Church of God, Anderson, IN; Raymond J. Bakke, Executive Director, International Urban Associates, Seattle, WA; Craig Barnes, Senior Pastor, National Presbyterian Church, Washington, DC; Marilyn Borst, Executive Director, Evangelicals for Middle East Understanding, Houston, TX; Don Bray, General Director, Global Partners, The Wesleyan Church, Indianapolis, IN; Gary M. Burge, Professor of Theology, Wheaton College & Graduate School, Wheaton, IL; Clive Calver, President, World Relief of the National Association of Evangelicals, Baltimore, MD; Tony Campolo, President, Evangelical Association for the Promotion of Education, St. Davids, PA; Paul-Gordon Chandler, President & CEO, Partners International, Spokane, WA; Tim Dearborn, Chairman, International Fellowship of Evangelical Mission Theologians, USA, Seattle, WA; John De Haan, Executive Director, Association of Evangelical Relief & Development Organizations (AERDO), Grand Rapids, MI; John R. Dellenback, Former Director, U.S. Peace Corps, U.S. House of Representatives, retired, Medford, OR; Christopher Doyle, President & CEO, American Leprosy Missions, Greenville, SC; Craig Hilton Dyer, President, Bright Hope International, Hoffman Estates, IL; David H. Engelhard, General Secretary, Christian Reformed Church in North America, Grand Rapids, MI; Colleen Townsend Evans, Author, Writer, Fresno, CA; Leighton Ford, President, Leighton Ford Ministries, Charlotte, NC; Vernon Grounds, Chancellor, Denver Seminary, Denver, CO; Jack Haberer, President Elect: Presbyterians for Renewal, Senior Pastor, Clear Lake Presbyterian Church, Houston, TX; Steve Hayner, Past President, Inter-Varsity, USA, Madison, WI; Gary T. Hipp, MD, Chief Executive Officer, Mission: Moving Mountains, Burnsville, MN; Paul Kennel, President, World Concern, Seattle, WA; Don Kruse, Vice President, Holy Land Christian Ecumenical Foundation, Chicago, IL; Peter Kuzmic, Distinguished Professor of World Missions & European Studies, Gordon-Conwell Seminary, South Hamilton, MA; Max Lange, President, Childcare International, Bellingham, WA; Jo Anne Lyon, Executive Director, World Hope International, Springfield, VA; Gordon MacDonald, Board Chairman, World Relief of the National Association of Evangelicals, Boston, MA; Michael A. Mata, Pastor of Leadership Development, Pasadena (CA) First Church of the Nazarene, Director, Urban Leadership Institute; Albert G. Miller, Midwest District Minister, The House of the Lord Pentecostal Church, Oberlin, OH; Paul Moore, President, CitiHope International, Andes, NY; Peter Moore, Dean and President, Trinity Episcopal School for Ministry, Ambridge, PA; Richard J. Mouw, President, Fuller Seminary, Pasadena, CA; David Neff, Editor, *Christianity Today,* Carol Stream, IL; Ronald W. Nikkel, President, Prison Fellowship International, Herndon, VA; John Ortberg, Teaching Pastor, Willow Creek Community Church, South Barrington, IL; Glenn Palmberg, President, Evangelical Covenant Church, Chicago, IL; Earl F. Palmer, Senior Pastor, University Presbyterian Church, Seattle, WA; Victor D. Pentz, Senior Minister, Peachtree Presbyterian Church, Atlanta, GA; John M. Perkins, President, John M. Perkins Foundation, Chairman Emeritus, Christian Community Development Association, Jackson, MI; Eugene F. Rivers, Special Assistant to the President, Pan-African Charismatic Evangelical Congress, Boston, MA; Leonard Rodgers, President, Venture International, Tempe, AZ; Andrew Ryskamp, Executive Director, Christian Reformed World Relief Committee — US, Grand Rapids, MI; Scott C. Sabin, Executive Director, Floresta USA, San Diego, CA; Cheryl J. Sanders, Senior Pastor, Third Street Church of God, Howard University School of

Divinity, Washington, DC; Amb. (r) Robert A. Seiple, Founder & President, The Institute for Global Engagement, St. Davids, PA; Ronald J. Sider, President, Evangelicals for Social Action, St. Davids, PA; Luci N. Shaw, Author, Lecturer, Writer in Residence, Regent College, Vancouver, BC, Canada; James Skillen, President, Center for Public Justice, Annapolis, MD; H. P. Spees, Chief Executive Officer, One by One Leadership, Fresno, CA; Glen Harold Stassen, Professor of Christian Ethics, Fuller Seminary, Pasadena, CA; Richard Stearns, President, World Vision US, Federal Way, WA; Amb. (r) Clyde D. Taylor, Member, International Christian Boards, Washington, DC; Dean Trulear, Pastor, Mt. Pleasant Baptist Church, Twin Oaks, PA; Harold Vogelaar, Resident Scholar in World Religions, Lutheran School of Theology at Chicago; Donald Wagner, Director, Center for Middle East Studies, North Park University, Chicago, IL; Robin & Nancy Wainwright, Board of Directors, Holy Land Trust, Pasadena, CA; Stuart Willcuts, CEO and President, Air Serv International, Warrenton, VA; Philip Yancey, Author, Evergreen, CO.]

SUMMARY

I have been converted by experiences and study. As an evangelical brought up on sermons and books explaining the chosenness of Israel in God's plan for history, I am now persuaded that the church cannot be entangled in a political agenda in the Middle East that destroys people and pursues injustice. The Old Testament continually calls God's people to protect "the alien, the orphan, and the widow." The New Testament says that the purity of our faith must be seen in how we treat "the foreign neighbor" (Luke 10:25–37). *The Palestinian is my neighbor.* Many Palestinians are my Christian brothers and sisters.

If Israel makes biblical claims to statehood, Israel must be an exemplar of biblical righteousness among the nations. At the very least, Israel must be comparable to the other nations in moral conduct. And if comparable, then Israel should be held to the same standards of justice we expect from countries such as South Africa, where our criticisms have been harsh.

Some Christians who have expressed criticisms such as these have been accused of anti-Semitism. Evangelicals who stand opposed to the secular nationalism of Israel are not discriminating against Jews as a people. On the contrary, evangelical critics are expressing dissatisfaction with the behavior of a nation that ought to know better — a nation whose possession of the Scriptures ought to give it more light. The prophets of the Old Testament, men like Isaiah and Jeremiah, loved Israel deeply. Yet this did not weaken their exhortations when Israel sinned.

I believe that evangelicals need to join these prophetic voices, and because of her rich spiritual heritage, Israel should become a light to the nations.

Because she has been abused in the past — exiled into foreign nations — Israel must not be the abuser today.

In the early 1990s, I spent an afternoon and evening walking through the back streets of a village outside Bethlehem with a young Palestinian Christian named In'am Bonoura. In'am then worked as a secretary at Bethlehem Bible College, and she gave me hours of her time, not simply to give a tour of her village, but to share something of her own thoughts about her country.

Two things stood out as we talked. In'am told me about her first visit to the United States. She was on a bus traveling through Indiana, and suddenly after four hours it hit her: she had never gone so far in one direction in her life. Israel had restricted her freedom of movement so much that the geographical scope of her world was "less than a couple hours wide." She cried when she realized how expansive and free she felt that afternoon north of Indianapolis.

We talked at length about America, its virtues and shortcomings, its relationship to Israel, and the role of the Christian church. We stopped on the road alongside the biblical Shepherds' Fields, and as I looked up at Bethlehem on the horizon, I found myself unable to answer some of In'am's questions. "How can America, your America, that believes in freedom, support Israel when it acts like this?" Such questions are frequent in the Middle East and easy to explain to Palestinians: The United States isn't a perfect country. We make mistakes even among our allies.

Then came the bombshell: "But why do American *Christians* support the Israelis as well? Why don't they help us? Why not even us, the Palestinian Christians?" As we walked on, I discovered to my shame that I had no answer. But at least I am confident today that evangelicals everywhere in America are going to change that record.

Chapter Thirteen

WHERE DO WE GO
FROM HERE?

Speak up for those who cannot speak for themselves; ensure justice for those who are perishing. Yes, speak up for the poor and helpless, and see that they get justice. — Proverbs 31:8–9 NLT

A number of years ago, an Israeli dentist was attending a professional conference in New York City. Seminars were being offered on dental research, techniques, and approaches to dentistry around the world. He was intrigued when he noted that another Israeli was on the seminar agenda, and so he attended with curiosity.

The seminar was about comparative enamel wear on the teeth of people living around the world. The researcher had come to some startling discoveries: In Israel, enamel loss through teeth grinding was astonishingly higher in Tel Aviv (his population sample) than in anywhere else in the Western world. In other words, Israelis (and we can assume Arabs too) are under so much stress that teeth grinding has reached almost epidemic proportions. Once I was walking through the back streets of Tel Aviv late at night and had this astounding image of people everywhere in their beds grinding their teeth in their sleep.

No one is happy in Israel/Palestine. The Israelis are not happy. Their quest for security — haunted as it is by the terrors of the past — have led them to forge a state that makes few proud. The Palestinians are not happy. Their quest for nationhood has put them at odds with Israel and led to terror and strife that likewise has lost the esteem of many. Turmoil victimizes the emotions of anyone who must live in the country. I have had close friends who work in Jerusalem suffer nervous breakdowns because of the stress. Others who serve the refugee camps experience surprising physical symptoms of what psychologists call "toxic anxiety." Israeli Jews in Chicago have confided to me that while they love Israel, they cannot bear the thought of making "that crazy place" their permanent home.

TIMES OF CRISIS

Tom Getman, World Vision's former director in Jerusalem, once hosted a wedding party in his Jerusalem home for his good friends Sami and Vera Taha. From their veranda, Tom and his wife Karen's home enjoyed one of the most picturesque views of Mount Zion. The party became concerned, however, when Sami was an hour late. Getman's own account:

> Sami the bridegroom came an hour late for his own party because his best friend Hisham's jewelry store in East Jerusalem was raided by 35 tax investigators, police and heavily armed soldiers at the very moment Sami went to pick him up. One of the family was still under arrest 48 hours later and 50 kilos of gold were confiscated with the charge "that you Arabs always lie and refuse to pay your taxes" even though Hisham's records were perfect and the tax payments current.
>
> The greatest inconsistency is that the services provided by the Israeli Jerusalem municipality [to Arab neighborhoods] are minimal while such harassment continues. [This event] may be rooted in the fact that several years ago another family member courageously video taped the beating of Palestinians by police behind his shop; as a result it was reported on CNN.[1]

When news of the episode was reported to the people at the party — Jews and Arabs — there was a stunned silence. An Israeli friend commented, "How can we live with ourselves when we are so abusive to the Palestinians? How can peace come if we continue to humiliate the other party?"

Small stories like this can be told a hundred times over in Israel/Palestine today. In the pages of this book, I have attempted to give a mere glimpse of what these stories look like. Home demolitions, land confiscation, arrests, beatings, and the absence of basic civic services have brought this country to a boiling point.

In an essay published in the journal *Commentary*, Daniel Pipes describes what he sees as "Israel's Moment of Truth."[2] In his mind, Israel has an opportunity today to resolve its most basic struggles with the Arabs. But if Israel does not, its own future will be in jeopardy. In a new study of Arab attitudes toward Israel conducted by the American University of Beirut, sixteen hundred Lebanese, Jordanians, Palestinians, and Syrians were asked about their attitudes toward peace. By a ratio of 69 to 28 (more than 2 to 1), respondents said that they did not want peace with Israel. If a resolution to these attitudes is not discovered, the lines of opposition will

---

1. T. Getman, "Reflection #49," e-mail publication of World Vision, Jerusalem.
2. D. Pipes, "Israel's Moment of Truth," *Commentary* 109, no. 2 (February 2000): 19–26.

harden and peace will slip from reach. The jeopardy for Israel is serious. Pipes writes:

> Israel today has money and weapons, the Arabs have will. Israelis want a resolution to conflict, Arabs want victory. Israel has high capabilities and low morale, the Arabs have low capabilities and high morale. Again and again, the record of world history shows, victory goes not to the side with greater firepower, but to the side with greater determination.

REAPING THE WHIRLWIND

The profound frustrations held for seven years among Palestinians finally exploded on September 28, 2000. Retired general Ariel Sharon, the leader of Israel's conservative Likud Party (and notorious leader of Israel's campaign against Lebanon), led hundreds of Israelis on a visit to the Muslim sanctuaries in the Old City, called the Haram al-Sharif (or The Noble Sanctuary) by Arabs. Here stands the famous Dome of the Rock and the Al-Aqsa Mosque, the third most holy site to Muslims. Sharon came, he said, in order to assert that Jewish control over even this area will never be given up to Arabs.

Immediately conflicts erupted as Muslims poured into the Haram, vowing to die for the sanctity of their holy sites. Israeli soldiers opened fire — first with rubber-coated bullets, then with real ammunition — and on the first day, four Arab men were killed. Within four days, riots had erupted throughout the country. The casualty count was stunning. In two weeks, 100 were dead and 2,000 hospitalized. In two months, 250 were dead and 5,000 hospitalized. Almost 95 percent of these were Arabs.[3]

Two factors distinguished this conflict from the previous Intifada. First, thousands of armed Palestinian police returned fire and wounded Israeli soldiers. This immediately escalated the struggle, and before long, Israeli troops were using field-grade weapons on their opponents: helicopter warships, missiles, and machine guns. Arab demonstrations were facing remarkable firepower and Israeli soldiers were freely using their weapons. Snipers stood on rooftops shooting demonstration leaders, and tanks squared off against rifles and stones. In fact, senior Israeli officials have even acknowledged that they use a tactic of hunting down and killing individual demonstrators, called "eliminations" by the authorities.[4] Today the Internet is filled

---

3. For a current number of deaths in this conflict, consult the regularly updated website of the electronic intifada (*electronicintifada.net*). This site will direct you to both the Palestinian Red Crescent Society and the Israeli Ministry of Foreign Affairs.

4. "Israel Acknowledges Hunting Down Arab Militants," *New York Times,* December 22, 2000.

with countless stories of these such attacks. A U.N. report issued six weeks into the conflict reported that Israeli attacks using heavy armor and rockets resulted in the partial or total destruction of 431 private homes, 13 public buildings, 10 factories, and 14 religious buildings.[5]

Second, for the first time, rioting broke out in Israeli cities outside the West Bank and Gaza. Arabs who were Israeli citizens, outraged by the astounding death toll and the Israeli use of military power, took to the streets. Moreover, for the first time, fighting broke out on the Jewish side. Israeli Jews attacked Israeli Arabs. Sarah Shartal, a young Israeli writing in the *Toronto Star,* described how she felt about this. For the first time, Israel saw the alternative to peace: civil war. Shartal writes:

> Also frightening is how Jewish Israelis are attacking Arab Israelis. Mosques, homes and businesses owned by Arab Israeli citizens have been attacked, looted and burned while Jewish Israeli citizens shout "Death to the Arabs." To date, our government has not protected its Arab citizens. When Jews from Nazareth Elite (a Jewish town near Nazareth) invaded Nazareth and started to loot local stores, local citizens came out to try to stop them. The army came in and shot the Arab victims of the attack, killing two of them.[6]

The deeper irony in this story is that just weeks before this clash, a major poll examined Israeli attitudes on life. Fully 70 percent felt that the peace process with the Arabs was not going well and because of this, over half (55 percent) claimed that their "mood was not good." Nevertheless, when asked about their personal situation in life, their financial and personal security, Israelis said things were fine. Eighty-three percent described their personal situation as "good." This public would have been enlightened had they asked the same questions of their Arab neighbors.

AN APARTHEID STATE?

In early September 2000, sixty progressive Israeli leaders met at Neveh Shalom (near Latrun) in order to discuss their country's slide into becoming an "apartheid state." Organized by the Israeli Committee Against House Demolitions and the Alternative Information Center, numerous scholars, lawyers, and social workers examined for the first time what they viewed as the formation of Israeli apartheid. The conference concluded with a public statement — and a warning — to both Israel and the United States to the

---

5. "The Palestinian Economy in Ruins, U.N. Says," *New York Times,* December 6, 2000.
6. *Toronto Star,* October 18, 2000.

effect that the present negotiations will likely frame the basis for future war. Their words:

> The establishment of a Palestinian state truncated by a massive system of by-pass roads, encircled by Israeli settlement blocs, subject to closures and restrictions on freedom of movement and commerce, with no control of its borders or natural resources, will only create a reality of apartheid; a Palestinian state as a bantustan.

The course of the present peace process may be leading to a separation of Israeli and Palestinian peoples that will mimic those results once found in South Africa. Palestinian areas (called Area A) are being encircled by Israeli-controlled regions (Area C) and policed by the military, and these realities will not change through the negotiations. Fertile land is being seized and segmented by bypass roads. Without contiguous borders, the hope of a Palestinian state will slowly evaporate. According to Amira Hass, the West Bank reporter for the Israeli newspaper *Ha'aretz,* the Palestinian economy is already destroyed and its citizens impoverished. In the current siege and fighting, Hass's view has proven true. Israeli tanks and armored personnel carriers have utterly wrecked the Palestinian infrastructure, sending the country, as one pastor told me, back to the 1940s. The "apartheid formula" has accomplished it. Control plus territorial confiscation plus separation equals apartheid.

The crucial feature about this warning is that it is coming from Israelis. Not only is a growing Jewish population in Israel aware of a moral problem at the heart of Israel's national program, but they also see the government's policies as detrimental to the well-being of Israel's future. Populations that have nowhere to go, no hope for the future, will soon become radicalized — often through religious fundamentalism — and grow a level of anger that is impossible to appease. David Grossman writing for the *New York Times* in November 2000 captured nicely the troubling dilemma of Israel:

> Anyone who talks to Palestinians in important positions is forced to admit that much of what they say is true. According to the map that was supposed to have been made by the Oslo Accords, the Palestinians would have ended up not with a real state, but with only a few blots of land, ringed and bisected by the presence of the Israeli occupier — which, after the bloody battles, would have engendered a sense of humiliation in every Palestinian heart. All these truths and many more have created a situation in which Israel must resort to the most convoluted logic (not to mention moral acrobatics) in order to defend itself.[7]

---

7. D. Grossman, "The Pain Israel Must Accept," *New York Times,* November 8, 2000.

BEN-GURION'S INSIGHT

This sort of discussion among Jews in Israel points to the national paralysis that inflicts the country. From the very beginning, Israel's founders recognized three dreams, three visions, that the state wanted to embrace: Israel was to be (1) a democracy; (2) a Jewish state; (3) and the owner of the historic land of Israel, from the Mediterranean to the Jordan River. David Ben-Gurion understood this vision, and he remarked that it would be impossible to hold all three of these at any one time. If Israel is to be a Jewish democracy, it could not have all the land. If Israel was to be a democracy and hold all the land with its Arab residents, it could not be exclusively Jewish. And if Israel wanted all the land and also be Jewish, then it could not be a democracy. The Arab citizenry would be shut out. By its very nature, Ben-Gurion argued, Israel had to live with genuine limitations.

When Israel was born in 1948, its leaders had to ask themselves: What sort of state do we want? From 1948 until 1967, they were able to make their original Zionist vision flourish. It was a Jewish democracy living with a majority Jewish population. But it had compromised something: the land. In 1967, however, Israel acquired all of the land and once again it had to ask itself a question: What sort of state do we want? Now Israel owned everything, and only two of the three visions were open to it. This dilemma rests at the heart of Israel today.

The first option is for Israel to keep all of its land, remain an exclusively Jewish state, and lose its identity as a democracy. Why? The Palestinian population has not been invited in. As conquerors know, captive populations must either be integrated into the national fabric, sent over the border, or killed. To Israel's credit, it has never considered the third agenda.

The second option is for Israel to keep all of its land and become a genuine democracy in which the Palestinians are given complete national participation. But if this choice is taken, surely the exclusively Jewish character of the state will be lost. If the Arab population of Israel joined with West Bank and Gaza, Arabs would outvote Jews in a generation. Will Israel take this risk?

The third option is for Israel to let go of much occupied land in the West Bank and remain a smaller Jewish state in which democracy is enjoyed by all its citizenry. This path opens the way for genuine Palestinian nationhood. Will Israel take this risk?

The Israeli national paralysis is that since 1967 it has tried to hold on to all three visions (land, democracy, and Jewishness) at the same time. Is holding all of this land intrinsic to its ideal of nationhood? Is the Jewish ethnicity critical to its self-understanding? Does it want to be a democracy?

Ben-Gurion argued — wisely — that the country would have to make a choice.

HOPE

Hope comes when I suddenly see my enemy as my neighbor. For Israel, this version of hope comes when Israelis see Arab families having the same dreams and fears as they have, and when Arabs understand the deepest security worries of Jews. But as Salim Munayer discovered, experiencing this change of vision may be a privilege that comes only to the young (see chap. 11).

Trust must be built, and sometimes these efforts must be ingenious. The Seeds of Peace is a nonprofit, nonpolitical organization founded in 1993 with a novel mission.[8] Each year three hundred outstanding students from Egypt, Israel, Jordan, Palestine, Morocco, Tunisia, Qatar, and Yemen are chosen by their governments from a pool of two thousand applicants. The students are selected on the basis of their scholarship and their leadership abilities. These young people are then flown to a private camp in the woods of Maine where they find a safe and supportive environment, where trust can be built, friendships won, and conflict resolution explored. World leaders always visit the camp, and during their administration, President Bill Clinton and Vice President Al Gore frequented the program. To date, fourteen hundred Arab and Israeli students have graduated from the program.[9]

Perhaps what makes this program (and others like it) so successful is that in a new context people who were once implacable enemies can discover new friendship and trust. On the night of October 10, 2000, ABC *Nightline's* Ted Koppel hosted a "Town Meeting" in Jerusalem and we listened to the dramatic plea of an Israeli girl, a graduate of Seeds for Peace, a girl who loves Israel — as she asked Israel's deputy defense minister to stop the killing. One of her fellow graduates, an Arab boy, had just been shot by an Israeli bullet days before. When Israelis plea for Palestinians, when Arabs plea for Jews, hope emerges.

Saeb Erekat, forty-two, is perhaps the lead Palestinian negotiator and considered by some to be Arafat's successor in the Palestinian Authority. In an interview with the *Wall Street Journal* at his office in Jericho, he took the unusual step of speaking of his fifteen-year-old daughter, Dalal.

---

8. See their website: *www.seedsofpeace.org.*
9. Because of its success, Seeds of Peace now has programs for Greek and Turkish youth as well as students from the Balkans.

My daughter attended an Israeli-Palestinian peace camp last year in Maine. After the flood hit Jericho, not one of my Israeli friends or counterparts in the peace talks called to ask me about my family or how I was doing. But 21 Israeli kids, 13 to 15 years old, called her. Every single one of the kids from that camp called Dalal to ask if she was OK, to see if we're OK. This is the future. This is what I am working to build, the culture of peace. It is why I'm in politics.[10]

FOUNDATIONS FOR PEACE

In a recent issue of *Sojourners* magazine, World Vision's Tom Getman outlined what he felt would be the essential elements that would make peace possible in Israel/Palestine today. A handful of critical items will lay a foundation on which a true peace can be built. Getman's outline:

- Palestinians will hear the cry of Israelis to live securely within their recognized state and to be healed of their ancient fears and anger.

- Israelis will heed the Palestinians who have lost their villages and homes, many of whom are living in refugee camps without access to Jerusalem.

- Refugees will be given "right to return" home and compensation for their losses, and ongoing demolitions, work restrictions, and water inequity will cease.

- Pilgrim and government visitors to Israel and Palestine will recognize and alleviate stark human needs while insisting on adherence to U.N. resolutions and rule of law in protecting people against rights violations in an apartheid system.

These points summarize in short compass what are undoubtedly four basic items that will remain on any peacemaker's agenda. But there are also two more. Former President Jimmy Carter, who led the original Camp David Accords in 1978, explained in the *Washington Post* that a primary assumption of that agreement (Reflected in U.N. Resolution 242) is that Israel would not acquire and settle occupied territory.[11] Carter recalls, "It was clear that Israeli settlements in the occupied territories were a direct violation of this agreement and were, according to a long-stated American position, both 'illegal and an obstacle to peace.'" Nowhere is this more obvious than Gaza. Here fifteen settlements host five thousand settlers who live in tension with 2.5 million Arabs. A parallel story can be told in the West Bank. During the Israeli occupation of Sinai, Jewish settlers likewise moved there and demanded rights of occupation. When Israel made peace with

---

10. A. D. Marcus, "Leader in Peace Talks Brings a New Style to Palestinian Politics," *Wall Street Journal*, January 22, 1998.
11. "For Israel Land or Peace," *Washington Post,* November 26, 2000, B07.

Egypt, these settlers were simply moved out. But hope still exists that these settlers might leave. In a recent (July 2002) Peace Now survey, 68 percent of them said that they would obey a democratic decision to withdraw and only 6 percent said they would resist. The majority (59 percent) said that they would agree to financial compensation for them to move.[12]

Israelis today are frustrated with settlers like these. In Hebron, for instance, the four hundred settlers in the heart of this Arab town must be moved. Israeli novelist A. B. Yehoshua addressed the Gaza settlers in an Israeli newspaper, "You are endangering yourselves and us in vain with your hopeless obstinancy."[13] Hence, another foundation for peace:

- Israeli settlements in Gaza and the West Bank must be stopped and many of them abandoned or handed over to the Palestinians so that Palestinian regions have real territorial unity not broken by settlements and bypass roads.

Finally, no peace agreement can ignore the importance of Jerusalem. The city is a religious center for three faiths: Islam, Judaism, and Christianity. Jerusalem is the cultural and ideological heart of both Arabs and Jews. For any one party to demand it, for any one side to claim the city as exclusively their own, is to handicap any overture to peace. In 1947, the United Nations proposed that the city be shared by both parties. At Camp David in 1978, both Sadat and Begin agreed that the city should remain undivided and shared, hosting a "municipal council representative of the inhabitants of the city supervising essential functions such as public utilities, public transportation, and tourism and ensuring that each community can maintain its own cultural and educational institutions."[14] Thus, our last foundation for peace:

- Jerusalem must be a shared city, celebrated by Jew, Muslim, and Christian, each of whom have equal access. It would be a "city set on a hill" that would directly model how the entire country might work toward reconciliation.

"Peace," according to Paul Beran of World Vision Jerusalem, "will mean victims become forgivers and perpetrators of crimes become confessors." This definition will become the foundation on which a future can be built, where a loving justice can be claimed.

---

12. For details, see *www.peace-now.org/SettlerSurvey/ExecutiveSummaryEng.doc* [an automated Word download].

13. *Time,* December 4, 2000, 57.

14. The paragraph, while affirmed in the 1978 negotiation, was excluded at the last minute due to its potential divisiveness.

WAS ISAIAH ANTI-SEMITIC?

I was surprised in May 1992 when I received a phone call from the Jewish Anti-Defamation League in New York City. An essay written along the same lines as this book had been published in a church journal, and much to my amazement it had been noted, catalogued, and found wanting among these leaders in New York. A rabbi phoned me at my office one afternoon and insisted that I clarify my viewpoints on Israel and Christian thought. The implication was clear: Criticism of Israel was intolerable, a subtle form of anti-Semitism. I was being called to account.

Recently I was having lunch with one of my students. Unexpectedly she told me that it was with some caution that she took my class. "My older brother warned me about you," she said. "You're the anti-Semitic professor at Wheaton, aren't you?"

Some who read this book will think the same thing. These pages report some very harsh events. They are critical of a political nation that makes religious, spiritual claims to justify its existence. Is Israel exempt from these criticisms? Is it wrong to lodge criticisms when we are talking about people with biblical ancestry?

One night I happened to be in Jerusalem during Pentecost and decided that since this was a holy season, it might be good to wander down to the Temple site and see what was going on. I stood in the Western Wall promenade for a while and then wandered down to the northern men's prayer area. Its crowded square was dense with song, prayer, and conversation. I slipped under the archway (Wilson's Arch), found a chair just inside, and began leafing through an Israeli Bible that was written in English. When I looked up, there next to me, through a wrought-iron gate, just two or three feet away, was an Israeli soldier reading his Scriptures aloud with his M-16 draped casually downward. I remember it well. The ammunition clip was locked into the weapon. The safety was on.

I flipped through the Bible wondering if I too might find some inspiration, some spiritually rewarding experience, for this great and sacred night. Then my eyes fell on Isaiah 1, and I began to read. Chapter after chapter, page after page, Isaiah was chastising the people of Israel because they had pursued nationhood at the expense of true spiritual devotion; they had pursued national religion without pursuing the demands of justice. Isaiah spares no words: God rejects all worship, all devotion, if it is not joined to righteousness. Through the prophet, God declares:

> When you stretch out your hands [in prayer],
> I will hide my eyes from you;

> even though you make many prayers,
>   I will not listen;
>   your hands are full of blood.
> Wash yourselves; make yourselves clean;
>   remove the evil of your doings
>   from before my eyes;
> cease to do evil,
>   learn to do good;
> seek justice,
>   rescue the oppressed,
> defend the orphan,
>   plead for the widow. (Isa. 1:15–17)

Guns and prayer were everywhere that night in Jerusalem, but no one was thinking about justice. Isaiah loved God's people, and he expected more of them. His sharp criticisms of Israel did not invalidate his commitment to them. Isaiah was not anti-Semitic. Not hardly. In fact, his commitment to the quality of Israel's nationhood was fueled by his understanding of what God wanted among his people no matter where they were.

I wish to join hands with Isaiah and, in the spirit of his commitment and concern, to remind Israel of its higher calling. A prophetic voice needs to be heard today in the Middle East, not an apocalyptic voice that announces the fulfillment of prophecies and the end times. Israel has strayed, and like an ox that has forgotten its master and its home, Israel has forgotten the voice of God (Isa. 1:3). I am convinced that if Isaiah were in Jerusalem today, his words would be unrelenting and his willingness to unearth Israel's sins would put his own well-being in jeopardy.

Indeed, those who criticize Israel will undoubtedly be surprised at the reactions — reactions not unlike those received by the Old Testament prophets.

INTERROGATION

Ben-Gurion International Airport in Tel Aviv is well-known for its security precautions, for good reason. The airport has witnessed many terrible terrorist atrocities. It is fascinating while standing in line to study the design of the interior of the building and discover its hidden security precautions, from viewing windows to bomb protection. Since I was traveling alone one spring, I knew that I would have to field the long list of questions that tourists rarely hear. My passport had far too many Israeli stamps in it. I arrived at the airport two and one-half hours before my departure home.

When I could not report to "security" that I had been residing in a typical tourist hotel and that my temporary residence had been a church hospice in Arab East Jerusalem, I quickly found that I had three security officers instead of one in front of me. "Have you talked to any Palestinians?" they asked. I mentioned that I had been traveling quite a bit interviewing Arab pastors from Galilee to Jerusalem. This comment was clearly a mistake. Then a fourth officer (apparently a supervisor) joined the group, and their conversation lapsed into Hebrew. I encouraged them to search everything I had to see that I was no security risk to the plane. But that wasn't enough. They wanted a list of Arabs whom I had talked to. My interview notes were in the attaché on my shoulder, and I remarked that under no circumstances would these notes be handed over. They were private, and I knew the fate of many Palestinians was at stake.

I had often heard about the "back rooms" at Ben-Gurion Airport, and many Arabs and Westerners had told me of extensive searches and questionings that went on there. I was soon to have a firsthand look. Four guards escorted me as if I were a criminal, and for ninety minutes they tore apart everything I owned, except for my notes, which stayed in my hand. It was clear that I had breached some protocol. I had been uncooperative, and now I had to pay up. Everything was stickered and dumped on the table for me to sort through. And throughout the hour and a half, young Israelis kept asking me questions about where I had been and why.

I suspected that one of the Israelis who was opening all of my toiletries was American. And so I asked him, "You're from the States, aren't you?"

He confided that he was — something about discovering his Judaism — but it was clear that he was breaking a rule by chatting with me. He looked around nervously and said he was from the East Coast. He had been in Israel for less than a year.

"This doesn't make sense, does it," I said. "We both know what this is about, tearing through my stuff."

He agreed with a furtive nod. Quietly he whispered, "These people are just afraid. And they don't know what else to do."

I pressed further, "Are you glad you're here?"

His reply was unexpected. He chuckled, shook his head in resignation, and said, "No. People back home don't know the half of this place."

INDEX OF SUBJECTS
AND NAMES

Abdullah I, King, 18, 27, 31, 39, 59, 131n.
Abraham, 11, 33, 60
children of, 10, 78, 167, 178, 183
God's promises to, 67–74, 92, 101, 168, 173, 179, 180, 182
Agriculture, 21, 23, 78, 136
Ahab, King, 91–93, 98, 100, 146, 179, 197
Al-Aqsa Uprising, 63, 244
Al Haq, 158, 219
Albright, Madeline, 53
Alexander the Great, 34, 62, 115
alien. See foreigner
Aloni, Shulamit, 159
al-Siryani, Majdi, 196, 205, 206, 226–28
alternative travel, 253–54
American Committee on Jerusalem, 54, 121n.
American Family Association, 240
Americans for Middle East Understanding, 255
Amir, Yigal, 51, 51n.
Amnesty International, 8n., 120n., 147n., 149, 150, 156, 158n., 164
Anglicans, 191, 198, 212, 248, 252, 253
anti-Semitism, 9, 14, 131, 188n., 198n., 235, 236, 258
anti-Zionism, 107
apartheid, 137, 141, 141n., 193, 263–65, 267
Arab Christians, xiv, 81n., 116, 190–204. See also Palestinian Christians
Arab Jews, 198–99
Arab Orthodox Society, 7, 209

Arafat, Yasir, 25n., 48–51, 53, 55, 63, 113, 138, 233, 234, 266
archaeology, 22, 80, 113n., 211
Armageddon, 11, 12, 48, 134, 239
Valley of, 3, 21
arrests, 8, 46, 47, 49, 96, 137–39, 152, 154–56
Arthur, Kay, 234
Assad, Bashar, 26
Assad, Hafez, President, 7, 26, 132
Assyria, xiii, 28, 34, 60, 83, 101
Ateek, Na'im, 104, 191n., 193, 214
Awad, Bishara, 210–11, 250
Aziz, Tariq, 29

Babylon, 28, 34, 60, 103, 104, 114
Baghdad, 28, 29, 253
Baker, James, 232
Balfour, Arthur, 37,
"Balfour Declaration," 37
Barak, Ehud, 53, 54, 63, 113, 147, 243n.
Bedouins, 23, 27, 201, 211, 227
Begin, Menachem, 17n., 39, 53, 63, 130n., 240, 244, 268
Beit Jala, 192, 211, 224–26
Beit-Sahour, 24, 121, 159, 161, 162, 192, 206, 220–22, 226–28
Beita, 94–98, 110
Ben-Gurion, David, 39, 40, 44, 109, 133, 136, 137, 265–66
Bereaved Parents Forum, the, 105
Bethlehem, ix, x, 9, 48, 52, 58, 119, 124, 139, 152, 161, 192, 210–11, 216–18

Bethlehem Bible College, 191, 201, 204, 211, 216, 250
Bir Zeit, 190, 192
Bir Zeit University, 147n., 194, 211–13, 254
Blackstone, William, 133, 134n.
Border Regiments, 4
Bridges for Peace, 12, 234, 241, 245–46
Britain, 37–39, 97, 117
Brueggemann, Walter, 98, 168, 174, 179, 183, 184n.
B'Tselem, xv, 143, 147
    Quarterly for Human Rights in the Occupied Territories, 153n., 155n., 157n.
Buffer zones, 2n., 25, 42, 43, 57, 63
building permits, 8, 52, 121–22, 142, 147–51
Bush, George, 49, 240
Bush, George W., 233, 234, 255
Byzantine, 9, 35, 118, 199
    Jerusalem, 116

caliph, 35, 116
Camp David, 43, 52–54, 63, 113, 268
    Peace Accords, 30, 63, 267
Canaan, 33, 67, 70–75, 82–84, 91, 113, 119
Carter, Jimmy, 30, 43, 53, 63, 162, 267
casualties, 95, 157, 158, 160, 262
    figures, 56, 160, 262
Chacour, Elias, 163n., 230–32
checkpoints, 46, 52, 122, 125, 145, 226
Chicago Sun Times, 222
Christ Church Jerusalem, 241
Christian Friends of Israel, 234, 241
Christian Zionism. *See* Zionism, Christian
Christianity Today, 68n., 240n., 241n., 247, 249–50
Christians' Israel Public Action Campaign, 241
church partnerships, 254
civil disobedience, 46

civil/human rights violations,
    arrests, 8, 46, 47, 55, 96, 152, 154–57
    deportations, 47, 97, 156–57
    discrimination, 138–41
    home demolitions, x, 7, 8, 62, 121, 144, 148, 149–51, 208, 230
    imprisonment, 46, 47, 107, 140, 152
    stealing land, 141–42
    stealing water, 142–43
    torture, 47, 152, 155–58, 161, 193
Clinton, Bill, 53, 266
closures, 124, 152–53, 264
CNN, xiii, 54, 150, 219, 261
Coalition of Women for Just Peace, 105
commandos, 159
Constantine, 35, 116
Coptics, 29, 30, 191, 253
Council for Christian Colleges and Universities, 251
"Courage to Refuse," 105–7
covenant, 13, 67
    promises, 69–72
    conditions, 72–74, 92, 103, 164
Crusades, 9, 35, 116, 119
curfew, 47, 152, 153
Cyprus, 36, 212, 225, 253

Damascus Gate, 4, 5, 115n., 117, 123, 151
David, King, 10, 13, 34, 61, 87–91, 113–14, 119
Day of Atonement. *See* Yom Kippur
Dead Sea, 20–23, 34, 58, 74
death squads, 159
"Declaration of Principles." *See* Oslo Peace Accords
Deir Yassin, 40–41, 213, 224
Democratic Choice, 121
detention. *See* civil/human rights violations; imprisonment
Dheisheh (camp), ix, x
Diaspora (dispersion), 170, 197
discrimination. *See* civil/human rights violations
Dispensationalism, 237, 239, 250

Dome of the Rock, 35, 112, 116, 194, 262
Duaybis, Cedar, 213–15

Eckstein, Yechiel, Rabbi, 234, 235, 241
economy, 46, 220
  Israeli, 20, 131, 136
  Palestinian, 27, 49, 200, 263n., 264
Egypt, 36
  modern, 7, 29–31, 37, 41–43, 59, 63, 268
  in biblical period, 33, 60, 70, 88, 90
Eighteen Benedictions, 169
Elijah, 77, 82, 91, 93, 98, 108, 143, 146
embargo, 29
EMEU (Evangelicals for Middle East Understanding), 7, 252–53, 257
End-times. *See* eschatology
eschatology, xii, 11, 12, 203, 238–40, 250, 270
"ethnic cleansing," 39, 41, 44, 109, 147
Eusebius, 28
Evangelical Council for Financial Accountability, 243
exile, 11, 14, 28, 34, 101, 107, 108, 115, 119
  of Palestinians, 43, 96, 98, 140, 204

Falwell, Jerry, 233–34, 240, 256
foreigners (aliens), 87–90
  Israel as, 13, 67, 70, 73, 75, 78
  Israel's neglect of, 110, 141
  prophets' concern for, 94, 101, 104
  rights and privileges of, 80, 84, 88–93
Friedman, Thomas, 131–32
France, 26, 36, 37, 41
Friends of Israel Gospel Ministries, 241
Friends of Jerusalem, 241

Galilee, 18–20, 22, 34, 43, 63, 191
  biblical, 80, 115, 126, 171–72
  demographics, 59
  Sea of, 19, 58, 143
Gaza, xiv, 10, 31, 44, 50–51, 106, 137, 138, 140, 154, 162, 265

Geneva International Human Rights Agreements, 98
ghetto, 9, 10
Golan Heights, 20, 42, 57, 59, 63, 88
Graham, Billy, 250
Greeks, 34, 69, 80, 115, 175
Greek Catholics. *See* Melkites
Greek Orthodox, 68, 168, 193, 222, 229
"green line," the, 42n., 105
Gulf War, 11–12, 48–50, 63
Gush Shalom, 105, 148–49, 159n.

Ha'aretz, 53n., 97, 123, 143, 148, 264
Haganah, 39
Hagee, John, 241
Halhoul, x, xi
Hashomer Hatzair, 106
Hasmonean kingdom, 34
Hebrew University, 97, 137
Hebron, 21, 38, 39, 51, 143, 152, 268
  biblical, 70, 76, 114
Hermon, 18–19, 56
  biblical, 86
Herod, King, 18, 22, 112, 115
Hizbullah, 25
holiness, 73, 74, 77, 113, 169
Holocaust, 9, 38, 83, 108, 235, 243
  Memorial (Yad Vashem), 41, 145, 224
Holy Sepulchre, Church of the, 35, 67, 68, 116, 124
Hopkins, Paul, 236
humility, x, 75, 78, 87
human rights violations. *See* civil/human rights violations
Hussein, Abdullah, 28
Hussein, King, 7, 27, 48, 58, 252
Hussein, Odai, 31
Hussein, Saddam, xi, 9, 12, 29, 48–49

identification (ID) cards, 122, 139, 140, 152, 155
Independence, 27, 33, 131, 136, 160
  War of, 39, 63, 117, 225

injustice, 92, 99, 105, 162, 197, 249, 258
Institute of Holy Land Studies, 245
International Christian Embassy, 195, 233, 234, 241–44
International Justice Mission (IJM), 251
interrogation, 152, 157, 270–71
Intifada, xv, 49, 50, 53, 63, 95, 139, 157, 260
    First, 45–48, 155
    Second, 54–56, 153, 262
Iraq, xi–xiii, 28, 29, 33, 48–50, 63
Isaac, Jad, 220–22
Isaiah, 33, 98, 102, 103, 125, 164, 188, 258, 269
Islam, 30, 35, 113, 215, 268
    Fundamentalist, 30, 264
Israel, xv, 3, 9, 133–35
    army (IDF), 11, 17, 106, 136, 156
    borders, 24–31, 37, 41, 153, 156, 208
    biblical, 33–36, 75–78, 80–92
    comparison with modern, 60–63, 133–64
    exclusivity, 87, 132, 136–38
    founding, 17, 52–53, 108, 136
    geography, 17–23
    history, biblical (outline), 33–34
    history, medieval, 35–36
    history, modern (timeline), 63
    infrastructure, 123
    population, 59, 138
    Protestant support for, 234
    Supreme Court, 97, 230
Israel Christian Advocacy Council, 240
Israel Vistas, 241
Israeli Center for Human Rights in the Occupied Territories, 147
Israeli Coalition Against Home Demolitions, 249
Israeli Committee Against Home Demolitions, 149, 151, 263
Israeli Defense Forces (IDF). *See* Israel, army

Jebusites, 67, 84, 91, 114, 118
Jenkins, Jerry B., 239
Jeremiah, 98, 101, 125, 136
Jerusalem, 112–29
    East, 7, 41, 60, 113, 120, 121, 148, 149
    West, 113, 117, 119, 139
    population, 118
Jerusalem Post, 29n., 95, 120n., 221, 234, 246
Jesus, 126, 171–78
    Jewishness of 10, 177–78
Jewish Anti-Defamation League, 269
Jewish National Land Fund, 39
Jews
    Messianic, 168n., 177, 201–3, 223, 224
    orthodox, 107, 202, 251
    practicing, 163
Jezebel, 92, 146
Jezreel Valley, 92
John Paul II, ix, x
Jordan, 8, 26, 35, 39, 63, 190
Jordan River, 18–22, 58, 74, 167, 265
Joshua, 22, 33, 82–85, 113, 189
Judah, 24
    tribe, 10, 84, 113
Judaism, xiii, 9–11, 69, 107, 118, 163, 177, 185, 198–99
Judea, 21, 61, 203
judgment, 85, 100–103, 143, 164, 186

Kac, A. W., 134
Kamel, Mohammed, 50
Khuttab, Jonathan, 218–20
Kibbutz Artzi Movement, 105
Kingdom of God, 171, 172–77
Kings Assembly in Jerusalem, 241
Kissinger, Henry, 43
Knesset, 10, 131, 138, 147, 229
Kollek, Teddy, 67, 119, 234, 244
Kort, Nora, 7, 208–10
Kuwait. *See* Gulf War

Labor Doves, 105
Laham, Maroun, 224–26
LaHaye, Tim, 239–40
Land
confiscation. *See* civil/human rights
violations, stealing land
and fidelity, 72–74, 86, 103, 135
inheritance, 71, 79, 87, 89, 91, 92,
102, 104, 170–75, 185
Jesus' teaching concerning, 172–77
ownership, 59, 75–77, 141, 142, 151,
198
"Land Day," 137
Last Days. *See* eschatology
Late Great Planet Earth, 3, 11, 134,
239
LAW: Palestinian Society for the
Protection of Human Rights,
249
League of Nations, 26, 63
Lebanon, 1–3, 24–26, 63, 153, 191,
243
invasion of, 43–45, 63, 108
Left Behind Series, 9, 240
Levy, David, 68
Likud Party, 54, 241n., 242, 244, 246,
262
Lindsay, Hal, 11
Lord's Supper, 10
Lückhoff, Johann, 242–43

Mamlukes, 36
Mandela Institute, 220
Mar Elias College, 232
"March of the Keys," ix. *See also*
civil/human rights violations, home
demolitions
Masada, 9, 22
Meir, Golda, 130–33
Melia Art and Training Center, 209
Melkites (Greek Catholics), xiii n., 191,
192, 195, 231, 253
Meretz, 105
Mishnah, 169
Morris, Benny, 40, 109, 145n.

Mubarak, Muhammed Hosni, 31
Muhammad, 30, 35, 199
Muslims, 25, 30, 59, 85, 119, 192. *See*
also Islam

Nablus, 58, 125, 192
Naboth, 91–92, 100, 197, 217
Nakbah, the ("catastrophe"), 52, 160
Nasser, Gamal Abdel, 30
National Association of Evangelicals,
241
National Christian Leadership
Conference for Israel, 241
National Religious Broadcasters, 241
Negev, 22–23
Netanyahu, Benjamin, 52, 63, 137, 147,
240–41
Netivot Shalom, 106
New Year, Jewish. *See* Rosh Hashanah
New York Times, 55, 95, 125, 132, 134,
241, 265
Nobel Peace Prize, 51, 230n.

Occupied Territories, 4, 49, 59, 60, 82,
105, 138, 142, 162, 267
Omar, Caliph, 36, 116, 119
"Operation Peace for Galilee." *See*
Lebanon, invasion of
Ornan, 91, 114
Orthodox Church, 191, 208, 225, 253
Greek, 168, 193, 221, 229
Oslo
"Declaration of Principles," 50, 63
Peace Accords, 50, 52, 63, 147, 234
Ottoman Empire, 24, 36–37, 117, 207
overcrowding, 120

Palestine Liberation Organization
(PLO), 25, 43, 46, 47, 48, 50, 53,
63
Palestinian Authority (PA), 51, 162,
245, 250, 256, 267
Palestinian Christians, 146n., 163n.,
164, 167, 190–204, 217. *See also*
Arab Christians

Palestinian Church, 190–204
Palestinian Conflict Resolution Center, 249
Palestinian infrastructure, 55, 123, 264
Palestinian Land Defense Committee, 249
Palestinian population, 8, 25–26, 57, 59, 122, 138, 191
Parliament, Israeli. *See* Knesset
partition, 37, 39, 114
Paul VI, Pope, 249
Paul, 181–89
Peace Coalition, 105
Pentecost, 199, 206, 238
Post-Zionists, 108–10
premillennialist, 239
propaganda, 40, 44
prophecy, xii, 3, 12, 133–35, 172–74, 238–40
Protestants, 192, 234, 235–55, 253
Pulitzer Prize, 132

Qumran, 22, 34
quotas, 119, 121, 153

Rabbis Against Home Demolitions, 106
Raheb, Mitri, 161, 167, 190, 216–18
Ramallah, 4, 55, 122, 125, 147, 192
Rapprochement Centre, 222
Reed, Ralph, 234, 235, 240
refugee camps, ix, 1, 25, 50, 150, 154, 160
refugees, x, 25, 27, 40, 42, 44–45, 145
refuseniks. See "Courage to Refuse"
residency cards 121, 122
Rizik, Najeeb Yousef, 228–30
Romans, 6, 22, 27, 34
Rosh Hashanah, 132
rubber bullets, 2, 47, 158
Ruether, Rosemary, 10, 70n., 87n., 104n.
Ryrie, Charles, 237

Sadat, Anwar, 30, 43, 53, 63, 269
Saladin, 18, 36, 116, 119

Salayta, Emil, 211–13
Samaria, 21, 133
    biblical, 34, 61, 85, 176
Saudi Arabia, 11, 35, 39, 49, 50, 150
Saul, King, 20, 33, 34, 80, 88, 237
Schultz, Jim, 195
Secret Police, Israeli (Shin Bet), 48, 152
Septuagint, 174n., 177n.
settlers, 7, 26, 37, 45, 51, 59, 67–68, 95, 119–21
Shamir, Yizhak, 39, 95, 97, 234, 244
Sharon, Ariel, 54–55, 63, 97, 142, 243, 262
Shenouda, Pope, 29
siege, 35, 38, 44, 55, 161, 233, 243
Sinai War, 41
Six-Day War, 11, 41–42, 48, 63
Solomon, King, 24, 34, 88–89, 112, 114–15, 133
Soviet Union, 18, 42, 50
Stern Gang, 39, 208
Swedish Save the Children Fund, 160
Syria, 7, 25–26, 41, 42, 57, 63, 190

Tabernacles, Festival (Feast), 10, 77, 242, 243
tear gas, 5, 46, 47, 48, 151, 158–59
Teggart, Sir Charles, 17–18, 63
Tel Aviv, 9, 106, 113, 121, 136
Temple, xi, 163, 170, 175, 182
    Herod's, 150, 172
    Solomon's, 88–91, 112, 114, 133
Temple Mount, 54, 116, 117
terrorists, 39, 57, 209, 234, 270
Thoene, Bodie, 9
Toronto Star, 123, 263
Truman, Harry S., 39
Tsemel, Leah, 154–55
Turks, 36–37. *See also* Ottoman Empire
Tutu, Desmond, Bishop, 137, 162

unemployment, ix, 212
UNICEF, xii
Unified National Command of the Uprising, 47

United Nations (UN), 38, 39, 42, 60,
114, 140, 269
condemnations, 41, 56, 97
figures, 39, 44, 58–59, 60
Resolution 242, 42, 49, 59, 267
Resolutions, x, 140n., 141n., 267
United States
alliance with Israel, 61
contribution to Israel, 31, 42, 161,
233–46
Uprising. *See* Intifada

violence, 7, 51, 96, 110, 124, 157–62

Wailing (Western) Wall, 117, 133
Walvoord, John, xi, 11, 12, 72, 118,
135, 237
War of Independence. *See* Independence,
war of
water, 142–43

websites. *See* Index of Websites
Weitz, Joseph, 39, 130
West Bank, 7, 21–22, 42, 48, 59, 63,
109, 137, 148. *See also* Judea;
Samaria
Women in Black, 105
World Vision, 142, 164, 212, 224,
248–49
World War I, 24, 26, 37, 38, 117,
207
World War II, 38, 117, 131

Yad Vashem, 41, 145, 224
Yehoshua, A. B., 268
Yom Kippur, 42, 132
Yom Kippur War, 42, 63

Zionism, 37, 93, 106, 108, 141, 163
Christian, 240–41, 246–47, 255
Zionist Confederation House, 209

INDEX OF SCRIPTURE

Genesis

12	69
12:1–3	69
12:2–3	11, 72
12:3	182
13:14–17	70
15	70
15:1–6	70
15:18–21	67, 70
15:20	71
15:20–21	91
17:7–9	70
17:8	71
17:9	71
19	86n.
19:38	88n.
23	71
23:2	75
26:2–4	71
28:13–15	71
48	23
49	23

Exodus

2:15	198
2:22	198
12:48	89
19:6	72, 185
20:8–10	76
23:12	89
23:22	185

Leviticus

18	73
20	73
18:24–30	73
18:28	77
19:10	89
19:33	80
19:33–34	90
19:23	104
20:22–26	73
23:27	89
24:22	90
25	76
25:2	76
25:23	75, 78
25:23–24	67
25:47–50	90
27:30–33	76

Numbers

9:14	89, 90
10:33	76
15:14	89
15:16	90
15:29	90
26:55	75
34:2	170
35:15	90
35:34	77
36:3	76

Deuteronomy

2:19	88n.
4:25–27	74
4:40	74
7:1–6	83
7:5	83
7:6	72
8–9	74
8:17–19	74
8:18	71
11:10	61
11:11–12	17, 74
12:5	76
12:9	76
12:11	76

12:21	*76*
14:22	*76*
14:23	*76*
14:24	*76*
14:29	*89*
18:9–15	*99*
18:15–22	*171*
18:19	*99*
24:14	*90*
24:19–21	*89*
26:5	*88*
26:9–15	*76*
26:12	*89*
27:19	*90*
28:12	*77*
28:24	*77*

Joshua

2	*83*
8:30–35	*84*
8:33	*89*
8:34–35	*84*
9	*84*
9:1–2	*83*
10:3–5	*84*
10:22–27	*84*
10:6–8	*84*
13	*84*
12:10	*84*
15:58	*x*
15:63	*84, 113*
17:5	*76*
20:9	*90*

Judges

1:21	*113*
3:7–8	*85*
4	*20*
8:21ff.	*87*
9:15	*24*
17–18	*85*
17–21	*85*
18	*23*
19–21	*86*
19:22	*86*
21:25	*85*

1 Samuel

8:10–12	*87*
8:13	*87*
8:14	*87*
8:15–18	*87*
8:16	*87*

2 Samuel

1:13	*87n.*
4:2–3	*87*
5:6–10	*113*
5:11	*113*
6:12–19	*114*
10:6–14	*88n.*
23	*87*
23:26	*87*
23:34	*88*
23:37	*88*
23:39	*88*

1 Kings

5:1–14	*24*
6	*114*
7:1–8	*114*
8:16	*76*
8:29	*76*
17:1	*78*
17:18	*101*
21	*91, 197, 217*
21:19	*91, 100*

2 Kings

24–25	*103n.*
25	*114*

1 Chronicles

11:10–47	*87*
21	*90*
21:18	*91*
21:20	*91*
21:24	*91*
21:25	*114*
22:1–5	*90, 114*
22:2	*88*
22:8	*98*
28:8	*89*
29:15	*88*

2 Chronicles _____
2:1–16	24
2:17	80, 88
6:26f	78
30:25	88
36:15f	115

Ezra _____
6	114

Nehemiah _____
1–6	114

Job _____
5:10	77
36:26f	77

Psalms _____
37:11 (36:11 LXX)	174n.
48	103
48:3	103
80:8	173
80:14	173
92:12	24
95:11	76
104:16	24
119:19	88
122	234
122:6	112
122:9	112
129:6	12
132:8	76
133:3	18
137	103

Proverbs _____
5:15	78
31:8–9	260

Isaiah _____
1:3	270
1:15–17	269
1:16–17	101
2:1–5	103n.
2:3	235
3:8	101, 112
3:9	101
3:14	101
5	176
5:1–7	102, 173
5:8	99
9:1–9	103n.
40:1	242
41:17	164
52:5	135
53	218
61:1–2	125
62:1	112
65:2	188
66:1	76

Jeremiah _____
3:19–20	101
7:5–7	94, 101
7:7	71
9:23–24	125
15:5	112
16:15	71, 103n.
52	103n., 114

Lamentations _____ 103

Ezekiel _____
22:7	105
22:29	105
36–37	103n.
47:22–23	104

Hosea _____
2:14–23	103n.
2:21–23	104
9:2–3	100
11:8–11	103n.

Joel _____
1:10–12	77

Amos _____
4:1–2	100
4:6	100
4:7	77
4:10	100
7:17	77, 100
9:14–15	103n.

Micah
2:1–3	*100*
6:8	*125*
7:20	*71*

Haggai
1:10	*77*

Zechariah
7:10	*105*
8:3–5	*126*

Malachi
3:5	*105*

Matthew
2:6	*174*
5:5	*1, 174, 174n.*
5:9	*1*
8:5	*20*
8:20	*174n.*
13:1	*112*
21:12–17	*227*
21:33–41	*172*
21:33–44	*115*
21:41	*173*
23	*227*
23:37–39	*172*

Mark
1:14–15	*172*
2:1	*20*
2:13	*20*
2:14	*20*
11:17	*172*
12:1–11	*173*
12:7	*173*
12:9	*173*
12:14–17	*171*
16:7	*172*

Luke
3:8	*178*
4:18–19	*126, 196*
10:25–37	*258*
12:13–15	*174*
13:6–9	*173n.*

19	*197*
19:11	*171*
19:41–42	*126*
19:42	*250*
21:20	*172*
24:21	*173*

John
1:17	*175*
1:51	*175*
2:1–11	*172*
2:21–22	*175*
4:10	*175*
4:20	*175*
5:1–9	*175*
5:45	*164*
6:1–34	*175*
6:15	*171*
6:35	*175*
7:37	*77*
14	*176*
14:23	*176*
15	*176, 176n.*
15:6	*176*

Acts
1:6	*173*
1:8	*180*
2	*205*
2:11	*198, 206*
7:54	*181*
7:57	*181*
7	*180*

Romans
2:24	*135*
2:25–29	*135*
4	*182*
4:13	*184*
4:13–14	*183*
4:16	*182*
8:17	*183*
9–11	*185, 187*
9:4	*182*
9:25–26	*186*
10:2–3	*187*
11	*10, 188*

Romans (continued)

11:1	*185*
11:1f	*182*
11:2	*185*
11:5	*185*
11:15	*186*
11:17–19	*186*
11:20	*186*
11:23	*187*
11:25	*187*
11:26–27	*187*
11:28	*10, 71n.*
11:28–29	*187*
11:29	*188*
11:32	*186*

1 Corinthians

16:1–4	*197*

2 Corinthians

8:1–15	*197*
11:22	*182*

Galatians

1:14	*181*
3	*182*
3:8	*72n., 182*
3:15–18	*183*
3:16	*183*
3:19f	*184*
3:24	*184*
3:28	*185*
6:16	*185*

Ephesians

2:11–17	*238*
2:11–22	*185*

Philippians

2	*218*
3:4	*182*
3:4–9	*186*

1 Thessalonians

2:13–16	*197*

Hebrews

3–4	*179*
8:13	*188*
11:8	*179*
11:8–16	*167*
11:9–10	*179*
11:13	*179*
11:13–16	*179*

James

1:1	*185*

1 Peter

1:1	*185*
1:4	*185*
2:9–10	*185*

Revelation

16:16	*21*

Enoch (Ethiopic)

26:1	*170*

4 Ezra

6:59	*184*

Jubilees

8:19	*170*

Num. Rabbah

23:7	*170n.*

Psalms of Solomon

17:26–28	*169*

INDEX OF WEBSITES

http://almashariq.hiof.no/general/700/770/779/historical/pcd0109/pcd0109.html, 25

www.alhaq.org, 158, 219

www.alhaq.org/frames_links.html, 156

www.ameu.org, 236

www.amnesty.org/ailib/aipub/1999/MDE, 8, 150

www.annadwa.org, 216, 254

www.arij.org, 222

www.assoc40.org, 144

www.BethlehemBibleCollege.edu, 211

www.birzeit.edu/links/index.html, 212

www.birzeitsociety.org, 212

www.bridgesforpeace.com, 12, 245, 246

www.btselem.org, xv, 143, 147

www.cam.ac.uk/societies/casi, xii

www.campus.northpark.edu/centers/middle/mesa.html, 251

www.cccu.org/students/mesp.htm, 252

www.christianitytoday.com, 250

www.churchworldservice.org/Reports2002/middle_east/luth-christmas-church.html, 193

www.coptic.net, 30

www.deiryassin.org, 40

www.electronicintifada.net, xv

www.emeu.net, 7, 252

www.fmep.org/maps/v11n4_Barak_Sharon_map.jpg, 54

www.fpc-wilmette.org/sanders/index/html, 193

www.geocities.com/SouthBeach/Lagoon/8522/palestine.html#1, 147

www.gush-shalom.org, 148

www.gush-shalom.org/demolition/demolition.html, 148

www.ijm.org, 251

www.intournet.co.il/icej, 242

www.israel.org/mfa/go.asp?MFAH0ia50, 55

www.jerusalem.muni.il/english/cap/toshavim.htm#Distribution, 120

www.jewsforjesus.com, 202

www.mecchurches.org, 253

www.megastories.com/iraq/index.htm, xiii, 29

www.mjaa.org, 201

www.msanews.mynet.net/MSANEWS/199811/19981130.12.html, 159

www.musalaha.org, 201

www.nazareth.muni.il, 198

www.netureikarta.org, 107

www.odci.gov/cia/publications/factbook, 138

www.palestinercs.org/bullet_types_images.htm, 158

www.palestinercs.org/Latest_CrisisUpdates_Figures&Graphs.htm, 55

www.peacenow.org.il/English.asp, 105

www.peacenow.org/SettlerSurvey/ExecutiveSummaryEng.doc, 268

www.sabeel.org/links.html, xv

www.seedsofpeace.org, 266

www.seruv.org.il/defaulteng.asp, 106

www.standforisrael.org/index.cfm?FuseAction=PressReleases.Home&PressRelease_id=3, 234

www.theage.com.au/articles/2002/05/01/1019441390497.html, 44

www.unfpa.org/swp/swpmain.htm, 60

www.whowillsavethechildren.org, 55

www.worldvision.org, 248, 249